Hands-On TypeScript for C# and .NET Core Developers

Transition from C# to TypeScript 3.1 and build applications with ASP.NET Core 2

Francesco Abbruzzese

BIRMINGHAM - MUMBAI

Hands-On TypeScript for C# and .NET Core Developers

Copyright © 2018 Packt Publishing

Commissioning Editor: Aaron Lazar
Acquisition Editor: Alok Dhuri
Content Development Editor: Zeeyan Pinheiro
Technical Editor: Ruvika Rao
Copy Editor: Safis Editing
Project Coordinator: Vaidehi Sawant
Proofreader: Safis Editing
Indexer: Rekha Nair
Graphics: Alishon Mendonsa
Production Coordinator: Nilesh Mohite

First published: October 2018

Production reference: 1301018

Published by Packt Publishing Ltd.
Livery Place
35 Livery Street
Birmingham
B3 2PB, UK.

ISBN 978-1-78913-028-7

www.packtpub.com

To my beloved parents, to whom I owe everything.

`mapt.io`

Mapt is an online digital library that gives you full access to over 5,000 books and videos, as well as industry leading tools to help you plan your personal development and advance your career. For more information, please visit our website.

Why subscribe?

- Spend less time learning and more time coding with practical eBooks and Videos from over 4,000 industry professionals

- Improve your learning with Skill Plans built especially for you

- Get a free eBook or video every month

- Mapt is fully searchable

- Copy and paste, print, and bookmark content

Packt.com

Did you know that Packt offers eBook versions of every book published, with PDF and ePub files available? You can upgrade to the eBook version at `www.packt.com` and as a print book customer, you are entitled to a discount on the eBook copy. Get in touch with us at `customercare@packtpub.com` for more details.

At `www.packt.com`, you can also read a collection of free technical articles, sign up for a range of free newsletters, and receive exclusive discounts and offers on Packt books and eBooks.

Contributors

About the author

Francesco Abbruzzese is an author of the MVC Controls Toolkit. He has also contributed to the diffusion and evangelization of the Microsoft web stack since the first version of ASP.NET MVC through tutorials, articles, and tools.

He writes about .NET and client-side technologies in his blog, *dotnet-programming*, and various online magazines/blogs. Now, his company, mvc-controls, implements and offers web applications, AI software, SAS products, tools, and services for web technologies associated with the Microsoft stack.

He moved from AI systems, where he implemented one of the first decision support systems for banks and financial institutions, to the video games arena, with top-ten titles such as Puma Street Soccer.

To my beloved parents, to whom I owe everything.

I would also like to thank my brother, my niece, and my friends, Lucio, Nico, Alfonso, and Carmen Maggi, for their support and encouragement.

I would also like to thank Alok Dhuri and Packt Publishing, who gave me the opportunity to write this book.

Last, but by no means least, I would like to thank Michele Aponte, Parth Ghiya, and Zeeyan Pinheiro, who reviewed this book, for their valuable advice, as well as Ruvika Rao, Ketan Kamble, and everyone at Packt Publishing who contributed to the production of this book.

About the reviewers

Michele Aponte has been passionately programming since 1993. She has worked as a Java, .NET, and JavaScript programmer for an Italian software house and numerous IT consulting companies. In 2013, she founded Blexin, with the aim of training users to migrate from their old solutions to new technologies. Michele believes in the value of sharing, and founded *DotNetCampania*, a Microsoft user group for which she organized many regional conferences for free, and even received recognition in the form of the MVP award.

You'll find Michele speaking at the most important Italian conferences on Microsoft and JavaScript technologies.

Parth Ghiya loves technologies and enjoys learning new things and facing the unknown. He has shown his expertise in multiple technologies, including mobile, web, and enterprise. He has been heading up projects in all domains with regard to security, high availability, and CI/CD. He has provided real-time data analysis, along with time-series and forecasting solutions.

In his spare time, he is an avid traveler, reader, and an immense foodie. He believes in technological independence and is a mentor, trainer, and contributor.

Packt is searching for authors like you

If you're interested in becoming an author for Packt, please visit `authors.packtpub.com` and apply today. We have worked with thousands of developers and tech professionals, just like you, to help them share their insight with the global tech community. You can make a general application, apply for a specific hot topic that we are recruiting an author for, or submit your own idea.

Table of Contents

Preface

JavaScript was initially conceived to enrich server-generated HTML pages with JavaScript widgets, including date pickers, autocomplete, tabs, and so on. With the increase in available internet bandwidth, and the enhanced computational power of desktops, laptops, mobile devices, and smartphones, in order to ensure faster responses to all user inputs, and to be in a position to better exploit all available resources, increasingly, application logic moved from the server-side to JavaScript code on the client machine. This was the case until the diffusion of single-page applications, where the entire application logic runs in JavaScript on the client machine and the server's role is limited to handling shared data, as well as authentication/authorization logic.

The increasing complexity of JavaScript code bases led to the definition of new JavaScript specifications and toolsets to bring JavaScript from the level of a scripting language to that of modern object-oriented languages, such as Java, C#, and C++. Among the significant changes and tools, the following are worthy of mention:

- The new ECMAScript 6 specifications that turn JavaScript into an advanced object-oriented language.
- The new TypeScript language that adds types to JavaScript to enable better compilation-time checks, and implements almost all new ECMAScript 6 features that are not yet supported by all browsers. What makes TypeScript great is that it is JavaScript of the future plus types, and that it transpiles to browser-compatible JavaScript.
- JavaScript library repositories, such as NPM, that are capable of automatically tracking dependencies among libraries.
- JavaScript test frameworks, such as Jasmine.
- The organization of JavaScript code into modules, and the usage tools called bundlers that facilitate the linking of several interdependent modules into a few JavaScript files to add to each HTML page.
- Frameworks, such as Angular, that contain everything needed to implement single-page applications.

Somewhat unfortunately, knowledge of these subjects is spread across a variety of locations, so it is very frustrating when you come to write modern rich-client web applications. For instance, if you decide to learn Angular, you'll discover that you need to learn TypeScript beforehand, and then you'll discover that a knowledge of TypeScript is not enough either, because you also need to learn more about ECMAScript 6 and JavaScript modules. Finally, if you have resisted hitherto, you'll discover that you also need to learn about bundling and WebPack.

This book consolidates in a single place all the knowledge you require to implement a modern rich-client web application using a non-trivial JavaScript/TypeScript code base—TypeScript, ECMAScript 6 features, JavaScript modules, TypeScript library development and testing, bundling modules with WebPack, and the Angular single-page application framework.

Who this book is for

This book was conceived mainly for ASP.NET developers who want to start developing rich-client applications using non-trivial TypeScript code bases. This book explains how to improve classic server-based web applications using well architected TypeScript code bases, and also how to build modern single-page applications in TypeScript with ASP.NET Core and Angular.

While the last part of the book focuses on Angular, the book covers TypeScript, ECMAScript 6 JavaScript features, JavaScript modules, and WebPack bundler, these being the starting points for learning any other single page application framework/library, such as React, Vue.js, Knockout.js, Aurelia, and Meteor. Hence, this book is also a useful tool for any ASP.NET developer who would like to learn any of the preceding frameworks/libraries, but who lacks some basic knowledge to embark on this learning path.

While most of the chapters use Visual Studio ASP.NET Core project templates, the book only requires a basic knowledge of Visual Studio, and C#, so it can be read by any web developer with a basic knowledge of ES5 JavaScript, a basic knowledge of any modern object-oriented language, such as C#, C++, or Java, and a basic knowledge of either Visual Studio or any another similar IDE.

What this book covers

Chapter 1, *Introduction to TypeScript*, explains how to install and configure TypeScript transpiler, TypeScript base types, variable declarations, and scoping. It also discusses TypeScript's mission, and how TypeScript types can help you to write, debug, and maintain your code bases.

Chapter 2, *Complex Types and Functions*, explains the basics of the language: arrays, tuples, interfaces, and function declarations. It also explains how to define new types by performing operations on existing types, and how to simplify your code with ECMAScript 6 destructuring and spread.

Chapter 3, *DOM Manipulation*, covers TypeScript types used to describe and manipulate the DOM, and how to use JavaScript libraries such as jQuery from TypeScript.

Chapter 4, *Using Classes and Interfaces*, covers TypeScript object programming, classes, interfaces, inheritance, and interface implementations. A complete code example explains how to architect a modular application with the help of abstract classes, interfaces, and inheritance.

Chapter 5, *Generics*, covers TypeScript generics, and how to define constraints on generics and type-mappings based on generics. TypeScript generics mimic C# generics, but, like C++ generics, they disappear in the compiled code.

Chapter 6, *Namespaces and Modules*, covers TypeScript's modular organization of code based either on namespaces, or on ECMAScript 6 modules. While TypeScript modules are completely based on ECMAScript 6 modules, they may run also in environments that do not support ECMAScript 6 modules, since ECMAScript 6 syntax may be processed by JavaScript bundlers such as WebPack, or transpiled in the syntax of AMD, CommonJS, or SystemJS loaders, that run on all platforms/browsers.

Chapter 7, *Bundling with WebPack*, contains a quite complete and practical description of WebPack, and of its more frequently used modules and loaders. Here, the reader can learn everything that is worth knowing in terms of using WebPack with most modern JavaScript frameworks/libraries.

Chapter 8, *Building TypeScript Libraries*, describes how to develop a TypeScript library package with Visual Studio Code, how to test it with Jasmine, and how to package it as an npm package.

Chapter 9, *Decorators and Advanced ES6 Features*, covers all ECMAScript 6 features, such as Symbols, Iterators/Generators, and Promises, that were not covered in previous chapters. The chapter also covers TypeScript's `async/await` notation, which is transpiled to Promise-based code, and TypeScript decorators and metadata that are important Angular building blocks.

Chapter 10, *Angular ASP.NET Core Project Template*, introduces Angular architecture, and describes all the parts an Angular CLI project is composed of, and how to configure a project. The chapter then lists all Angular building blocks, focusing on modules, components, and data binding.

Chapter 11, *Input and Interactions*, explains how to take and validate user input, and how to customize standard data binding behavior with pipes and life cycle hooks. The chapter also covers the interaction of components through JavaScript and custom events.

Chapter 12, *Angular Advanced Features*, covers the details of attribute and structural directive usage and definition. The chapter also explains how to customize components with content projection (that is, filling predefined holes with input content), and how to improve the user interface with Angular animations, giving all details of Angular animation syntax.

Chapter 13, *Navigation and Services*, covers all Angular features conceived for complex applications, navigation among application pages, and how to dynamically load Angular modules. It also covers how components can communicate with the server using Angular HTTP Client class, and how HTTP Client and other services can be injected into components' constructors with the help of dependency injection. It also describes how to test components and other Angular classes.

To get the most out of this book

We would be needing the Visual Studio Community edition (version 15.8.7 or higher) software and Visual Studio Code (version 1.28 or higher).

Download the example code files

You can download the example code files for this book from your account at `www.packt.com`. If you purchased this book elsewhere, you can visit `www.packt.com/support` and register to have the files emailed directly to you.

You can download the code files by following these steps:

1. Log in or register at www.packt.com.
2. Select the **SUPPORT** tab.
3. Click on **Code Downloads & Errata**.
4. Enter the name of the book in the **Search** box and follow the onscreen instructions.

Once the file is downloaded, please make sure that you unzip or extract the folder using the latest version of:

- WinRAR/7-Zip for Windows
- Zipeg/iZip/UnRarX for Mac
- 7-Zip/PeaZip for Linux

The code bundle for the book is also hosted on GitHub at https://github.com/PacktPublishing/Hands-On-TypeScript-for-CSharp-and-.NET-Core-Developers. In case there's an update to the code, it will be updated on the existing GitHub repository.

We also have other code bundles from our rich catalog of books and videos available at https://github.com/PacktPublishing/. Check them out!

Download the color images

We also provide a PDF file that has color images of the screenshots/diagrams used in this book. You can download it here: http://www.packtpub.com/sites/default/files/downloads/9781789130287_ColorImages.pdf.

Code in Action

Visit the following link to check out videos of the code being run: http://bit.ly/2RlN1Yw.

Conventions used

There are a number of text conventions used throughout this book.

CodeInText: Indicates code words in text, database table names, folder names, filenames, file extensions, pathnames, dummy URLs, user input, and Twitter handles. Here is an example: "The name, surname, and secondName variables are public properties, while fullName is a public method."

A block of code is set as follows:

```
class Person {
        name: string;
        surname: string;
        secondName?: string;
        fullname(): string {
            return this.secondName !== undefined ?
                this.name + " " + this.secondName + " " + this.surname :
                this.name + " " + this.surname;
        }
```

Any command-line input or output is written as follows:

```
npm install <package name>@<package version>
```

Bold: Indicates a new term, an important word, or words that you see on screen. For example, words in menus or dialog boxes appear in the text like this. Here is an example: "Right-click on the `domlist` folder and select **Open with Code.**"

 Warnings or important notes appear like this.

 Tips and tricks appear like this.

Get in touch

Feedback from our readers is always welcome.

General feedback: If you have questions about any aspect of this book, mention the book title in the subject of your message and email us at customercare@packtpub.com.

Errata: Although we have taken every care to ensure the accuracy of our content, mistakes do happen. If you have found a mistake in this book, we would be grateful if you would report this to us. Please visit www.packt.com/submit-errata, selecting your book, clicking on the Errata Submission Form link, and entering the details.

Piracy: If you come across any illegal copies of our works in any form on the internet, we would be grateful if you would provide us with the location address or website name. Please contact us at `copyright@packt.com` with a link to the material.

If you are interested in becoming an author: If there is a topic that you have expertise in and you are interested in either writing or contributing to a book, please visit `authors.packtpub.com`.

Reviews

Please leave a review. Once you have read and used this book, why not leave a review on the site that you purchased it from? Potential readers can then see and use your unbiased opinion to make purchase decisions, we at Packt can understand what you think about our products, and our authors can see your feedback on their book. Thank you!

For more information about Packt, please visit `packt.com`.

Introduction to TypeScript
1

The implementation of large JavaScript code bases in modern, rich client web applications has always pushed more in the direction of preventing hard-to- find bugs, with exhaustive checking at compile time. TypeScript meets this requirement by transforming JavaScript into a strongly typed language; that is, into a language that requires declarations and type specifications for all variables and properties. In fact, strong typing allows compile-time type checking that prevents the misuse of variables and functions while variable declarations avoid the variable names misspelling that often causes these bugs in JavaScript.

This chapter explains the TypeScript manifest, how to install it and add it to your ASP.NET core projects, how to organize files and compile them to JavaScript, and the basics of TypeScript configuration. Then the chapter introduces the basics of types and variable declarations.

The following topics will be covered in this chapter:

- Installation on Windows and the TypeScript mission
- Adding TypeScript to ASP.NET core web projects and debugging it
- Basics of TypeScript configuration
- Simple types, enums, and basics of Union types
- Variable declarations, scoping, expressions, casting, and string interpolation

Basics and installation

This section discusses the main motivations behind TypeScript and how to install the TypeScript SDK. Installation concerns just developers' machines since TypeScript code is completely compiled into JavaScript code and doesn't need any runtime library to be executed.

Adding types to JavaScript

TypeScript is a language that is transpiled to JavaScript; that is, TypeScript code is processed to generate JavaScript code.

As a first approximation, you may imagine that TypeScript code is obtained by adding type declarations of variables to usual JavaScript code. For instance, let's consider this JavaScript code:

```
var firstName = "Francesco";
var surName = "Abbruzzese";

function fullName(x, y, spaces){
    x + Array(spaces+1).join(' ') + y;
}
>fullName(firstName, surName, 3)
>"Francesco   Abbruzzese"
```

TypeScript adds a type declaration to the `firstName` and `surName` variable declarations, and it also adds types to the `fullName` function arguments, and to the function's return value:

```
var firstName: string = "Francesco";
var surName: string = "Abbruzzese";

function fullName(x: string, y: string, spaces: number): string{
    x + Array(spaces+1).join(' ') + y;
}
```

TypeScript and JavaScript code are very similar, the only difference being the colon followed by the type immediately after each variable or argument declaration and each function declaration.

In this very simple example, the JavaScript code generated by TypeScript transpilation is identical to the code written directly in JavaScript, so what is the advantage of using TypeScript?

Simple: type checking! The TypeScript compiler verifies type compatibility, thus immediately discovering errors that might otherwise manifest themselves with strange behaviors at runtime.

Suppose, for instance, that we call `fullName` with its arguments in the wrong order:

```
fullName(3, firstName, surName)
```

The TypeScript transpiler immediately discovers the error since 3 is not a string and `surName` is not a number, while JavaScript tries to automatically convert types and gets the wrong result:

```
>fullName(3, firstName, surName)
>"3Francesco"
```

TypeScript types are used just to perform compile-time checks, and do not influence JavaScript code generated by the transpiler. In a few words, types disappear completely in the transpiled code. This is by design, because TypeScript was conceived to maintain the same JavaScript semantics and principles while helping with compile-time checks.

Using JavaScript of the future now!

While TypeScript was initially conceived to perform better compile-time checks than JavaScript, very soon its mission was extended to mitigate the different support for new JavaScript standards which are at the moment, ECMAScript 6-8. TypeScript includes most of ECMAScript 6-8's important features, but you may target the transpiled code at previous JavaScript versions. When a feature is not available in the target JavaScript version, the TypeScript transpiler creates code that simulates this feature in the target JavaScript version.

For instance, TypeScript includes ECMAScript 6 classes that will be covered in `Chapter` `4`, *Using Classes and Interfaces*, and ECMAScript 8 async/await, which will be covered in the *Promises and async/await notation* section of `Chapter` `9`, *Decorators and Advanced ES6 Features*. Here is an example of async/await use:

```
async function asyncAwaitExample(url: string): string {
    let response= await fetch(url);
    return await response.text();
}
```

The syntax is completely analogous to C# `async/await`.

Since TypeScript was conceived to be JavaScript + compile-time type checks, all its current and future versions will include only runtime features that are part of some ECMAScript standard.

Installing the Visual Studio 2017 TypeScript SDK

As a default, Visual Studio 2017 installers automatically install TypeScript SDK, and as long as you keep Visual Studio updated, you should always have a recent version of the TypeScript SDK. Anyway, if for some reason TypeScript was not installed, or if you want to be sure you have the latest version of the TypeScript SDK, proceed as follows.

Go to **Program and Functionalities** in your computer's **Control Panel** and verify that TypeScript SDK is installed, and which version is installed:

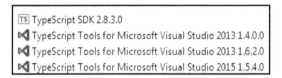

In this case, TypeScript is already installed and its version is 2.8.3.0.

Open **Visual Studio 2017** and go to **Tools** | **Extensions and Updates**:

When the **Extensions and Updates** window opens, in the left-hand menu, select **Online** | **Visual Studio Gallery** | **Tools**, and then type TypeScript in the text box in the upper-right corner.

A few seconds after you finish typing `TypeScript`, you should see all available versions of the TypeScript SDK. Select the most recent version:

In this case, the most recent version is 2.8.3.

If the version you found is more recent than the one already installed, click on the list item to select it, and then click on the **Download** button that appears to download the TypeScript SDK installer. When the download completes, double-click on the installer to install the SDK.

Installation of Node.js-based TypeScript compiler

In the *Using VS Code* section of `Chapter 8`, *Building Typescript Libraries*, we will learn TypeScript development without Visual Studio. In this case, we need the Node.js-based TypeScript compiler that is independent of Visual Studio.

As a first step, go to the Node.js website at `https://nodejs.org/en/` and download the recommended version of Node.js.

Once installation is complete, open a Windows Command Prompt and type `node -v` to verify Node.js has been installed properly, and to verify its version.

We also need `npm`, the Node.js packages handler (a kind of NuGet for Node.js packages). `npm` is automatically installed with Node.js. Type `npm -v` in the Windows Command Prompt to verify its proper installation and its version.

Here is the result of typing these commands in a Windows Command Prompt:

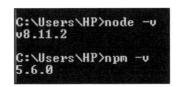

```
C:\Users\HP>node -v
v8.11.2

C:\Users\HP>npm -v
5.6.0
```

Now, installing TypeScript compiler is quite easy; just type `npm install -g typescript`. This will install the last version of the TypeScript compiler globally on your computer.

If you need a different version of the TypeScript compiler for a specific project, you may install it locally for that project folder, while all other projects will continue using the version installed globally. This can be done as follows:

1. Open Command Prompt in the project folder.
2. Suppose the version you would like to install is 2.7.1, then type the following command:

```
npm install --save-dev typescript@2.7.1
```

Adding TypeScript to your web projects

Once you have the TypeScript SDK installed, adding a TypeScript code file to an ASP.NET Core project is straightforward. Your TypeScript file will be compiled in a JavaScript file that you may call, as usual, in any View. However, you may debug your code and put breakpoints directly in the TypeScript source.

Your first TypeScript file

Let's open Visual Studio and create an ASP.NET Core project 2.x named
`TypeScriptTests`:

Click **OK**, and in the new window that appears, select an MVC 2.x application with **No Authentication** (we need just a View for where to call our code):

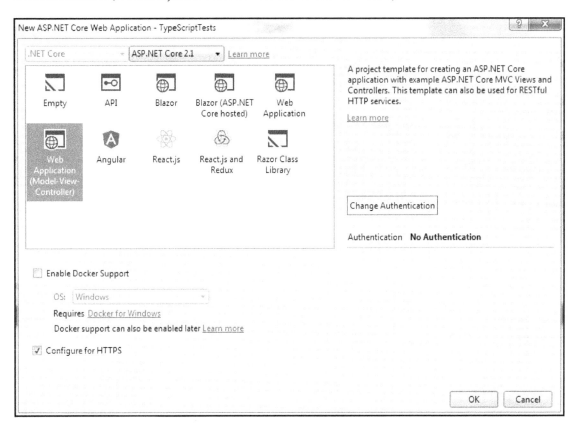

Once the project finishes loading, run it to verify that the project has been scaffolded properly. Then, in the solution explorer, right-click on the wwwroot node and select **Add | New Folder** to add a new folder named ts:

Finally, right-click on the `ts` folder and select **Add New Item**. The following window opens:

In the left-hand menu, select **ASP.NET Core | Web | Scripts**. Then select the **TypeScript File** and name it `tests.ts`.

Let's add some test code to the newly added `test.ts` file:

```
var firstName: string = "Francesco";
var surName: string = "Abbruzzese";

function fullName(x: string, y: string, spaces: number): string {
    return x + Array(spaces+1).join(' ') + y;
}

alert(fullName(firstName, surName, 3)+" Hello");
```

Thanks to declarations and strong typing, the Visual Studio editor helps us with IntelliSense:

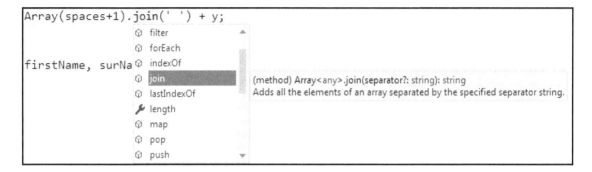

As soon as we save the file, Visual Studio invokes the TypeScript compiler to transpile our file into a `test.js` JavaScript file:

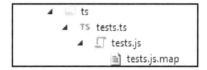

In the case of errors, the JavaScript file is not generated and all errors are displayed in the editor as soon as we save the file. Let's try this behavior by misspelling the `join` method:

```
function fullName(x: string, y: string, spaces: number): string {
    return x + Array(spaces+1).joine(' ') + y;
}
```

When we build the project, all TypeScript errors are also added to the **Error List** panel, as follows:

Running and debugging TypeScript code

Running and debugging TypeScript code is straightforward. It is enough to add the transpiled JavaScript file to a view. Let's add our previous `test.js` file to the bottom of the `Home/Index.cshtml` view:

```
@section Scripts{
    <script src="~/ts/tests.js"></script>
}
```

It is worth remembering that `Script` is a section defined in the `Layout` view of the ASP.NET Core MVC template. It allows all views to place the JavaScript code they need in the right place in the `Layout` view. When you run the project, an alert box should appear as soon as the website's default page is loaded in the browser, as shown in the following screenshot:

Thanks to the `test.js.map` map file generated by the TypeScript compiler, it is possible to debug the TypeScript source instead of the JavaScript transpiled code. In fact, map files contain all the information needed to map each position in the transpiled file into a position in the source file. Map files are not a peculiarity of TypeScript but a well-recognized standard, since they are also used for mapping minimized JavaScript files to their sources.

Let's place a breakpoint on the last instruction of `test.ts` and run the project:

```
function fullName(x: string, y: string, spaces: number): string {
    return x + Array(spaces+1).join(' ') + y;
}

alert(fullName(firstName, surName, 3)+" Hello");
```

Once the breakpoint is hit, you may benefit from all the Visual Studio debugging features you are used to when debugging C# code.

You may see values by hovering over variables with the mouse:

```
var firstName: string = "Francesco";
var surName: string = "Abbruzzese";
        surName "Abbruzzese"
```

Or, you can use a **Watch 1** window:

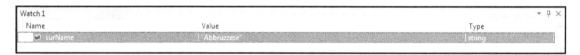

You also have access to the calls stack, to an immediate window, to the intellitrace, and to all other C# code features you are used to.

TypeScript compiler options

As a default, Visual Studio compiles all TypeScript files in your project into JavaScript files with the same names, but with the `.js` extension, and they are placed in the same folder. Moreover, for each `.js` file, it creates a file with the same name but with a `.js.map` extension that is called a map file. Map files map locations in the generated JavaScript files to locations in their TypeSctipt sources, thus enabling debugging on the TypeScript sources. This default behavior of the TypeScript compiler may be changed in two ways: either by forcing Visual Studio to invoke the TypeScript compiler with different parameters, or by specifying the desired options in a configuration file.

Specifying parameters for the TypeScript compiler

All parameters Visual Studio uses to invoke the TypeScript compiler may be edited in the project properties by right-clicking on the project icon and selecting **Properties**:

In the window that appears, select **TypeScript Build**. Here, you may change several options:

- The **TypeScript version** from the ones installed.
- The **ECMAScript version** of the JavaScript code generated. At the moment, **ECMAScript 5** is supported by all mainstream browsers, while higher versions have incomplete support, so it is the advised choice for most applications.

- Whether to **compile on save** or not. If this option is deselected, TypeScript files are compiled only when the whole project is built. This possibility may be useful in complex projects in which the TypeScript build is quite slow because after transpilation, large files are first minimized and then bundled into chunks.
- To keep, or not, all TypeScript source comments in the generated JavaScript files.
- To choose a different directory for both the JavaScript and map files created by the compiler.
- To emit JavaScript code, or not, in the case of errors.
- To emit map files or not. If you want to debug TypeScript sources, you should always emit map files.
- The directory in which to look for TypeScript files to compile. If this directory is not provided, the project root is taken.

Let's unselect the **Compile on save** option, save the changes, modify something in the test.ts file (for instance, change the Hello string to Hello world), and verify that the file is not compiled on save. Have a look at the last modification date of the test.js file. After this test, do not forget to select the **Compile on save** option again.

Now, let's try to put all the files generated by the TypeScript compiler in the js folder:

After that, if you change something in the test.ts file and save it, test.js and test.js.map will appear in the .js folder:

TypeScript configuration file

A TypeScript configuration file allows us to specify several more options. We may specify several input directories instead of just one, we may specify paths/files to be excluded from compilation, or we may specify several more compilations flags.

If you want Visual Studio to invoke the TypeScript compiler automatically, you must give the project TypeScript configuration file its default name, which, `tsconfig.json`. Otherwise, you must invoke the TypeScript compiler manually and pass it the configuration file name as a command-line parameter.

In order to add a TypeScript configuration file to your project, right-click on the project icon in the project explorer and select **Add New Item**:

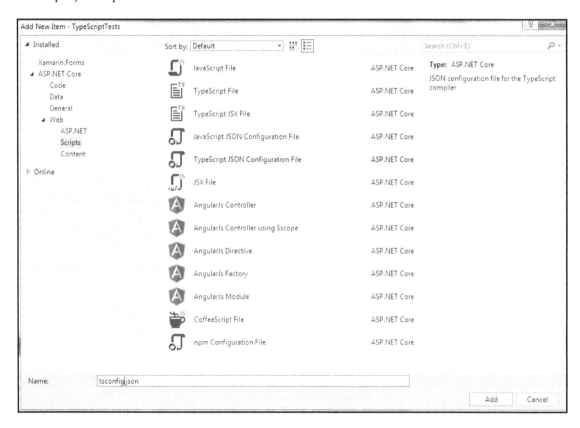

Then select **TypeScript JSON Configuration File**. The configuration file should appear in the project root. Replace its content with the following code:

```
{
    "compileOnSave": true,
    "compilerOptions": {
        "noImplicitAny": false,
        "noEmitOnError": true,
        "removeComments": false,
        "sourceMap": true,
```

```
            "target": "es5",
            "outDir": "wwwroot/js"
        },
        "include": [
            "wwwroot/ts/**/*.ts"
        ],
        "exclude": [
            "**/node_modules"
        ]
    }
```

compileOnSave enables compilation on save, while compilerOptions contains all compiler flags. It is easy to recognize the same options we discussed previously:

- noEmitOnError: No code generation in the case of errors.
- removeComments: It removes/keeps comments in JavaScript-emitted code.
- sourceMap: It enables/disables map files.
- target: It specifies the JavaScript version of the emitted code; in our case, ECMAScript 5.
- outDir: It specifies where to place the emitted files. If omitted, this is next to their sources.
- noImplicitAny: It will be discussed later on in this chapter.

Intellisense suggests the allowed options and values, so there is no need to remember their exact names.

include specifies a list of directory or file patterns to include in the compilation. Each entry is a pattern that may match several directories/files, since entries may contain wildcards: * matches a single name, while ** matches any path. In our case, there is a single pattern that selects all files contained in wwwroot/ts and in all its subdirectories (because of the **), whose extension is .ts.

exclude specifies a list of patterns to remove from the ones added within other options (for instance, with the include option). In our case, a unique pattern excludes all files contained in any directory called node_modules located at any depth, since these directories usually include JavaScript packages downloaded with the **NPM Package Manager**.

There is also a files option to add a list of files (just files, not patterns) to the compilation:

```
"files":[
    "file1.ts",
    "dir/file2.ts",
```

```
    . . .
]
```

If no `files` or `include` options are specified, the whole project root is taken.

Save `tsconfig.json` and modify `tests.ts`. When the file is saved, it should be compiled according to the options contained in `tsconfig.json`.

Once a `tsconfig.json` has been added, all options in the **TypeScript Build** panel of the project properties are disabled:

One or more tsconfig.json or jsconfig.json files detected. Project properties are disabled.

TypeScript version: 2.8

General

ECMAScript version:

JSX compilation in TSX files:

Module System:

☑ Compile on save

☑ Allow implicit 'any' types

Output

☑ Keep comments in TypeScript compiler output

☐ Combine JavaScript output into file:

☐ Redirect TypeScript compiler output to directory: Browse...

☐ Generate declaration files

☐ Do not emit outputs if any errors are reported

Debugging

☑ Generate source maps

☐ Specify root directory of source maps: Browse...

☐ Specify root directory of TypeScript files: Browse...

You may use this panel just to select the TypeScript version; that is, the compiler that is automatically invoked by Visual Studio. All other options must be specified in the configuration file you added.

Basic types

TypeScript primitive types obviously include JavaScript primitive types, namely Boolean, number, string, null, and undefined. However, TypeScript adds a few new primitive types and slightly changes the semantics of primitive types. All type declaration examples in the remainder of the chapter may be tested by adding them to our `test.ts` file.

TypeScript type system

The TypeScript type system is similar to one of the other object-oriented languages, such as C#. There is a root type called `any` that is similar, but not completely equivalent, to the C# `Object`. All primitive types are direct descendants of `any`, while all complex types, such as the `Date` type, for instance, descend from the `object` type, which , in turn, is a direct descendant of `any`:

```
var myDate: Date = new Date(); //a Date is a complex type
var myString: string = "this is a string"; //string is a simple type
var myNumber: number = 10; //number is a simple type
var myBoolean: boolean = true; //boolean is a simple type

/* Correct all types descend from any */
var x: any = myDate;
x = myString;
x = myNumber;
x = myBoolean;

/* Correct all comlex types descend from object */
var myObject: object = myDate;

/* Wrong! Simple types do not descend from object */

myObject = myString;
myObject = myNumber;
myObject = myBoolean;
```

The last three statements are wrong since primitive types do not descend from objects; the Visual Studio TypeScript editor should immediately signal the following errors:

```
myObject = myString;
myOb:
     [●] var myObject: object

     (TS) Type 'string' is not assignable to type 'object'.
```

Errors are underlined in red, and it is enough to hover the mouse over them to see a detailed error message. So, the C# Object is similar to the TypeScript any and not to the TypeScript object.

any and unknown

While any may be considered the TypeScript root type, the semantics of any are quite different from the usual semantics of other languages' root types. In fact, while other languages' root types allow almost no operations on them, any allows all operations. It is a way to prevent any type check, and was conceived this way to allow compatibility of some code chunks with JavaScript. In fact, once something has been declared as any, it may be processed as it can in simple JavaScript, with no preoccupations about compilation-time type checks.

TypeScript 3.0 also introduces the unknown type, which behaves more like a usual root type since no operations are allowed on a variable declared as unknown, and all values may be assigned to an unknown variable. Thus, from version 3.0 onward, TypeScript has two root types that can be assigned to each other, any and unknown. any disables type checks and allows all operations, while unknown behaves like a usual root type.

Strings, numbers, and Booleans

Strings, numbers, and Booleans have the usual JavaScript semantics; there are no integers or decimals, but all numbers are represented by the number type, which is a 64-bit floating point, and Boolean may have just the true and false values:

```
var myString: string = "this is a string"; //string is a simple type
var myNumber: number = 10; //number is a 64 bit floating point simple type
var myBoolean: boolean = true; //boolean is a simple type whose only values
are: true, false.
```

The null and undefined subtypes

Like in JavaScript, `null` and `undefined` denote both the two types and the only values these types may have:

```
/* correct null type may assume just the null value */
var myNull: null = null;

/* correct undefined type may assume just the undefined value */
var myUndefined: undefined = undefined;

/* Wrong! */
myNull = 10;
myUndefined = 10;
```

As a default, `null` and `undefined` are subtypes of all types (including all custom types defined by the user), so we may assign them to any variable/property.

As in JavaScript, `undefined` is the implicit value assigned to any object that was not initialized yet:

```
/* value is undefined since variable was not initialized */
var notInitialized: number;
```

However, if the `strictNullChecks` compiler option is explicitly set to `true`, `null` and `undefined` aren't subtypes of all types anymore, so `null` and `undefined` become illegal values for all other types.

Let's add this option to our project's `tsconfig.ts`:

```
{
    "compileOnSave": true,
    "compilerOptions": {
        "noImplicitAny": false,
        "strictNullChecks": true,
        "noEmitOnError": true,
        "removeComments": false,
        "sourceMap": true,
        "target": "es5",
        "outDir": "wwwroot/js"
    },
    "include": [
        "wwwroot/ts/**/*.ts"
    ],
    "exclude": [
        "**/node_modules",
        "**/*.spec.ts"
```

```
        ]
    }
```

Then add this code to `tests.ts`:

```
/* Wrong! */

var nullCheck: string = null;
var undefinedCheck: string = undefined;
```

Both declarations will be signaled as wrong, since now `null` and `undefined` are illegal values for a string.

If you want a specific string variable to accept null and/or undefined values, you may use another TypeScript feature: union types.

Basics of union types

In order to keep most of the JavaScript flexibility without renouncing compile-time type checks, TypeScript allows the definition of new types as unions of other types. For example:

```
/* Both statements are correct */
var stringOrNumber: string | number = "Hellow";
stringOrNumber = 10;
```

A Union Type may assume all values allowed by all its member types, so `stringOrNumber` may assume both `string` and `number` values. Without union types, `stringOrNumber` should have been declared `any`, thus renouncing completely any type checks.

We may mix more than two types in a Union Type so for instance, if we set `strictNullChecks` but we want a specific string variable to also take `null` and `undefined` values, we may declare it as follows:

```
var nullCheck: string|null|undefined = null;
var undefinedCheck: string | null | undefined = undefined;
```

Now both statements are correct. We may also define aliases for union types:

```
type NullableString = string | null;

type ExtendedString = string | null | undefined;

var nullCheck: NullableString = null;
var undefinedCheck: ExtendedString = undefined;
```

This way, we factor out their definitions into a single place and avoid tedious repetitions.

 If you set the `strictNullChecks` options and use Union Types and Type aliases to specify when `null` and `undefined` are allowed, you have a better compile-time check and you may avoid hard-to-find bugs.

Union Types may also be defined as unions of either numeric constants or string constants. Here is a string constants example:

```
type fontStype = "Plain" | "Bold" | "Italic" | "Underlined";

var myFontType: fontStype = "Bold"; //Right

myFontType = "Red"; //Wrong
```

And here is a numeric constants example:

```
type dice = 1 | 2 | 3 | 4 | 5 | 6;

var myDice: dice =5; //Right

myDice = 7; //Wrong
```

void

`void` is a type that can't assume any value except for `null` or `undefined`. It make no sense to declare a variable of type `void`. This type should be used just to declare a function that must return no value:

```
function sayHello(): void {
    alert("Hello world");
}
```

If a function whose return value has been declared `void` actually returns a value along some paths, an error is signaled at compile time:

```
/* Wrong! */
function sayHelloWrong(): void {
    alert("Hello world");
    return 1;
}
```

Also, the converse is true; a function whose return type has been declared, say `number`, but which doesn't return a value along some paths, will trigger a compile-time error:

```
/* Wrong! */
function wrongNumer(x: number): number {
    if (x > 0) return x;
}
```

The error may be removed either by adding the missing `return` statement or by adding `void` to the return value:

```
/* Correct! */
function wrongNumer(x: number): number|void {
    if (x > 0) return x;
}
```

never

`never` is the type whose values never occur! It is the return type of functions that never return, either because of an endless loop or because they always throw an exception:

```
/* never return type is explicitly declared */
function error(message: string): never {
    throw message;
}
/* never return type is inferred by compiler */
function alwaysinError() {
    return error("there was an error");
}
```

You may verify that the compiler automatically infers the `never` return type of the second function by hovering the mouse over the function name:

```
/* never return type is explicitly declared */
function error(message: string): never {
    throw message;
}
/* never return type is inferred by compiler */
function alwaysinError() {
    return error
                  function alwaysinError(): never
}
```

Here is an endless loop:

```
function endlessLoop(): never
{
    while (true)
    {
        ...
        ...
    }
}
```

Here is a function that may return or may die in an endless loop:

```
function endlessLoop(x: string): never|number {
    while (true) {
        if (x == "stop") return 1;
    }
}
```

Enums

TypeScript also provides C#-style enum types:

```
enum YesNoAnswer { unknown, yes, no};
var myAnswer: YesNoAnswer = YesNoAnswer.unknown;
```

Like in C#, enum values are translated into integers. As a default, the first value is assigned 0, the second value 1, and so on. However, the default start value may be changed:

```
enum YesNoAnswer { unknown=1, yes , no}; //yes=2, no=3
```

You may also provide default integers for all enum values:

```
enum YesNoAnswer { unknown=1, yes=3 , no=5};
```

Integers may also be specified through expressions involving the previously defined variables and values of the same enum:

```
enum YesNoAnswer { unknown=1, yes=unknown+2 , no=yes+2};
```

The TypeScript compiler generates a variable with the same name as the enum and does something like this:

```
YesNoAnswer = {};
YesNoAnswer["unknown"] = 1;
YesNoAnswer["yes"] = 3;
YesNoAnswer["no"] = 5;
```

That's why we may use expressions such as `YesNoAnswer.unknown` to refer to the enum values.

We may also translate the integer associated with each enum value to the string representing its name:

>YesNoAnswer[3]
>"yes"

This is because the TypeScript compiler generates also something like:

```
YesNoAnswer[1] = "unknown";
YesNoAnswer[3] = "yes";
YesNoAnswer[5] = "no";
```

If the enum is defined to be constant, the `YesNoAnswer` variable and all associated properties are not generated, and each occurrence of `YesNoAnswer.unknown`, `YesNoAnswer.yes`, and `YesNoAnswer.no` in the code is replaced by its associated integer at compile time in the generated JavaScript code:

```
const enum YesNoAnswer { unknown=1, yes=3 , no=5};
var myAnswer: YesNoAnswer = YesNoAnswer.unknown;

/* when the enum is const this is wrong*/
var valueName: string = YesNoAnswer[1];
```

However, in this case, expressions like `YesNoAnswer[3]` are not allowed anymore:

```
/* when the enum is const this is wrong*/
var valueName: string = YesNoAnswer[1];
```
                        (TS) A const enum member can only be accessed using a string literal.

Moreover, all integers defining the constant enum values must be constant the compiler may compute at compile time.

Thus, the following is correct:

```
const enum YesNoAnswer { unknown=1, yes=unknown+2 , no=yes+2};
```

However, we can't assign the `startEnum` variable, whose value changes at runtime, to `unknown`:

```
var startEnum : number;
. . .
. . .
. . .
const enum YesNoAnswer { unknown=startEnum, yes=unknown+2 , no=yes+2};
```

Otherwise, we get a compilation error:

```
const enum YesNoAnswer { unknown = startEnum, yes=unknown+2 , no=yes+2};

                              [●] var startEnum: number

                              (TS) In 'const' enum declarations member initializer must be constant expression.
```

Thus, `const enum` generates less JavaScript code at the price of less flexibility.

`enum` values may be combined with the bitwise operators `&`, `|`, and `~`:

```
const enum YesNoAnswer { unknown = 1, yes = unknown + 2, no = yes + 2 };

var myAnswer: YesNoAnswer = YesNoAnswer.unknown | YesNoAnswer.yes;
```

Thus, we may define the equivalent of C# bit flags:

```
const enum TextTransformation {
    None = 0,
    Bold = 1,
    Italic = Bold << 1, //2
    Underline = Italic << 1, //4
    Overline = Italic << 1, //8
    LineThrough = Overline << 1, // 16
    HasLine = Underline | Overline | LineThrough
}

function HasBold(x: TextTransformation): boolean {
    return (x & TextTransformation.Bold) == TextTransformation.Bold;
}
```

The `HasBold` function shows how bit properties may be tested in exactly the same way as in C#.

Declarations and scoping

TypeScript declarations and scoping rules are one of the ECMAScript 6 version of JavaScript, with the only addition of type specifications after the declared objects. Also, TypeScript expressions support some new ECMAScript 6 features, such as string interpolation. In case the JavaScript target is a lower version, all ECMAScript 6-specific features are simulated by the TypeScript transpiler, which automatically generates the equivalent JavaScript code.

Declarations

In the previous example, we have already seen declarations based on the var keyword:

```
var myString: string;
```

Declarations may also initialize the variables with expressions involving both constants and other previously defined variables:

```
var firstName: string = "Francesco";
var surName: string = "Abbruzzese";

function fullName(x: string, y: string, spaces: number): string {
    return x + Array(spaces+1).join(' ') + y;
}

var label: string = fullName(firstName, surName, 3);
```

A single var statement may also contain several declarations:

```
var aString: string = "this is a string",
    aNumber: number,
    anInteger: number = 1;
```

The first and third variables have been initialized, while the second one is still undefined.

TypeScript also supports ECMAScript 6 declarations based on const and let:

```
const aConstString: string = "this is a string",
    aConstNumber: number=1.5,
    aConstInteger: number = 1;
```

`const` has the purpose of defining constants, so variables declared with `const` are read-only and can't be modified:

```
aConstInteger = 2;
         □ const aConstInteger: number

         (TS) Cannot assign to 'aConstInteger' because it is a constant or a read-only property.
```

Since constants can't be modified, they must always be initialized in their declarations:

```
const aConstString: string = "this is a string",
      aConstNumber: number,
      aCo
         □ const aConstNumber: number

         (TS) 'const' declarations must be initialized.
```

Declarations based on `let` have the same syntax and almost the same semantics as `var`-based declarations:

```
let aString: string = "this is a string",
    aNumber: number,
    anInteger: number = 1;
```

The difference between `var` and `let` is just in the scoping rules. We will analyze scoping rules in detail in a short time.

Obligatoriness of declarations and noImplicitAny

In JavaScript, when an undeclared variable is used, it is automatically declared in global scope, often causing hard-to-find bugs.

For this reason, in TypeScript, variables can be used just after they have been declared:

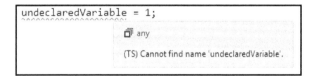

```
undeclaredVariable = 1;
              □ any

              (TS) Cannot find name 'undeclaredVariable'.
```

When a variable is initialized, its type may be automatically inferred, so it may be omitted:

```
var thisIsAString = "a string";
            [●] var thisIsAString: string
```

However, when a variable is not initialized, the specification of the variable type is not obligatory! The type assigned to a not initialized variable when the type is not specified explicitly depends on the noImplicitAny compiler option, or, more specifically:

- When noImplicitAny is false, the variable is assigned the any type.
- When noImplicitAny is true, the compiler tries to infer the type of the variable from the type of the first expression that is assigned to that variable.

For example, if the configuration file of the TypeScriptTests project sets noImplicitAny to false and we omit type specifications:

```
var untypedVar;
```

any is assumed, as you may verify by hovering the mouse over the untypedVar variable:

```
var untypedVar;
            [●] var untypedVar: any
```

However, if you set noImplicitAny to true in tsconfig.json, and you slightly change the code:

```
let untypedVar;

untypedVar = 1.2;
var test1: number = untypedVar + 2;
            [●] let untypedVar: number
```

The number type is automatically inferred because the first value assigned to untypedVar is a number (namely, 1.2). Thus, no error is signaled in the next statement, in which untypedVar is added to a constant number.

Rely on automatic type inference only when a variable is initialized in the declaration so that there are absolutely no doubts about its type. Otherwise, always declare variable types, since hard-to-find bugs might occur in subsequent code modifications.

Variable scoping

Scoping rules are different for the old `var` and the ECMAScript 6 `let` and `const`. All of them have global scope when declared outside any of the functions and blocks:

```
/*global scope, visible also outside the file they are declared in.*/
var firstName = "Francesco";
var surName = "Abbruzzese";

function fullName(x, y, spaces){
    x + Array(spaces+1).join(' ') + y;
}
```

However, variables defined with `var` are visible within the inner function they are defined in, while variables defined with `let` and `const` are visible just in the inner block they are defined in:

```
function scopeTest(x: number) {
    if (x > 0) {
        var result: number = x;
    }
    else {
        result = -x; //correct result is visible within the whole function
    }
    return result; //correct result is visible within the whole function
}

function scopeTestLet(x: number) {

    if (x > 0) {
        let result: number = x;
    }
    else {
        result = -x; //error result is undefined here
    }
    return result; //error result is undefined here
}
```

In the case of `for` loops, if the loop variables are declared with `let`, different variable instances are defined for each loop iteration:

```
for (let i = 0; i < 5; i++) {
    setTimeout(function(){ console.log(i) }, 1000);
}
```

A new variable named `i` is created at each iteration. So, we have five different variables with the values 0, 1, 2, 3, 4. Due to `setTimeout`, all variables are logged to the console after 1 second (1000 milliseconds), when the `for` loop is already ended. The five different copies of `i` remain unchanged and also retain their values after the `for` loop has ended, so the result in the console will be this:

```
>0
>1
>2
>3
>4
```

Now let's see by substituting `let` with `var`:

```
for (var i = 0; i < 5; i++) {
    setTimeout(function(){ console.log(i) }, 1000);
}
```

Then there would be a unique `i`, whose scope is the function containing the `for` loop. Accordingly, after the loop ends, the value of this unique variable would be 5. Therefore, since all five occurrences of the `setTimeout` statement capture this variable, and since all values are logged after the end of the `for` loop, the result in the console will be this:

```
>5
>5
>5
>5
>5
```

As in C#, variables may always be redefined outside their scope, since variables defined this way are considered different:

```
for (let i = 0; i < 5; i++) {
    setTimeout(function(){ console.log(i) }, 1000);
}
let i: string ="this is a string";
```

In a difference from C#, a new variable with the same name may also appear in the same scope. In this case, the newer definition overrides the previous one:

```
var firstName = "francesco";
var firstName = "peter"; //correct, new definition overrides previous one.
```

However, overrides are allowed only if the two variables have the same type:

```
var firstName: string = "Francesco";
var firstName: number = 1";
```

      [✎] var firstName: string

      (TS) Subsequent variable declarations must have the same type. Variable 'firstName' must be of type 'string', but here has type 'number'.

Expressions – type assertions, and string interpolation

The syntax of TypeScript expressions is exactly the same as the syntax of JavaScript expressions. This syntax is also identical to the expression syntax of other languages, such as C# and C++. However, TypeScript contains one more unary operator: the type assertion operator. This operator doesn't generate any JavaScript code; it simply replaces the type inferred by the TypeScript compiler with a type assertion provided by the developer:

```
function tryConvertNumber(x: string): string | number {
    var res = parseFloat(x);
    if (isNaN(res)) return x;
    else return res;
}
let numberAsAString: string = "5";

let newNumber: number = <number>tryConvertNumber(numberAsAString);
```

In this case, the compiler is not able to infer that the result of the function call is actually a number, so the developer, who knows it from the logic of the code, avoids a type error by asserting the right type. Type assertions also have an `as` syntax:

```
let newNumber: number = tryConvertNumber(letbumberAsAString) as number;
```

The two syntaxes are completely equivalent. It is worth pointing out that while syntax is very similar to C#, semantics are completely different. In fact, while C# attempts an actual type conversion; TypeScript does not attempt any type conversion, it just replaces its inferred type with the one provided by the developer.

String interpolation is another expression enhancement provided by TypeScript. Actually, it is already part of ECMAScript 6, but TypeScript also provides it when targeting lower JavaScript versions. String interpolation is also available in C# from version 6.0 onward and is a kind of enhanced string format:

```
let person = {
    name: "francesco",
    surname: "abbruzzese",
    title: "Mr."
};

let hello: string = `Hello ${person.title + ' ' + person.name}
${person.name}`;
```

String templates are enclosed between backticks, `, instead of the usual quotes with strings. Each ${} may contain any expression that evaluates to a string. The content of each ${} is evaluated and replaces the ${} in the final string. In our example, the final string is this:

```
>Hello Mr. francesco abbruzzese
```

Summary

TypeScript enhances JavaScript with types, and with features that are only available in the more recent ECMAScript standards. You may install the TypeScript SDK in Visual Studio to take advantage of the same user interface you are used to with C#, or you may install it with Node.js. Adding TypeScript to your ASP.NET projects is straightforward; it is enough to add .ts files to it. Compiler options may be specified within Visual Studio project options, or with a specific JSON configuration file. According to the compiler settings, JavaScript files are generated either on saving the respective .ts files or when the project is built, and may be placed in your Views in the usual way.

TypeScript declarations are very similar to JavaScript declarations, the only differences being that they are obligatory and are the specifications of types. Simple types are the same as JavaScript, with only the addition of any, unknown, void, never, and the C#-like enum.

Scoping rules include let and const ECMAScript 6 block-level scoping, together with the usual var-based scoping.

TypeScript enhances JavaScript expressions with type assertions and ECMAScript 6 string interpolation.

Questions

1. What are the main benefits of adding types to JavaScript?
2. Is it possible to get the type of a TypeScript variable at runtime? How?
3. At the moment, is there any chance the TypeScript team will add something like C# operator overloading so users may define custom behavior for + and – when applied to their custom types? Why?
4. Is there a way to define a variable that might contain both numbers and strings? What is the best way to do it?
5. What is the return type of a function that returns no value?
6. What is the scope of a variable that has not been declared?
7. How many instances of the counter variable are generated by a `var`-based `for` loop that iterates 100 times? How many instances are generated by the `let` version of the same loop?
8. Is this assertion true: TypeScript string variables are always allowed to have a `null` value? Explain.
9. What is the most space-efficient way to define an `enum` (the one that generates the least code and requires the least runtime memory)?
10. How do you declare that the values of an `enum` are C#-like bit flags?

Further reading

This chapter, as does the remainder of the book, assumes a minimum familiarity with both ASP.NET Core and JavaScript basics. To learn about them, you may refer to *Learning ASP.NET Core 2.0* (`https://www.packtpub.com/application-development/javascript-and-jquery-7-days-video`), and to Microsoft's official documentation (`https://docs.microsoft.com/en-US/aspnet/core/?view=aspnetcore-2.1`) for ASP.NET Core. Also, refer to *JavaScript (and jQuery) in 7 Days* (`https://www.packtpub.com/application-development/javascript-and-jquery-7-days-video`) to learn the basics of JavaScript and jQuery.

To learn more about TypeScript's design goals, please refer to the official design goals stated by the TypeScript development team: `https://github.com/Microsoft/TypeScript/wiki/TypeScript-Design-Goals`.

Complex Types and Functions

2

This chapter covers complex types, such as arrays, tuples for returning multiple values, and indexable types. We will look at how to define and use interfaces, and how to build new types via the union or intersection of existing types. Thanks to this union and intersection of types, type-checking can benefit from the flexibility of JavaScript variables, in that they can hold several different types—ES6-style function definitions, with ES6 pattern matching, destructuring, and spread, features supported by TypeScript. These features help developers to write more concise and readable code, and deploy more flexible functions. All of the concepts that we explore will be explained simply, with concise examples.

The following topics will be covered in this chapter:

- Using arrays and tuples
- Defining and using interfaces, indexable types, and type inference
- Union and discriminated unions
- Intersection of types
- Objects and arrays destructuring, spread operator
- Functions

Technical requirements

To follow along with the examples in this chapter, you will need to have the following installed on your machine:

- Visual Studio 2017 with the latest ASP.NET Core tools
- Visual Studio TypeScript SDK

All code snippets in this chapter can be tested by adding new TypeScript files to the previous chapter's `TypeScriptTests` project, or to a new ASP.NET Core project. The code can be executed by adding the JavaScript files produced by the TypeScript compiler to any project View, and then by monitoring what happens with the Visual Studio debugger.

All the code used in this chapter can be downloaded from the following GitHub link: `https://github.com/PacktPublishing/Hands-On-TypeScript-for-CSharp-and-.NET-Core-Developers`.

Arrays and tuples

TypeScript arrays are operated exactly the same way as JavaScript arrays, the only difference being that the former's types are explicitly declared.

TypeScript also introduces tuples, notwithstanding they are not part of any ECMAScript standard (remember that, according to its manifest, the TypeScript language should contain either type elements or features approved in an ECMAScript standard). While other languages such as C# support tuples, since they allow functions to return multiple values, tuples were never considered in any ECMAScript standard. The main reason for this is that they appear unnecessary in a language such as JavaScript, where multiple values are easily handled by arrays, in the form of `["this is a string", 12]`, which may contain heterogeneous objects. TypeScript, instead, needs a tuples syntax to constrain value types. TypeScript arrays and tuples are described in detail in two dedicated subsections.

Array declaration

TypeScript arrays are almost completely analogous to JavaScript arrays; the only differences are that all array elements must have the same type, and that array variables must be declared together with the array type. In turn, the type of an array is denoted with the type of its elements, followed by the `[]` symbols. Thus, array variables may be declared as follows:

```
let names: string[] = ["Francesco", "Mary", "John"];
let ages: number[] = [14, 18, 35, 40];
let outcomes: number[];

outcomes = [];
```

The following screenshot shows how the `names` array appears in the Visual Studio debugger:

```
let names: string[] = ["Francesco", "Mary", "John"];
let ages    names Array(3) ["Francesco", "Mary", "John"]
let outcom     length    3
                 0        "Francesco"
outcomes =       1        "Mary"
                 2        "John"
               _proto_   Array(0) [, ...]
```

Analogously to simple types, declarations may initialize the variable or not.

If the variable type is inferred by its initialization, the type may be omitted as follows:

```
let someStrings = ["a string", "another string"];
```

The type inferred by TypeScript can be shown by hovering the mouse over the variable definition:

```
let someStrings = ["a string", "another string"];
        [◉] let someStrings: string[]
```

If the values specified in the initial array have different types, then the right union type is inferred. To demonstrate this, consider the following piece of code:

```
let numbersAndStrings = ["a string", 12];
```

The preceding statement is the same as the following:

```
let numbersAndStrings: (string|number)[] = ["a string", 12];
```

The following screenshot shows how the union type, inferred for the variable by TypeScript, can be revealed by hovering the mouse over the variable:

```
let numbersAndStrings = ["a string", 12];
        [◉] let numbersAndStrings: (string | number)[]
```

Don't forget the parentheses when specifying arrays of union types, since the `[]` operator has precedence over `|`. For instance, if you omit the parentheses in `(string|number)[]`, the assumed type will be `string|(number[])`, which is either a string or an array of numbers.

When the type can't be inferred because the initial array is empty, the behavior of the TypeScript compiler depends on the value of the `noImplicitAny` compiler option. If it is true, `any[]` is assumed, as shown here:

```
let cantInferTypes = [];
                         [☞] let cantInferTypes: any[]
```

If it is false, an array of impossible values is assumed; that is, `never[]`:

```
let cantInferTypes = [];
                         [☞] let cantInferTypes: never[]
```

Such a type is completely useless, since we can't add any value to such an array:

```
cantInferTypes.push(3);
                         (TS) Argument of type '3' is not assignable to parameter of type 'never'.
```

 Do not rely on type inference when the initial array is empty, since this might cause errors during subsequent software maintenance.

Tuples

Tuples are part of several languages. C# introduced an ad hoc syntax for tuples in v7.0. JavaScript has no special syntax for tuples, since they are handled with arrays, while TypeScript needs an ad hoc syntax to specify type constraints. Tuples are declared with a syntax along the following lines:

```
var result: [number, boolean];
var resultWithValue: [number, boolean] = [12, true];
```

Specifying the type is obligatory; otherwise, the TypeScript compiler can't distinguish between tuples and arrays, and assumes an array by default. Tuples elements can be accessed through the usual array syntax, as follows:

```
var success: boolean = resultWithValue[1];
```

Later in this chapter, when describing destructuring in the *Destructuring and spread* section, we will see a smarter way to access tuples elements.

A typical application of tuples is in the definition of functions that perform computations that might fail:

```
var result: number;
...
function stringToNumber(s: string): [number, boolean]
{
    var res = parseFloat(s);
    if (isNaN(res)) return [0, false];
    else return [res, true];
}

result = stringToNumber("5.7")
if (result[1]) console.log(result[0])
else console.log("error")

result = stringToNumber("not a number")
if (result[1]) console.log(result[0])
else console.log("error")
```

The Boolean part of the tuple returned by the function contains the success/failure information that is used by the calling code to decide whether to print the result or an error message.

The following output is shown in the browser console when the preceding code is executed in Chrome:

Up to now, this chapter has described TypeScript's counterpart of JavaScript predefined types. The next section introduces TypeScript interfaces, which are the simplest way to define custom types.

Interfaces and type inference

In versions of JavaScript prior to and including the fifth version, objects have no specific types attached to them. We can use prototypes and constructor functions to create objects with predefined shapes (that is, with properties and functions attached to them), but further properties and functions may be attached to them at any point. ECMAScript 6 introduces classes that will be described later in this book, but their usage is not obligatory, and the developer may continue using also untyped objects.

TypeScript introduces interfaces to describe the shape of both untyped and typed objects. Thus, TypeScript interfaces can be used as in C# to define the functionality to be implemented by classes, as well as to assign types to untyped objects based on their structure. In short, TypeScript interfaces assign names to structural features of usual JavaScript objects.

Interfaces basics

Let's define a new TypeScript file, called `Interface.ts`, to collect all interfaces examples.

The syntax for defining interfaces is straightforward, and mimics object syntax, as shown here:

```
interface Person {
  name: string;
  surname: string;
}
```

The preceding definition says that every object having `name` and `surmame` properties of the `string` type is a `Person`. Once defined, the interface may be used to prescribe constraints on objects. For instance, we can prescribe that a function that computes the `fullname` function may only accept objects that are `Person`; that is, objects with `name` and `surname` properties that are strings:

```
function fullName(x: Person): string {
    return x.name + " " + x.surname;
}
```

The usage of the interface prevents errors and wrong calls to the function. Moreover, we get IntelliSense assistance while coding the function:

In most object languages, when we call `fullname`, we need to declare explicitly that the object passed is a `Person`:

```
let testObject: Person = {
    name: "John",
    surname: "Smith"
};
alert(fullName(testObject));
```

In TypeScript, however, there is no need to declare `testObject` as `Person`:

```
let testObject = {
    name: "John",
    surname: "Smith",
    age: 42
};
alert(fullName(testObject));
```

In fact, the TypeScript compiler is able to understand that `testObject` is a `Person` from the fact that `testObject` has all the properties required by the `Person` interface. In general, an object, that hasn't been explicitly declared as a certain type is assumed to belong to an interface type if it has all of the properties prescribed by that interface. This TypeScript feature is called **structural subtyping**.

Readonly properties

In the preceding `Person` example, it would be useful to prevent all functions that process `Person` objects from modifying `name` and `surname`, since `Person`, `name`, and `surmame` do not usually change. This is easily achieved with the `readonly` keyword, as follows:

```
interface Person {
    readonly name: string;
    readonly surname: string;
}
```

Now, if, for some reason, an error might cause an unwanted modification, then a compilation time error is signalled immediately:

```
function errorFullName(x: Person): string {
    if (x.name = "") return x.surname;
    else if
    else ret
}
```
(property) Person.name: string

(TS) Cannot assign to 'name' because it is a constant or a read-only property.

If there are a few functions that need to modify `name` and/or `surname`, then we can define a new interface:

```
interface PersonToModify {
    name: string;
    surname: string
}
function changeName(x: PersonToModify, newName: string): void {
    x.name=newName;
}
```

`Person` and `PersonToModify` are assignable to each other thanks to structural subtyping. This means that we can use the most appropriate one for each function definition, that is, `Person` for `fullName`, and `PersonToModify` for `changeName`, with no risk of causing incompatibilities:

```
let me: Person ={
    name: "francesco",
     surname: "abbruzzese"
}

changeName(me, "frank");
alert(fullName(me));
```

Optional properties

TypeScript allows the definition of optional properties in interfaces. This might appear meaningless, since interfaces only prescribe that an object must simply have some properties, so any additional property is optional. But actually, by explicitly defining some optional properties, we have the benefit of being able to refer to them without casting the object to `any`. For instance, in order to handle a possible second name without optional properties, we would be forced writing something like the following:

```
function fullName(x: Person): string {
    if((x as any).secondName)
        return x.name + " " + (x as any).secondName + " " + x.surname;
    else
        return x.name + " " + x.surname;
}
```

The preceding code also carries the risk of misspelling `secondName`, since no check on the correctness of this property is done. Optional properties allow a better solution:

```
interface Person {
    readonly name: string,
    readonly secondName?: string;
    readonly surname: string;
}

function fullName(x: Person): string {
    if(x.secondName)
        return x.name + " " + x.secondName + " " + x.surname;
    else
        return x.name + " " + x.surname;
}
```

Properties are declared as optional simply by adding a question mark at the end of their names.

Excess property check

Since interfaces just prescribe that their properties be present in all declared objects of that interface type, then an object declared as a `Person` interface type may also contain other properties that are not defined in `Person`; for example, an `age` property that is not contained in `Person`. Thus, the following code will compile and work properly:

```
let testObject: Person = {
    name: "John",
    surname: "Smith",
    age: 42
};
alert(fullName(testObject));
```

So, we might expect that, for the same reason, the following equivalent code should also compile properly:

```
alert(fullName({
    name: "John",
    surname: "Smith",
    age: 42
}));
```

But upon compilation, we find that an error message is displayed instead:

```
    name: "John",
    surname: "Smith",
    age: 42
}));      🔧 (property) age: number

          (TS) Argument of type '{ name: string; surname: string; age: number; }' is not assignable to parameter of type 'Person'.
          Object literal may only specify known properties, and 'age' does not exist in type 'Person'.
```

In general, when a literal object (that is, an object that is not contained in a variable or returned by a function, but that is explicitly written) is assigned to a function parameter, or to a variable declared as interface, only properties explicitly mentioned in that interface are allowed. The explanation behind this apparently strange feature, referred to as **excess property check**, is as follows:

- It is not very useful to add properties to a literal object that the subsequent code is not able to access. In our example, the `age` property can't be accessed by the `fullName` function, and since the `fullName` function is the only user of the literal object, then the `age` property is totally useless, because `fullname` can only access properties declared in the `Person` interface. If we already know that the object might contain an `age` property that the function needs to process, then the correct way to proceed is to declare `age` as an optional interface property.
- This behavior prevents properties being misspelled in the object literal. In fact, if, for instance, `name` is misspelled as `neme`, an error is signaled since `neme` is not an interface property.

Defining function properties in interfaces

Interface property types may also include functions, as follows:

```
interface Point {
    x: number;
    y: number;
    Distance(p1: Point, p2: Point): number;
}

let myPoint: Point =
    {
        x:1,
        y:1,
        Distance: function(p1: Point, p2: Point): number{
            return Math.sqrt((p1.x - p2.x) * (p1.x - p2.x) +
                (p1.y - p2.y) * (p1.y - p2.y));
        }
    };
```

Function properties are declared simply by providing the function signature. All objects of any interface must provide implementations for all function signatures specified by that interface.

Interfaces that specify a single unnamed function type, with no further properties, are identified with the single function type they contain, as shown here:

```
interface CombineStrings {
    (string1: string, string2: string): string;
}

let concat: CombineStrings =
    function (string1: string, string2: string) {
        return string1 + string2;
    };
alert(concat("12", "34"));
```

In this case, the function is not associated with any property, but the function signature is inserted as the unique content of the interface declaration. This is the TypeScript equivalent of C# delegates. TypeScript chooses to use interfaces for defining functions because of structural subtyping; that is, because, in TypeScript, interfaces are the standard way to give names to entity shapes.

Indexable types

Indexable types are another way that interfaces are used to classify entities according to their shape.

Arrays use integers to index other types, but we know that JavaScript also uses strings indexers. For example, we can create a phone book with simple statements, such as the following:

```
tel["John smith"]= "3512421934";
```

TypeScript strongly types indexers with the help of interfaces:

```
interface PhoneBook {
    [index: string]: string
}
let myPhoneBook: PhoneBook = {};
myPhoneBook["John smith"] = "3512421934";
```

Since `PhoneBook` is an interface, that is, just a shape description, we cannot create instances of it, but we must create instances of types that support the interface, so we assign { } to `myPhoneBook`.

We can also have something more complex, such as the type returned by the indexer:

```
interface ContactData {
    tel: string;
    Country: string;
    Address: string;
}
interface ComplexPhoneBook {
    [index: string]: ContactData
}
let myComplexPhoneBook: ComplexPhoneBook = {};
myComplexPhoneBook["John smith"] = {
    tel: "3512421934",
    Country: "United Kingdom",
    Address: "........."
}
```

If the indexer is an integer, we must create an object that supports integer indexers, or in other words, an array:

```
interface ToDoList {
    [number: number]: string
}
let myToDoList: ToDoList = ["todo 1", "todo 1"];
myToDoList[3] = "todo 3";
```

However, once an array is assigned to a `ToDoList` variable, we cannot use all array methods, and are instead limited to indexing operations:

```
let myToDoList: ToDoList = ["todo 1", "todo 1"];
myToDoList[3] = "todo 3";

myToDoList.push("todo 4"); //wrong
```

In order to use `push`, we need to perform a type assertion as follows:

```
(myToDoList as string[]).push("todo  4"); //correct
```

Strings and integers are the only permissible indexers, but we may define indexers that support both of them:

```
interface HybridComplexPhoneBook {
    [index: string]: ContactData
    [index: number]: ContactData
}
let myHybridPhoneBook: HybridComplexPhoneBook = {};
myComplexPhoneBook["John smith"] = {
    name: "John smith",
```

```
        tel: "3512421934",
        Country: "United Kingdom",
        Address: "........."
    }
    myComplexPhoneBook[1] = {
        name: "Francesco Abbruzzese",
        tel: "3333333333",
        Country: "United Kingdom",
        Address: "........."
    };
```

However, in this case, we can't actually retrieve myComplexPhoneBook[1] with myComplexPhoneBook["Francesco Abbruzzese"], because the 1 integer is transformed into the "1" string, and the string is indexed under "1" and not under "Francesco Abbruzzese". For the same reason, the type returned by the number indexer must be coherent with the one specified for the string indexer; that is, it must be either the same type or a subtype of it:

```
interface WrongComplexPhoneBook {
    [index: string]: ContactData
    [index: number]: string
}
    [●] (parameter) index: number

    (TS) Numeric index type 'string' is not assignable to string index type 'ContactData'.
```

Since, in JavaScript, a["name"] is the same as a.name , indexers are used also to add an indefinite number of properties to an object. Clearly, no TypeScript check or IntelliSense is available on the indefinite number of property names added through indexers, so TypeScript gives us the ability to mix properties added through indexers, with properties whose names are known in advance:

```
interface ProductDataScheet {
    [index: string]: string;
    name: string;
    code: string;
    description: string;
}

let myProductDataScheet: ProductDataScheet={
    name: "fast trigger",
    code: "trg-101",
    description: "trigger.....",
```

```
    responseTime: "10 microS"
}
```

Each product data sheet has `name`, `code`, and `description` variables that are added explicitly, but it also has properties that depend on the product itself—those that are modeled with a string indexer. This way, we can get name check and IntelliSense functionality on the `name`, `code`, and `description` variables, but TypeScript allows the addition of any other property without signalling errors, because of the string indexer. However, since the indexer returns a string type, all other properties must be assignable to the type string; that is, they must be either strings, or string literal types:

```
let wrongProductDataScheet: ProductDataScheet = {
    name: "fast trigger",
    code: "trg-101",
    description: "trigger.....",
    availability: 10 //wrong not assignable to string
}
```

Interface inheritance

Interfaces can inherit their prescriptions from other interfaces, as follows:

```
interface Employed extends Person {
    Code: string;
    Department: string
}
```

In the preceding definition, `Employed` has all `Person` properties, plus `Code` and `Department`. It is worth pointing out that, since interfaces define constraints, interface inheritance is just another way to add more constraints.

Inheritance is declared with the `extends` keyword. An interface can inherit from several other interfaces. So, we can modify the previous example as follows:

```
interface PhysicalObject {
    weight: number;
    height: number;
    width: number;
    length: number;
}

interface Employed extends Person, PhysicalObject {
    code: string;
    department: string;
    role: string;
```

```
    }
    let marketingDirector: Employed =
    {
        code: "145",
        department: "marketing",
        role: "director",
        name: "John",
        surname: "Smith",
        weight: 80,
        width: 50,
        height: 170,
        length: 30
    }
```

Any object declared as `Employed` must satisfy all constraints coming from `Employed` itself, plus all constraints coming from `Person` and `PhysicalObject`. If any non-optional property coming from one of these interfaces is missing, an error is signaled:

```
let marketingDirector: Employed =
{
        [⊘] let marketingDirector: Employed
    cc
    de   (TS) Type '{ code: string; department: string; role: string; name: string; surname: string; width: number; h...' is not assignable to type 'Employed'.
            Property 'weight' is missing in type '{ code: string; department: string; role: string; name: string; surname: string; width: number; h...'.
    rc
    name: "John",
    surname: "Smith",
    width: 50,
    height: 170,
    length: 30
}
```

Operations on types

`Chapter 1`, *Introduction to TypeScript,* introduced the TypeScript union of simple types as a simple way of retaining the flexibility of JavaScript variables after the addition of strong typing. Type unions are also easily extended to all the types we describe in this chapter, including arrays, tuples, and interfaces, and to all types that will be introduced in the remainder of the book. However, in the case of more complex types, such as interfaces, we can also define the intersection of types. In fact, while it is hard to imagine a meaning for the intersection of, say, `number` and `string`, it would be quite spontaneous to define the intersection of two interfaces as a type that keeps all prescriptions of both interfaces. For instance, the intersection of `Person` with `PhysicalObject` should be a type that is both `Person` and `PhysicalObject`; that is, a type that contains all properties prescribed by both interfaces.

Type intersections are easy to process, since we can perform on them all operations that are possible on all member types. For instance, we can apply any function that accepts `Person` or `PhysicalObject` as argument to the intersection of these two types, since this intersection is a subtype of both `Person` and `PhysicalObject`.

The situation is more complex for union types. For instance, we can apply neither `number` operations nor `string` operations on a `string|number` before having tested, if it is a `number` or a `string`. TypeScript has ad hoc features, called **type guards**, to properly handle union types.

Let's create a new TypeScript file named `TypesOperations.ts` to test all examples on type operations. As usual, let's add the JavaScript file, obtained by transpiling `TypesOperations.ts`, to any View of your web project.

Intersection types

Intersection types are easy to understand with the `Person` and `PhysicalObject` interfaces that we already defined:

```
interface Person {
    readonly name: string;
    readonly secondName?: string;
    readonly surname: string;
}

interface PhysicalObject {
    weight: number;
    height: number;
    width: number;
    length: number;
}

type PhysicalPerson = Person & PhysicalObject;
```

A `PhysicalPerson` must have both `Person` and `PhysicalObject` properties. Due to structural subtyping, we don't need to explicitly declare an object as a `PhysicalPerson`; rather, any object containing all needed properties may be assigned to a `PhysicalPerson` variable or parameter:

```
let myIntersectionObject = {
    name: "John",
    surname: "Smith",
    weight: 80,
    width: 50,
```

```
        height: 170,
        length: 30
};

let myPhysicalPerson: PhysicalPerson = myIntersectionObject;
```

Moreover, structural subtyping implies that the intersection of `PhysicalPerson` and `Person` is equivalent to the following:

```
interface PhysicalPerson1 extends Person, PhysicalObject {
};
```

In fact, let's try defining `Employed` as the following:

```
interface Employed extends Person, PhysicalObject {
    code: string;
    department: string;
    role: string;
}
let myEmployed: Employed =
{
    code: "145",
    department: "marketing",
    role: "director",
    name: "John",
    surname: "Smith",
    weight: 80,
    width: 50,
    height: 170,
    length: 30
}
```

Then, we can assign `myEmployed` to `myPhysicalPerson`, as shown here:

```
myPhysicalPerson = myEmployed;
```

Among all types analyzed so far, only interfaces may be used to define intersection types. Later on in this book, we will see that intersection types may be applied also to classes. As for unions, all intersections can involve more than two base types:

```
type MultipleIntersection = typ1 & type2 & ... & typeN;
```

Union types and type guards

So far in this chapter, union types have been used to define functions that are able to accept both `strings` and `numbers`, and to add `null` and `undefined` to simple types when `strictNullChecks` is set. Another typical usage of union types are functions that accept either a type or an array of objects of the same type:

```
function showErrors(x: string | string[]): void{
    if (typeof x == "string") {
        alert(<string>x);
    }
    else {
        for (let s of <string[]>x) alert(s);
    }
}
```

Since we don't know if x is `string` or `string[]`, the function uses type assertions (namely `<string>x`, and `<string[]>x`) to access operations that works only for strings or only for arrays. The good news is that in the preceding example, type assertions may be omitted:

```
function showErrors(x: string | string[]): void{
    if (typeof x == "string") {
        alert(x);
    }
    else {
        for(let s of x) alert(y);
    }
}
```

In fact, `typeof x == "string"` is considered a type guard; that is, a declaration to the TypeScript compiler that, in the code block contained in that branch of the condition, x must be assumed a `string`. The final `else` doesn't contain any type guard, but being the last option, it is assumed that x is not a type already processed in any other branch (`if`, or `else if`). In the preceding example, this leaves only the possibility that x is a `string[]`. Thus, the type assertion may also be omitted in the `else` statement, since the compiler already knows x must be a `string[]`.

In JavaScript, `typeof` can discriminate only between simple types, so it can't be used to solve the problem in general. Luckily, TypeScript allows other kinds of type guards: `instanceof` type guards and user-defined type guards. `instanceof` discriminates between instances of classes, so `instanceof` type guards will be described in the chapter dedicated to TypeScript classes. User-defined type guards, instead being completely custom, can be used with all types. In particular, they are the basic option for discriminating interfaces. For instance, consider the following definitions:

```
interface Company {
    name: string;
    vat?: string;
    registration: string;
}
type Customer = Company | Person;
```

Then, we may add the following function, as a type guard, for discriminating `Company`:

```
function isCompany(x: Customer): x is Company
{
    return (<Company>x).registration !== undefined;
}
```

A user-defined type guard is a Boolean function, accepting a type, that admits subtypes as its unique argument, and that returns `true` whenever the instance passed is the subtype it discriminates. The discriminated type is declared by replacing the `bool` return type with a clause in line with the `x is Company` syntax.

User-defined type guards are used in the same way as `typeof` type guards:

```
function swowCustomer(x: Customer) {
    if (isCompany(x)) alert(x.name);
    else alert(x.name + " " + x.surname);
}
```

Discriminated unions

In the previous example, types of a union are discriminated by checking the existence of a property, and by defining a custom type guard. If the union type and its member types are conceived to work together, we can also add a common property to all member types whose values can be used to discriminate among them. The common property is called the **discriminant of the union type**. This solution is more elegant, and the TypeScript compiler automatically recognizes the pattern as a **discriminated union**, so there is no need to define custom type guards. For instance, suppose we have the following:

```
interface Rectangle {
    kind: "rectangle";
    width: number;
    height: number;
}
interface Circle {
    kind: "circle";
    radius: number;
}
interface Triangle {
    kind: "triangle";
    side1: number;
    side2: number;
    side3: number;
}

type SimpleShape = Triangle | Rectangle | Circle;
```

`kind` is the common property. TypeScripts automatically infers the following to be true:

- `"rectangle" | "triangle" | "circle"` is a string literal type
- `kind` in `Rectangle` restricts the literal type to the single value `"rectangle"` subtype; `kind` in `Circle` restricts the literal type to the single value `"circle"` subtype; and `kind` in `Triangle` restricts the literal type to the single value `"triangle"` subtype
- `SimpleType` is a discriminated union based on the `kind` discriminant property

At this point, conditions on the `kind` property can be used as type guards, removing the need to define custom type guards, since TypeScript has all information needed to process them properly:

```
function simpleShapeArea(s: SimpleShape): number {
    switch (s.kind) {
        case "rectangle": return s.height * s.width;
        case "circle": return Math.PI * s.radius ** 2;
```

```
        case "triangle": //Heron's formula
            return Math.sqrt((s.side1 + s.side2 + s.side3) +
                (-s.side1 + s.side2 + s.side3) +
                (s.side1 - s.side2 + s.side3) +
                (s.side1 + s.side2 - s.side3)
            ) / 4;
    }
}
```

In this case, conditions are more conveniently expressed with a `switch` statement, since we have a single property that can assume a finite set of values.

Destructuring and spreads

Destructuring syntax is a way to extract multiple property values from objects, or multiple elements from arrays, with a single instruction. It is available in C# starting from v7.0, and was introduced to JavaScript by the ECMAScript 2015 specifications. TypeScript also makes destructuring available on previous JavaScript versions, by generating equivalent instructions. Moreover, it also extends destructuring to TypeScript tuples.

Destructuring may be used in variable definitions, assignments, and when passing values to a function; that is, wherever a value is assigned to a variable or parameter.

Let's create a new TypeScript file named `DestructuringAndSpread.ts` to test some examples on destructuring and spread. Then, as usual, add the JavaScript file obtained by transpiling `DestructuringAndSpread.ts` to any View of your web project.

Array destructuring

The simplest form of array destructuring extracts some initial elements from an array:

```
let fruits = ["banana", "apple", "pear", "strawberry", "cherry", "peach"];

let first, second, third;

[first, second, third] = fruits;
```

Running the project and looking at the variable values, we see the following:

Name	Value
first	"banana"
second	"apple"
third	"pear"

We can also mix variable definition and destructuring, as shown here:

```
let [newfirst, newsecond, newthird] = fruits;
```

The preceding statement both defines and initializes `newfirst`, `newsecond`, and `newthird` with destructuring.

Array elements may be jumped by using commas, as shown here:

```
let [, , , fourth, , sixth] = fruits;
```

We can extract the last elements into a vector by using a variable, preceded by the . . . operator:

```
let rest: string[];
[first, second, , ...rest] = fruits;
```

The first element goes into `first`, the second one into `second`, the third one is jumped, and the remaining elements are placed into the `rest` array, as shown in the following screenshot:

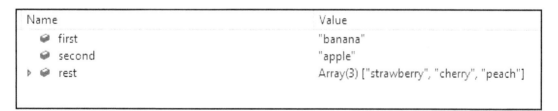

Name	Value
first	"banana"
second	"apple"
▷ rest	Array(3) ["strawberry", "cherry", "peach"]

Array spreads

A spread is the inverse operation of destructuring, since it allows the insertion of arrays into other arrays. It uses the same . . . syntax used to extract an array—the difference being that, in the case of the spread, the . . . operator is used in the right side of the assignment.

The following is an example of a spread:

```
let firstArray: string[] = ["a", "b", "c"];
let secondArray: string[] = ["f", "g", "h"];

let arraySpread = [...firstArray, "d", ...secondArray, "i"];
```

A new array is obtained by combining elements and spread arrays in the order they appear, without modifying the included arrays:

Name	Value	Type
▷ ● firstArray	Array(3) ["a", "b", "c"]	Object
▷ ● secondArray	Array(3) ["f", "g", "h"]	Object
◢ ● arraySpread	Array(8) ["a", "b", "c", ...]	Object
● length	8	number
● 0	"a"	string
● 1	"b"	string
● 2	"c"	string
● 3	"d"	string
● 4	"f"	string
● 5	"g"	string
● 6	"h"	string
● 7	"i"	string
▷ ● __proto__	Array(0) [, ...]	Object

Tuples destructuring

Since tuples use the same array syntax, destructuring extends to tuples using the exact same syntax. The only difference here is that, in this case, the . . . operator is meaningless, since tuple elements belonging to different types can't be assigned to a homogeneous array.

The example of the stringToNumber function tuples can be rewritten in a more elegant way with the help of destructuring:

```
function stringToNumber1(s: string): [number, boolean] {
    var res = parseFloat(s);
    if (isNaN(res)) return [0, false];
    else return [res, true];
}

let [toShow, ok] = stringToNumber1("5.7")
if (ok) console.log(toShow)
else console.log("error")
```

Object destructuring

Object destructuring is almost completely analogous to array destructuring, except that in this case, we can't use commas to jump properties:

```
interface PersonalDetails{
    firstname: string;
    secondname?: string;
    address: string;
    surname: string;
}

let mary: PersonalDetails = {
    firstname: "mary",
    surname: "smith",
    address: "....."
}

let surname: string, secondname: string | undefined;

({ surname, secondname } = mary);
```

However, in the object case, parentheses must surround the statement, since JavaScript interprets a leading { as the start of a block. `secondname` must be defined `string|undefined` if the `strictNullChecks` compiler option is set, since it is an optional `PersonalDetails` property, so the variable may also take the `undefined` value.

Variables can be given names that differ from the property names by specifying the variable names after a colon:

```
let marySurname: string, marySecondname: string | undefined;
({ surname: marySurname, secondname: marySecondname} = mary);
```

As with array destructuring, we can mix variable definitions and initialization with destructuring:

```
let { surname: newMarySurname, secondname: newMarySecondname } = mary;
```

In this case, we must omit the surrounding parentheses, since the { is not leading. Variable types are automatically inferred by the corresponding property types, but we can also specify them explicitly if we need a supertype of the corresponding property type, as follows:

```
let { surname: newMarySurname, secondname: newMarySecondname }:
    { surname: string, secondname?: string } = mary;
```

Since the colon after the property name may be used to provide the variable name, type must be assigned to the whole object after the destructuring syntax.

We can also specify default values for optional properties, as follows:

```
({ surname: marySurname, secondname: marySecondname = "no second name" } =
mary);
```

Also, objects support the . . . operator, which, in this case, assigns all properties whose names have not been mentioned in the destructuring syntax to another object:

```
let { firstname: maryName, ...maryOthers } = mary;
```

The properties of `maryOthers` are easily verified by hovering the mouse over the variable, as demonstrated previously:

```
let { firstname: maryName, ...maryOthers } = mary;

               [●] let maryOthers: {
                      secondname?: string | undefined;
                      address: string;
                      surname: string;
                   }
```

Object spreads

Similarly to array spreads, an object spread allows the insertion of all properties of various objects into another object:

```
interface Product {
    name: string;
    price: number;
    description: string
}

let laptop: Product = {
    name: "surface pro",
    price: 400,
    description: "....."
}
let quantity = 2;
let sale = {
    quantity: quantity ,
```

```
    ...laptop,
    totalPrice: quantity * laptop.price
}
```

The following is the result of executing the preceding code:

Name	Value	Type
⊿ ● sale	Object {quantity: 2, name: "surface pro", price: 400, ...}	Object
● description	"....."	string
● name	"surface pro"	string
● price	400	number
● quantity	2	number
● totalPrice	800	number
▷ ● __proto__	Object {constructor: , __defineGetter__: , __defineSetter__	Object

The same property may appear several times, and since values are processed from left to right, the rightmost values win. Therefore, it is easy to apply a discount to the previous example, as follows:

```
let saleDiscount= 0.8;
let discountedSale = {
    quantity: quantity,
    ...laptop,
    price: laptop.price * saleDiscount,
    totalPrice: quantity * laptop.price * saleDiscount
}
```

The result of the executing previous code is shown in the following screenshot:

Name	Value	Type
▷ ● sale	Object {quantity: 2, name: "surface pro", price: 400, ...}	Object
⊿ ● discountedSale	Object {quantity: 2, name: "surface pro", price: 320, ...}	Object
● description	"....."	string
● name	"surface pro"	string
● price	320	number
● quantity	2	number
● totalPrice	640	number
▷ ● __proto__	Object {constructor: , __defineGetter__: , __defineSetter__	Object

Object spread is the easiest way to clone objects:

```
let laptopClone = { ...laptop };
```

It can also be used to apply defaults, as shown here:

```
let optionsDefaults = {
    option1: "default1",
    option2: "default2"
}

let options = {
    ...optionsDefaults,
    option2: "custom value"
}
```

Functions

As demonstrated in the previous examples, TypeScript functions extend the usual syntax of JavaScript functions by adding type declarations to the function arguments and to the function return value, as in the following example:

```
function fullName(x: string, y: string, spaces: number): string {
    return x + Array(spaces+1).join(' ') + y;
}
```

The possibility we have in JavaScript to pass different argument lists is not undermined by strong typing, since TypeScript introduces a limited kind of function overloading. Actually, all TypeScript function overloads compile into a unique JavaScript function, since JavaScript doesn't allow function overloading. Function overloads can't be defined at all in JavaScript, since each function has an indefinite number of optional parameters, so there would be no way to distinguish between functions with the same name. Thus, TypeScript function overloads have one purpose—listing all possible parameter usages and types so that the TypeScript compiler can perform type checking on each function reference.

TypeScript adds also extensions introduced by ECMAScript 6, such as optional arguments with default values, destructuring on the function arguments, and arrow functions. Arrow function syntax is similar to classic JavaScript anonymous function syntax, but the former binds `this` in a different way. As usual, when the target JavaScript version is less than 6, these features are simulated by equivalent JavaScript code.

Let's create a new TypeScript file named `TypeScriptFunctions.ts` to test all of these examples on functions. Then, as usual, add the JavaScript file obtained by transpiling `TypeScriptFunctions.ts` to any View of your web project.

Anonymous functions and function types

As in JavaScript, anonymous functions may be assigned to variables as follows:

```
let repeatStringUntyped = function (s: string, n: number): string {
    let result = "";
    for (let i = 1; i < n; i++) result += s;
    return result;
}
```

There is no need to declare the variable type if we declare both the types of arguments and the return type in the anonymous function, because of TypeScript's automatic type inference. However, if one specifies the variable type arguments, then all types may be omitted in the anonymous function:

```
let repeatStringTyped: (s: string, n: number) => string = function (s, n):
string {
    let result = "";
    for (let i = 1; i < n; i++) result += s;
    return result;
}
```

The syntax for specifying function types consists of the typed argument list with the return type after the => symbol.

Function types may be given names either with the `type` keyword or by using the interface syntax described previously:

```
type SingleStringAggregator = (s: string, n: number) => string;

interface SingleStringAggregatorInterface {
    (s: string, n: number) : string
}
```

The way the function type is specified with the interface syntax differs in the usage of : in place of =>.

After this, we can write something like the following:

```
let repeatStringWithNamedType: SingleStringAggregatorInterface = function
(s, n): string {
    let result = "";
    for (let i = 1; i < n; i++) result += s;
    return result;
}
```

Optional arguments and destructuring

In JavaScript, function arguments may be omitted when calling a function, in the event of which they are assumed to be undefined. In TypeScript, optional arguments must be explicitly declared, otherwise a compile-time error is signaled when the function is called with fewer arguments. The syntax is based on the ? symbol, as in the case of optional interface properties. As in JavaScript, optional arguments must follow all obligatory arguments:

```
function buildFullName(firstname: string,
    surname: string, secondName?: string): string {
    if (secondName === undefined) return firstname + " " + surname;
    else return firstname + " " + secondname+ " " + surname;
}

alert(buildFullName("Francesco", "Abbruzzese"));
```

Since the function parameter is not specified in the call, its value is undefined. The undefined type is automatically added to any optional parameter when the strictNullChecks compiler option is set:

```
function buildFullName(firstname: string,
    surname: string, secondName?: string): string {
    if (secondName ===        [•] (parameter) secondName: string | undefined      " + surname;
    else return firstna...                                    ...name;
}
```

All optional arguments may be assigned default values, as follows:

```
function repeatString(s: string, n: number = 2): string {
    let result = "";
    for (let i = 1; i < n; i++) result += s;
    return result;
}
alert(repeatString("Hello"));
```

In this case, the ? parameter must be omitted. The syntax closely resembles the optional argument syntax seen in C#.

TypeScript allows also ECMAScript 6 syntax to be used for capturing an indefinite number of arguments at end of the list. The syntax is based on the . . . symbol:

```
function stringConcat(s1: string, s2: string, ...others: string[]): string
{
    let result: string = s1 + s2;
    for (let s of others) result += s;
    return result;
}
alert(stringConcat("First")); // wrong!
alert(stringConcat("First", "Second"));
alert(stringConcat("First", "Second", "Third"));
alert(stringConcat("First", "Second", "Third", "Fourth"));
```

Since argument bindings are assignments, we can apply destructuring to them as follows:

```
function PrintCompleteName({ firstname, secondname = "", surname }:
CompleteName): string {
    return firstname + " " + secondname + " " + surname;
}
let myName = {
    firstname: "francesco",
    surname: "abbruzzese"
}
alert(PrintCompleteName(myName));
```

Function overloads

Often, the same JavaScript library functions may accept different argument lists that they interpret and process differently. For instance, the jQuery on method offers the following possibilities:

```
.on( eventsString [, selector ] [, data ], handler )
.on( eventsObject [, selector ] [, data ] )
```

Here, the first argument is a string in the first call scheme, while in the second, it is an object. Moreover, the first scheme has two optional arguments in the middle of the list. TypeScript function overloads retain this JavaScript flexibility, while ensuring a type check for each call scheme.

For instance, suppose we would like to define a unique function that is able to repeat the same string several times, and to add an indefinite number of strings. As a first step, we define the needed overloads without a body:

```
function aggregateStrings(s: string, n: number): string;
function aggregateStrings(s1: string, s2: string, ...others: string[]):
string;
```

Immediately after all overloads, we must place a unique function implementation that has a number of arguments equal to the maximum of the argument numbers of all overloads, and whose argument types are the union of all types each overload has in each position. For the previous example, we have three arguments, as follows:

```
function aggregateStrings(s: string, x: string | number, ...others:
string[]): string {
    ...
}
```

Here, the second argument has the union type of the second arguments of both overloads. No other union type is needed, since the first argument is a string in both overloads, and the third argument is contained in the second overload only.

Also, the return type must be the union of all return type of all overloads, but in the previous example, all overloads return a string.

In the function body, type guards are used both to detect the overload that has been called, and to assert the right types:

```
function aggregateStrings(s: string, n: number): string;
function aggregateStrings(s1: string, s2: string, ...others: string[]):
string;
function aggregateStrings(s: string, x: string | number, ...others:
string[]): string {
    if (typeof x == "number") {
        let result = "";
        for (let i = 1; i < x; i++) result += s;
        return result;
    }
    else {
        let result: string = s + x;
        for (let cs of others) result += cs;
        return result;
    }
}
```

In the previous, fairly simple example, a type guard on the second argument is sufficient.

At each call, TypeScript performs a type check by comparing the call with each overload, but not with the actual implementation. Thus, for instance, the following call is wrong:

```
aggregateStrings("first", 2, "last");//wrong
```

This happens because, despite the fact that it is compatible with the function implementation, it is not compatible with any of the overloads.

Arrow functions

TypeScript allows the arrow syntax for anonymous functions that was introduced by ECMAScript 6. Arrow syntax completely avoids the brackets that enclose the function body when the function consists of the only return statement:

```
let addition = (x: number, y: number) => x + y;
```

Also, it is a much more elegant option for when the functions contain several statements:

```
let additions = (x: number, y: number, ...others: number[]) => {
    let result: number = x + y;
    for (let x of others) result += x;
    return result;
}
```

Arrow syntax is completely analogous to the lambda functions in C# syntax.

Arrow functions differ slightly from the usual anonymous JavaScript functions. More specifically, since they are designed to be defined inside the scope of other statements or functions, they can capture not only all local variable defined there, in the way that usual anonymous functions do, but can also capture the this variable from the scope they are defined in.

For instance, in the case of instances of classes (the subject of a later chapter in this book), this is bound with the current object when used in any class method. Now, if a method itself returns an anonymous function, then this will no longer be bound to the current object, since the function returned is not a class method.

However, if one uses the arrow syntax, then this will be captured from the external scope; that is, from the class method, and everything works properly:

```
class Product {
    name: string;
    price: number;
```

```
        constructor(name: string, price: number) {
            this.price = price;
            this.name = name;
        }
        finalPriceProcessor() { return (n: number) => n * this.price; }
    }
    var product = new Product("laptop", 1000);
    var priceProcessor = product.finalPriceProcessor();
    alert(priceProcessor(2));
```

In the preceding code, if the arrow function is replaced by the following line, then the price will be displayed as NaN, because this would have the wrong binding:

```
    function(n: number) {return n * this.price;}
```

Summary

TypeScript strongly types arrays, and defines tuples to handle aggregates of heterogeneous objects. JavaScript objects are strongly typed with interfaces according to their shapes, that is, to their properties and methods. Interfaces are used also to strongly type indexable types and functions.

The intersection and union of types allows TypeScript to retain the flexibility of JavaScript, without reverting to strong typing. Type guards and discriminated unions simplify the usage of unions, avoiding the usage of too many type assertions. Indeed, type guards and discriminated unions factor out a type assertion to a whole block of code.

The destructuring and spread operators introduced in ECMAScript 6 simplify both the construction of complex entities, and the extraction of information from such complex entities.

Finally, TypeScript adds both strong typing and overloads to JavaScript functions, and also adds advanced ECMAScript features, including argument default values, the capturing of an indefinite number of arguments, and arrow functions.

Questions

1. What is the JavaScript equivalent of TypeScript's tuples?
2. How many ways of defining the type of a function do you know?
3. Is it obligatory to define the interface implemented by an object *before* passing it to a function that requires a specific interface?
4. How does TypeScript handle functions that may be called with different lists of arguments?
5. Are arrow functions completely equivalent to the usual anonymous functions?
6. What are the usages you know for the . . . symbol?
7. Can commas be used for jumping arguments in array destructuring?
8. Can commas be used for jumping arguments in object destructuring?

Further reading

More details about the ECMAScript 6 features of destructuring and spread can be found at `https://developer.mozilla.org/en-US/docs/Web/JavaScript/Reference/Operators/Destructuring_assignment`, an article on the Mozilla Developer Network.

A detailed discussion about the usage of `this` in JavaScript can be found in Yehuda Katz's article *Understanding JavaScript Function Invocation and this,* available at `https://yehudakatz.com/2011/08/11/understanding-javascript-function-invocation-and-this/`.

DOM Manipulation 3

In this chapter, the reader will learn how to manipulate the DOM, either with plain TypeScript, or by calling jQuery from TypeScript. All concepts are explained with complete examples that involve both TypeScript code and HTML code. The reader will also learn how to continue using his/her favorite JavaScript libraries from TypeScript thanks to declaration files.

The following topics will be covered in this chapter:

- DOM basic TypeScript types
- How to perform DOM manipulation with plain TypeScript
- How to use JavaScript libraries from TypeScript
- How to perform DOM manipulation from TypeScript with jQuery

Technical requirements

The following are the tools required while working on this chapter:

- Visual Studio 2017 with the latest ASP.NET Core tools
- Visual Studio TypeScript SDK
- `@types/jquery` will be installed in the project with `npm`

All code examples in this chapter may be tested by doing the following:

1. Create a new ASP.NET Core MVC project, called `DOMManipulation`, without authentication:

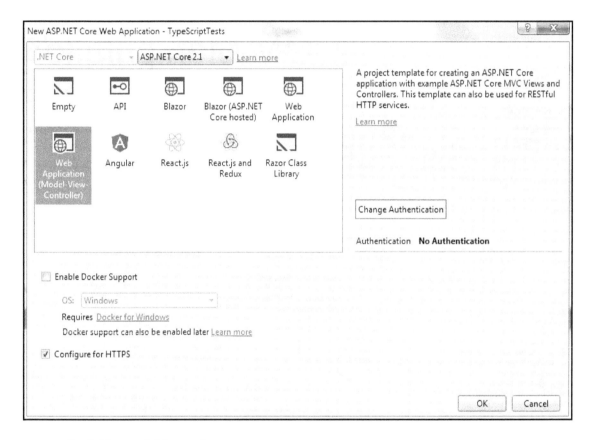

2. Add a `ts` folder under `wwwroot`:

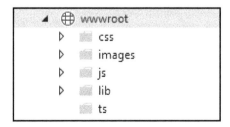

3. Add the following `tsconfig.json` in the project root:

```
{
    "compileOnSave": true,
     "compilerOptions": {
         "noImplicitAny": true,
         "strictNullChecks": true,
         "noEmitOnError": true,
         "removeComments": false,
         "sourceMap": true,
         "target": "es5",
         "outDir": "wwwroot/js"
    },
    "include": [
        "wwwroot/ts/**/*.ts"
    ],
    "exclude": [
        "**/node_modules",
        "**/*.spec.ts"
    ]
}
```

All the code used in this chapter can be downloaded from the following GitHub link: `https://github.com/PacktPublishing/Hands-On-TypeScript-for-CSharp-and-.NET-Core-Developers.`

Check out the following video to see the Code in Action: `http://bit.ly/2EQRy3L.`

DOM types

TypeScript automatically loads types and variable declarations that describe both the DOM and JavaScript's predefined functions, types, objects, and variables. They are collected in various declaration libraries that are specific to various JavaScript ECMAScript versions. As a default, the right libraries to load are selected according to the target JavaScript version specified in the `target` compiler option, but the developer may manually specify all declaration libraries to load through the `lib` compiler option. All types and variables used to describe the DOM and ECMAScript functionalities have exactly the same names and parameters described in the official JavaScript specifications, so they may be used exactly as in JavaScript. The right type names to use in declarations may be discovered either with Visual Studio suggestions or by referring to some DOM specifications, such as the one provided in the Mozilla documentation: `https://developer.mozilla.org/en-US/docs/Web/API/Document_Object_Model.`

Let's add a `DOMTests.ts` file to your project. With the help of Visual Studio IntelliSense, you may use it to give a particular look to all methods and properties of the DOM interfaces described in this section. In order to prevent all test elements defined here from interfering with the remainder of the code in other TypeScript files, please enclose your tests inside a function as shown in the following code:

```
(function () {

//your tests here

})();
```

TypeScript predefined declarations

The TypeScript compiler automatically adds all declarations of the objects and variables that should be available in the target ECMAScript target. For instance, if the target declared in the TypeScript configuration file is `es5`, TypeScript adds the following declaration sets:

- `dom`, which contains all interfaces and variables in the DOM specifications
- `es5`, which contains all interfaces defined in the ECMAScript 5 specifications

The target-specific declarations modules may be overridden by inserting the desired declarations module list in the `lib` compiler option in the TypeScript configuration file. For instance, the following configuration may be used if one wants to use ECMAScript 6 promises, while keeping an ECMAScript 5 target:

```
{
    "compileOnSave": true,
    "compilerOptions": {
        "noImplicitAny": true,
        "strictNullChecks": true,
        "noEmitOnError": true,
        "removeComments": false,
        "sourceMap": true,
        "target": "es5",
        "lib": ["dom", "es5", "es2015.promise"],
        ...
    }
    ...
}
```

However, in this case, one should provide a polyfill for all browsers that do not support Promises, since the `lib` list adds just TypeScript declarations. Code and/or polyfills that actually implement the missing features must be added manually by the developer.

All available declaration modules are suggested by Visual Studio IntelliSense:

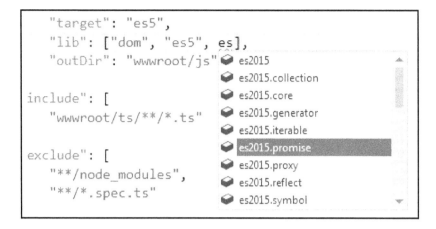

DOM basic types

HTML documents and types are a specialization of the abstract DOM types, which are an abstraction of both XML and HTML types. DOM documents are substantially trees. A whole document is represented by the `Document` interface while each tree node is represented by a `Node` interface. Documents may contain several subtypes of `Node`: comments represented by the `Comment` interface, elements (such as <span>, <div>, and XML elements) represented by the `Element` interface, element attributes represented by the `Attr` interface, and the text content of both elements and attributes represented by the `Text` interface. Most of the methods needed to manipulate the DOM are inherited by the `Node` interface:

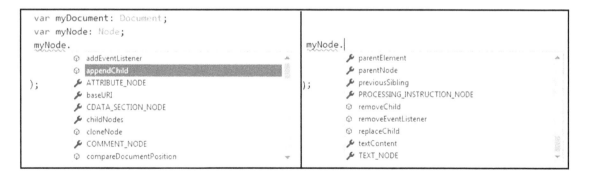

In particular, the `Node` interface includes all methods to add, delete, replace, and clone nodes and to add and remove event handlers, and all properties needed to navigate in the node tree, such as `parentNode`, `childNodes`, `previousSibling`, and `nectSibling`. All uppercase properties are numeric constants that encode all types of nodes with a constant. For instance, `TEXT_NODE` contains the constant `3`, which represents `Text` nodes, while `ELEMENT_NODE` contains `1`, which represents an `Element` node. The type of each node is contained in its `nodeType` property. The total number of `Node` subtypes is `12`, each node type being encoded by an integer between `1` and `12`.

The `document` interface contains all properties and methods needed to process the document as a whole:

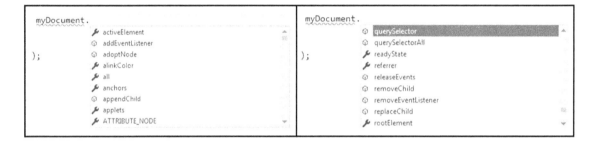

In particular, the `document` interface contains methods to add/remove event handlers to/from the whole document, and methods to create document elements.
The `document` interface also includes properties that contain a list of all scripts, all forms, all anchors, the currently active element, the document character set, and its document type declaration. It is also worth mentioning methods such as `querySelector` and `querySelectorAll`, used to query the whole document with CSS syntax.

Other interfaces worth mentioning are the `Event` interface, which is the base type of all DOM events, and the `DOMException` interface, which is the base type for all DOM-generated exceptions.

HTML specific types

The DOM type hierarchy includes types and variables that are specific for HTML documents, XML documents, and SVG documents (SVG is an XML-based format for 2D graphics). Most of the types in these three DOMs are supported by all modern mainstream browsers. This chapter briefly describes just the HTML DOM features. The reader is referred to the links provided at the end of chapter for further details, and for a discussion of XML and SVG DOM.

All HTML elements are subtypes of `HTMLElement`, which adds a few HTML-specific properties to `Element`, such as `tabindex`, `style`, `title`, if the element is hidden or editable, all elemental geometric properties (width, height, position, and so on), its drag and drop properties, and a few more minor properties. Each HTML tag has its associate interface that descends from `HTMLElement` and adds to it all tag-specific properties (`HTMLBodyElement`,
`HTMLDivElement, HTMLSpanElement, HTMLImageElement, HTMLBodyElement, HTMLFor mElement, HTMLInputElement,` and so on).

The HTML document has the `HTMLDocument` type, which adds to `Document` a few HTML specific properties, such as `domain` (current domain), `URL` (current URL), `readyState` (document loading state), `defaultView`, which contains a reference to the window object, and so on. The current document is contained in the global `document` variable.

The `Window` interface contains information and methods connected to the browser status, and to the way the document is displayed. Specifically, the `history` property contains a `History` interface that allows the interaction with the browser navigation status (getting/setting the current URL, moving back and forth in the browser history, and so on). The `clientInformation` property contains some user settings (such as whether cookies are enabled or not). The `screen` property contains information about the window dimensions and other graphic settings. It is also worth mentioning all properties related to the browser page scrolling status:

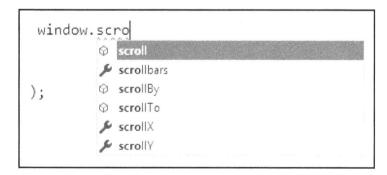

The `getSelection` method returns a `Selection` object describing the current text selection, if any.

The current `Window` settings are collected in a `Window` object contained in the `window` global variable.

Basic DOM operations

In this section, we describe a simple implementation of a to do list as an example of how to perform DOM manipulation with TypeScript without the help of any JavaScript library or framework.

Let's add a `plainToDo.ts` file to your project. In order to avoid the creation of global variables that might interfere with other JavaScript code, create a function to enclose the whole code. This is the so-called **JavaScript Module Pattern**, whose main purpose is avoiding unwanted interactions between JavaScript code modules (for more details, see `https://addyosmani.com/resources/essentialjsdesignpatterns/book/#modulepatternjavascript`). Later on, in `Chapter 6`, *Namespaces and Modules*, we will show better options offered by TypeScript:

```
(function () {
    //put code here
})();
```

Then, replace the content of the `/Home/Index.csHTML` view with this:

```
@{
    ViewData["Title"] = "To Do";
}

<h1>@ViewData["Title"]</h1>
<ul lass="list-group" style="min-height:200px" id="main_list">
    @*<li class="list-group-item">
            <button type="button" class="btn btn-sm">
                <span class="glyphicon glyphicon-minus" aria-
hidden="true"></span>
            </button>
            <span>to do content here</span>
        </li>*@
</ul>
<div class="row">
    <div class="col-sm-12">
        <div class="input-group">
            <input type="text" class="form-control" placeholder="Insert
here to do..." id="main_input">
            <span class="input-group-btn">
                <button class="btn btn-primaryt" type="button"
id="main_add">Add to do</button>
            </span>
        </div>
    </div>
</div>
```

```
@section Scripts{
<script src="~/js/plainToDo.js"></script>
}
```

The `li` tag commented out between the `@*` `*@` is the schema of all to do items that will be added dynamically. Each to do item has a button that, when clicked, removes the item. New to do items are added by first inserting the to do text into the input with the ID `main_input` and then by clicking the button with the ID `main_add`. Each new to do item is appended as the last child of the `ul` tag with the ID `main_list`.

DOM manipulation utilities

If one decides to not use any JavaScript framework and proceed with plain TypeScript, the first step of any project is the design of all necessary DOM traversal and manipulation utilities. In the case of this simple to do example, one just needs a function that finds a node ancestor with a given tag name:

```
function findAncestor(n: HTMLElement|null, tag: string): HTMLElement | null
{
        while (n != null && n.tagName != "BODY") {
                if (n.tagName == tag) return n;
                n = n.parentNode as HTMLElement;
        }
        return null;
}
```

The `findAncestor` function passes an element and then the tag name of the ancestor to be found. The first argument is `HTMLElement|null`, instead of `HTMLElement`, because `strictNullChecks` is `true` (so, `null` is not an element of other types) and the function should also work properly with a `null` argument.

If one hovers the mouse over the n parameter inside `while`, one sees that the type of n is considered to be `HTMLElement` instead of `HTMLElement|null` because the n `!=null` condition in the `while` acts as a type guard, so the TypeScript compiler understands n can't be `null` inside the `while` loop:

```
while (n != null && n.tagName != "BODY") {
        if (n.tagName == tag) return n;
        n =     [●] (parameter) n: HTMLElement    ient;
}
return null;
```

Since the `parentNode` property is inherited from `Node`, its type is `Node` so it must be cast to `HTMLElement` before being assigned to n. This can always be done because the parent of an `HTMLElement` must be another `HTMLElement`.

If the ancestor with the required tag name is not found, the function returns `null`.

In more complex projects, a function that finds an ancestor satisfying a generic CSS selector might be needed. This is easily achieved by using the `matches` method and its variants for Webkit browsers:

```
function findAncestorExt(n: HTMLElement | null, selector: string):
HTMLElement | null {
        while (n != null && n.tagName != "BODY") {
            if (n.matches && n.matches(selector)) return n;
            else if (n.webkitMatchesSelector &&
n.webkitMatchesSelector(selector)) return n;
            n = n.parentNode as HTMLElement;
        }
        return null;
    }
```

Removing an item

Items removal requires an event handler that intercepts the click events of all items' remove buttons. A unique event handler for the click event placed on the `main_list ul` element is the easiest way to handle the click events of all present and future to do items, because all mouse events are bubbled up to all ancestors.

As a first step, we get the `main_list ul` element:

```
let listRoot = document.getElementById("main_list") as HTMLElement;
```

The `as HTMLElement` type assertion is necessary because `getElementById` in general returns `HTMLElement | null`. The `null` value is returned when the element is not found, which is impossible in this case. If one omits the type assertion and goes on with the code, TypeScript signals an error at the first call of an `HTMLElement` method, saying that the method is also not available for `null`. So, either one is sure the element exists, and one adds an `as HTMLElement` type assertion, or one encloses the subsequent code in a not `null` type guard:

```
if(listRoot != null){
    //HTMLElement methods and properties here
}
```

At this point, we can add the event listener:

```
let listRoot = document.getElementById("main_list") as HTMLElement;

listRoot.addEventListener("click",
(evt: MouseEvent) =>
{
    let button = findAncestor(evt.target as HTMLElement, "BUTTON") ;
    let target = findAncestor(button, "LI");
    if (target != null && target.parentNode != null)
        target.parentNode.removeChild(target);
});
```

The evt.target property contains the source of the event, which in this case must be an HTMLElement. However, in general, evt.target is one of the ancestor interfaces of HTMLElement, so a type assertion that requires an HTMLElement is needed before passing it to findAncestor. When one clicks the remove button, one might also click the icon span that is inside the button, so evt.target might contain either the button or the icon span. findAncestor returns the clicked button in both cases.

Accordingly, whenever the user clicks the remove button, a not null button is passed to the second call to findAncestor that returns the li the button is in, that is, the li element to remove. The right way to remove an element is by calling removeChild on its parent node. There is also a remove() shortcut method that may be called on the node itself, but it is not supported by all browsers.

If, instead, the user clicks a location inside the li but outside the remove button, then the first call to findAncestor returns null, which in turn causes null to also be returned by the second call to findAncestor. So, in this case nothing happens.

Both target and target.parentNode are HTMLElement|null, but the TypeScript compiler returns no error when the parentNode and removeChild HTMLElement members are called because of the target != null && target.parentNode != null type guard, which ensures they may be safely called.

The preceding code may be tested by uncommenting the test li element inside the ul, in the /Home/Index.csHTML View, and by running the project.

Adding a new item

The addition of new to do items requires the addition of an event listener to the `main_add` button, which contains the code to assemble all HTML parts of the to do item:

```
let mainAdd = document.getElementById("main_add");
if (mainAdd != null) mainAdd.addEventListener("click",
        (evt: MouseEvent) =>
        {
            //assemble here the to do item, and append it to the ul element
        });
```

As a first step, one may build the `span` with the to do item text:

```
let textSpan = document.createElement("span");
//create span with text
textSpan.innerText = " "+(document.getElementById("main_input") as
HTMLInputElement).value;
```

The to do text is taken from the `main_input` input. The `as HTMLInputElement` type assertion excludes the `null` possibility (`main_input` must exist!).

Since the whole application uses Bootstrap CSS, icons within buttons are implemented with Bootstrap icon classes. In Bootstrap, all icons are implemented by adding the `glyphicon` and `glyphicon-xxxx` CSS classes to an inline element such as a `span`. Here, `glyphicon` is a CSS class that contains the style settings that are common to all icons, while `glyphicon-xxxx` is a CSS class associated to each different icon supported by Bootstrap.

Thus, we implement the remove button with a `span` element with the minus Bootstrap icon:

```
//create span with icon to put inside button
let iconSpan = document.createElement("span");
iconSpan.setAttribute("aria-hidden", "true");
iconSpan.setAttribute("class", "glyphicon glyphicon-minus");
```

The `aria-xxx` attributes are a set of attributes that define ways to make web content and web applications more accessible to people with disabilities. `aria-hidden` set to `true` makes the span with the icon invisible to non-visual HTML rendering, such as HTML readers for sightless people. In fact, HTML readers describe buttons, either with text they contain, or with their HTML `title`.

Then, one creates the item remove button and appends the icon span to it:

```
//create remove button
let button = document.createElement("button");
```

```
button.setAttribute("type", "button");
button.setAttribute("class", "btn btn-sm");
button.setAttribute("title", "remove");

//append icon inside button
button.appendChild(iconSpan);
```

The remove button must have an HTML `title`, since it has no text inside of it, and each HTML element must have a textual description to be used by HTML readers for sightless people.

Then, one creates the `li` element and appends to it, first the remove button, and then the text span:

```
//create li
let liElement = document.createElement("li");
liElement.setAttribute("class", "list-group-item");

//append button and text span tu li
liElement.appendChild(button);
liElement.appendChild(textSpan);
```

Finally, the `li` element may be appended to the `ul`:

```
//append li to ul
listRoot.appendChild(liElement);
```

Now, the to do list should be ready for a complete test!

The new element may be added also before another child instead of being added as the last child, by calling the `insertBefore` method:

```
//insert before otherSibling
listRoot.insertBefore(otherSibling, liElement);

//insert after otherSibling
if (otherSibling.nextSibling)
    listRoot.insertBefore(otherSibling.nextSibling, liElement);
else
    listRoot.appendChild(liElement);

//insert as first child
if (listRoot.firstChild)
    listRoot.insertBefore(listRoot.firstChild, liElement);
else
    listRoot.appendChild(liElement);
```

Declaration files and JavaScript libraries

Usually, large applications are not designed starting from scratch as we have done in the previous section, but use either complete JavaScript frameworks, such as Angular, Ember.js, and Aurelia; sophisticated user interface libraries such as Vue.js, React.js, Meteor, and Knockout.js; or utility libraries such as jQuery. While Angular is the subject of the third part of the book, jQuery is briefly covered in the next section.

Whatever JavaScript libraries or frameworks are used, the developer has the problem of informing the TypeScript compiler about public functions, methods, interfaces, and variables they contain; otherwise, any attempt to use them would result in a compilation error.

This is done by providing declaration files that describe the types used by the libraries with the TypeScript syntax. Since declaration files do not generate any JavaScript code but just inform the TypeScript compiler about existing types, they may contain just declarations that generate no JavaScript code, such as interfaces, function types, and named union/intersection types.

Moreover, they may contain special global variable/constant/function declarations that generate no memory allocation:

```
declare myVar: string;
declare myConst: number;
declare function myfunction(x: HTMLDivElement): string;
```

They are preceded by the `declare` keyword and can't be initialized, since initialization would require the generation of JavaScript code. For the same reason, functions must not contain any body. Moreover, when a function has several overloads, a more general signature must come after more specific signatures:

```
declare function myfunction(x: HTMLDivElement): string;
declare function myfunction(x: HTMLElement): number;
declare function myfunction(x: any): any;
```

TypeScript declaration files have the `d.ts` extension and are available for substantially all JavaScript libraries.

Where to find declaration files

Declaration files either are published inside the JavaScript library package they describe, or are available in the `DefinitelyTyped` GitHub repository: `https://github.com/DefinitelyTyped/DefinitelyTyped`.

All declaration files in `DefinitelyTyped` are also published as npm packages with names such as `@types/<library name>`. For instance, the declaration file for jQuery is available in npm with the name `@types/jquery`: `https://www.npmjs.com/package/@types/jquery`.

If, instead, the declaration file is contained inside the same npm package, typically it has the same name as the package's main JavaScript file but with the `d.ts` extension. For instance, if the main package file is `./lib/main.js`, the associated TypeScript declaration file should be `./lib/main.d.ts`. This is not obligatory, but if the declaration filename doesn't conform with this rule, then its name must be explicitly declared in the npm `package.json`, under the `types` attribute:

```
{
    "name": "myPackage",
    "version": "2.1.0",
    "main": "./lib/main.js",
    "types": "./lib/maintypes.d.ts"
}
```

How to use TypeScript declaration files

In order to use TypeScript declaration files, it is enough to install the npm packages they are defined in. Once this is done, all symbols contained there become available in all TypeScript files. This works properly both if one uses a `@types/<library name>` package and if declaration files are contained directly in the JavaScript library's npm package.

As an example, let's install the `@types/jquery` TypeScript definition that will be used in the next section. First of all, we must add a `package.json` to the web project:

1. Right-click on the project root (which should be named `DOMManipulation`), and select **Add** | **New item**
2. Then, under **Web** | **Scripts**, select **npm Configuration File**
3. Accept the default `package.json` name and click the **Add** button

The new file should open with the default content:

```
{
  "version": "1.0.0",
  "name": "ASP.NET",
  "private": true,
    "devDependencies": {
    }
}
```

There is no need to modify the default content. Just add `@types/jquery` under `devDependencies`:

```
{
  "version": "1.0.0",
  "name": "ASP.NET",
  "private": true,
    "devDependencies": {
        "@types/jquery": "^3.3.4"
    }
}
```

The last available version number should be suggested by Visual Studio IntelliSense. Once the file is saved, the package added to `devDependencies` should install automatically. Once the package installation completes, all jQuery symbols are available in all TypeScript files with no need for further action!

It is worth pointing out that `jQuery.js` must be added to all views that use jQuery, since the `@types/jquery` package adds just TypeScript definitions, but no JavaScript code. Luckily, ASP.NET core project templates, as a default, add jQuery in the **Layout View**, so one has `jQuery.js` already available in all Views.

DOM operations with jQuery

This section describes a jQuery implementation of the previous section's to do list. It is just an example of how to use jQuery with TypeScript, not a jQuery primer. It can be skipped by readers that do not have any knowledge of jQuery and who are not interested in using it. Readers who would like learn or to improve their knowledge of jQuery may find some useful references at the end of the chapter.

Once `@types/jquery` has been installed, following the instructions in the previous section, using jQuery from TypeScript is straightforward. Let's add a `jQueryToDo.ts` under the `ts` folder and modify the scripts section of `Views/Home/Index.csHTML` to use the JavaScript file from `jQueryToDo.ts`:

```
@section Scripts{
    <script src="~/js/jQueryToDo.js"></script>
}
```

Then, enclose all code within a function to avoid the creation of global variables:

```
(function ($) {
    //put jquery based code here
})(jQuery);
```

This time, the function binds the `jQuery` global variable to its `$` parameter. This is a jQuery best practice for using the `$` abbreviation without risking errors due to collision with some other global symbol with the same `$` abbreviation.

The jQuery code for item removal is straightforward:

```
let listRoot = $("#main_list");
listRoot.on("click", (event) => {
    let button = $(event.target).closest("BUTTON");
    if (button.length === 0) return;
    button.closest("LI").remove();
});
```

In fact, jQuery already has the powerful `.closest()` method to do the job of the previous `findAncestor` function.

Also, the code for adding a new item simplifies a lot, since one may append the HTML for the new item directly in string format with no need to manually handle the creation of all nodes with their attributes:

```
let mainAdd = $("#main_add");
    mainAdd.click(event => {
        let toAdd =
            `<li class="list-group-item">
                <button type="button" class="btn btn-sm" title="remove">
                    <span class="glyphicon glyphicon-minus" aria-
hidden="true"></span>
                </button>
                <span>${$("#main_input").val()}</span>
            </li>`;
        listRoot.append(toAdd);
    });
```

This code uses string interpolation based on the back quotes and `${}` syntax (see the *Declarations and scoping* section in `Chapter 1`, *Introduction to TypeScript*) to insert the desired text into a generic template for the to do item.

Following are the output screenshots of the code that we have been working on:

- Adding an entry in our to do list:

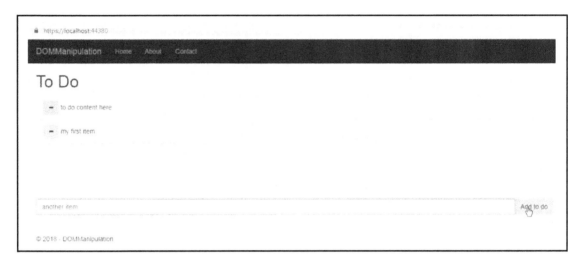

- Removing an entry from our to do list:

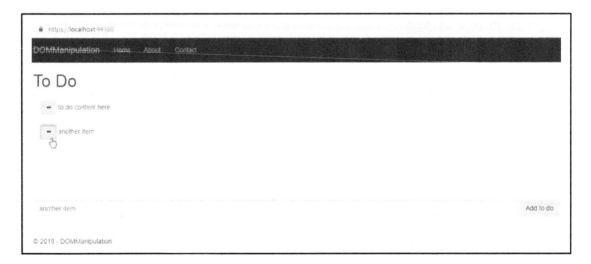

Summary

As a default, the TypeScript SDK has definitions for all W3C DOM types, and for all predefined types of the target JavaScript version. However, the predefined types added may be controlled manually through the `lib` compiler option.

DOM manipulation may be performed with the usual properties and methods, but while paying attention to all types involved. In particular, if the `strictNullChecks` compiler option is `true`, the compiler automatically detects missing `null` checks. The price to pay for this verification is that the developer must provide type assertions whenever they are sure a value can't be `null`, and accordingly the `null` check is superfluous.

JavaScript libraries and frameworks, such as jQuery, may be used by providing TypeScript declaration files that describe the public types they expose. Declaration files are either included in the library packages themselves or they are available from the `DefinitelyTyped` repository. In both cases, they may be used by installing npm packages.

The next chapter describes TypeScript's object-oriented features, and how to build modular applications with the help of TypeScript classes, interfaces, and inheritance.

Questions

1. If `node` and `child` are `HTMLElement`, is this statement always correct: `node.parentNode.appendChild(child)`? If not, what is the right way to proceed?
2. Can a variable declaration appear in a TypeScript declaration file? If yes, what is the right syntax? Why?
3. Do you remember a property or method that belongs to `HTMLDocument`, but not to its `Document` ancestor?
4. Are there specific operations to perform before using jQuery in a TypeScript project?
5. How do you verify that an `HTMLElement` satisfies a CSS selector without using jQuery?
6. Does `HTMLelement` have an `insertAfter` method? If yes, what is its syntax? If not, how do you simulate it?
7. What is the easiest way to create templates for HTML fragments in TypeScript?

Further reading

A good reference for all DOM types supported by TypeScript is the Mozilla documentation: `https://developer.mozilla.org/en-US/docs/Web/API/Document_Object_Model`. Available TypeScript declaration files may be found in the DefinitelyTyped GitHub repository: `https://github.com/DefinitelyTyped/DefinitelyTyped`, or on npm: `https://www.npmjs.com/search?q=%40types`. A good quick start for jQuery is **Learning jQuery 3** (`https://www.packtpub.com/web-development/learning-jquery-3x-fifth-edition`).

Using Classes and Interfaces

This chapter explains the basics of object-oriented programming in TypeScript, and TypeScript classes and their differences from and similarities to C# classes. The reader will first become familiar with the new concepts with simple class examples, and then they will move on to how to represent a whole application domain with a network of classes, abstract classes, and interfaces.

TypeScript classes are ECMAScript 6 classes with the addition of type specifications. When the target is a lower JavaScript version, the TypeScript transpiler takes care of implementing classes with equivalent code, such as prototypes and constructor functions. Classes, and, in general, all TypeScript object-oriented features, help make TypeScript applications modular and easy to maintain, thereby enabling the construction of large TypeScript code bases and rich client applications with advanced client frameworks, such as Angular, that are the subject of the last part of this book.

The following topics will be covered in this chapter:

- Defining and using classes, constructors, properties, methods, and accessibility
- Static members and static parts of a class
- Defining and using inheritance and interface implementation
- Using abstract classes/methods and interfaces for a modular design
- Advanced type-compatibility and type guards

Technical requirements

We will need the following tools for this chapter:

- Visual Studio 2017 with the latest ASP.NET Core tools
- Visual Studio TypeScript SDK

All examples in this chapter use the same `Chapter 2`, *Complex Types and Functions*, `DOMManipulation` project. Some previous code will be re-engineered in a more modular way with the use of classes and interfaces, and new examples will be added.

All the code used in this chapter can be downloaded from the following GitHub link: `https://github.com/PacktPublishing/Hands-On-TypeScript-for-CSharp-and-.NET-Core-Developers`.

Check out the following video to see the Code in Action: `http://bit.ly/2CLU7lb`.

Classes

Classes are the building blocks of object-oriented programming. While an interface declares just the shape and the behavior of objects, a class not only specifies a shape and a behavior but also gives the code to implement that behavior, and a way to create objects with that behavior and shape. In a few words, we may say that interfaces are just specifications while classes are specifications plus implementation.

ES6 specifications extend ES5 specifications by adding classes to JavaScript. However, when the JavaScript target is ES5, TypeScript generates equivalent code based on the JavaScript constructor functions. The TypeScript class syntax mimics the one of ES6 classes, the only difference being the addition of types to all class parts. This is by design since TypeScript is the JavaScript of the future plus types.

Classes define types, whose instances are JavaScript objects that may be created with the new keyword:

```
var x: <class name> = new <class name>(/* parentheses may enclose
parameters */);
```

TypeScript classes are defined as follows:

```
class <class name>
{
    //class definition
}
```

Before continuing, add a `ClassTest.ts` TypeScript file to the `DOMManipulation` project. All code snippets in this section may be tested by adding them to this file. As usual, to avoid interaction with other TypeScript code, please enclose the whole code inside a function:

```
(function () {
    //code here
})();
```

Classes are made of public and private members, and each member may be either a property or a function. Function members are called methods. Private members may be accessed and used only by other methods of the same class, so only the public members are visible from outside a class. Accordingly, just public members define the specification part of a class. More specifically, all public properties and signatures of all public methods define an interface, which is the specification part of the class.

For instance, suppose we have the following class:

```
class Person {
    name: string;
    surname: string;
    secondName?: string;
    fullname(): string {
        return this.secondName !== undefined ?
            this.name + " " + this.secondName + " " + this.surname :
            this.name + " " + this.surname;
    }
}
```

Most object-oriented languages, such as C# or C++, as a default, consider members private. TypeScript, instead, considers members public. The `name`, `surname`, and `secondName` variables are public properties, while `fullName` is a public method. Like C# methods, it may refer to other private and public class members through the `this` keyword, however, unlike C#, where the `this` keyword may be omitted in TypeScript, the usage of `this` is obligatory.

An instance of the `Person` type may be created with the following:

```
var myPerson: Person = new Person();
```

The preceding snippet may be simplified as the following:

```
var myPerson= new Person();
```

This is because the type is inferred automatically by the TypeScript compiler as being the same type on the right-hand side of the = statement. In both cases, `myPerson` is a JavaScript object containing all members declared in the `Person` class definition.

The interface part of the `Person` class is the interface:

```
{
        name: string;
        surname: string;
        secondName?: string;
        fullname(): string;
}
```

In TypeScript, a class can be used wherever an interface is allowed. For instance, one may use `Person` in the definition of other interfaces that extend `Person` members:

```
interface Employed extends Person
{
    department: string;
    code: string;
}
```

`Employed` is defined by extending `Person` as if `Person` were an interface, so all members of `Employed` are inherited by `Person`. This makes sense since the preceding statement refers just to the interface part of `Person`:

```
{
        name: string;
        surname: string;
        secondName?: string;
        fullname(): string;
}
```

Declaring `secondName` as an optional property in `Person` extends its type from `string` to `string|undefined`. However, when `Person` is used as an interface, for instance, in the `Employed` interface definition, `secondName` actually becomes an optional property, since one may create an `Employed` object without the `secondName` property:

```
var x: Employed = {
        name: "Frank",
        surname: "Abbruzzese",
        department: "marketing",
        code: "1254",
        fullname:  function() {return "Frank Abbruzzese";}
}
```

Thus, declaring a public class property as optional only affects the interface part of the class.

Constructors

Like in most object languages (C#, C++, Java), in TypeScript, classes have constructors containing code that is executed whenever each class instance is created with `new`. TypeScript constructors appear as a method named `constructor`, which returns no value:

```
class Person {
    name: string;
    surname: string;
    secondName?: string;
    constructor(name: string, surname: string, secondName?: string) {
        this.name = name;
        this.surname = surname;
        this.secondName = secondName;
    }
    fullname(): string {
        return this.secondName !== undefined ?
            this.name + " " + this.secondName + " " + this.surname :
            this.name + " " + this.surname;
    }
}
```

Constructor parameters conform to all rules of function parameters that were exposed in the *Functions* section of `Chapter 2`, *Complex Types and Functions*. So they may have optional parameters with or without default values, an undefinite number of arguments, and several overloads, and they can use the spread operator. For instance, the following is a constructor with several overloads:

```
conctructor(s: string, n: number): void
conctructor(s1: string, s2: string, ...others: string[]): void
conctructor(s: string, x: string | number, ...others: string[]){
//This is the actual constructor that handles
//paramters of all constructors
}
```

In the preceding example, there are two constructor overloads, and the second one admits an indefinite number of parameters that are collected in the `others` array. The actual implementation that comes after the two constructors must handle both constructors by checking the types of the parameters it receives. For more details on overloads, please refer to the *Functions* section in `Chapter 2`, *Complex Types and Functions*.

Each constructor overload specifies a different set of arguments to be passed in the new statement. For instance, we may create a Person instance in two ways, since the `secondName` parameter is optional:

```
var myPerson: Person = new Person("John", "Smith");
var anotherPerson = new Person("George", "Smith", "Carl");
```

Unlike C# and C++, TypeScript has no concept of the destructor/finalizer that is called when an instance is destroyed by the garbage collector. This is a consequence of JavaScript having no such concepts. In turn, the absence of destructors/finalizers in JavaScript is tied to the following consideration: languages that use garbage collection, such as C# and Java, need a destructor/finalizer just to release external resources that aren't handled automatically by the garbage collector, but JavaScript, being designed to run in browsers, can't have the responsibility of releasing external resources, for security reasons. However, nowadays, thanks to Node.js, JavaScript is also being used outside browsers, and the lack of destructors/finalizers has become a serious limitation.

Members definition and modifiers

Class members may be either functions, in which case they are called methods, or memory locations, in which case they are called properties. Methods, like functions and constructors, may have several overloads. Please refer to the *Functions* section of Chapter 2, *Complex Types and Functions*, for more details on how to handle overloads. From our side, the class members may be invoked by prefixing their names with an expression that evaluates to a class instance followed by a dot:

```
var myPerson = new Person("John", "Smith");

var fname = myPerson.fullname();
var name = myPerson.name;
```

Only members declared as public may be invoked from outside the class. As a default, members are declared public, but for better readability they may be explicitly declared public with the `public` modifier that must precede the member definition. So, the previous `Person` class with explicit public declarations becomes the following:

```
class Person {
    public name: string;
    public surname: string;
    public secondName?: string;
    constructor(name: string, surname: string, secondName?: string) {
        this.name = name;
        this.surname = surname;
```

```
            this.secondName = secondName;
        }
        public fullname(): string {
            return this.secondName !== undefined ?
                this.name + " " + this.secondName + " " + this.surname :
                this.name + " " + this.surname;
        }
    }
```

Members may also be declared private or protected by replacing the `public` modifier with the `private` and `protected` modifiers. Private members may be used only from within the class they are defined in. Usually, they encode implementation details that must not be visible from outside the class. Hiding implementation details in object-oriented languages is called **encapsulation**. Encapsulation ensures modularity because, if needed, implementation details encoded by private members may be changed without affecting the code outside the class, since private members can't be referenced from outside the class.

For instance, the `Person` class might use a private method that uppercases the first letter of a name, surname, and second name before assembling the full name:

```
        private titleCase(x: string): string {
            return x.substr(0, 1).toUpperCase() + x.substr(1);
        }
        public fullname(): string {
            return this.secondName !== undefined ?
                this.titleCase(this.name) + " " +
    this.titleCase(this.secondName)
                    + " " + this.titleCase(this.surname) :
                this.titleCase(this.name) + " " +
    this.titleCase(this.surname);
        }
```

The preceding example shows a private method, but classes may also have private properties to store data structures whose implementation details must be encapsulated.

Protected members work like private members, with the only difference being that, unlike private members, they are visible to all inheriting classes. Inheritage is discussed later on in a dedicated section of this chapter.

Properties may also have the `readonly` modifier, in which case code may only read them, but can't assign them a value. Read-only properties may be assigned a value only in the class constructor, that is, when a class instance is created. Since a `Person` usually doesn't change `name`, `surname`, and `secondName`, one may define all these properties as read-only:

```
public readonly name: string;
public readonly surname: string;
public readonly secondName?: string;
```

Or simply the following, since, as a default, members are considered public:

```
readonly name: string;
readonly surname: string;
readonly secondName?: string;
```

Implicit property definition

In the `Person` class, the `name`, `surname`, and `secondName` identifiers are both constructor parameters and class properties. Moreover, the value of each constructor parameter is assigned to the property with its same name. Since this is a common pattern, TypeScript gives the possibility to define the class properties while defining the constructor itself! It is enough to precede the parameter definition with one or more of the `public`, `private`, `protected`, and `readonly` modifiers. When this is done, TypeScript automatically defines properties with the same names of the parameters, each with the modifiers specified before the parameter definition. Then the TypeScript transpiler automatically creates the code to assign each parameter value to its corresponding property.

Thus, the `Person` class may be rewritten in a simpler way:

```
class Person {
    constructor(readonly name: string, readonly surname: string,
        readonly secondName?: string) {
    }
    public fullname(): string {
        return this.secondName !== undefined ?
            this.name + " " + this.secondName + " " + this.surname :
            this.name + " " + this.surname;
    }
}
```

The constructor is empty since all previous assignment instructions are now created automatically.

In case parameters are not read-only, one may replace the `readonly` modifier with the `public` modifier, since at least one modifier must be specified to trigger the automatic property definition:

```
constructor(public name: string, public surname: string,
        public secondName?: string) {
}
```

Accessors

C#-style getters and setters are part of ECMAScript 5 specifications and are supported by all mainstream browsers. Getters and setters simulate an object property by running code whenever the virtual property is set and by computing a value whenever the property value is required.

TypeScript supports getters and setters in classes only if the JavaScript target is ECMAScript 5 or greater. No attempt is made to simulate them on lower JavaScript versions, since a perfect simulation that works in all situations is impossible. The syntax for getters and setters is straightforward:

```
class MyClass{
    ...
    get <property name>(): <property type>{
        ...
        return....
    }
    set <property name>(x: <property type>)
    {
        ...
    }
    ....
}
//after that one may write:
var instance = new MyClass();
instance.<property name> = ....;
var test = instance.<property name>;
```

For example, the `fullname` method in the `Person` class may be substituted by a virtual property implemented with a getter:

```
class Person {
        constructor(readonly name: string, readonly surname: string,
            readonly secondName?: string) {
        }
        get fullname(): string {
```

```
            return this.secondName !== undefined ?
                this.name + " " + this.secondName + " " + this.surname :
                this.name + " " + this.surname;
        }
    }
```

After that, `fullname` may be retrieved as a standard property with a statement such as:

```
    var x = myPerson.fullname;
```

Instead of the following:

```
    var x = myPerson.fullname();
```

Since `fullname` has no setter, it is considered read-only and can't be assigned a value. Analogously, when there is a setter but no getter, the property is considered write-only and its value can't be read.

The `Person` class may be modified so that `fullname` can be written too, but this requires that `name`, `surname`, and `secondName` are also not declared read-only, since when `fullname` is assigned a value, they must be modified:

```
    class Person {
        constructor(public name: string, public surname: string,
            public secondName?: string) {
        }
        get fullname(): string {
            return this.secondName !== undefined ?
                this.name + " " + this.secondName + " " + this.surname :
                this.name + " " + this.surname;
        }
        set fullname(value: string) {
            var arr=value.replace(/\s\s+/g, ' ').split(' ');
            if (arr.length == 2) {
                this.name = arr[0];
                this.surname = arr[1];
                this.secondName = undefined;
            }
            else if (arr.length == 3) {
                this.name = arr[0];
                this.surname = arr[2];
                this.secondName = arr[1];
            }
            else throw "wrong fullname assignement";
        }
    }
```

`.replace(/\s\s+/g, ' ')` removes multiple spaces, then the string is split into its words, and the words are assigned to `name`, `secondName`, and `surname`. When there are just two words, `secondName` is assumed to be absent. If the number of arguments is neither two nor three, an exception is thrown. It is worth pointing out that the preceding implementation doesn't work when `name`, `surname`, or `secondName` contain more than one word each, since in this case it is impossible to understand which word is part of `name`, `surname`, or `secondName`. Thus, in practical implementations, the class version containing just the `fullname` getter should be preferred.

Static members and static parts of a class

Other object-oriented languages such as C# and C++ as well as TypeScript, allow static members. Readers fluent in C# should know what static members are, so this section gives just a simple recall, focusing on the peculiarities of TypeScript.

All class members considered so far are called **instance members**, since they are tied to a specific instance of the class. The meaning of **tied** is different for properties and methods:

- Properties have different values for each class instance. Thus, for instance, the string one gets with `myPerson.name` depends on and is specific to the class instance contained in the `myPerson` variable.
- The method's code is the same for all instances, but methods are tied to a specific instance through the `this` symbol. In other words, when a method is invoked on a specific class instance, all occurrences of `this` in that method are bound to that instance. Thus when one invokes `myPerson.fullname()`, all occurrences of `this` in the `fullname` method are bound to the class instance contained in `myPerson`, so the `fullname` method uses the `name`, `surname`, and `secondName` of the specific instance contained in `myPerson` to assemble a full name.

On the other hand, static methods can't use `this`, and static properties are not tied to any instance, they are simply tied to the class itself that acts as a container that groups together functions and variables that are conceptually related to the class itself. Static class methods and properties are accessed through the class name itself instead of a variable containing a class instance:

```
let test1 = <class name>.<static method>();
let test2 = <class name>.<static property>;
```

Members are declared static by prefixing their definition with the `static` modifier. For instance, supposing that the `Person` class models some kind of community, one might add a static property containing the administrator of the community:

```
class Person {
    static administrator: Person = new Person("John", "Smith");
    constructor(readonly name: string, readonly surname: string,
        readonly secondName?: string) {
    }
    public fullname(): string {
        return this.secondName !== undefined ?
            this.name + " " + this.secondName + " " + this.surname :
            this.name + " " + this.surname;
    }
}
```

With the preceding definition, one may get the community administrator with the following:

```
let admin = Person.administrator;
```

What is the type of a class object?

An expression of the `Person.administrator` type may work only if `Person` is not only a TypeScript type but also a runtime JavaScript value. Let's assign the `Person` value to a variable:

```
let personMaker = Person;
```

Then let's hover the mouse on `personMaker`:

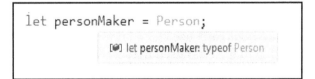

So the type of the `Person` value is `typeof Person`, a type that TypeScript creates automatically, to assign a type to the `Person` value. More insights on the nature of the `Person` value may be gained by using Visual Studio IntelliSense:

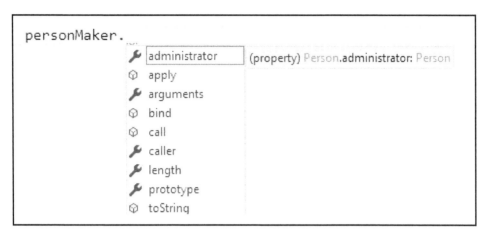

It appears to be a function because of the `call`, `bind`, and `apply` methods. Moreover, it has all static members defined on `Person` (just the `administrator` property).

It turns out that the `Person` value is the constructor function used to create `Person` instances. In fact, we may use also `personMaker` to create `Person` instances:

```
let aPerson: Person = new personMaker("Frank", "Smith");
```

The class constructor with all the class static members attached is a part of the class that is common to all class instances. For this reason, it is called the **static part** of a class. TypeScript puts the static part of a class in a variable that has the same name as the class.

Inheriting from a class and implementing interfaces

Similar to C#, TypeScript supports inheritage, implementing interfaces, and abstract classes and methods. This section recalls the preceding concepts and shows how they are implemented in TypeScript and how to use them to design modular applications.

Implementing interfaces

A class may declare that it implements one or more interfaces with the following syntax:

```
class <class name> implements <interface1> [, <interface1>]...{
    ...
    ...
}
```

The `implements` keyword is followed by one or more comma-separated interface references. After that, the class must contain all methods and properties prescribed by each interface, and all of them must be declared as public. Interfaces prescribe only public members because they constrain the class' external surface, which is how the class may be used by the remainder of the code, not how class features are implemented.

Interface implementation may help build modular code, because different classes that implement a common interface may be processed by exactly the same code, thus that code may be factored out, instead of being replicated for each different class. For instance, if one defines the following `IPrintable` interface:

```
interface IPrintable {
    getString(): string;
}
```

Then one may write code that may print any mix of objects belonging to classes that implement `IPrintable` in a human-readable format, thereby implementing code that works properly on a wider range of arguments.

Here is an implementation of `IPrintable` for the `Person` class:

```
class Person implements IPrintable {
    static administrator: Person = new Person("John", "Smith");
    constructor(readonly name: string, readonly surname: string,
        readonly secondName?: string) {
    }
    public fullname(): string {
        return this.secondName !== undefined ?
            this.name + " " + this.secondName + " " + this.surname :
            this.name + " " + this.surname;
    }
    public getString(): string {
        return "\n" + this.fullname() + "\n";
    }
}
```

Inheriting from a class

Classes may inherit from a single parent class, in which case they get all public and protected members of the parent class. The syntax for specifying a parent class to inherit from is the same as interface inheritage:

```
class <class name> extends <parent class> {
    ...
    ...
}
```

As in other object-oriented languages, inheritage is limited to a single parent class to avoid potential conflicts between members with the same name coming from different parents. Inheritage promotes modularity, since common code shared by several classes may be factored out into a single parent class.

Inheriting classes are called subclasses or derived classes, while their parent classes are called superclasses. Descendant classes are subtypes of their superclasses, so it is allowed to to move an instance of a class into a variable whose type is a superclass of that instance.

When a derived class instance is created, the constructor of its superclass, if any, must be called to initialize all superclass members. In order to ensure superclass properties, initialization-derived classes must call `super(....)`, passing it all parameters of the superclass constructor, as shown in the following code:

```
constructor (par1: type1, ....)
{
    ...
    super(...);
    ...
}
```

As an example of inheritage, we may define a `Teacher` class that inherits from the `Person` class:

```
class Teacher extends Person {
        constructor(public course: string, name: string, surname: string,
            secondName?: string) {
            super(name, surname, secondName);
        }

    }
```

The preceding example shows that specialization hierarchies implicit in the application domain are often a good guide for defining superclass-derived class relations.

However, this is just a heuristic, not a general rule. In fact, as the complete example at the end of this section shows, useful, superclass-derived class relations may be defined in absence of such specialization hierarchies. The only general rule is, *define parent classes to factor out common code that might be used by several derived classes*. A superclass should also be defined when it has a single derived class, if the code factored out in the superclass might be used by future derived classes that might be added during the application evolution, and maintenance.

The `Teacher` class defined in the preceding example also inherits the `IPrintable` implementation of `Person`, however, the `getString` method inherited by `Person` doesn't give a complete human-readable picture of a `Teacher` instance, since it doesn't provide any information about the teacher course. Luckily, each derived class may redefine any method inherited by its superclass. In this case, we say that the method provided by the derived class overrides the method defined in the superclass:

```
class Teacher extends Person {
    constructor(public course: string, name: string, surname: string,
        secondName?: string) {
        super(name, surname, secondName);
    }
    getString(): string {
        return super.getString() + "techer of: " +
            this.course + "\n";
    }
}
let myPrintable: IPrintable = new Teacher("TypeScript", "Francesco",
"Abbruzzese");
let humanReadable = myPrintable.getString();
```

In the preceding example, `humanReadable` will contain the complete information about the teacher, since `myPrintable` uses the `getString` definition provided in the `Teacher` class.

All methods of a derived class may call superclass implementations of any overridden method by prefixing the method name with `super.`. The `Teacher` example uses `super.getString()` to get its superclass human-readable string and then add its information specific to `Teacher`.

Abstract classes and methods

Abstract classes are entities in between classes and interfaces. Namely, they are classes that do not specify an implementation for some of their methods. The methods without implementation are called abstracts. One cannot create instances of abstract classes since they are incomplete, so they just factor out some code to be used by derived classes that provide implementation for all their abstract methods.

Each abstract class definition must be prefixed with the `abstract` modifier. Also, each abstract method of an abstract class must be prefixed with the `abstract` modifier:

```
abstract class Product {
    constructor(public availability: number) {
    }
    abstract unitPrice(): number;
    totalPrice(quantity: number): [number, number] {
        if (quantity > this.availability) quantity = this.availability;
        let unitPrice = this.unitPrice();
        if (quantity >= 5) unitPrice *= 0.95;
        else if (quantity >= 10) unitPrice *= 0.90;
        else if (quantity >= 20) unitPrice *= 0.80;
        else if (quantity >= 100) unitPrice *= 0.65;
        return [quantity, quantity * unitPrice];
    }
    buy(quantity: number): [number, number] {
        let result = this.totalPrice(quantity);
        this.availability -= result[0];
        return result;
    }
}
```

The `Product` abstract class factors out the `availability` property, the `totalPrice` methods that contain the logics to compute the price as a function of the unitary price, required quantity, and availability, and the `buy` method that updates `availability` after a purchase. Both `buy` and `totalPrice` return a pair with the actual quantity that can be sold, and the total price of the purchase.

The `unitPrice` method is declared abstract because the logic to compute the product unit price as a function of the product's features depends on the specific type of product, so it may be provided only by a derived class that describes each specific type of product. For instance, the unit price of a computer may depend on the quantity of RAM, video RAM, hard disk, and other features, while the price of a table may depend on its dimensions and type.

Abstract methods offer the possibility to plug derived classes' specific logics into the general logic of the superclass.

Modular design with inheritance, interfaces, and abstract classes

The remainder of the section shows how to implement a modular version of the previous chapter's to-do list. Let's open the DOMManipulation project and add a lib folder under the .ts folder. The lib folder will contain library TypeScript files that may be reused in other projects, while the code specific to the project will be placed in a TypeScript file named modularToDoList.ts, placed directly in the ts folder. Let's add the following TypeScript files under the newly created lib folder: AbstractLists.ts, jQueryList.ts, plainList.ts:

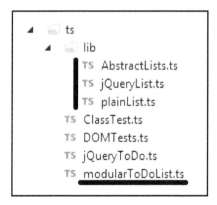

Let's start with the library code. We need classes/interfaces that abstract HTML node lists that may be manipulated somehow with HTML buttons. One may split the specifications into two parts:

- Insert and remove operations on a list of HTML nodes
- Buttons and input-field logic that trigger the HTML nodes' operations and provide the content for all insertion operations

Each part may be implemented with a different class—a class that manipulates a node list, whose methods are invoked by the class that handles the needed buttons and input. The connection between the two classes may be created by passing an instance of the node-list manipulation class into the constructor of the buttons/input handling class.

As a first step, let's concentrate on the node list manipulation class. Is it better to implement a similar class directly, or to define an interface containing all node list operations, and then to design one or several classes that implement this interface?

Since node-list manipulation class instances must be passed to the buttons/input-handling class, the usage of an interface might be a good idea, because this way the same buttons/input-handling class would be able to work properly with several implementations of a node-list manipulation interface. However, does one need different implementations of the node-list manipulation interface or is a single implementation adequate for all applications? Let's see:

- In general, each item on the list might be connected somehow with other HTML that, for instance, might handle a detail view of the item and/or might need event handlers attached to it for the same reasons. Thus, all list-manipulation implementation might depend on the preceding application-specific details.
- A plain JavaScript DOM manipulation implementation is faster than any implementation based on a framework such as jQuery. On the other hand, a jQuery implementation might be more adequate for applications that must be compatible with legacy browsers.

Accordingly, it makes sense to have several implementations of node-list manipulation methods, so the idea of using an interface appears to be a winning one. A possible definition of a similar interface might be as follows:

```
interface ItemList {
    appendItem(itemData: any): void;
    prependItem(itemData: any): void;
    appendBefore(node: HTMLElement, itemData: any): void;
    appendAfter(node: HTMLElement, itemData: any): void;
    removeItem(node: HTMLElement): void;
    itemTemplate: (x: any) => HTMLElement;
    readonly itemsParent: HTMLElement;
}
```

There is a single removal operation but there are four possible insertion operations: prepending at the beginning of the list, appending at the end of the list, and inserting after/before another item. Each insertion operation accepts a data item whose properties are used to fill holes in an HTML template. The data item is modelled with the `any` type since it may be anything, while the HTML template is contained in the `itemTemplate` property, and is modelled as a function that transforms the data item into an `HTMLElement` (with all its descendent nodes). The interface also has the `itemsParent` read-only property that returns the parent node all items will be appended to. `itemsParent` will be passed in the constructor of all classes that implement the `ItemList` interface.

Let's place the preceding interface in the `AbstractLists.ts` file, which will also contain the input/button-handling class, while the `plainList.ts` and `jQueryList.ts` files will contain a plain TypeScript implementation and a jQuery-based implementation of `ItemList`, respectively.

Let's move on to the input/button-handling class. Is it possible to implement a complete class that solves the problem once and for all, or is the best option an incomplete class that may be completed in a way that depends on the specific application?

If only the incomplete option is viable, the class must be defined as abstract, and all application-specific stuff must be enclosed in abstract methods. There are at least the following two operations that depend on the specific context:

- How does one assemble the content of various input fields into a data item to pass to the various `ItemList` insertion methods?
- The HTML template function to be placed in the `itemTemplate` property of `ItemList`

Thus, the input/button-handling class must be abstract and must have at least two abstract methods. Let's start writing its skeleton:

```
abstract class AppendGrid {
    protected abstract itemTemplate(x: any): HTMLElement;
    protected abstract extractDataToAdd(): any;
}
```

The two abstract methods have been declared `protected` since they don't need to be accessed from outside the class but just from the descendant classes that provide their implementations.

The class has been called `AppendGrid`, since it will handle just the `appendItem` and `prependItem` operations. In fact, the `appendBefore/After` operation requires a more complex button logic, so the best option to handle them is to write a further class that inherits from `AppendGrid` (this will not be done here, but the willing reader is invited to try it).

Since we need to find the item the button was clicked on, and since one might click some content inside a button instead of the button, `AppendGrid` needs a `findAncestor` method to find an ancestor that satisfies a given CSS selector (the button, and the item root element):

```
abstract class AppendGrid {
    abstract itemTemplate(x: any): HTMLElement;
    abstract extractDataToAdd(): any;
```

```
private static findAncestor(n: HTMLElement | null,
            selector: string): HTMLElement | null {
    while (n != null && n.tagName != "BODY") {
        if (n.matches && n.matches(selector)) return n;
        else if (n.webkitMatchesSelector
            && n.webkitMatchesSelector(selector)) return n;
        n = n.parentNode as HTMLElement;
    }
    return null;
}
}
```

The findAncestor method handles all browser variants of the matches method, and has been declared static since it is not tied to a specific instance of the class since it doesn't use the this keyword inside of it. The constructor of the AppendGrid class must pass all information needed to connect an instance of the class with the HTML of the page, namely the following:

- The ItemList to work on.
- The **Add** button, since it needs to add a click handler to it.
- A CSS selector to help the findAncestor method find the root of the item the remove button was clicked in, so it can be removed.
- HTMLElement that contains all input fields to be processed by extractDataToAdd, to assemble the data item to pass to all insertion methods.
- An optional prepend button to be used when a prepend operation is needed. This button is optional, since not all implementations need the prepend operation.

Accordingly, the following constructor skeleton should work:

```
constructor(
        protected list: ItemList,
        protected addButton: HTMLElement,
        protected itemRootSelector: string,
        protected addItemDataRoot: HTMLElement,
        protected addBeforeButton?: HTMLElement) {
    }
```

Inside the constructor, the `itemTemplate` method must be assigned to the `itemTemplate` property of `list`, so `ItemList` has the right HTML template to create new items. Then, the click handlers must be added to both the add and the prepend buttons. Finally, a click-handler must be added to `list.itemsParent`, so it can intercept the click events of all remove buttons because of JavaScript event-bubbling:

```
constructor(protected list: ItemList,
    protected addButton: HTMLElement,
    protected itemRootSelector: string,
    protected addItemDataRoot: HTMLElement,
    protected addBeforeButton?: HTMLElement) {
    this.list.itemTemplate = this.itemTemplate;
    this.list.itemsParent.addEventListener("click",
        (evt: MouseEvent) => {
            let button = AppendGrid.findAncestor(
                evt.target as HTMLElement,
                "button");
            let target = AppendGrid.findAncestor(
                button,
                itemRootSelector);
            if (target != null )
                list.removeItem(target);
        });
    this.addButton.addEventListener("click",
        (evt: MouseEvent) => {
            list.appendItem(this.extractDataToAdd());
        });
    if (this.addBeforeButton) {
        this.addBeforeButton.addEventListener("click",
            (evt: MouseEvent) => {
                list.prependItem(this.extractDataToAdd());
            });
    }
}
```

The data item to be passed to all `ItemList` insertion methods is obtained by calling the abstract `extractDataToAdd` method, whose implementation will be provided by each application-specific descendant of `AppendGrid`. `findAncestor` is called the first time to verify that the click event comes from inside a button, then to find the root of the item to remove by exploiting the `itemRootSelector` CSS selector.

The complete definition of the class is as follows:

```
abstract class AppendGrid {
    constructor(protected list: ItemList,
        protected addButton: HTMLElement,
```

```
            protected itemRootSelector: string,
            protected addItemDataRoot: HTMLElement,
            protected addBeforeButton?: HTMLElement) {
        this.list.itemTemplate = this.itemTemplate;
        this.list.itemsParent.addEventListener("click",
            (evt: MouseEvent) => {
                let button = AppendGrid.findAncestor(
                    evt.target as HTMLElement,
                    "button");
                let target = AppendGrid.findAncestor(
                    button,
                    itemRootSelector);
                if (target != null )
                    list.removeItem(target);
            });
        this.addButton.addEventListener("click",
            (evt: MouseEvent) => {
                list.appendItem(this.extractDataToAdd());
            });
        if (this.addBeforeButton) {
            this.addBeforeButton.addEventListener("click",
                (evt: MouseEvent) => {
                    list.prependItem(this.extractDataToAdd());
                });
        }
    }
    protected abstract itemTemplate(x: any): HTMLElement;
    protected abstract extractDataToAdd(): any;
    private static findAncestor(n: HTMLElement | null,
                    selector: string): HTMLElement | null {
        while (n != null && n.tagName != "BODY") {
            if (n.matches && n.matches(selector)) return n;
            else if (n.webkitMatchesSelector
                && n.webkitMatchesSelector(selector)) return n;
            n = n.parentNode as HTMLElement;
        }
        return null;
    }
}
```

Here is a plain TypeScript implementation of ItemList to be placed in plainList.ts:

```
class PlainList implements ItemList {
    itemTemplate: (x: any) => HTMLElement;
    constructor(readonly itemsParent: HTMLElement) {
    }
    removeItem(node: HTMLElement): void {
        this.itemsParent.removeChild(node);
```

```
    }
    appendItem(itemData: any): void {
        this.itemsParent.appendChild(this.itemTemplate(itemData));
    }
    prependItem(itemData: any): void {
        if (this.itemsParent.childElementCount === 0)
            this.appendItem(itemData);
        else
            this.itemsParent.insertBefore(
                this.itemTemplate(itemData),
                (this.itemsParent.firstChild as HTMLElement));
    }
    appendBefore(node: HTMLElement, itemData: any): void {
        this.itemsParent.insertBefore(
            this.itemTemplate(itemData),
            node);
    }
    appendAfter(node: HTMLElement, itemData: any): void {
        if (node.nextSibling)
            this.itemsParent.insertBefore(
                this.itemTemplate(itemData),
                node.nextSibling);
        else this.appendItem(itemData);
    }
}
```

All insertion operations are expressed in terms of `HTMLElement.appendChild`, and `HTMLElement.insertBefore`, since they are the only plain JavaScript insertion operations available for `HTMLElement`.

The jQuery implementation, to be placed in `jQueryList.ts`, is simpler since all methods are just wrappers around already existing jQuery methods:

```
class JQueryList implements ItemList {
    itemTemplate: (x: any) => HTMLElement;
    constructor(readonly itemsParent: HTMLElement) {
    }
    removeItem(node: HTMLElement): void {
        $(this.itemsParent).remove();
    }
    appendItem(itemData: any): void {
        $(this.itemsParent)
            .append(this.itemTemplate(itemData));
    }
    prependItem(itemData: any): void {
        $(this.itemsParent)
            .prepend(this.itemTemplate(itemData));
```

```
    }
    appendBefore(node: HTMLElement, itemData: any): void {
        $(node).before(this.itemTemplate(itemData));
    }
    appendAfter(node: HTMLElement, itemData: any): void {
        $(node).after(this.itemTemplate(itemData));
    }
}
```

Both implementations accept `HTMLElement` to be used as the parent of all items as the only parameter of their constructors. This `HTMLElement` is enough to bind each class instance to the HTML of the web page.

The preceding implementations complete the library part of the code. The application part of the code must be applied to the same `Views\Home\Index.cshtml` page used in *Chapter 3*, *DOM Manipulation*.

The TypeScript code will be placed in the previously created `modularToDoList.ts`. The whole code will be placed within the body of a function, since all application classes and variables don't need to be visible to other TypeScript files:

```
(function () {
    //Whole application code here
})();
```

The main part of the code is a class that inherits from `AppendGrid` and provides implementations for the abstract methods, `extractDataToAdd` and `itemTemplate`. The skeleton of this class is as follows:

```
class MyULAppendGrid extends AppendGrid {
    constructor(list: ItemList,
        addButton: HTMLElement,
        itemRootselector: string,
        addItemDataRoot: HTMLElement,
        addBeforeButton?: HTMLElement) {
        super(list, addButton,
            itemRootselector,
                addItemDataRoot,
            addBeforeButton);
    }
    extractDataToAdd(): any {
        //method implementation here
    }
    itemTemplate(x: any): HTMLElement {
        //method implementation here
    }
}
```

The application class constructor just takes all needed parameters and passes them to the parent class by invoking `super`. `extractDataToAdd` must assemble the data item by using the content of all input fields contained inside `addItemDataRoot HTMLelement`. In this case, the item data consists simply of the string contained in the `main_input` input field, so `addItemDataRoot` is this input field, and `extractDataToAdd` only needs to extract its content:

```
extractDataToAdd(): any {
    return (this.addItemDataRoot as HTMLInputElement).value;
}
```

In `itemTemplate`, one may use string interpolation to build the HTML string that represents the element to be created by the template. Then, the needed `HTMLElement` is obtained by assigning this string to the `innerHTML` property of a dummy element:

```
itemTemplate(x: any): HTMLElement {
    let str = x as string;
    let toAdd =
    `<li class="list-group-item">
        <button type="button" class="btn btn-sm" title="remove">
            <span class="glyphicon glyphicon-minus" aria-hidden="true">
            </span>
        </button>
        <span>${str}</span>
    </li>`;
    let temp = document.createElement('ul');
    temp.innerHTML = toAdd;
    return temp.firstChild as HTMLElement;
}
```

The item data is cast to a string and then used for string interpolation. Since the element to create is `li`, one is forced to use a `ul` or `ol` dummy element. As soon as `toAdd` is assigned to `innerHTML`, the browser builds the HTML automatically, represented by the string, and uses it as content of the dummy element, so it is enough to return the first child of the dummy element.

Now we need to create an instance of an `ItemList` implementation:

```
var mainList = new PlainList(
        document.getElementById('main_list') as HTMLElement);
```

The `main_list` variable is the ID of the `ul` tag that will contain all the to-do items. Then we must get all HTML elements that are needed by the `MyULAppendGrid` constructor together with `mainList`, which is the add button and the new item input field, since the example has no prepend button:

```
var addButton =
    document.getElementById('main_add') as HTMLElement;
var addInput =
    document.getElementById('main_input') as HTMLElement;
```

The type-assertion is needed since `getElementById` returns `HTMLElement|null`, and the HTML elements exists for sure. At this point, it is enough to create an instance of `MyULAppendGrid` to attach all handlers needed to start the application:

```
var mainGrid = new MyULAppendGrid(mainList, addButton,
        "li", addInput);
```

The `li` tag is passed as the CSS selector to locate the item root, since it is the only `li` element contained in each item.

Before running the application, we must add all needed JavaScript files to `Views\Home\Index.cshtml`:

```
@section Scripts{
<script src="~/js/lib/AbstractLists.js"></script>
<script src="~/js/lib/plainList.js"></script>
<script src="~/js/modularToDoList.js"></script>
}
```

The jQuery implementation of `ItemList` may be tested by replacing `~/js/lib/plainList.js` with `~/js/lib/jQueryList.js`. It is worth mentioning that the TypeScript compiler automatically creates the `lib` folder under `js` to replicate the same folder-organization of the source TypeScript files.

Advanced type-compatibility

This section lists additional type-compatibility rules and type guards that come with classes and class inheritage.

Descendant classes are subtypes of their superclasses, so one may write something such as the following:

```
let aTeacherOrPerson: Person = new Teacher("TypeScript", "Francesco",
"Abbruzzese");
```

In `ClassTest.ts`, `Teacher` inherits from `Person`. On the other hand, one may use the `instanceof` type guard to discriminate among descendant classes:

```
let myCourse: string | null;
if (aTeacherOrPerson instanceof Teacher)
    myCourse = aTeacherOrPerson.course;
else
    myCourse = null;
```

Inside the `if` branch, `aTeacherOrPerson` is assumed to be of the `Teacher` type because of the new `instanceof` type guard. `instanceof` returns `true` if the object on its left is an instance of the class on its right, or an instance of descendant of that class. Thus, for instance, `x instanceof Person` returns true if x is `Teacher`, or a descendant of `Teacher`.

As already discussed, one can write the following:

```
var anotherPerson = new Person("George", "Smith", "Carl");
```

This means `anotherPerson` is inferred to be `Person` by the TypeScript transpiler. However, let's see what happens if one writes the following:

```
let mixedArray1 =
    [new Teacher("TypeScript", "Francesco", "Abbruzzese"),
    new Person("John", "Smith")
    ];
```

By hovering the mouse, we see that `mixedArray1` is assumed to be `Person[]`:

```
let mixedArray1 =
    [ne    [👁] let mixedArray1: Person[]    ", "Francesco", "Abbruzzese"),
    new   .......( ...... ,. ....h")
    ];
```

In fact, among all types of the array elements, `Person` is the one that is a superset of all other elements. What if one adds also a string that is a type that has no common ancestor with all other types? Let's see:

```
let mixedArray1 =
    [new Teacher("TypeScript", "Francesco", "Abbruzzese"),
    new Person("John", "Smith"),
    "simple string"
    ];
```

One gets `(string|Person)[]`:

```
let mixedArray1 =
    [new Te   [●] let mixedArray1: (string | Person)[]   esco", "Abbruzzese"),
    new Pe
    "simple string"
    ];
```

That is, the TypeScript transpiler uses union types to get a common ancestor.

As a general rule, when an expression involves several concurrent types, the TypeScript transpiler finds their closest common ancestor, possibly using the type union operator, |.

However, TypeScript only uses types that are actually concurrent types of the expression, it doesn't use superclasses that are external to the expression.

For instance, if we build an array containing just `Teacher`, and another subclass of `Person`, say `Customer`, but no `Person`, the inferred type will not be `Person[]` but `(Teacher|Customer)[]`, since `Person` is not a possible concurrent type of the expression.

The structural sub-typing of interfaces not only applies to single objects but also to whole classes. This means that there is no need to declare explicitly with the `implements` statement that a class implements an interface, but the same fact that the class has all members required by an interface is enough for TypeScript compiler to understand that the class actually implements that interface. For example, if we remove `implements` `ItemList` from `PlainList`, and `JQueryList` classes of the previous section example no error is signalled and the code compiles and runs properly.

It is good practice to declare explicitly all interfaces implemented by a class. This way, if the class is modified in a way that might break an interface implementation, an error is signalled immediately, thus avoiding error propagations that might cause hard-to-find bugs.

Summary

TypeScript supports all typical object-oriented concepts. Each class is both a type and a set of instructions on how to build instances of that type. Classes have constructors and instance members that may be properties, accessors, or methods. Each of them may have the `private`, `protected`, or `public` modifier. Private members are accessible only from inside a class, the protected ones are also from inheriting classes, while public members are publicly available from the remainder of the code. Properties may be decorated with the `readonly` modifier, in which case they are read-only and may be assigned a value only from inside the class constructor. Properties that are assigned a value from constructor parameters may be declared in the constructor itself together with the parameters they take the value from.

Class instances are created with the `new` keyword followed by the class name with all constructor parameters specified and enclosed between parentheses just after the class name.

Instance members are accessed from other class methods by prefixing their names with the `this` keyword followed by a dot. From outside the class, public members may be accessed by attaching a dot followed by the member name to an expression evaluating to a class instance.

TypeScript supports static members which, together with the class constructor, constitute the static part of the class that is implemented as a JavaScript constructor function.

TypeScript supports inheritage, interface implementation with classes, and abstract classes, which, together with the `protected` and `private` modifiers, are the building blocks to factor out common code and to hide implementation details, thus enabling a modular software design. Classes may override inherited methods and recall the original version of all overridden methods, thus handling exceptions to general procedures, and their further specialization. `instanceof` type guards may be used to discriminate among descendant classes.

The next chapter will look at TypeScript generics that mimic C# generics and C++ templates. Generics enable the definition of code that may be applied to different types, thus factoring out behaviors that apply to several types into unique functions or classes. Generics are a powerful feature that reduces an application's development time and improves its modularity.

Questions

1. What is the difference between the private and protected modifiers? Can an abstract method be defined as private?
2. Are you able to state a simple rule on when to add the static modifier to a class method?
3. Can a class have different constructor overloads? If not, why? If yes, how?
4. Can one create an instance of an abstract class? Why?
5. Can an abstract class have a constructor? Why?
6. How can a descendant class call the original version of an overridden method?
7. How does a descendant class provide all constructor parameters to its parent class constructor?
8. Is it possible to define a public write-only property in a class? How?
9. When and why is it convenient to define an interface and classes that implement it?
10. How many interfaces can a class implement? How many classes can a class inherit from simultaneously?

Further reading

This chapter about TypeScript classes is quite self-contained and should enable any developer with some experience in any object-oriented language, such as C#, to use object-oriented programming in TypeScript. The reader that feels the need to better understand object-oriented principles and best practices is referred to a general book on the subject: *Learning Object-Oriented Programming*: https://www.packtpub.com/application-development/learning-object-oriented-programming.

5
Generics

The word **generics** refers to using variable types, that is, parameters that at a later time will be bound to actual types. Parametric types were first introduced in C++ templates, then they took the name generics in Java and in C#. The main difference between C++ and Java/C# implementation is that C++ parametric types disappear at runtime; only the complete types obtained by substituting actual types to all template parameters survive at runtime.

On the contrary, in C# and Java, data structures (classes, interfaces, functions) based on generics are legal runtime types. In fact, any C# programmers with some experience in reflection know that a generic class can be dynamically instantiated at runtime with actual types.

TypeScript has a generics implementation that mimics C# syntax, but, as in C++, TypeScript generics live just at compilation time and disappear at runtime, for two simple reasons:

- The TypeScript manifest prescribes that all type-related stuff must disappear at runtime
- JavaScript has no generic-like entities that might host TypeScript generic types at runtime

Accordingly, TypeScript generics are just a compilation-time help that recover compilation-time type checks in situations that should otherwise be handled with the `any` type. This chapter shows that, notwithstanding this limitation, TypeScript generics are a very useful tool. The chapter focuses both on the motivations behind generics and on their implementation and properties in TypeScript.

The following topics will be covered in this chapter:

- How to improve type checking with generic functions and interfaces
- How to define general-purpose classes with generic classes
- How to improve type checking with generic constraints
- The `keyof` and `keyof` constraints

Technical requirements

We need the following tools and packages for this chapter:

- Visual Studio 2017 with the last ASP.NET Core tools
- Visual Studio TypeScript SDK

For the examples in this chapter, please copy the `DOMManipulation` project from `Chapter 4`, *Using Classes and Interfaces*. Some previous code will be re-engineered with the help of generics, and new examples will be added.

All the code used in this chapter can be downloaded from the following GitHub link: `https://github.com/PacktPublishing/Hands-On-TypeScript-for-CSharp-and-.NET-Core-Developers`.

Check out the following video to see the Code in Action: `http://bit.ly/2JnifM5`.

Generic functions and interfaces

The example at the end of the *Inheriting from a class and implementing interfaces* section of `Chapter 4`, *Using Classes and Interfaces*, uses the following interface:

```
interface ItemList {
   appendItem(itemData: any): void;
    prependItem(itemData: any): void;
    appendBefore(node: HTMLElement, itemData: any): void;
    appendAfter(node: HTMLElement, itemData: any): void;
    removeItem(node: HTMLElement): void;
    itemTemplate: (x: any) => HTMLElement;
    readonly itemsParent: HTMLElement;
}
```

Various methods accept an `itemData` parameter, which represents a general data item whose fields have to be be used to assemble new elements to add to the DOM list represented by the interface. Its type is `any` since the data item may have any type. However, by using `any`, one misses several opportunities:

- The type of `itemData` can be any type but it is exactly the same type in all methods with an `itemData` parameter. This constraint is not represented anywhere in the interface.

- There is no compilation-time type check on the `itemData` parameter in both the code that uses, and in the one that implements, the interface.

These problems might be solved by defining a variable type, that is, by saying something such as—the type of `itemData` is a `T` type that will be specified later on before using the interface. This is exactly what generics were conceived for! Using generics, the `ItemList` interface can be rewritten as:

```
interface ItemList<T> {
    appendItem(itemData: T): void;
    prependItem(itemData: T): void;
    appendBefore(node: HTMLElement, itemData: T): void;
    appendAfter(node: HTMLElement, itemData: T): void;
    removeItem(node: HTMLElement): void;
    itemTemplate: (x: T) => HTMLElement;
    readonly itemsParent: HTMLElement;
}
```

The list of all type variables used by the interface is enclosed between the <> operator after the interface name, then these type variables are used as normal types. The `ItemList` interface needs just one type variable, but, in general, one may have several comma-separated variables within <>. So the general syntax is:

```
interface |interface name|<T1, T2, ...>
{
    ...
    |member name|  : T1;
    ...
    |member name|  : T2;
    ...
    |method name|(..., |parameter name|: T3,..)
}
```

Once declared within <>, type variables can be used in every place that might accept a type—members types, methods parameters types, and so on.

Type variables are called **generics**, while interfaces that use type variables are called **generic interfaces**.

The next section proposes a generics-based version of the whole example the `ItemList` interface was taken from. The remainder of this section gives you a feel of how to write code involving variable types with a simple example involving a single generic function. In fact, TypeScript also allows generic functions with a similar syntax—a list of generics enclosed between <> immediately after the function name, and then all generics can be used to replace types in the function parameter list, in place of the function return type, and in the function body.

The main difficulty in writing code containing generics is that generics don't allow any operation since the allowed operations depend on the types that will replace them. However, we will show that this problem can be solved in several ways, thus enabling the developer to write very useful and non-trivial code that manipulates generics.

A generic function for aggregating array elements

Aggregating a collection of data items of a T type means using all collection elements to create an instance of a new type, M, by applying a recursion rule to a current partial result and to each element of the collection. Each time the recursion rule is applied to an element of the collection and to the current partial result, a new partial result is obtained. At the end of the process, the last partial result becomes the result of the aggregation.

Examples of aggregations are computing the total value of an array of invoices, or finding the person whose surname-name pair comes first in lexicographical order.

Since the types involved are two (T and M) variable types, the aggregation function must be a generic function with two generics. Its first argument must be the array of items of the T type, while the second argument must be the aggregation rule to use. Thus the aggregation function skeleton should be something like:

```
function aggregate<M, T>(items: T[],
    rule: (x: M | undefined, t: T) => M): M | undefined {
    //code here
}
```

The aggregation rule must also accept `undefined` as the first argument since when the first array element is processed, the partial result is `undefined`. The result of the aggregation is `undefined` when the array is empty, so the result type of the function must also be `M | undefined`.

Let's create an `aggregate.ts` file under the `ts/lib` folder to host the function code. The `lib` folder is the right place for the function implementation since it is a general utility. The function implementation is straightforward:

```
function aggregate<M, T>(items: T[],
    rule: (x: M | undefined, t: T) => M): M | undefined {
    var partialResult: M | undefined;
    for (let y of items)
        partialResult = rule(partialResult, y);
    return partialResult;
}
```

It is worth pointing out how the preceding code solves the problem of processing objects whose type structure is unknown, that is, objects whose allowed operations are very limited—assignments, passing them to a function, accessing an element of an array, and so on. The preceding code uses two basic techniques:

- Accessing an array of elements of the variable type, since this operation doesn't depend on the specific structure of the type that will be bound to `T`.
- Manipulating the variable type instances with the function contained in the `rule` parameter whose implementation will be provided when the generic types have been bound to actual types. This way, the generic instances are processed by code that is specific to the types that actually replace the generics.

The remainder of this chapter will cover other techniques to process objects with an unknown structure.

Let's write some code to test the aggregation function on the invoices sum problem. First of all, let's create an `invoices.ts` file directly under the `ts` folder, and let's recall all JavaScript files needed to run the code under the `Views/Home/About.cshtml` view, so it is executed as soon as the user goes to the **About** page:

```
@section Scripts{
    <script src="~/js/lib/aggregate.js"></script>
    <script src="~/js/invoices.js"></script>
}
```

As a first step, create a very simple `Invoice` class:

```
class Invoice {
    constructor(readonly amount: number,
        readonly description: string,
        readonly reference: string) {
    }
}
```

Then, create an array of invoices:

```
let testInvoices: Invoice[] =
    [
        new Invoice(600, "computer", "i1"),
        new Invoice(100, "printer", "i2"),
        new Invoice(500, "installation service", "i3")
    ];
```

Now, the sum of all invoice amounts is easily computed by invoking a proper instantiation of the `aggregate` function:

```
let invoicesTotal =
    aggregate<number, Invoice>(testInvoices,
        (x: number | undefined, y: Invoice) =>
            x === undefined ? y.amount : x + y.amount);
```

The aggregation rule is passed as an arrow function. If the partial aggregation is `undefined`, it returns the amount of the current invoice, since this happens at the start of the aggregation process; otherwise, the amount of the current invoice is added to the current partial aggregation.

We may also remove the instantiation of the function generics since their types can be inferred automatically by the TypeScript compiler, in a way that is completely analogous to the C# generics inference:

```
let invoicesTotal =
    aggregate(testInvoices,
        (x: number | undefined, y: Invoice) =>
            x === undefined ? y.amount : x + y.amount);
```

In fact, `T` is inferred by the type of `testInvoices`, while `M` is inferred by the type of the arrow function.

> In the case of generic functions, it is always convenient to test whether TypeScript is able to automatically infer all generics, and to specify them explicitly only if the compiler complaint it is not able to infer them (the complaint message is immediately shown by Visual Studio IntelliSense). Automatic inference rarely works with generic interfaces, but it works for generic classes when all generic types contained in the class are inferred from the types of the class constructor parameters.

The code may be tested by showing `invoicesTotal` in an `alert` function:

```
alert(invoicesTotal);
```

At this point, the `aggregate` function can be tested by running the project and going to the **About** page.

Generic classes

Generic classes can be defined in the exactly same way as generic interfaces, by enclosing all generics inside the <> symbols, and then using them in the class definition. As an example of designing a complete application that uses both generic interfaces and classes, this section proposes rewriting the `dom` manipulation example at the end of the *Inheriting from a class and implementing interfaces* section of `Chapter 4`, *Using Classes and Interfaces*.

As discussed in the previous section, the `ItemList` interface can be redefined as a generic interface to avoid representing data items with the `any` type:

```
interface ItemList<T> {
    appendItem(itemData: T): void;
    prependItem(itemData: T): void;
    appendBefore(node: HTMLElement, itemData: T): void;
    appendAfter(node: HTMLElement, itemData: T): void;
    removeItem(node: HTMLElement): void;
    itemTemplate: (x: T) => HTMLElement;
    readonly itemsParent: HTMLElement;
}
```

After that, the `PlainList` interface implementation can be redefined as a generic class:

```
class PlainList<T> implements ItemList<T> {
    itemTemplate: (x: T) => HTMLElement;
    constructor(readonly itemsParent: HTMLElement) {
    }
    removeItem(node: HTMLElement): void {
        this.itemsParent.removeChild(node);
    }
    appendItem(itemData: T): void {
        this.itemsParent.appendChild(this.itemTemplate(itemData));
    }
    prependItem(itemData: any): void {
        if (this.itemsParent.childElementCount === 0)
            this.appendItem(itemData);
        else
            this.itemsParent.insertBefore(
                this.itemTemplate(itemData),
                (this.itemsParent.firstChild as HTMLElement));
    }
    appendBefore(node: HTMLElement, itemData: T): void {
```

```
                this.itemsParent.insertBefore(
                    this.itemTemplate(itemData),
                    node);
        }
        appendAfter(node: HTMLElement, itemData: T): void {
            if (node.nextSibling)
                this.itemsParent.insertBefore(
                    this.itemTemplate(itemData),
                    node.nextSibling);
            else this.appendItem(itemData);
        }
    }
```

It is worth pointing out that the `T` generic defined in the class is used to instantiate the
`ItemList` generic interface that that class must implement. In general, expressions
involving generics (in the preceding class, the simple term `T`) can be used to instantiate
other generics (in the preceding class, the generic of the `ItemList` interface) contained later
in the code.

The modification of the `JQueryList` class is left to the reader. Let's move to the
`AppendGrid` class contained in `AbstractLists.ts`:

```
    abstract class AppendGrid<T> {
        constructor(protected list: ItemList<T>,
            protected addButton: HTMLElement,
            protected itemRootSelector: string,
            protected addItemDataRoot: HTMLElement,
            protected addBeforeButton?: HTMLElement) {
            this.list.itemTemplate = this.itemTemplate;
            this.list.itemsParent.addEventListener("click",
                (evt: MouseEvent) => {
                    let button = AppendGrid.findAncestor(
                        evt.target as HTMLElement,
                        "button");
                    let target = AppendGrid.findAncestor(
                        button,
                        itemRootSelector);
                    if (target != null )
                        list.removeItem(target);
                });
            this.addButton.addEventListener("click",
                (evt: MouseEvent) => {
                    list.appendItem(this.extractDataToAdd());
                });
            if (this.addBeforeButton) {
                this.addBeforeButton.addEventListener("click",
                    (evt: MouseEvent) => {
```

```
            list.prependItem(this.extractDataToAdd());
        });
    }
}
protected abstract itemTemplate(x: T): HTMLElement;
protected abstract extractDataToAdd(): T;
private static findAncestor(n: HTMLElement | null,
            selector: string): HTMLElement | null {
    while (n != null && n.tagName != "BODY") {
        if (n.matches && n.matches(selector)) return n;
        else if (n.webkitMatchesSelector
            && n.webkitMatchesSelector(selector)) return n;
        n = n.parentNode as HTMLElement;
    }
    return null;
}
}
```

The preceding code shows two further techniques to manipulate generic variables:

- The manipulation of generic type instances can be assigned to other generic interfaces or classes. The `AppendGrid` generic class assigns the manipulation of `T` to an instance of the `ItemList<T>` generic interface that somehow knows how to deal with `T`.

- The details of how to manipulate a `T` generic variable are hidden in abstract methods, so that their implementations are delayed until a concrete subclass that binds `T` to a concrete type is able to provide implementations of them that are specific for the type bound to `T`. `AppendGrid<T>` delays the responsibility of assembling `T` (`itemTemplate` abstract method) and the responsibility of using instances of `T` to instantiate an HTML template (`extractDataToAdd` abstract method) to its `AppendGrid<string>` that, being specific for the `string` type that binds `T`, can provide an implementation of both `itemTemplate` and `extractDataToAdd`.

The application-specific `MyULAppendGrid` class in `modularToDoList.ts` binds `T` to `string`, and furnishes all details that depend on the specific nature of `T` (implementation of both `itemTemplate` and `extractDataToAdd`):

```
class MyULAppendGrid extends AppendGrid<string> {
    constructor(list: ItemList<string>,
        addButton: HTMLElement,
        itemRootselector: string,
        addItemDataRoot: HTMLElement,
        addBeforeButton?: HTMLElement) {
        super(list, addButton,
```

```
                    itemRootselector,
                     addItemDataRoot,
                    addBeforeButton);
        }
        extractDataToAdd(): string{
            return (this.addItemDataRoot as HTMLInputElement).value;
        }
        itemTemplate(str: string): HTMLElement {
            let toAdd =
            `<li class="list-group-item">
                <button type="button" class="btn btn-sm" title="remove">
                    <span class="glyphicon glyphicon-minus" aria-
hidden="true">
                    </span>
                </button>
                <span>${str}</span>
            </li>`;
            let temp = document.createElement('ul');
            temp.innerHTML = toAdd;
            return temp.firstChild as HTMLElement;
        }
    }
```

The remainder of the application code in `modularToDoList.ts` remains unchanged.

Generic constraints

Previous sections listed some techniques to manipulate generic type instances notwithstanding the complete lack of knowledge of the operations and properties supported by the type that later on will replace the generic. Sometimes, the techniques exposed so far are not sufficient to encode an abstract behavior, and sometimes one may need more than one technique, namely:

- Invoking specific members that must be contained in the type that will bind the generic type
- Creating an instance of the type that will bind the generic type

The first need can be satisfied by declaring that the generic type can be bound only by types that have the required members. Since interfaces are TypeScript's way of expressing constraints on the members contained in objects, constraints on members translate into requiring interface implementations.

Type constraints

The types that can bind a generic variable may be constrained to a given interface with the following syntax:

```
<T extends |interface name|, T1, ....>
```

The following is a simple example:

```
interface IConcatenable<T> {
    concat(x: T) : T;
}

function concatenateAll<T extends IConcatenable<T>>(...list: T[]):
T|undefined {
    if (list.length == 0) return undefined;
    let curr: T = list[0];
    for (let i = 1; i < list.length; i++)
        curr = curr.concat(list[i]);
    return curr;
}
```

The preceding example shows that the interface that constrains a generic can itself contain the same generic.

The type that will bind T doesn't need to implement explicitly the interface declared in the constraint, but, due to TypeScript's structural subtyping, it is enough that the type that will bind T contains all members prescribed by the interface.

For example, strings and arrays both have a concat method but don't explicitly implement IConcatenable<T>. This is enough for them to be bindable to T in the concatenateAll generic function:

```
let stringConcat = concatenateAll<string>("a", "b", "c");
let arrayConcat = concatenateAll<number[]>([1, 2, 3], [4, 5], [6, 7]);
```

The type in a constraint can also contain other previously listed generic variables, as shown in the following code:

```
class Widget<T, K extends ItemList<T>>{
...
}
```

Moreover, in the constraint, the type that follows the `extends` keyword doesn't need to be an interface but can be any type of expression. Thus, in general, the type that will bind `T` is required to be a subtype of the type specified by that type expression:

```
type computerMemory = "4" | "8" | "16" | "32" | "64" | "128";

class computerFamily<K extends computerMemory>
{
    ...
}
```

`K` is a type that specifies the available memory size. The fact that `K` must be a subtype of `computerMemory` means that the possible memory sizes must be a subset of the ones listed in `computerMemory`, since subtype means more specific, for example, a particular case of `computerMemory`. Thus, an acceptable value for `K` might be `"8"` | `"16"`.

The idea is that `new Computer<"8"|"16">()` should create a computer family that is available in two memory sizes: 8 and 16.

So let's suppose that each instance of `computerFamily` is used to track the available quantities of all memory-size variants of the family. We need a dictionary to store the available quantity for each memory size:

```
type computerMemory = "4" | "8" | "16" | "32" | "64" | "128";
interface IndexableQuantity {
    [s: string]: number;
}
```

Now, the complete code that meets the required specifications is:

```
type computerMemory = "4" | "8" | "16" | "32" | "64" | "128";
interface IndexableQuantity {
    [s: string]: number;
}
class computerFamily<K extends computerMemory>
{
    private map: IndexableQuantity = {};
    setAvailable(model: K, quantity: number) {
        this.map[model] = quantity;
    }
    getAvailable(model: K): number {
        return this.map[model] || 0;
    }
    buy(model: K): boolean {
        var av = this.getAvailable(model);
        if (av > 0) {
```

```
            this.setAvailable(model, av - 1);
            return true;
        }
        else return false;
    }
}
```

After the preceding definitions, we can write:

```
let myComputerFamily = new computerFamily<"8" | "16">();

myComputerFamily.setAvailable("16", 100); //Correct "16" is in "8" | "16"

myComputerFamily.setAvailable("32", 100); //Wrong. Visual Studio signals an
error
```

Creating instances of generic variables

JavaScript libraries often use the options pattern. All functionality options are represented by option classes, and have global default values represented by default option class instances. This way, the developer doesn't need to specify a whole option object that might contain hundreds of properties, but just the properties that differ from the default.

For instance, in the case of a graphic library, a very simplified option class might be something such as:

```
class GraphicStyle {
    pencilWidth: number;
    pencilType: string;
    foregroundColor: string;
    backgroundColor: string;
    colors(): string {
        return this.foregroundColor + " " + this.backgroundColor;
    }
    pencil(): string {
        return this.pencilWidth + " " + this.backgroundColor;
    }
}
```

The instance containing the default settings might be something such as:

```
let defaultGraphicStyle = new GraphicStyle();
defaultGraphicStyle.pencilType = "continuous";
defaultGraphicStyle.pencilWidth = 2;
defaultGraphicStyle.foregroundColor = "black";
defaultGraphicStyle.backgroundColor = "white";
```

When one calls a graphic routine, say, for drawing a circle with a "dotted" pencil style while taking the defaults for all other properties, one just needs to specify what changes with respect to the defaults with an object:

```
{
    pencilType: "dotted"
}
```

If the option object is simple, such as the one in the example, there is no big difference between specifying one property instead of four, but usually option classes may have hundreds of properties. Moreover, the modularity of the code improves if one defines an option object by specifying which properties differ from the ones of a default option object. In fact, a few changes in such a single default object can simultaneously change the behavior of several chunks of code. For better modularity, usually there is a hierarchy of defaults – global default, section default, page default, picture default, object default, and so on – where each default is specified through its differences with respect to the previous default.

The basic option pattern operation is: cloning a default instance, and applying to it all changes provided by the developer to get either another default in the hierarchy or the final option object.

Is it possible to build a class that performs the preceding operation? A similar class might have a skeleton such as the one in the following code:

```
class OptionCloner<O>{
    ....
    clone(x: O): O {
        ...
    }
    overrideDefaults(defaults: O,
        overrides: any): O {
        ...
    }
}
```

The first method just clones an option instance, while the second one applies the needed changes specified by an `any` type object. The generic O is replaced by the actual option type, in order to specialize the `OptionCloner` class for a specific type.

How can `OptionCloner<O>` create an instance? Something such as `new O()` yields an error for two reasons:

- While an actual class name such as `GraphicStyle` represents a type, it is also a variable containing the class constructor function (see the *Static members and static part of a class* section in `Chapter 4`, *Using Classes and Interfaces*). `O` only represents a type, so it can't be used in an expression. After the `new` keyword, the TypeScript compiler expects a constructor function, not a type. More specifically, the constructor function associated to the `O` type.
- TypeScript, might infer that we are referring to the constructor function of `O`, and not to the `O` type because of the `new` keyword before `O`, but it can't infer the constructor parameter types and number. So, for instance, TypeScript can't infer automatically that the `O` class constructor has no parameters.

In order to overcome the preceding problems, TypeScript has a specific way to refer to the type of a constructor function:

```
type myType = new (par1: type1, ...) : T;
```

Where `T` is the type created by the constructor function. In the option case, the type should be `new (): O` since option constructors have no parameters. One will pass the constructor function for the `O` type in the constructor of `OptionCloner`, this way, TypeScript will automatically infer `O` from the type of the constructor function passed as an argument:

```
class OptionCloner<O>{
    constructor(readonly builder: { new(): O; }) {
    }
    ...
}
```

After that, one might create an instance specific for `GraphicStyle` with:

```
var graphicStylecloner= new OptionCloner(GraphicStyle);
```

The complete implementation of `OptionCloner<O>` is:

```
class OptionCloner<O>{
    constructor(readonly builder: { new(): O; }) {
    }
    clone(x: O): O {
        let result = new this.builder();
        for (let att in x) {
            let p = x[att];
            if (typeof p !== "function")
                result[att] = x[att];
```

```
        }
        return result;
    }
    overrideDefaults(defaults: O,
        overrides: any): O {
        let result = this.clone(defaults);
        for (let att in overrides)
            (result as any)[att] = overrides[att];
        return result;
    }
}
```

The `new this.builder()` method invokes the `O` constructor, which has been passed in the `OptionCloner<O>` constructor. The `clone` method copies the content of each property, but doesn't copy methods (because of the `typeof if`) or accessors (because set/get properties are not enumerated in `let att in x`). Moreover, `overrideDefaults` first clones the options object and then applies all overrides.

The following is a complete example of the usage of `OptionCloner<O>`:

```
var graphicStylecloner = new OptionCloner(GraphicStyle);

let overridenStyle =
graphicStylecloner.overrideDefaults(defaultGraphicStyle,
    {
        pencilType: "dotted",
        foregroundColor: "red"

    }).pencil();
```

The keyof constraints

The `overrideDefaults` method of `OptionCloner<O>` uses an `any` type to represent an object that contains a subset of the properties of `O`. This prevents compilation-time check of the property names. In order to solve this and other similar problems, TypeScript has two operators defined on types: the , `keyof O` index type query operator and the, `O[k]` indexed access operator.

Furthermore, `keyof O` returns the subtype of `string` that just contains all public property names of `O`. Thus `keyof GraphicStyle` is the following type:

```
"pencilType"|"pencilWidth"|"foregroundColor"|"backgroundColor"
```

The `pencilType` shown in the preceding code contains the names of all public properties of `GraphicStyle`. Similarly, `GraphicStyle["pencilWidth"])` is the type of the property of `GraphicStyle` whose property name is `pencilWidth`, which is an integer value.

In turn, `keyof` and the indexed access operator, `O[]`, are used to define generalizations of indexable types described in the *Interfaces and type inference* section of `Chapter 2`, *Complex Types and Functions*, which are called **mapped types**:

```
type LikeGraphicStyle = {
    [s in keyof GraphicStyle]: GraphicStyle[s];
}
```

`LikeGraphicStyle` is a type that contains the same public members of `GraphicStyle`. One may use generics to define a generic type that contains all the public property of any class. This is exactly what the `interface<T>` operator does, it extracts the interface part of a class:

```
type interface<T> =
{
    [P in keyof T]: T[P]
}
```

Thus, `interface<GraphicStyle>` is exactly the same as `LikeGraphicStyle`.

In a similar way, one can define the `Readonly<T>` generic type that contains all properties of `T` but made read-only:

```
type Readonly<T> = {
    readonly [P in keyof T]: T[P];
}
```

And `Partial<T>` contains all types of `T` but are made optionals:

```
type Partial<T> = {
    [P in keyof T]?: T[P];
}
```

`Readonly<T>` and `Partial<T>` are so useful that they are included in TypeScript standard library (see the *DOM types/TypeScript predefined declarations* section in `Chapter 3`, *DOM Manipulation*), so the developer doesn't need to define them.

`Partial<T>` is what one needs to improve the `overrideDefaults` method of `OptionCloner<O>`:

```
overrideDefaults(defaults: O,
    overrides: Partial<O>): O {
    let result = this.clone(defaults);
    for (let att in overrides) {
        let source = overrides[att];
        if(source !== undefined && typeof source != "function")
            (result as any)[att] = source;
    }
    return result;
}
```

Now, property names and types of the object passed in the `overrides` argument are checked by TypeScript compiler. In addition to this, `overrideDefaults` contains a check on functions, since `Partial<O>` contains the methods of `O`.

The TypeScript standard types library contains two more generic types, `Pick` and `Record`:

```
type Pick<T, K extends keyof T> = {
    [P in K]: T[P];
}

type Record<K extends string, T> = {
    [P in K]: T;
}
```

`Pick` extracts a subset of the members of `T`:

```
let
ColorStyle=Pick<GraphicStyle,"foregroundColor"|"backgroundColor"|"colors">
```

The preceding code extracts all color-related members of `GraphicStyle`. It is useful to restrict the member access within some routines. So if we define an input parameter of a graphic routine that manipulates colors as `ColorStyle`, the TypeScript transpiler will automatically check that this routine uses just color-related properties.

`Record<K extends string,  T>` defines a collection of elements of the `T` type, indexed by a finite set of string keys:

```
type DocumentVersions = Record<"current"| "previous" | "previousPrevious",
documentType>;
```

Summary

TypeScript allows C#-like generics and generic types. More specifically, the user may define generic functions, interfaces, and classes. Constraints on generics are defined with the `extends` keyword followed by a type expression made of both ground types and other generic types. Variable types are manipulated either with the help of functions whose implementations will be furnished after the variable type instantiation is known, or by constraining the variable type with an interface, thus enabling all interface operations on the variable type.

The `keyof` and `T[]` operators, together with generic types, allow the explicit manipulation of type properties, and the definition of mapped types such as `interface<T>`, `Partial<T>`, `Readonly<T>`, `Pick<K extends string, T>`, and `Record<T>`.

The next chapter discusses how to design large code bases, keeping them modular and maintainable with the help of two alternative techniques, namespaces and modules, and how to choose between them.

Questions

1. Is it possible to create new types dynamically by instantiating a generic type at runtime? Why? How?
2. What techniques do you know to manipulate a variable type?
3. What techniques do you know to create an instance of a variable type?
4. Are you able to define a generic `Nullable<T>` type that contains all members of `T` and transforms them into nullable properties (for instance, if a property is of the `string` type, it is transformed into `string|null`)?
5. How do you define the subtype of `string` that contains as possible values the member names of the K type plus the member names of the T type?
6. Do you know a syntax for denoting a type that has all public members of two types (hint: see the *Operations on types* section in `Chapter 2`, *Complex Types and Functions*)?
7. Are you able to define the `NullableMixin<T, K>` generic type that contains all public members of `T` plus all members of `K` transformed into nullable types?
8. Are you able to define a `CreateMixinInstance<K, T>(x: K, y: T): NullableMixin<T, K>` function that creates instances of `NullableMixin<T, K>` (hint: loop on all properties of `T`, then on all properties of `K`, and add the needed type assertions)?

6
Namespaces and Modules

This chapter explains how to use namespaces and modules to avoid name collisions in large code bases. TypeScript namespaces are completely analogous to C# namespaces, while modules are an advanced feature introduced by ES6 specifications to overcome namespaces' pitfalls. Modules are a fundamental building block of Angular applications, which is the topic of the last part of this book. Moreover, notwithstanding ES6 modules are not fully supported by all browsers a they may be processed by JavaScript bundlers such as WebPack (described in `Chapter 7`, *Bundling with WebPack*), that assemble JavaScript modules in a way similar to object code-linkers to yield optimized JavaScript code chunks to add to the various web pages.

The following topics will be covered in this chapter:

- Defining namespaces and references to other namespaces
- Defining and using ES6-style modules
- Dynamic-loading modules
- How to define modules and namespaces in declaration files

Technical requirements

We need the following tools and packages for this chapter:

- Visual Studio 2017 with the latest ASP.NET Core tools
- Visual Studio TypeScript SDK

For the examples in this chapter, please perform two copies of the `DOMManipulation` project from the previous chapter. They will be used to re-engineer the code, one using namespaces and one using modules.

All the code used in this chapter can be downloaded from the following GitHub link: `https://github.com/PacktPublishing/Hands-On-TypeScript-for-CSharp-and-`. `NET-Core-Developers`.

Check out the following video to see the Code in Action: `http://bit.ly/2OkabwI`.

Namespaces

In several examples in this book, the code was enclosed inside a function body:

```
(function () {
   //code here
})();
```

This way, all symbols being declared inside a function body are local to that function and are not visible outside of the function body in other TypeScript files. This is a best practice in JavaScript. In fact, global symbols shared between several files, possibly written by different people, may cause unwanted interactions, thereby causing hard-to-find bugs.

Therefore, global symbols must be carefully planned with the whole development team. It is best practice to organize all symbols that must be shared among several files into trees rooted in a few global symbols that are agreed upon by the whole development team. For instance, jQuery is the root symbol of the jQuery library and all public symbols of this library are available as nested properties of the `jQuery` symbol. This way, collisions are avoided and the code is kept modular.

In the body of a JavaScript global root function, symbols are defined by attaching them to the `window` object:

```
(function () {
   class Person  {
      . . .
   }
   (window as any)["Person"] = Person;
})();
```

The preceding code defines globally the constructor function of the `Person` class, but doesn't export the `Person` type outside the function body. In any case, the `Person` global symbol might collide with other names defined in other files by other developers, so shared classes are typically attached to nested properties of a few global symbols.

C# resolves the name-collision problem by organizing all symbols into symbol-trees with namespaces. TypeScript has C#-style namespaces, which similarly to C# namespaces solve the name collision problem, but in TypeScript they also solve the problem of controlling what is visible from outside the namespace:

```
namespace Anagraphic {

    export interface IPrintable {
        getString(): string;
    }

    export class Person implements IPrintable {
        ...
    }
    class Teacher extends Person {
        ...
    }
    let myPrintable: IPrintable =
            new Teacher("TypeScript", "Francesco", "Abbruzzese");
    export let humanReadable = myPrintable.getString();
}
```

Only the symbols whose definitions are prefixed with the `export` keyword are visible from outside the `Anagraphic` namespace, and their names must be prefixed with the namespace name. In this case, only the `IPrintable` interface, the `Person` class, and the `humanReadable` variable are visible from outside `Anagraphic`, and their names must be prefixed with `Anagraphic`, as shown in the following example:

```
alert(Anagraphic.humanReadable );
let myPrintable: Anagraphic.IPrintable = new
Anagraphic.Person("Francesco", "Abbruzzese");
```

The compiler doesn't complain that `myPrintable` has already been defined since the `myPrintable` instance type defined inside of the `Anagraphic` file is not visible from outside of `Anagraphic`.

Namespaces may also be nested, but the internal namespaces need the export keyword in their definition, otherwise they are not visible from outside of their outer namespace:

```
namespace Anagraphic {

    export interface IPrintable {
        getString(): string;
    }

    export class Person implements IPrintable {
```

```
        ...
    }
    export namespace Courses {
        export class Teacher extends Person {
            ...
        }
        let myPrintable: IPrintable =
            new Teacher("TypeScript", "Francesco", "Abbruzzese");
        export let humanReadable = myPrintable.getString();
    }
}
```

In the preceding example, `Teacher` and `humanReadable` are visible from outside of both the `Courses` and `Anagraphic` namespaces and may be used as shown in the following code:

```
new Anagraphic.Courses.Teacher("TypeScript", "Francesco", "Abbruzzese");

let test = Anagraphic.Courses.humanReadable;
```

A long chain of namespaces may be avoided by defining shorthands, called **aliases**, with the `import` keyword, as in the following example:

```
import myCourses = Anagraphic.Courses;
...
...
let myTeacher = new myCourses.Teacher("TypeScript", "Francesco",
"Abbruzzese");
```

Or:

```
import Teacher = Anagraphic.Courses.Teacher;
...
...
let myTeacher = new Teacher("TypeScript", "Francesco", "Abbruzzese");
```

 The same namespace may be split into different files, that is, different TypeScript files may contribute to the same namespace. However, the various files contributing to the same namespace only see each other's exported names. In other words, local symbols are not available from within other files contributing to the same namespace.

Here is an example of multi-file definition:

```
//File 1
namespace Anagraphic {
```

```
    . . .

    export class Person implements IPrintable {
        . . .
    }
    . . .
}

//File 2
namespace Anagraphic {
    . . .
    let myPerson = new Person("Francesco", "Abbruzzese");
    . . .
}
```

DOM manipulation re-engineered with namespaces

This subsection shows how to re-engineer the DOM manipulation project in the previous chapter to use namespaces. Please use a copy instead of modifying the original project.

Let's start with the library files under the `lib` folder. All classes in `AbstractLists.ts` might be placed in a namespace named `DOMLists`:

```
namespace DOMLists {
    export interface ItemList<T> {
        . . .
    }

    export abstract class AppendGrid<T> {
        . . .
    }
}
```

The plain JavaScript implementation might be placed in a nested namespace, `DOMLists/Plain`. Moreover, since the fact that the implementation is based on plain JavaScript is now clear from the namespace it is in, the class name may be changed to `ItemListImplementation`:

```
namespace DOMLists {
    export namespace Plain {
        export class ItemListImplementation<T> implements ItemList<T> {
            . . .
        }
```

```
        }
    }
```

The jQuery implementation might have the same class name but a different nested namespace, DOMLists/JQuery:

```
namespace DOMLists {
    export namespace JQuery {
        export class ItemListImplementation<T> implements ItemList<T> {
            ...
            ...
        }
    }
}
```

Finally, the application code might be placed in an App namespace that might define adequate aliases to easily access the needed libraries:

```
namespace App {
    import ListImplementation = DOMLists.Plain.ItemListImplementation;
    class MyULAppendGrid extends DOMLists.AppendGrid<string> {
        constructor(list: DOMLists.ItemList<string>,
            addButton: HTMLElement,
            itemRootselector: string,
            addItemDataRoot: HTMLElement,
            addBeforeButton?: HTMLElement) {
            super(list, addButton,
                itemRootselector,
                addItemDataRoot,
                addBeforeButton);
        }
        ...
        ...
    }

    var mainList = new ListImplementation(
        document.getElementById('main_list') as HTMLElement);
    ...
    ...
}
```

The preceding code defines an alias for the list implementation, so it is enough to change the definition of this alias to move to a jQuery implementation, with no need to modify the remainder of the file. It is worth pointing out that MyULAppendGrid has no export keyword, since it doesn't need to be reused by other TypeScript files.

Pitfalls of namespaces and ES6 modules

JavaScript files depend on each other, and, in large code bases, tracking their dependencies to decide which files to add to each HTML page, and in which order, is not a trivial task. Moreover, the maintenance of large sets of JavaScript files whose dependencies are not explicitly represented in the code itself is a nightmare that considerably limits the possibility to re-engineer the code as an application evolves.

The situation worsens if one tries to optimize the downloading time of JavaScript files. In fact, the only ways to optimize this time, other than the obvious minimization of JavaScript files, are the following:

- To bundle together several files in a way to reduce the number of download operations.
- To try downloading some files in parallel, while respecting all precedence constraints coming from the dependencies graph. In fact, if a file A depends on files B and C, then B and C must be downloaded and executed before A is executed.

Defining a single bundle per HTML page doesn't optimize cache usage, since common files are copied in several bundles instead of being cached once in the browser. An optimal strategy should factor out files used by several pages in separate bundles so that, when passing from one page to another, they may be found in the cache instead of being downloaded several times as part of different bundles.

Bundling, cache optimization, and parallel downloading may be taken care of by automatic tools, but this would require dependency relations be explicitly represented somehow.

This led the JavaScript community to create the concept of a JavaScript module as a chunk of JavaScript code that explicitly represents its dependencies, and that can be asynchronously downloaded. General paradigms to represent modules and to asynchronously download several JavaScript files simultaneously were conceived, such as **Asynchronous Module Definition** (**AMD**) and CommonJS. The first paradigm was implemented by the famous `requireJS` software, while the second one was chosen in Node.js. `systemjs` is an evolution of both paradigms that is compatible with both.

Together with asynchronous module-loaders, JavaScript communities started conceiving module-bundlers, which can bundle several modules together to reduce download time while optimizing cache usage.

Finally, asynchronous module-loaders arrived to a standardization with ECMAScript 6 modules, which are also the module choice of TypeScript. TypeScript uses ECMAScript 6-type modules, which are the subject of this section.

At the moment, ES6 modules are supported by the latest versions of most desktop and mobile browsers, such as Chrome, Edge, Firefox, Safari, iOS Safari, and Chrome for Android. However, TypeScript is able to also simulate ES6 modules with all other module systems we mentioned before. The way TypeScript modules are translated into JavaScript is controlled by the `module` compiler option. However, if the target is not ES6 but AMD, CommonJS, or System (`systemjs`), it is the developer's responsibility to install and configure the software that implements them, since they are not natively supported by any browser.

At the moment, using an ES6 module target is the best choice, since it is considered a best practice to handle modules with a modern bundler that understands ES6 modules and uses them to aggregate modules into bundles that are subsequently handled by the bundler at runtime. This way, an ES6 target also works with browsers that don't support ES6 modules. `Chapter 7`, *Bundling with WebPack*, is dedicated to what appears to be the de facto standard for bundling JavaScript applications: WebPack.

Namespaces usage is simpler and require less knowledge of JavaScript tools, so they are adequate for simpler websites based mainly on server-side code that uses JavaScript just to improve HTML page graphics. On the other hand, modules are necessary in client-rich applications where the whole presentation layer, such as **Single-Page Applications (SPAs)**, is moved to the client side, since in this case both JavaScript files' optimization and dependencies tracking may become very complex tasks.

Before continuing this section, please make another copy of the `DOMManipulation` project from the previous chapter for this section's examples.

Exporting module symbols

A TypeScript file doesn't require any syntax to be interpreted as a module, but a TypeScript file is considered a module just because another file tries to load it as a module. Like for namespaces, symbols are visible to the importing modules only if declarations are preceded by the `export` keyword. Unlike with namespaces, a module's code doesn't need to be enclosed in any syntactic container (such as the `namespace...{}` container) – the boundary of a module is defined by the file it is in:

```
//Anagraphic.ts file
export interface IPrintable {
    getString(): string;
```

```
    }

    export class Person implements IPrintable {
        ...
    }
    class Teacher extends Person {
        ...
    }
    let myPrintable: IPrintable = new Teacher("TypeScript", "Francesco",
"Abbruzzese");
    export let humanReadable = myPrintable.getString();
```

Thus, in the preceding module, just `IPrintable`, `Person`, and `humanReadable` are visible to importing modules, while `Teacher` and `myPrintable` are invisible. The name of the module is the name of the file containing it, that is, `Anagraphic`.

Different from namespaces, symbols to export may also be defined after their declarations. For instance, one may declare that the `Teacher` symbol must also be exported as follows:

```
export {Teacher }
```

While exporting, symbol names may also be changed with the `as` keyword:

```
export { Teacher as Tutor }
```

The usage of the `export` keyword in a module is similar to namespaces, but exported symbols are visible just to other modules that directly import that module. For instance, if A imports B and B imports C, just the exported symbols of B are accessible to A. The C symbols are not automatically visible to A.

However, a module may re-export some or all symbols of another module. For instance, another module may export all symbols of the `Anagraphic` module, as follows:

```
export * from "./Anagraphic"
```

Or some of its symbols:

```
export {Teacher} from "./Anagraphic"
```

As with internal exports, names of re-exported symbols may be changed while exporting them:

```
export {Teacher as Tutor} from "./Anagraphic"
```

The path to the imported module that follows the `from` keyword must not contain the file extension, and should be relative to the module that contains the `export` statement to avoid problems when files are copied in different locations.

Importing module symbols

The simplest way to import symbols from another module is something like the following:

```
//this is module AnagraphicImporter.ts

import * as Anagraphic from "./Anagraphic"
```

The preceding code imports all symbols that are exported by `Anagraphic.ts`.

The path to the imported module that follows the `from` keyword must not contain a file extension, and should be relative to the module that contains the `import` statement, to avoid problems when files are copied in different locations.

All symbols imported from `./Anagraphic` are available through the identifier specified after the `as` keyword, that in the preceding example is `Anagraphic` with expressions such as `Anagraphic.<imported module symbols>`. For instance have a look at the following code snippet:

```
let aPrintable: Anagraphic.IPrintable =
    new Anagraphic.Person("John", "Smith");

alert(Anagraphic.humanReadable);
```

Only all `./Anagraphic` exported symbols are visible, and they are visible with the names they were exported. For example, the `./Anagraphic Teacher` class is visible with the `Tutor` name since its name was changed in the export statement:

```
var teacher =
    new Anagraphic.Tutor("Francesco", "Abbruzzese", "TypeScript");
```

The general format of this `import` statement is as follows:

```
import * as <new name> from "<path to the module without file extension>"
```

It is also possible to import just some symbols with a statement such as the following:

```
//this is module AnagraphicImporter1.ts

import { Person, Tutor, IPrintable} from "./Anagraphic"
```

The preceding code imports all symbols separated by commas within the `{}` symbols.

 In order to get suggestions on the symbols that are possible to import, let's write `import {} from "./Anagraphic` first, and then fill in the `{}` list. This immediately informs Visual Studio on the module one is importing from, so Visual Studio may compute the list of all its exported symbols and may provide suggestions while one is typing the elements to import.

With the preceding `import` statement, imported symbols are available as they are without being prefixed by any name:

```
let aPrintable: IPrintable =
    new Person("John", "Smith");

var teacher =
    new Tutor("Francesco", "Abbruzzese", "TypeScript");
```

Also possible providing alias while importing symbols by adding `as` clauses after symbols, as shown in the following example:

```
//this is module AnagraphicImporter2.ts

import { Person as Human, Tutor, IPrintable } from "./Anagraphic"

let aPrintable: IPrintable =
    new Human("John", "Smith");

var teacher =
    new Tutor("Francesco", "Abbruzzese", "TypeScript");
```

Default export and import

Often modules have a single object that, through its properties, allows access to the resources contained in the modules. For instance, jQuery, when it is loaded as a CommonJS or AMD module, exports just the `jQuery` symbol.

Similar situations may be handled by defining an exported symbol as a default export, with a syntax like the one in the following example:

```
export default jQuery;
```

Default exports may be imported with a simplified syntax:

```
import $ from "./jQuery";
...
...
alert($("#myInput").val());
```

The general format for importing a default export is the following:

```
import <new name for the default export> from "<path to the module to
import without file extension>";
```

A default export may be defined not only in modules that export a single symbol, but also in modules that export several symbols. For example, the `Anagraphic.ts` module may be modified to export the `Person` symbol as its default export:

```
//this is module Anagraphic1.ts

...

export default class Person implements IPrintable {
    ...
}
...
...
```

Default exports can only be imported with the default import statement. Thus, after the preceding modification, the syntax to import `Person`, `Tutor`, and `IPrintable` must be modified as follows:

```
//this is module AnagraphicImporter3.ts

import Human from "./Anagraphic1"
import {Tutor, IPrintable } from "./Anagraphic1"

let aPrintable: IPrintable =
    new Human("John", "Smith");

var teacher =
    new Tutor("Francesco", "Abbruzzese", "TypeScript");
```

Using ES6 modules in browsers

The TypeScript compiler may be configured to handle modules through JavaScript ES6 modules by setting the `"module"` compiler option to `es6`. The resultant JavaScript target code may be used directly in browsers that support ES6 modules, or it may be processed with JavaScript bundlers that organize modules into bigger chunks and generate code that also works on browsers that do not support ES6 modules.

When one uses ES6 modules without a JavaScript bundler, HTML pages must contain just references to all root modules, since all their dependencies are handled automatically by the browser's ES6 loader. Moreover, the script tag must have the type set to module, as in the following example:

```
<script type="module" src="/js/myMainModule.js"></script>
```

Currently, browsers require the `.js` extension in all import statements:

```
import * as Abstracts from "./lib/AbstractLists.js"
```

Unluckily, the code generated by TypeScript doesn't add any file extensions automatically. At the moment, there is no compiler option to require the automatic addition of the `.js` extension, so if one doesn't plan to use a JavaScript bundler, the `.js` extension must be added directly into the TypeScript import statement.

Accordingly, there is only one way to generate an ES6 import statement such as the following:

```
import * as Abstracts from "./lib/AbstractLists.js"
```

To do so, locate the following TypeScript import statement:

```
import * as Abstracts from "./lib/AbstractLists"
```

Replace the preceding code with this:

```
import * as Abstracts from "./lib/AbstractLists.js"
```

Hopefully, future TypeScript versions will fix this problem by defining adequate compiler options. On the other hand, in practical applications the problem discussed here is irrelevant, since, as discussed in the next chapter, it is a best practice to always use a modern JavaScript bundler, and JavaScript bundlers properly handle ES6 import statements without the `.js` extension.

DOM manipulation re-engineered with modules

This subsection shows how to re-engineer the DOM manipulation project from the previous chapter to use modules. Please create a copy instead of modifying the original project.

Since this book doesn't cover outdated module systems, such as AMD, CommonJS, or SystemJS, but favors modern JavaScript bundlers, such as WebPack, let's configure TypeScript to generate code compatible with ES6 modules, by setting the `"module"` compiler option to `es6` in `tsconfig.json`:

```
{
    "compileOnSave": true,
    "compilerOptions": {
        "noImplicitAny": true,
        "strictNullChecks": true,
        "noEmitOnError": true,
        "removeComments": false,
        "sourceMap": true,
        "target": "es5",
        "module": "es6",
        "outDir": "wwwroot/js"
    },
    "include": [
        "wwwroot/ts/**/*.ts"
    ],
    "exclude": [
        "**/node_modules",
        "**/*.spec.ts"
    ]
}
```

Accordingly, the browser used to test the code must support ES6 modules. Recent versions of Chrome, Edge, Safari, and Firefox will do the job. The next chapter will show how modern JavaScript bundlers, such as WebPack, make ES6-compatible code that also runs in browsers that do not support ES6 modules.

In what follows, all code omitted and replaced by . . . remains the same as in the version of the DOM manipulation project from the previous chapter.

Let's start with the library files under the `lib` folder. All classes in `AbstractLists.ts` must be exported:

```
export interface ItemList<T> {
    ...
}
```

```
export abstract class AppendGrid<T> {
    ...
}
```

The jQueryList.ts implementation of ItemList<T> must use default exports since each of them exports a single symbol:

```
//this is lib/plainList.ts module

import * as Abstracts from "./AbstractLists.js"

export default class DOMList<T> implements Abstracts.ItemList<T> {
    ...
}
```

Also, the plainList.ts implementation of ItemList<T> must use default exports since each of them exports a single symbol:

```
//this is lib/jQueryList.ts module

import * as Abstracts from "./AbstractLists.js"

export default class DOMList<T> implements Abstracts.ItemList<T> {
    ...
}
```

The main module looks something like this:

```
// this modularToDoList.ts module

import * as Abstracts from "./lib/AbstractLists.js"
import DOMList from "./lib/plainList.js"

class MyULAppendGrid extends Abstracts.AppendGrid<string> {
    constructor(list: Abstracts.ItemList<string>,
            addButton: HTMLElement,
            itemRootselector: string,
            addItemDataRoot: HTMLElement,
            addBeforeButton?: HTMLElement) {
            super(list, addButton,
                itemRootselector,
                 addItemDataRoot,
                addBeforeButton);
        }
        ...
    }

var mainList = new DOMList(
```

```
        document.getElementById('main_list') as HTMLElement);
    var addButton =
        document.getElementById('main_add') as HTMLElement;
    var addInput =
        document.getElementById('main_input') as HTMLElement;

    var mainGrid = new MyULAppendGrid(mainList, addButton,
        "li", addInput);
```

One may pass from plain list implementation to jQuery implementation by changing the following code:

```
import DOMList from "./lib/plainList.js"
```

In the module header, simply replace the preceding code with this:

```
import DOMList from "./lib/jQueryList.js"
```

There is no need to change anything in the subsequent code.

The magic of ES6 modules is that `Index.cshtml` needs to recall just the main module; the ES6 browser engine will do the job of tracking dependencies and loading all needed modules:

```
@section Scripts{
<script type="module" src="~/js/modularToDoList.js"></script>
}
```

Loading modules

So far, just two options were considered to specify the location of a module to load in an `import` statement, relative to the importing module and absolute path:

```
//relative to current module
import DOMList from "./lib/jQueryList"

//absolute path
import DOMList from "c:/wwwroot/myWbSite/lib/jQueryList"
```

Absolute paths should be avoided since copying or moving the whole file tree into a different location would break the code, so the only viable option analyzed was a path relative to the importing module. Organizing the whole code with relative paths is straightforward if one has full control of how to place each file.

Unluckily, this is not the the case when one uses third-party libraries with their own import statements and their own dependencies, since library authors don't know where their files will be placed, and where the files of other dependencies will be placed. For instance, in the case of npm library packages, each dependency of A is loaded in the node_modules folder of the A package folder only if it has not already been loaded in the node_modules folder of an ancestor of A, where the term ancestor refers to a package that A has either a direct or indirect dependency on. Thus, when using npm packages as project libraries, resolving a module location requires a search in several folders, the node_modules folder of the importing package, plus the node_modules folders of all its ancestor packages.

In order to handle library packages, and npm packages in particular, TypeScript adds a third option to relative and absolute paths called non-relative paths. Each path that is not absolute and doesn't start either with / or . is considered a non-relative path:

```
//non-relative path
import $ from "jQuery"

//non-relative path
import * as gridUtilities from "grid/utilities"
```

Modules imported with non-relative paths are resolved with loading strategies that may be configured in several ways.

ES6 doesn't support non-relative paths natively, but requires the usage of module bundlers that perform the module resolution for it. Accordingly, complex projects that need library packages must use module bundlers such as WebPack if TypeScript is configured with "module": "es6". On the other hand, a different "module" setting requires an external module loader, since browsers natively support just es6 modules. That's why basically all modern projects use "module": "es6" and a bundler such as WebPack.

Compile-time and runtime module-resolution

Module-resolution is performed in two different situations by two different agents, as follows:

- The TypeScript compiler resolves imported modules to get all definitions they contain, in order to interpret and compile all references to imported symbols properly. The same job is performed by Visual Studio IntelliSense, during file editing. During this stage, modules may resort either to TypeScript files (.ts) or to TypeScript definition files (.d.ts) since the purpose of this stage is just getting types and definitions. It is worth remembering that TypeScript definition files (.d.ts) are files that contain just TypeScript declarations of libraries whose TypeScript sources are not available. They generate no code but give to the TypeScript transpiler all information needed to compile statements that use symbols from that library. We already used TypeScript definition files for jQuery in `Chapter 3`, *DOM Manipulation*.
- Either the browser ES6 loader or an external JavaScript loader, or a module bundler, resolves the modules to get the actual code to run. During this stage, modules should resort just to JavaScript files since the actual code to run is needed.

Accordingly, coherence between the two previous stages may be ensured only if compile-time module-resolution performed by the TypeScript compiler is able to mimic the same resolution strategies performed on the actual JavaScript files by the runtime loaders/bundlers.

More specifically, in the case of relative paths, coherence just requires that the relative positions of the .ts files and of their target .js files be the same, that is, the .ts file's tree and the generated .js file's tree must differ only for the extensions of all files (.ts in the first tree and .js in the second tree). If and only if this constraint is satisfied, for each import statement the runtime loader will load the JavaScript file that results from the compilation of the TypeScript file loaded by the TypeScript compiler when it processes the same import statement.

For example, if the TypeScript files tree is:

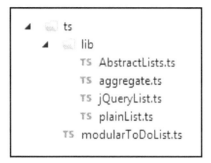

The tree of the generated JavaScript files must have a completely parallel structure:

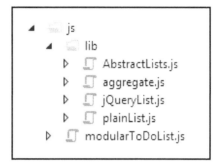

In order to understand why, let's suppose a file contains a statement such as the following:

```
import * as Abstracts from "./lib/AbstractLists"
```

Then, when this statement is processed by the TypeScript compiler, the compiler loads the `ts/lib/AbstractLists.ts` file to get all definitions it contains, and when the same statement is processed at runtime, the browser loads the file that contains the corresponding JavaScript code to be executed, that is, the file created by the compilation of `ts/lib/AbstractLists.ts`, which is `js/lib/AbstractLists.js`.

In the case of non-relative paths, there are two possibilities:

- The JavaScript file's tree and the TypeScript file's tree are completely parallel, as in the case of relative paths. In this case, the TypeScript module-resolution strategy must be identical to the strategy executed by the runtime loader/bundler.

- The JavaScript file's tree differs slightly from the TypeScript file's tree because of a post-processing of the JavaScript files immediately after the compilation (for instance, some JavaScript files are moved to a common folder immediately after compilation). In this case, it should be possible to configure the TypeScript compiler module-loader in a way that compensates for these slight differences.

Due to the flexibility requirements discussed here, the TypeScript module resolver was created to mimic the module-resolution strategies of all main loaders/bundlers, and to remap paths into different paths.

The TypeScript compiler module-resolution strategies for non-relative paths and their configuration are discussed in the next subsection.

Non-relative path module-resolution

Non-relative paths such as `lib/MyLib` are resolved by attempting to transform each non-relative path into an absolute path in various ways. For instance, the TypeScript resolution algorithm might attempt to add a prefix such as `c://projects/myProject/wwwroot`, getting an absolute path of `c://projects/myProject/wwwroot/lib/MyLib`.

The TypeScript compiler performs several attempts to get an absolute path from each not-relative path, till an existing file is found, or no further attempt is possible. The way the various absolute paths are built, and the order in which they are tried, depends on various compiler options, which we will discuss in this subsection.

For each absolute path created during the search, various file extensions are tried, and the path may also be interpreted as the directory name of an `npm` package, in which case the TypeScript declaration file contained in that package, if any, is taken. More specifically, the attempts made on each absolute path depend on the `moduleResolution` compiler option.

If `moduleResolution` is set to `Classic`, the algorithm first tries the `.ts` extension and then the `.d.ts` extension:

```
c://projects/myProject/wwwroot/lib/MyLib.ts
c://projects/myProject/wwwroot/lib/MyLib.d.ts
```

If none of the preceding files is found, the absolute path is rejected and another one is tried, if possible, otherwise module-resolution fails, and a complaint message appears in the Visual Studio editor.

If moduleResolution is set to Node after attempting the .ts and the .d.ts extensions, if no match is found, the absolute path is interpreted as the folder name of an npm package. At this point, the name of the file containing TypeScript definitions is searched in the package configuration file:

```
c://projects/myProject/wwwroot/lib/MyLib/package.json
```

If the .json file contains a types property whose value is the name of a declaration file, say myDeaclarations.d.ts, then the following file is taken:

```
c://projects/myProject/wwwroot/lib/MyMyLib/myDeaclarations.d.ts
```

If either the directory contains no package.json file or if the configuration file contains no valid target property, the algorithm assumes TypeScript definitions might be contained in a file named index (the default name for the main file of an npm package), and the following paths are attempted:

```
c://projects/myProject/wwwroot/lib/MyLib/index.ts
c://projects/myProject/wwwroot/lib/MyLib/index.d.ts
```

If these attempts also fail, the initial absolute path (c://projects/myProject/wwwroot/lib/MyLib) is rejected and, if possible, another absolute path is tried. Otherwise module resolution fails, and a complaint message appears.

The algorithm that generates various absolute paths for resolving each non-relative path works as follows:

1. As a first attempt, the module name, say MyLib, is matched against the entries of an object specified in the paths compiler option, as in the following example:

```
{ "compilerOptions":
 {
 "baseUrl": ".", // This must be specified if "paths" is.
 "paths": {
 "MyLib": ["wwwroot/lib/MyLib", <other paths>]
 // This mapping is relative to "baseUrl",
 ...<other entries>...
 }
 }
}
```

2. If the module name matches an entry, all paths specified between the square brackets of that entry are attempted. All paths specified as entry values are relative to the path provided in the `baseUrl` compiler option, which, in turn, is relative to the position of `tsconfig.json`. So, if in the example, `tsconfig.json` is in the `c://projects/myProject` directory, the final path to try is `c://projects/myProject` + `wwwroot/lib/MyLib`, which is `c://projects/myProject/wwwroot/lib/MyLib`. `paths` may also contain a `*` wildcard entry that matches all module names, as in the following example:

```
"baseUrl": ".",
"paths": {
    "*": [
      "*",
      "lib/*"
    ]
}
```

3. In this case, each module is searched first under `"baseUrl"` and then under `baseUrl+"lib/*"`. If the search among all entries fails, or if no `"paths"` option is provided, the path contained in the `"baseUrl"` option itself is used as a prefix for the non-relative path. Thus, if the directory specified by `"baseUrl"` is `"c://projects/myProject"`, and if the non-relative path is `"lib/MyLib"`, the absolute path obtained will be `"c://projects/myProject/lib/MyLib"`. If the `"baseUrl"` step fails, the algorithm reverts to a search relative to the position of the importing module that depends on the value of the `moduleResolution` compiler option. Suppose the importing module is located in the `c://projects/myProject/wwwroot/lib/MyLib` directory, and the non-relative path of the module to search is `dependencyLib`. If `moduleResolution` is set to `Classic`, the following absolute paths are tried:

```
c://projects/myProject/wwwroot/lib/MyLib/dependencyLib
c://projects/myProject/wwwroot/lib/dependencyLib
c://projects/myProject/wwwroot/dependencyLib
c://projects/myProject/dependencyLib
c://projects/dependencyLib
c://dependencyLib
```

4. That is, the algorithm tries all ancestor directories of the importing module. If, instead, `moduleResolution` is set to `Node`, then the algorithm mimics the Node.js modules search, by looking in all relevant `node_modules` directories. That is, it starts with the `node_modules` directory under the directory of the importing module, and then it moves up to all `node_modules` directories that are under all its ancestor directories:

```
c://projects/myProject/wwwroot/lib/MyLib/node_modules/dependencyLib
c://projects/myProject/wwwroot/lib/node_modules/dependencyLib
c://projects/myProject/wwwroot/node_modules/dependencyLib
c://projects/myProject/node_modules/dependencyLib
c://projects/node_modules/dependencyLib
c://node_modules/dependencyLib
```

In case of errors, the whole module-resolution process may be traced by setting the `traceResolution` compiler option to `true`.

Dynamic-loading module

The DOM manipulation project described in the *DOM manipulation re-engineered with modules* subsection allows several different implementations of the `ItemList<T>` interface. With module imports, one may select just one of them, but it would be smarter to select the more appropriate implementation at runtime depending on the features supported by the browser and on other JavaScript libraries available in the JavaScript environment. Unluckily, import statements must be placed in the file header, and the string containing the module to import must be static, so the imported module can't depend on any runtime check. At runtime import, statements are processed by loaders/bundlers before any JavaScript module code is executed to decide which modules must be loaded/bundled. Code-execution starts after all modules have been loaded.

Starting from version 2.4, TypeScript includes an `import()` function that may be called anywhere in the code to load modules dynamically. The module to load is specified by a string argument similar to one of the static `import` statements, but this time it may be a JavaScript variable whose value is decided at runtime.

The inclusion of the `import` function in JavaScript was done after a proposal to include the same `import` function in the JavaScript standard reached stage 3 of the TC39 process for evolving the JavaScript language. The dynamic import feature should be included in ECMAScript 2018/2019.

When the `"module"` TypeScript compiler option is set to `"amd"`, `"commonjs"`, or `"system"`, the import function is translated into analogous dynamic load functions available in the AMD, CommonJS, or SystemJS loaders. The import function can't be used with `"module"` set to `"es6"` since the JavaScript ES6 standard has no dynamic load function, but `"es6"` must be promoted to `"esnext"`. `"esnext"` includes all features contained in `"es6"` plus other features included in future ECMAScript versions; among them is the dynamic import function.

When `"module"` is set to `"esnext"`, the TypeScript compiler generates code for the JavaScript-native `import` function which, at the moment, is not supported by all mainstream browsers. Luckily, the JavaScript-native `import` function is supported by the WebPack bundler, which uses it to define dynamically loadable chunks in a way that is compatible with all browsers.

The `import` function requires that the browser supports Promises, or that a Promises polyfill is available. Luckily, Promises are supported by recent versions of all mainstream browsers with the exception of Internet Explorer (just Internet Explorer; Edge supports Promises). However, the availability of Promises must also be declared to TypeScript that would, otherwise, show a complaint message when the `import` function is used. This may be achieved by setting the `"target"` compiler option to at least `"es6"` (or `"es2015"`, which has the same meaning) in `tsconfig.json`:

```
{
    ...
    "compilerOptions": {
        "noImplicitAny": true,
        "strictNullChecks": true,
        "noEmitOnError": true,
        "removeComments": false,
        "sourceMap": true,
        "target": "es6",
        "module": "esnext",
        "outDir": "wwwroot/js"
    },
    ...
}
```

Or by explicitly specifying Promises among the definitions libraries to be used in the `lib` compiler option:

```
{
    ...,
    "compilerOptions": {
```

```
            "noImplicitAny": true,
            "strictNullChecks": true,
            "noEmitOnError": true,
            "removeComments": false,
            "sourceMap": true,
            "target": "es5",
            "module": "esnext",
            "lib": ["dom", "es5", "es2015.promise"],
            "outDir": "wwwroot/js"
        },
        ...
    }
```

The syntax for using the import function is the following:

```
import (<module name/path>)
    .then(x =>{
        //do something with the loaded module
    })
    .catch(error =>{
        //error handling
    })
```

import causes an asynchronous call, and returns immediately, without waiting for the module to be loaded. Therefore, the code that uses the loaded module must be placed in the arrow function contained in the then that is called after the asynchronous operation returns with its x parameter bound to an object whose properties are all symbols exported by the loaded module. In case the loaded module has a default export, this default export is placed in a property called default.

In case the attempt to load the module results in a failure, the arrow function contained in catch is called with its error parameter bound to the exception thrown because of the error.

Actually, the import function returns a Promise object and the then and catch functions are methods of this Promise object. Promises are discussed in the *Promises and async/await notation* section of Chapter 9, *Decorators and Advanced ES6 Features*, together with the async/await constructs that provide a simpler way to handle asynchronous calls.

Let's modify the DOM manipulation example in the *DOM manipulation re-engineered with modules* subsection to use the dynamic import function to load an ItemList<T> implementation.

`tsconfig.json` must be modified to allow both Promises and the dynamic import function:

```
{
    ...
    "target": "es5",
    "module": "esnext",
    "lib": ["dom", "es5", "es2015.promise"],
    ...
}
```

Open the `modularToDoList.ts` file and remove the following static import statement:

```
import DOMList from "./lib/plainList.js"
```

The static import will be replaced by a dynamic import. As a first step, let's write a dynamic load that is equivalent to the static import removed. Let's locate the following code:

```
var mainList = new DOMList(
        document.getElementById('main_list') as HTMLElement);
    var addButton =
        document.getElementById('main_add') as HTMLElement;
    var addInput =
        document.getElementById('main_input') as HTMLElement;

    var mainGrid = new MyULAppendGrid(mainList, addButton,
        "li", addInput);
```

Replace the preceding code with the following:

```
import("./lib/plainList.js")
 .then(x => {
 var mainList = new x.default(
 document.getElementById('main_list') as HTMLElement);
 var addButton =
 document.getElementById('main_add') as HTMLElement;
 var addInput =
 document.getElementById('main_input') as HTMLElement;

 var mainGrid = new MyULAppendGrid(mainList, addButton,
 "li", addInput);
 })
 .catch(reason => {
 alert("an error occurred");
 });
```

This imports the exact same module dynamically. The old `DOMList` constructor function is now contained in `x.default`, since the `plainList` module exports it as a default export. Since the module name is passed to the import function as a static string (`./lib/plainList.js`), the TypeScript compiler is able to locate the module at compile time, and to infer the type of `x.default`:

```
import("./lib/plainList.js")
    .then(x => {
        var mainList = new x.default(
            document.getEleme
                                    constructor DOMList<{}>(itemsParent: HTMLElement): DOMList<{}>
        var addButton =
            document.getElementById('main_add') as HTMLElement;
```

Obviously, replacing a static import with a dynamic import that does the exact same thing makes no sense, so let's do something smarter: let's load the jQuery implementation, if jQuery is available in the environment, otherwise let's go back to `./lib/plainList.js`:

```
import((window as any).jQuery ? "./lib/jQueryList.js" :
"./lib/plainList.js")
    . . .
    . . .
```

This time, the TypeScript compiler is not able to infer the type of `x.default`:

```
import((window as any).jQuery ? "./lib/jQueryList.js" : "./lib/plainList.js")
    .then(x => {
        var mainList: Abstracts.ItemList<string> = new x.default(
            document.getElementById('main_list') as HTMLEle
                                                              any
        var addButton =
            document.getElementById('main_add') as HTMLElement;
```

That's why it is necessary to explicitly specify the type of `mainList`. The complete code is as follows:

```
import((window as any).jQuery ? "./lib/jQueryList.js" :
"./lib/plainList.js")
    .then(x => {
        var mainList: Abstracts.ItemList<string> = new x.default(
            document.getElementById('main_list') as HTMLElement);
        var addButton =
```

```
                document.getElementById('main_add') as HTMLElement;
        var addInput =
                document.getElementById('main_input') as HTMLElement;

        var mainGrid = new MyULAppendGrid(mainList, addButton,
            "li", addInput);
    })
    .catch(reason => {
        alert("an error occurred");
    });
```

The preceding code runs only in browsers that support dynamic import natively, such as a recent version of Google Chrome. The next chapter explains how to run the same code in any browser with the help of the WebPack bundler.

Writing declaration files

TypeScript declaration files were introduced in the *Declaration files and JavaScript libraries* section of `Chapter 3`, *DOM Manipulation*, as a way to describe types of libraries that are only available in JavaScript. That section covered where to find them and how to use them. This section, instead, gives some more details on how to write them in case they are not already available somewhere.

The rule of thumb for deciding how to declare entities in declaration file is as follows:

> *Declarations contain just the structure of objects without the code that implements their behavior. Declarations of entities that require memory allocation must be preceded by the declare keyword.*

Type aliases are declared as they are, since they are already pure declarations:

```
type size = "small"|"average"|"large";
```

Since interfaces do not contain implementations and do not require memory allocation, they are declared as they would be declared in TypeScript code files:

```
interface Person {
    name: string;
    surname: string;
}
```

Functions, instead, when encountered by the TypeScript compiler, usually cause memory allocation and generate executable code (also if their bodies are empty). Accordingly, their declarations must be preceded by the `declare` keyword, and the function body must be completely removed in order to prevent normal code-generation:

```
declare function myfunction(x: HTMLDivElement): string;
```

In case a function has several overloads, all overloads must be listed, and the more specific ones must come first:

```
declare function myfunction(x: HTMLDivElement): string;
declare function myfunction(x: HTMLElement): number;
declare function myfunction(x: any): any;
```

Classes, like `function` cause memory allocation because their class constructor is a function, and they have implementations, so they must be preceded by the `declare` keyword, and the implementation of their constructors, methods, getters, and setters must be removed:

```
declare class Person {
    public name: string;
    public surname: string;
    public secondName?: string;
    constructor(name: string, surname: string,
        secondName?: string);
    get fullname(): string;
    set fullname(value: string);
    getString(): string;
}
```

> Parameter properties cannot be used in declarations; that's why, in the preceding example class, the `name`, `surname`, and `secondName` properties were declared separately instead of being declared directly in the constructor.

Variables cause memory allocation but have no implementation, so they need just the `declare` keyword:

```
declare myPrintable: IPrintable
```

Also enums cause memory allocation, since JavaScript objects are created to implement them, but they have no implementation, so they must be preceded by the `declare` keyword:

```
declare enum YesNoAnswer { unknown=1, yes , no};
```

Namespaces require memory allocation too, since they are implemented as a JavaScript variable whose value is a JavaScript object, but they have no implementation:

```
declare namespace Anagraphic {

    interface IPrintable {
        getString(): string;
    }

    class Person implements IPrintable {
        static administrator: Person;
        constructor(readonly name: string, readonly surname: string;
        public fullname(): string;
        public getString(): string;
    }
}
```

 Symbols contained in a declared namespace must not be preceded by any `declare` or `export` keywords, since it is implicit, they are declarations, and since there is no need to declare symbols that must not be exported. All symbols contained in a namespace declaration are implicitly considered exported. In particular, nested namespaces must not be preceded by the `declare` keyword.

Modules do not cause memory allocation and have no implementation (just symbols inside modules have implementations), so they are declared as they are:

```
import * as Abstracts from "./AbstractLists.js"

export default declare class DOMList<T> implements Abstracts.ItemList<T> {
    itemTemplate: (x: T) => HTMLElement;
    constructor(readonly itemsParent: HTMLElement);
    removeItem(node: HTMLElement): void;
    appendItem(itemData: T): void ;
    prependItem(itemData: any): void;
    appendBefore(node: HTMLElement, itemData: T): void;
    appendAfter(node: HTMLElement, itemData: T): void;
}
```

In the case of modules, the `declare` and `export` statements can't be omitted, since a module might mix both declarations and standard code (nothing in the module informs the compiler that it is just a declaration of modules). In ambient modules, described in the next subsection, that are explicitly defined to be declarations, instead, symbols don't need the `declare` keyword but they need the `export` keyword since there are various ways to export a symbol (export statements may be separated from the symbol definitions, and may redefine their names or may define them as default exports).

Ambient modules

Library packages usually contain several JavaScript modules, so when they are compatible with TypeScript, the JavaScript file's tree must have an analogous tree made of the corresponding TypeScript declaration files. In order to simplify the usage of TypeScript libraries, often all module declarations are collected in a single declaration file. Each module declaration in this unique declaration file is called an **ambient module**.

Ambient modules may be imported and may contain imports with only non-relative paths. Since each ambient module has no actual file location associated with it, a more flexible resolution strategy is needed. Usually, since library packages are implemented as npm packages, the Node resolution strategy works fine.

The syntax for declaring ambient modules in a single declaration file is as follows:

```
declare module "<non-relative path>"{
...
}
declare module "<non-relative path>"{
...
}
...
```

As an example, suppose we would like to distribute just the JavaScript targets of library files in the DOM manipulation example: lib/AbstractLists.js, lib/plainList.js, and lib/jQueryList.js. We might define a unique TypeScript declaration file like the following:

```
declare module "lib/AbstractLists.js" {
    export interface ItemList<T> {
        appendItem(itemData: T): void;
        prependItem(itemData: any): void;
        appendBefore(node: HTMLElement, itemData: T): void;
        appendAfter(node: HTMLElement, itemData: T): void;
        removeItem(node: HTMLElement): void;
        itemTemplate: (x: T) => HTMLElement;
        readonly itemsParent: HTMLElement;
    }
    export abstract class AppendGrid<T> {
        protected list: ItemList<T>;
        protected addButton: HTMLElement;
        protected itemRootSelector: string;
        protected addItemDataRoot: HTMLElement;
        protected addBeforeButton?: HTMLElement;
        constructor(list: ItemList<T>,
            addButton: HTMLElement,
```

```
                    itemRootSelector: string,
                    addItemDataRoot: HTMLElement,
                    addBeforeButton?: HTMLElement);
            protected abstract itemTemplate(x: T): HTMLElement;
            protected abstract extractDataToAdd(): T;
        }
    }
    declare module "lib/jQueryList.js" {
        import * as Abstracts from "lib/AbstractLists.js"

        export default class DOMList<T> implements Abstracts.ItemList<T> {
            readonly itemsParent: HTMLElement
            itemTemplate: (x: T) => HTMLElement;
            constructor(itemsParent: HTMLElement);
            removeItem(node: HTMLElement): void;
            appendItem(itemData: T): void;
            prependItem(itemData: any): void;
            appendBefore(node: HTMLElement, itemData: T): void;
            appendAfter(node: HTMLElement, itemData: T): void;
        }
    }
    declare module "lib/plainList.js" {
        import * as Abstracts from "lib/AbstractLists.js"

        export default class DOMList<T> implements Abstracts.ItemList<T> {
            readonly itemsParent: HTMLElement
            itemTemplate: (x: T) => HTMLElement;
            constructor(itemsParent: HTMLElement);
            removeItem(node: HTMLElement): void;
            appendItem(itemData: T): void;
            prependItem(itemData: any): void;
            appendBefore(node: HTMLElement, itemData: T): void;
            appendAfter(node: HTMLElement, itemData: T): void;
        }
    }
```

It is enough to place this file in a directory that is processed by the TypeScript compiler, according to the configuration contained in `tsconfig.json`.

The `import` statements in `modularToDoList.ts` must be modified to use just non-relative paths:

```
import * as Abstracts from "lib/AbstractLists.js"
import DOMList from "lib/plainList.js"
```

While the preceding code compiles properly, it doesn't run in a browser that supports ES6 JavaScript native import. Since ES6 specifications do not allow non-relative paths, a module bundler that is able to process non-relative paths is needed! This example will be revisited in `Chapter 7`, *Bundling with WebPack*, which is dedicated to JavaScript bundlers.

Ambient modules are quite common in the `@Type` packages that contain only TypeScript definitions. Please refer to the *Declaration files and JavaScript libraries* section in `Chapter 3`, *DOM Manipulation*, for more details on `@Type` packages.

Some libraries, such as jQuery, may be loaded both as modules and as a set of global symbols. The declaration files that describe similar libraries contain both ambient modules and global definitions, which may or may not be organized into namespaces.

For example, the jQuery declaration file looks like the following:

```
declare module 'jquery' {
    export = jQuery;
}
...
...
  interface JQuery<...> extends ...
{
    ...
}
```

That is, the same jQuery symbol is declared globally, and exported by the `jquery` module. The following statement exports all symbols contained as public properties of x. If x is either a class or an interface, or all symbols exported by x if x is a namespace:

```
export = x;
```

Automatic generation of declaration files

When a library has been implemented in TypeScript, it is a best practice to just distribute the resultant JavaScript files and all TypeScript declaration files needed to use the library from TypeScript. The main reasons for this choice are as follows:

- This way the library may also be used by JavaScript applications
- The potentially different TypeScript compiler settings used by the application that uses the library might break the TypeScript code

For this reason, the TypeScript compiler offers the option to automatically generate the declaration files corresponding to all compiled files. It is enough to set the `"declaration"` compiler option to `true`, and to specify a directory in which to put the declaration files with the `"declarationDir"` compiler option. The path specified in `"declarationDir"` is relative to the TypeScript configuration file.

For instance, suppose the `src` folder contains the `MyLib.ts` source file and that TypeScript configuration file contains the following settings:

```
{
    ...
    "compilerOptions":{
        ...
        "declarationDir": "./decs/es6",
        "declaration": true,
        "outDir":"./dest/es6",
        "module": "es6"
        ...
    }
    ...
}
```

Then, the compiled `MyLib.js` file will be generated in the `dest/es6` folder, while the `MyLib.d.ts` file containing all TypeScript declarations needed to use `MyLib.js` from TypeScript will be generated in the `decs/es6` folder.

Summary

As in several languages, such as C# and C++, TypeScript namespaces were conceived to avoid name collisions among different libraries and application parts in large code bases. However, they don't solve another important problem of large code bases: dependency-tracking. TypeScript modules solve both these problems, but projects based on modules require an advanced knowledge of JavaScript bundlers, and are more difficult to configure and build. Namespaces should be preferred in simpler applications based mainly on server-side processing that uses JavaScript to improve HTML page graphics, while modules should be preferred in complex, rich-client applications, such as SPAs, that move the whole presentation layer to the client side.

TypeScript modules mimic ES6-native modules but may also generate JavaScript code based on other non-native module systems, such as AMD, CommonJS, and SystemJS. The choice of which module system to use in the generated JavaScript is independent of the JavaScript version chosen with the "target" compiler option, since it is controlled with the different "module" compiler option. The TypeScript dynamic import allows us to choose which module to load depending on the features supported by the browser, and on which JavaScript libraries are available in the final environment.

Several modules may be declared in a single file thanks to the ambient module feature. This is the favorite choice for @Types packages that contain TypeScript definitions only. The same declaration file may declare a library both as a module and as a set of global symbols, thanks to the export = statement and to ambient modules.

The next chapter will discuss how to use WebPack to organize several JavaScript/TypeScript modules into bigger chunks, in order to optimize JavaScript download time and to use modules in browsers that do not support ES6 modules.

Questions

1. What is the problem solved by namespaces, and what is the JavaScript equivalent of namespaces?
2. Can you list the main pitfalls of namespaces? How are they solved by modules?
3. How can you import all symbols exported by the A module without being forced to prefix the names of all symbols in A with another identifier in the subsequent code (for example, if A contains a Person class, we don't want to write something such as new prefix.Person(...), but we would like to write simply new Person(...))?
4. When is module-resolution performed? At compile time? At runtime?
5. When and why are non-relative paths needed in import statements?
6. What is the main advantage of a dynamic import? When is it needed?
7. Is a dynamic import part of the ES6 specifications?
8. Can TypeScript's dynamic import be used by a browser that doesn't support JavaScript-native dynamic import? How?
9. Do enums require the declare keyword when declared in TypeScript declaration files? Why?
10. Are non-relative paths supported in JavaScript ES6 import statements? If not, what tools are needed to use non-relative paths in practical projects?

Further reading

A discussion on using JavaScript just to improve HTML page graphics in server-based applications, and some tips on how to do it, may be found in this article on my blog: `http://www.dotnet-programming.com/post/2013/12/10/JavaScript-Intensive-Web-Applications-2-Enhancing-Html-with-JavaScript.aspx`. The *Writing declaration files* section just describe the syntax of declaration files. Tips and techniques for generating declaration files of existing libraries may be found in the TypeScript official documentation here: `https://www.typescriptlang.org/docs/handbook/declaration-files/introduction.html`.

The ECMAScript proposal for modules' dynamic import can be found here: `https://github.com/tc39/proposal-dynamic-import`. More information on the whole TC39 committee and process can be found here: `https://www.ecma-international.org/memento/tc39-m.htm`.

This chapter just covers ES6-native JavaScript modules, since modern applications use them together with modern JavaScript bundlers such as WebPack. Information on the other module systems supported by TypeScript may be found in the following references:

- The `require.js` implementation of the AMD protocol: `https://requirejs.org/`
- SystemJS: `https://github.com/systemjs/systemjs`
- CommonJS usage, and on Node.js module-resolution strategies: `https://nodejs.org/en/docs/`

Bundling with WebPack

7

Bundlers link all modules that compose a JavaScript application or library into one or more bigger chunks of JavaScript code. Their outputted code chunks can then be added as they are to HTML pages and/or automatically loaded at a later time by the bundler runtime. In both cases, neither ES6-compliant browsers nor JavaScript module loaders are needed anymore since all loading operations are performed by the bundler runtime inserted in the code chunks. Bundlers are able to process both ES6 modules and modules based on JavaScript libraries such as AMD, CommonJS, and SystemJS. Starting from the roots module, they recursively track all dependencies until they reach the leaf modules with no dependencies. Once a module's tree has been built for each root module, each tree is transformed into a unique, independent JavaScript file called a bundle, that may be added to any HTML page.

Modules that are common to several dependency trees may be factored out in further bundles instead of being replicated within each separated bundle in order to optimize JavaScript download time and caching. This topic is covered in the *Optimizing bundles* section.

Bundlers also handle dynamic module import statements. This topic is covered in the *Runtime loading* section. The most used bundlers are Browserify, WebPack, and Rollup. This chapter, and the whole book, covers just WebPack, which became a de facto standard. This chapter explains how to use WebPack to bundle several TypeScript/JavaScript files/modules into a few transpiled JavaScript files in order to optimize HTML page-loading and JavaScript caching. This chapter also explains how to use WebPack to bundle other resources, such as CSS files, HTML files, and images to improve performance. WebPack is a fundamental building block of Angular applications, which are the topic of the last part of the book.

More specifically, the following topics will be covered in this chapter:

- Basics of JavaScript and TypeScript bundling
- Optimizing multiple bundles with common chunks
- Bundling dynamic import instructions
- Configuring WebPack for production and for development
- Bundling CSS, images, and HTML

Technical requirements

We'll need the following tools for this chapter:

- Visual Studio 2017 with the last ASP.NET Core tools
- Visual Studio TypeScript SDK
- Node.Js and `npm` package manager

Node.js and `npm` are both contained in Node.js installation packages you may find at `https://nodejs.org/en/`. Please select the recommended version and follow the simple steps contained at the beginning of the *Installation of Node.js based TypeScript* compiler subsection of `Chapter 1`, *Introduction to TypeScript*, in order to verify that both Node.js and `npm` were properly installed.

All the code used in this chapter can be downloaded from the following GitHub link: `https://github.com/PacktPublishing/Hands-On-TypeScript-for-CSharp-and-.NET-Core-Developers`.

Check out the following video to see the Code in Action: `http://bit.ly/2qjSR10`.

Bundling TypeScript and JavaScript

This section uses the `DOMManipulation` project version based on modules created in the *Pitfalls of namespaces and ES6 modules* section of `Chapter 6`, *Namespaces and Modules*.

WebPack is installed with `npm`. It is enough to add it to the `package.json` file of the `DOMManiupation` example, which should look like this:

```
{
  "version": "1.0.0",
  "name": "ASP.NET",
  "private": true,
```

```
    "devDependencies": {
        "@types/jquery": "^3.3.4",
    }
}
```

It was already used to load the package containing jQuery and TypeScript definitions. Anyway, it is worth recalling how to add `package.json` to a Visual Studio project:

1. Right-click on the project root (it should be named `DOMManipulation`) and select **Add | New Item**.
2. Under **Web | Scripts** select **npm Configuration File**
3. Accept the default `package.json` name and click the **Add** button. Let's add three more packages under `devDependencies`:

```
{
    "version": "1.0.0",
    "name": "ASP.NET",
    "private": true,
        "devDependencies": {
            "@types/jquery": "^3.3.4",
            "webpack": "^4.16.4",
            "webpack-cli": "^3.1.0",
            "path": "^0.12.7",
        },
}
```

Feel free to specify more recent versions suggested by Visual Studio IntelliSense. `"webpack"` contains the actual WebPack, while `"webpack-cli"` contains its standard user interface. Without `"webpack-cli"`, one would be forced to write a custom Node program that calls WebPack processor. `"path"` is a Node.js library containing some helpers to manipulate file and directory names that will be useful in writing down WebPack configuration files. Once the file is saved, all node packages are installed. During the downloading and installation of the packages, the `npm` folder within the dependencies node in the solution explorer will have a danger signal with an explanation point on it, meaning that at least one `npm` package is not ready for usage. The end of the download/installation process is signaled both in the Visual Studio output window and by the removal of the danger signal on the `npm` folder inside the dependencies node.

WebPack could be invoked by opening a console window in the project (not solution) root and passing the following command:

```
node   node_modules/webpack/bin/webpack
```

This invokes the Node.js interpreter on the `node_modules/webpack/bin/webpack.js` JavaScript file. This must be done when the current directory is the project directory, since the WebPack configuration file will be placed there and all paths that will be specified are relative to this directory.

One may avoid specifying the whole path to `webpack.js` by defining a script in `package.json`:

```
{
  "version": "1.0.0",
  "name": "ASP.NET",
  "private": true,
    "devDependencies": {
        "@types/jquery": "^3.3.4",
        "webpack": "^4.16.4",
        "webpack-cli": "^3.1.0",
        "path": "^0.12.7"
    },
    "scripts": {
        "build": "webpack"
    }
}
```

Now WebPack may be invoked, while in the project root, with the following command:

```
npm run-script build
```

The next step before invoking WebPack is the specification of a configuration file. Right-click on the project icon in the solution explorer and add `webpack.config.js` in the project root. `webpack.config.js` is the default name searched automatically by WebPack to load the configuration information. A different name may be specified, but then this name must be passed as a parameter to the `"webpack"` command.

`webpack.config.js` is a JavaScript file that has the structure of a Node.js module:

```
//other module Node.js imports
...
const path = require("path");
...
//compute or define some useful values:
...
const bundleOutputDir = "./wwwroot/dist";
```

```
...

module.exports = {
    ...
    ...
};
```

Each node module, once imported with the `require` function, returns a JavaScript object as a value. For instance, `path` will contain an object whose methods are all the path/directory names helpers contained in the `path` package. Also, `webpack.config.js` must return an object that, in this case, will contain the WebPack configuration. The object to return as the module value is specified by assigning it to `module.exports`, as shown in the preceding code snippet.

The most important information of the configuration object is the modules to be used as root of the dependencies tree in our `modularToDoList.js` example. Once all the dependency trees are built, all modules in each tree are bundled together into unique JavaScript files called bundles:

```
module.exports = {
    entry: {
        main: "./wwwroot/ts/modularToDoList"
    },
    ...
....
}
```

In the preceding example, `main` is the bundle name. Relative paths must be computed relative to the `webpack.config.js` file. A bundle may also contain several dependency tree roots:

```
module.exports = {
    entry: {
        main: ["<root 1>", "<root 2>", ...]
    },
    ...
....
}
```

This way, we might place the whole JavaScript that is specific for a given web page into a single bundle.

Several bundles may be computed simultaneously:

```
module.exports = {
    entry: {
```

```
                <bundle 1>: ["<root 1>", "<root 2>", ...],
                <bundle 2>: "./.....",
                <bundle 3>: "./.....",
                ...
        },
        ...
    ....
    }
```

The various bundles might contain, for instance, the JavaScript of different web pages.

Another essential piece of information is how to name the bundle files and in which directories to place them. This information is placed in the output configuration property:

```
const path = require("path");
const bundleOutputDir = "./wwwroot/dist";
module.exports = {
    entry: {
        main: "./wwwroot/ts/modularToDoList"
    },
    output: {
        filename: "[name].bundle.js",
        path: path.join(__dirname, bundleOutputDir)
    }
}
```

In the preceding example, all bundles are placed in the `"wwwroot/dist"` directory in the project root. `__dirname` is a Node.js variable containing the directory that `"webpack.config.js"` is in, which in our case is the project root. `path.join` builds an absolute path from `__dirname` and the relative path, `bundleOutputDir`.

The bundle file name is obtained by adding `.bundle.js` to the bundle name, since `[name]` stands for a variable containing the bundle name. If `entry` contains the definition of several bundles, all of them will be placed in the directory specified in the output and all of them will have a name like `[name].bundle.js`. There are other variables that may be used in the bundle file name:

- `[hash]`: A hash that depends on the file content. Adding a hash in the file name prevents the browser caching after the file content changes.
- `[id]`: A numeric ID assigned automatically to all objects generated by WebPack. Unlike `[hash]`, it does not change when the file content changes so it can't be used to prevent caching. It is useful for objects that have no name assigned by the developer.

Another important configuration property is `mode`, which may be either `"production"` or `"development"`:

```
...
module.exports = {
    ...
    mode: "development"
    ..-
}
```

It is important to specify the `mode`, since various WebPack modules assume different defaults depending on whether the build is done for production or for further development. For instance, when `mode` is set to `"production"`, all bundles are minimized as a default. A detailed discussion on the more appropriate settings for production and development is given in the *Production and development configurations* section. If no `mode` property is assigned, `"production"` is assumed.

After having also added `mode: 'development'`, we may invoke WebPack to bundle all files. Let's open a **Package Manager Console** in Visual Studio (**Tools | NuGet Package Manager | Package Manager Console**) and issue the `dir` command to verify what is the current directory, since WebPack must be invoked from the project root directory. Normally, the current directory should be the solution directory, so we need `cd DOMManipulation` to move to the project root.

Now it is enough to run `npm run-script build`, since we added `"scripts": { "build": "webpack"}` in our `package.json`. After successfully executing the command, the console should show something like this:

```
Entrypoint main = main.bundle.js
[./wwwroot/js/lib/AbstractLists.js] 1.66 KiB {main} [built]
[./wwwroot/js/lib/plainList.js] 1.14 KiB {main} [built]
[./wwwroot/js/modularToDoList.js] 1.89 KiB {main} [built]
PM> |
```

This means that a bundle called `main.bundle.js` has been created that contains the three modules listed. In fact, a new folder named `dist` should appear under `wwwroot`, and it should contain the `main.bundle.js` file.

Now let's go to the `Home/Index.cshtml` view and find the old script:

```
@section Scripts{
    <script type="module" src="~/js/modularToDoList.js"></script>
}
```

Replace the preceding code with the following:

```
@section Scripts{
    <script type="text/javascript" src="~/dist/main.bundle.js"></script>
}
```

The new code also runs in browsers such as Internet Explorer that do not support ES6-native modules!

What if we want to debug the JavaScript code?

Debuggers are able to work with the `main.bundle.js` code that was created by WebPack, not with the original files used to create it. WebPack may be configured to generate a source map that connects `main.bundle.js` to the original files, which would enable the debugger to work with the original files.

Let's add the following property to the WebPack configuration file:

```
devtool: "source-map"
```

If the WebPack build is run again, a new file named `main.bundle.js.map` appears next to `main.bundle.js`, which contains the source map. The source map may be included in the bundle itself, instead of creating another file, with the following configuration:

```
devtool: "in-line-source-map"
```

After the project is run, breakpoint inserted either in the original TypeScript files or in the JavaScript files generated by their compilation are not hit, but the code may be debugged with the Browser debugger. Browser debugger should show a `webpack://` node containing all original files, where we may place breakpoints. However, this way we also have access to the Javascript files generated by TypeScript compiler, not to the TypeScript sources!

WebPack is able to connect the source map generated by the TypeScript compiler and its source map to get an overall source map that connects `main.bundle.js` directly with the TypeScript sources, but it must be informed that such source files exist. At the moment, it is not aware of any TypeScript sources since it was invoked directly on the JavaScript files generated by the TypeScript compiler.

The next subsection introduces the concept of the loader and uses it to invoke WebPack directly on the TypeScript sources, so it may create more appropriate source maps.

WebPack loaders – bundling TypeScript files

WebPack bundles JavaScript to yield JavaScript, so any kind of file to be processed by WebPack must be transformed into JavaScript before it may be bundled properly. Loaders do the job of transforming other file types into JavaScript before they are processed by the WebPack-bundling engine.

Loaders are similar to ASP.NET Core middleware; they are transformation blocks with an input and an output that may be stacked so that the output of a loader becomes the input of the subsequent loader. Some loaders are included in WebPack, while others must me installed as separate `npm` packages.

There are two TypeScript loaders: `"ts-loader"` and `"awesome-typescript-loader"`. This section uses the second one, since it was designed to be faster. All loaders call the TypeScript compiler to do their job, but they can't use the Visual Studio TypeScript compiler since they need it as an `npm` package. Thus, the TypeScript compiler `npm` package must be added together with the `"awesome-typescript-loader"` package in the `package.json` project:

```
{
    ...
    "devDependencies": {
        ...
        "typescript": "^3.0.1",
        "awesome-typescript-loader": "^5.2.0"
    },
    ...
}
```

Feel free to choose any more recent version suggested by Visual Studio IntelliSense.

Before using the TypeScript loader, all `.js` extensions in the paths of the import statements must be removed from the `AbstractLists.ts`, `jQueryList.ts`, `plainList.ts`, and `modularToDoList.ts` files. In fact, the `.js` extension might confuse the loader that looks for `.ts` files. After this modification, WebPack must be instructed to look automatically for `.ts` and `.js` extensions when paths have no extensions with the following configuration option:

```
resolve: { extensions: ['.js', '.ts'] }
```

The `resolve` property collects all configuration options that affect the WebPack module's resolution algorithm. It is discussed in more detail in the last subsection of this section.

Finally, WebPack must be instructed to use `"awesome-typescript-loader"` by adding the following configuration:

```
module: {
    rules: [
        { test: /\.ts$/, use: 'awesome-typescript-loader' },
    ]
}
```

The `rules` array inside the `module` property contains rules that specify which loaders to apply to which file types. The type of file is identified by the regular expression contained in the `test` property of each rule, while the loaders to apply are listed in the `use` property. When several loaders must be stacked, their names may be separated bay a `!`:

```
{ test: /\.ts$/, use: 'awesome-typescript-loader!<another loader>' }
```

Loaders are applied in inverse order, starting from the last one and ending with the first one. Thus, in the preceding example `"awesome-typescript-loader"` is the last loader applied.

Loaders may have options that are specified as a web query string after the module name:

```
{ test: /\.ts$/, use: 'awesome-typescript-loader?silent=true' }
```

The `silent` option prevents TypeScript messages from being printed in the console. Several options are separated by the `&` symbol, like in actual query strings:

```
test: /\.ts$/, use: 'awesome-typescript-loader?silent=true&<another option>'}
```

The use of a loader may also be specified by adding the whole string one might insert in the `use` property directly after the filename, separated by a `!`. For instance, check out the following `import` statement:

```
import * as Abstracts from "./lib/AbstractLists!awesome-typescript-loader?silent=true"
```

It causes the `AbstractList` file be processed by `"awesome-typescript-loader"` with the `silent` option also if its file name doesn't match any `module.rule`.

Several loaders may also be specified with an array instead of being chained in the same string, with the syntax shown in the following example:

```
{
        test: /\.ts$/,
        use: [
          {
            loader: 'awesome-typescript-loader',
            options: {
              silent: true
            }
          },
          { loader: '<another loader>' }
        ]
      }
```

After the last modification, the WebPack configuration file of the DOMManipulation project should be as follows:

```
const path = require("path");
const bundleOutputDir = "./wwwroot/dist";
module.exports = {
    entry: {
        main: "./wwwroot/ts/modularToDoList"
    },
    output: {
        filename: "[name].bundle.js",
        path: path.join(__dirname, bundleOutputDir)
    },
    resolve: { extensions: ['.js', '.ts'] },
    module: {
        rules: [
            { test: /\.ts$/, use: 'awesome-typescript-loader' },
        ]
    },
    mode: "development"
}
```

Going to the project folder and building the project with the run-script npm build should now produce a source map that refers directly to the original TypeScript files. Unluckily, the way WebPack, generated source maps refer to file names is not compatible with Visual Studio, so Visual Studio debugger is still unable to set breakpoints. The next subsection introduces the concept of the WebPack plugin, discusses a plugin that allows the customization of WebPack source maps, and shows how to configure it to recover the Visual Studio debugger.

WebPack plugins – recovering the Visual Studio debugger

While loaders just preprocess files, WebPack plugins hook the WebPack bundling process and modify it somehow. Some plugins are contained in the WebPack package, while others are independent npm packages. Plugins are JavaScript constructor functions that must be loaded with a require(...) instruction. Plugin options are passed as parameters of these constructor functions when they are invoked to create instances. Then plugin instances are inserted as array elements in the plugins property of the WebPack configuration, according to the following schema:

```
const pluginConstructorFunction= require('<plugin name');
....
module.exports = {
    ...
    plugins: [
        ...
        new pluginConstructorFunction(...<options>...),
        ...
    ],
    ...
}
```

The plugin that customizes WebPack source maps is called SourceMapDevToolPlugin. It is not contained in an external package, but its constructor function is available as a property of the 'webpack' object:

```
const webpack = require('webpack');
const SourceMapDevToolPlugin = webpack.SourceMapDevToolPlugin;
....
const bundleOutputDir = "./wwwroot/dist";
```

All its options are passed into a unique JavaScript object:

```
plugins: [
        new SourceMapDevToolPlugin({
            // Remove the line below if you prefer inline source maps
            filename: '[file].map',
            // Point sourcemap entries to the original file locations on
disk
            moduleFilenameTemplate: path.relative(bundleOutputDir,
'[resourcePath]')
        })
    ]
```

The `filename` option is a template for generating the source map file names. `[file]` is a variable containing the bundle file name. If this option is omitted, an inline map is created.

`moduleFilenameTemplate` is a template for the format of the original source file names contained in the source maps. For Visual Studio debugger to work properly, these names must be the paths relative to the source map location. `[resourcePath]` is a variable bound to each of the sources paths, relative to the WebPack configuration file (`"./wwwroot/ts/lib/AbstractLists.ts"` and so on), and the `path.relative` function recomputes this path as relative to `"./wwwroot/dist"`, which is relative to the source map file (`"../ts/lib/AbstractLists.ts"` and so on).

Now, after completing the WebPack build, the Visual Studio debugger starts working properly! In order to test it, let's place a breakpoint within the `appendItem` method in `"wwwroot/ts/lib/plainList.ts"`, run the project, and add a new to-do item. The breakpoint is actually hit:

```
appendItem(itemData: T): void {
    this.itemsParent.appendChild(this.itemTemplate(itemData));

}
```

The WebPack module's resolution algorithm

The `resolve` option specifies how WebPack resolves module names. The *WebPack loaders – bundling TypeScript files* subsection already introduced its `extensions` sub-option that specifies how to complete paths with no extension:

```
resolve: { extensions: ['.js', '.ts'] }
```

All extensions specified in the array are tried, in the order they are listed, until an existing file is found.

As already discussed in the *Modules loading* section of Chapter 6, *Namespaces and Modules*, absolute and relative paths are trivially solved. The difficult part is solving non-relative paths. The alias sub-option is analogous to the TypeScript path option, the main difference being that paths in path are relative to the path contained in the baseUrl option, while the paths specified in the alias sub-option are taken as they are. However, baseUrl may be easily defined and used as follows:

```
...
const baseUrl = path.join(__dirname, "wwwroot");
...
{
    ...
    resolve: {
        extensions: ['.js', '.ts'],
        alias: {
            utilities: path.join(baseUrl, "js/utilities/")
        },
        ...
    },
    ...
}
```

Another difference with the TypeScript path is that all paths in alias are also used to replace subpaths. For instance:

```
utilisties/myModule
```

The preceding code is resolved to:

```
/wwwroot/js/utilities/myModule
```

In order to exclude subpaths replacement, a $ postfix may be added at the end of the alias:

```
alias: {
    utilities: path.join(baseUrl, "js/utilities/"),
    myUtility$: path.join(baseUrl, "js/utilities/MyUtility")
}
```

In the preceding case, the myUtility value may replace just the "myUtility" string.

The standard paths in which to search module names that were not found in `alias` are specified with the `modules` sub-option:

```
resolve: {
        extensions: ['.js', '.ts'],
        ...
        modules: [<path1>, <path2>, ...]
        ...
    }
```

All paths are searched in the order in which they are listed until a match is found. If a path is absolute, it is chained to the module name to get the actual module path; if a path is non-relative, a Node.js-like search, similar to the one described for TypeScript in the *Modules loading* section of Chapter 6, *Namespaces and Modules*, is adopted. If `<path1>` is `node_modules`, and if a node placed in `c://projects/myProject/wwwroot/lib/MyLib` is importing a module called `dependencyLib`, the following paths are tried:

```
c://projects/myProject/wwwroot/lib/MyLib/node_modules/dependencyLib
c://projects/myProject/wwwroot/lib/node_modules/dependencyLib
c://projects/myProject/wwwroot/node_modules/dependencyLib
c://projects/myProject/node_modules/dependencyLib
c://projects/node_modules/dependencyLib
c://node_modules/dependencyLib
```

If a path contains an extensions, it is tried as it is; otherwise, all extensions contained in the `extensions` sub-option are tried. If no extension succeed, the algorithm interprets the path as a folder containing a library package. Accordingly, the algorithm searches for a package-configuration file:

```
c://projects/myProject/wwwroot/lib/MyLib/package.json
```

If the JSON file contains a `main` property, the file path specified there, say `myMain.js`, is appended to the directory:

```
c://projects/myProject/wwwroot/lib/MyMyLib/myMain.js
```

If either the directory contains no `package.json` file or the configuration file contains no valid `main` property, the algorithm assumes the default `index` file name, which is tried with all extensions specified in the `extensions` sub-option:

```
c://projects/myProject/wwwroot/lib/MyLib/index.js
c://projects/myProject/wwwroot/lib/MyLib/index.ts
```

The `main` property name may be changed by specifying a different property name in the `mainFields` sub-option whose value must be an array, since several alternative names may be specified. Analogously, the `mainFiles` sub-option is used to specify an array of alternative names to replace the `index` default file name.

The default value of the `modules` sub-property is `node_modules`:

```
resolve: {
        extensions: ['.js', '.ts'],
        ...
        modules: ['node_modules']
        ...
    }
```

This way, the default WebPack strategy matches perfectly, TypeScript Node `moduleResolution` setting strategy described in the *Modules loading* section of Chapter 6, *Namespaces and Modules*. This is the adequate strategy when all library files are provided through npm packages.

Since libraries are typically packaged and provided as npm packages, usually there is no need to change the WebPack `modules` default setting, while the TypeScript `moduleResolution` compiler option must be set to Node.

Internal project modules are easily handled with relative paths with the possible help of the WebPack `alias` and TypeScript `paths` compiler option.

WebPack has also a `resolveLoader` option that works and has exactly the same sub-options of `resolve`, but which is used for resolving WebPack loaders' names. Its defaults are:

```
module.exports = {
  ...
  resolveLoader: {
    modules: [ 'node_modules' ],
    extensions: [ '.js', '.json' ],
    mainFields: [ 'loader', 'main' ]
  }
  ...
};
```

Since loaders are provided through npm packages, usually there is no need to modify the preceding defaults.

Integrating WebPack in ASP.NET Core middleware

ASP.NET Core offers the `Microsoft.AspNetCore.SpaServices` package, which helps its interaction with WebPack. It contains an ASP.NET Core middleware that takes care of launching the WebPack build each time the project is run in development mode, passing it useful options and possibly enabling WebPack Hot Modules Replacement (simply called HMR). With HMR set to on, WebPack automatically detects changes in all source files processed and automatically sends patches to the client in order to immediately update all assets on the client side. Thus, if a CSS file is packaged with WebPack (see the *Bundling CSS, images, and HTML* section), any change made in it is immediately visible in the page shown by the development browser.

Before modifying the project of the previous section, let's make a copy of it. Then right-click on the `dependencies` node in the solution explorer and select **Manage Nuget Packages...**. In the window that opens, select the **Browse** tab and search `Microsoft.AspNetCore.SpaServices`. It is necessary to install the version with the same number of the ASP.NET Core version used in the project. Thus, if the project was created with the 2.1.0 version of ASP.NET Core, the `Microsoft.AspNetCore.SpaServices` version must also be 2.1.0.

Now WebPack middleware must be installed in the `Configure` method of `Startup.cs`. As a first step, let it add the following using clause to `Startup.cs`:

```
using Microsoft.AspNetCore.SpaServices.Webpack;
```

Then the code in-between the following comments must be placed exactly after the `app.UseHttpsRedirection();` instruction in the `Configure` method:

```
app.UseHttpsRedirection();

//code to add start
if (env.IsDevelopment())
{
    app.UseWebpackDevMiddleware(new WebpackDevMiddlewareOptions
    {
        HotModuleReplacement = false
    });
}
//code to add end
```

The `WebpackDevMiddlewareOptions` object passed to the middleware contains options that are reflected on the WebPack configuration and on the way WebPack is invoked `Microsoft.AspNetCore.SpaServices` needs some `npm` packages to interact properly with WebPack. Let's add them to `package.json`:

```
{
    ...
    "devDependencies": {
        ...
        "aspnet-webpack": "^3.0.0",
        "webpack-hot-middleware": "^2.22.3",
        "webpack-dev-middleware": "^3.1.3",
        ...
    },
    ...
}
```

Feel free to install the latest versions suggested by Visual Studio IntelliSense.

Now, as soon as the project is run, a WebPack build should be invoked automatically by the WebPack middleware. The correct invocation of WebPack may be tested by removing all files contained in the `"wwwroot/dist"` folder. When the project is run, all files in `"wwwroot/dist"` are recreated and the to-do list continues working properly!

Watch mode and Hot Modules Replacement

If the `HotModuleReplacement` property of the option object is set to `true`, WebPack is invoked in watch mode and with **Hot Modules Replacement** (**HMR**) on. Accordingly, WebPack would look for changes in the sources it processed to creates all bundles, and when any change is detected it takes care of sending a patch to update all assets on the client side.

For HMR to work properly, WebPack must be informed on the path of the web server that will be used to serve its bundles, in our case the `dist/` path (that is, all bundles are served from `http://localhost:<port number>/dist/`). This information must be placed in the `publicPath` property of the WebPack configuration `output` option object, as shown:

```
...,
output: {
        filename: "[name].bundle.js",
        path: path.join(__dirname, bundleOutputDir),
        publicPath: 'dist/'
    },
    ...
```

HMR is very useful for testing modifications to CSS files. This will be shown in the *Bundling CSS, images, and HTML* section. Taking advantage of HMR with TypeScript or JavaScript files is more difficult, since when the new version of a module replaces the old one, in general, a lot of other JavaScript variables and properties still have pointers to objects contained in the old module version and this may break the code. So either the whole application must be reset to its initial state, or all pointers must be updated to point to the corresponding objects of the new module version. Most SPA engines support HMR and take care of resetting the application state whenever a new module version is loaded.

Supporting HMR on TypeScript/JavaScript modules in server-based applications that have no framework that orchestrates modules-loading is quite difficult and it is not worth the effort, since refreshing the browser is simpler than writing ad hoc code for properly handling HMR in the various application parts. This is because in server-based applications, browser refreshes are usually fast.

This is not the case for Single-Page Applications, which load more and more assets while the whole application continues running in the same web page. Thus, while an incremental update approach such as HMR is not very useful in a server-based application, it becomes a must when developing Single-Page Applications.

The remainder of this subsection shows how HMR works with TypeScript files by applying HMR to changes in the `plainList.ts` module. For HMR to work, a small snippet of code must be added to a file that imports the modules to reload with HMR, in our case to `modularToDoList.ts`. However, as a first step, the overall code must be modified so that it is possible to easily replace all pointers involving objects from `plainList.ts`. It turns out that the only object imported by `plainList.ts` is its `DOMList<T>` class, which is used to create an instance of `DOMList<string>` whose occurrences must be replaced when a new version of the module is loaded.

The only pointer to this instance is contained in the `list` protected property of `AppendGrid<T>` in the `AbstractLists.ts` file. It is enough to add a method that changes this property to `AppendGrid<T>` so that one may recall it whenever a new version of the `plainList.ts` module is downloaded:

```
public replaceList(list: ItemList<T>): void {
        this.list = list;
}
```

We need to make some necessary changes to the constructor of `AppendGrid<T>`:

```
constructor(protected list: ItemList<T>,
        ...
        ...) {
        ...
```

```
        ...
        this.addButton.addEventListener("click",
            (evt: MouseEvent) => {
                list.appendItem(this.extractDataToAdd());
            });
        if (this.addBeforeButton) {
            this.addBeforeButton.addEventListener("click",
                (evt: MouseEvent) => {
                    list.prependItem(this.extractDataToAdd());
                });
        }
    }
```

All references to the `list` constructor parameter must be replaced with `this.list`, since only `this.list` may be changed by invoking the `replaceList` method:

```
    constructor(protected list: ItemList<T>,
        ...
        ...) {
        ...
        ...
        this.addButton.addEventListener("click",
            (evt: MouseEvent) => {
                this.list.appendItem(this.extractDataToAdd());
            });
        if (this.addBeforeButton) {
            this.addBeforeButton.addEventListener("click",
                (evt: MouseEvent) => {
                    this.list.prependItem(this.extractDataToAdd());
                });
        }
    }
```

Now it is time to add the hot replacement script to `modularToDoList.ts`. It is enough to add the following code at the end of the file:

```
if (module.hot) {
    module.hot.accept("./lib/plainList", () => {
        mainList = new DOMList(
            document.getElementById('main_list') as HTMLElement);
        mainGrid.replaceList(mainList);
    });
}
```

The `module` variable is part of the WebPack runtime, and its `hot` property is not null if, and only if, HMR is enabled. In this case, all overloads of the `module.hot.accept` function may be used to declare which modules accept hot replacements, and a function to invoke after each hot replacement. In this function, a new instance of `DOMList` replaces the instance created with the old version of the module.

The preceding code doesn't compile because the `module` variable lacks a TypeScript declaration. The problem is easily fixed by adding the `@types/webpack-env` NPM package, which contains the TypeScript declarations of all symbols used by the WebPack runtime. Let's add it to `package.json` and select the latest version suggested by Visual Studio IntelliSense. After that, `modularToDoList.ts` should compile properly.

Let's run the the project and add some to do items. Now let's modify the `removeItem` method in `plainList.ts` so that an alert box is shown whenever an item is removed:

```
removeItem(node: HTMLElement): void {
        alert("remove");
        this.itemsParent.removeChild(node);
}
```

As soon as the file is saved, the Visual Studio output window shows that some processing is going on and informs us of a hot replacement of the `plainList.ts` module. After that, let's try to remove an item. An alert box with the `remove` string appears, proving that the modification has been put in place on the client side!

WebPack runtime also supplies a method to provide code to execute just before a module is replaced by a newer version:

```
module.hot.dispose(() => {/*disposal code here */});
```

The disposal code is used either to reset data structures containing references to objects related to the old module version and/or to extract the state of the old module version so that it may be used to configure the new version of the same module.

HMR may also be configured without the help of ASP.NET Core and WebPack ASP.NET Core middleware. References on how to proceed without WebPack ASP.NET Core middleware are provided in the *Further reading* section.

Optimizing bundles

When files must be organized in several different bundles, for instance, because the different bundles must be served in different web pages that need different JavaScript/TypeScript libraries, some optimization problems arise:

- Some modules belongs to external libraries that will not be modified during the project's development. Thus, it makes no sense to process them during the frequent builds of the JavaScript/TypeScript project files. It makes more sense to organize them in separate bundles that are processed once and for all when all the library packages are installed.
- If some modules are part of several bundles, it makes sense to factor them out into a separate bundle instead of duplicating them in all bundles. This way, the browser may cache them once and for all and they are not downloaded several times as parts of different bundles, thus reducing the average download time.

The subsections that follow describe two optimization techniques specific to the two goals specified here.

Library bundling – DllPlugin

`DllPlugin` causes WebPack to organize all external library modules into separate library bundles. Since these library modules do not change during the development process they can be bundled when the project starts, thus saving the time to bundle them in all subsequent project builds. Since library packages are usually larger than the application-specific code, the time saved in each build with this technique is significant. Depending on the project needs, one or more library bundles may be defined. Each library bundle is generated by a different bundling process that has its own WebPack configuration file and that uses the WebPack `DllPlugin` to generate a kind of table of contents, called a **manifest**. Each manifest contains all the information needed to communicate with the modules contained in the library bundle.

The main application WebPack configuration file references the manifests of all library bundles and uses them to solve dependencies and to generate the code needed to interact with the modules contained in the library bundles.

In the deployment stage, each main bundle will be distributed together with the library bundles it depends on. For instance, each page of the `DOMManipulation` project used in the previous section depends on the jQuery and Bootstrap libraries, so they may be organized into library bundles that will replace the script that refers jQuery, and Bootstrap separately in the `_Layout` view.

It is simpler to use the Node.js package version of both Bootstrap and jQuery from a WebPack configuration file instead of the ones contained in the `wwwroot/lib` folder. So let's add Bootstrap and jQuery `npm` packages to `package.json`:

```
{
    ...
    "devDependencies": {
        ...
        "jquery": "3.3.1",
        "bootstrap": "3.3.7"
    }
    ...
}
```

Please select exactly the same version of the files contained in `wwwroot/lib` to avoid incompatibility problems. (Bootstrap 4 is definitely not compatible with the project.)

Library bundles each need their own WebPack configuration file, so let's add another WebPack configuration file named `webpack.config.vendor.js` in the project root. Then add a new script to invoke WebPack on this configuration file in `package.json`:

```
{
    ...
    "scripts": {
        "build": "webpack",
        "build_vendor": "webpack --config webpack.config.vendor.js"
    }
}
```

The `build_vendor` script will be invoked just once, since no source file contained in the bundle will be modified during project development!

The following is the content of `webpack.config.vendor.js`:

```
const path = require('path');
const webpack = require('webpack');

module.exports = {
    resolve: {
        extensions: ['.js']
    },
    entry: {
        vendor: ['bootstrap', 'jquery'],
    },
    output: {
        path: path.join(__dirname, 'wwwroot', 'dist'),
        publicPath: 'dist/',
```

```
            filename: '[name].js',
            library: '[name]_[hash]',
        },
    plugins: [
        new webpack.ProvidePlugin({ $: 'jquery', jQuery: 'jquery' }),
        new webpack.DllPlugin({
            path: path.join(__dirname, 'wwwroot', 'dist', '[name]-
manifest.json'),
            name: '[name]_[hash]'
        })
    ]
};
```

Almost everything is quite standard, and only `.js` extensions are resolved since usually external libraries only contain JavaScript and TypeScript declaration files. `vendor` is the name of the bundle that contains two root files modules.

The `library` property in `output` and the `name` property in `DllPlugin` must contain names that univocally identify the library bundle. The two values may be different but they must be unique. Unicity is enforced by attaching the file hash to the bundle name. The `path` property of `DllPlugin` specifies the path of the manifest associated to the library bundle.

jQuery is compatible with modules, but Bootstrap that depends on jQuery uses `JQuery` and `$` global symbols instead of requiring jQuery as a module. `ProvidePlugin` automatically generates a dependency on jQuery (or on another different module with a different name mentioned as a value in the object passed to the `ProvidePlugin`) whenever either `$` or the `jQuery` variables (or any other identifier used as property name in the object passed to the `ProvidePlugin`) are found in a module. In other words, `ProvidePlugin` infers dependencies from the usage of global symbols.

Now let's move to the project root as the current directory and launch the `build_vendor` script we defined in the script section of the `package.json` project:

```
npm run-script build_vendor
```

Two new files are created under the `www/dist` directory, namely `vendor.js` and the associated manifest, `vendor-manifest.json`.

Let's go to `Views/Shared/_Layout` View and find the following code:

```
<environment include="Development">
    <script src="~/lib/jquery/dist/jquery.js"></script>
    ...
</environment>
<environment exclude="Development">
```

```
        ...
        <script src="~/js/site.min.js" asp-append-version="true"></script>
    </environment>
```

Replace the preceding code with the newly-created library bundle:

```
<script src="~/dist/vendor.js"></script>
```

At this point, jQuery and Bootstrap are no longer available in the global environment, and they will be executed just if a module imports them. All modules that use jQuery must import it. Accordingly, a jQuery import statement must be added to the lib/jQueryList.ts module:

```
import * as $ from "jquery";
```

Bootstrap must be imported for its side effects, and also if its functions are not referenced by any module. As a consequence, at least one module per web page must import it, so the simplest option is to place it in the root TypeScript module of each page. Accordingly, let's add a Bootstrap import statement to the modularToDoList.ts root module:

```
import 'bootstrap';
```

No symbols were specified before 'bootstrap' since Bootstrap is imported just for its side-effects and not for using its definitions.

Now it is enough to add a reference to the library bundle manifest into the webpack.config.js WebPack configuration file:

```
    ...
    module.exports = {
        ...
        plugins: [
            ...
            new webpack.DllReferencePlugin({
                context: __dirname,
                manifest: require('./wwwroot/dist/vendor-manifest.json')
            })
        ]
    };
```

The manifest property gets the library manifest, while context specifies the reference path for all modules' entry points contained in the manifest.

Try running the project—everything should work properly.

Automatic common chunk extraction – SplitChunksPlugin

`SplitChunksPlugin` does the job of automatically factoring out common chunks from various bundles. It is able to automatically extract all external libraries in separate bundles, but it is not convenient to have the overhead of bundling all library files at each build during development. Therefore, it is recommended to leave the job of bundling all external libraries to the `DllPlugin` that prepares all libraries bundle in separate build processes that may be performed just once per project.

There is no need to add `SplitChunksPlugin` to the plugins property in the configuration file, since WebPack invokes it automatically if the following configuration snippet is added to the WebPack configuration file:

```
optimization: {
    splitChunks: {
        //SplitChunksPlugin configuration here
    }
}
```

Very often, the plugin works well without any option specified because all default options were carefully conceived. The plugin has general settings, but also allows the specification of `cacheGroups` whose settings may override the general settings. Each `cacheGroup` has two properties that select whether a module is processed with the more specific settings of the group:

- `test`: A regular expression that must be satisfied by the module path. It is optional; if it is not specified, the compatibility test is always considered successful.
- `priority`: An integer. If a module satisfies the compatibility test of several cache groups, the one with the highest priority is selected. If no priority is specified, `0` is assumed.

`cacheGroups` are specified here:

```
optimization: {
    splitChunks: {
        ...
        cacheGroups: {
            myCachedGroup: {
                test:...
                priority: 1,
                ...
```

```
            },
            ...
        }
    }
}
```

There are two default `cacheGroups`:

```
optimization: {
    splitChunks: {
        cacheGroups: {
            vendors: {
                test: /[\\/]node_modules[\\/]/,
                priority: -10
            },
            default: {
                minChunks: 2,
                priority: -20,
                reuseExistingChunk: true
            }
        }
    }
}
```

They are automatically added to the `cachedGoups` list, but, if needed, they may be removed as follows:

```
cacheGroups: {
    ...
    default: false,
    ...
}
```

However, usually there is no need to remove them since they may be overridden by specifying `cacheGroups` with a higher priority.

The `vendors cacheGroups` is designed to match all external npm library modules, since the regular expression checks that they are under a `node_modules` path. Several library modules that satisfy the general settings (since `vendors cacheGroup` has no specific settings) are put together in the same chunk.

If no custom `cacheGroup` is defined, modules that fail the `vendors` test are processed with the `default` group. The `default` group contains the `minChunks: 2` option, which instructs WebPack to factor out a module from its original bundles into a new shared bundle, but only if it is shared between at least two bundles. The `reuseExistingChunk` setting may be applied just to `cacheGroups` (it may not be used as a general setting), and gives the preference to always reuse an existing chunk that already contains modules common to the same bundles instead of creating a new one.

As a default, the name of a chunk is obtained by chaining the names of all entries that share its modules with the name of the `cachedGroup` that was applied to create the chunk. As a default, names are separated by the ~ symbol. Thus, for instance, a chunk formed by extracting common modules between `bundle1`, `bundle2`, and `bundle4`, and by applying `default cachedGroup` as a default will have the name `default~bundle1~bundle2~bundle4`. The separator character may be customized through the `automaticNameDelimiter` property that may be applied either to `splitChunks` or to any `cachedGroup`.

Default names may be changed by assigning a string value to the `name` property in a specific `cachedGroup`. In this case, all modules processed by the settings of that group will be included into a unique chunk with that name. If, for instance, the following group is defined:

```
cacheGroups: {
        single_vendor: {
          name: "vendor"
          test: /[\\/]node_modules[\\/]/,
          priority: 10
        }
    }
```

Then all library modules will be placed into a unique chunk called **vendor**.

Other properties that may be applied to either `splitChunks` or just to a specific `cachedGroup` are:

- `minChunks`: The minimum number of bundles that must share some modules to factor them out in a separate chunk. The root default is 1, but the `default` group has a value of 2.
- `minSize`: Minimum size a set of modules must have to be grouped in a separate chunk. The default value is 30000.
- `maxSize`: The maximum size a chunk may have. If bigger, it is broken into smaller pieces. The default value is 0, meaning no upper limit.

- chunks: Filters the modules that are processed by SplitChunksPlugin. If its value is 'all', all modules are processed; if its value is 'async', only modules imported dynamically are processed; and if its value is 'init', only modules that are imported statically are processed. Its value may be also a function that is passed each module name, and must return true if the module must be processed and false otherwise. The default value is 'async'.
- maxInitialRequests: Maximum number of statically-imported chunks generated by each single entry. The default is 3.
- maxAsyncRequests: Maximum number of dynamically imported chunks generated by each single entry. The default is 5.

The SplitChunksPlugin algorithm tries to factor out chunks that conform with all specified constraints.

Let's try to apply SplitChunksPlugin to the DOMManipulation example already used in this section. The library modules have already been factored out by DllPlugin, so we need some shared modules to test the plugin on them. Let's create a fake.ts TypeScript file directly under wwwroot/ts directory and copy there the same content of modularToDoList.ts. This way, both fake.ts and modularToDoList.ts will share the AbstractLists.ts and plainList.ts modules. There are two shared modules, but the default group is unable to factor out these two modules since their overall size is less than 30000.

Therefore, they may be factored out only by defining a custom group, say common, that overrides the 30000 minimum size limit. Let's do it by adding the following code to webpack.config.js:

```
...
optimization: {
      splitChunks: {
          chunks: 'all',
          cacheGroups: {
              common: {
                  minChunks: 2,
                  minSize: 0
              }
          }
      }
},
...
```

Chunks set to `'all'` ensure statically-imported modules are processed. Since there are automatically-generated chunks, let's specify a different name template for chunks to distinguish them from the original entries. This can be done by adding a `chunkFilename` property to the `output` settings, as follows:

```
...
output: {
    filename: "[name].bundle.js",
    chunkFilename: "[name].chunk.js",
    path: path.join(__dirname, bundleOutputDir),
    publicPath: 'dist/'
},
...
```

A new chunk, called `common~fake~main.chunk.js`, should be generated. It is needed by the main entry bundle, so the scripts loaded by the `/Home/Index.cshtml` View must be modified as follows:

```
@section Scripts{
    <script src="~/dist/common~fake~main.chunk.js"></script>
    <script type="text/javascript" src="~/dist/main.bundle.js"></script>
}
```

Once the project is run, the `common~fake~main.chunk.js` actually appears and the to-do list works properly.

Dynamic loading

WebPack is able to process the dynamic `import(...)` function discussed in the *Dynamic module loading* subsection of Chapter 6, *Namespaces and Modules*. It replaces all calls with analogous calls performed by WebPack runtime so that modules that use the `import(...)` function become compatible with browsers that do not support that function. Several dynamically-imported modules may be grouped into unique chunks, according to the `SplitChunksPlugin` settings. In any case, the module to import is placed in a chunk that is given a name automatically by WebPack, and whose file name is determined by the `output.chunkFilename` setting. A custom name may be given by means of special comments, as follows:

```
import(/* webpackChunkName: "plainList" */ "./lib/plainList")
    .then(
        ...
    );
```

WebPack is able to process efficiently just dynamic import instructions whose module name is passed as a constant string. So if the choice among which module to load must be taken at runtime, the only solution is the usage of conditional statements that select different dynamic import instruction, each with its constant module name.

Let's modify the `DOMManipulation` example already used throughout this section to dynamically load the `./lib/plainList` module. As a first step, the TypeScript configuration file must be set to support promises and dynamic imports:

```
{
    ...,
    "compilerOptions": {
        ...,
        "module": "esnext",
        "lib": ["dom", "es5", "es2015.promise"],
        ...
    },
    ...
}
```

Then, let's open `modularToDoList.ts` and comment out the static import statement:

```
//import DOMList from "./lib/plainList"
```

Then comment out the following code at the end of the file:

```
/*
var mainList = new DOMList(
        ...
if (module.hot) {
    ...
});
*/
```

Replace the preceding code with the following:

```
import(/* webpackChunkName: "plainList" */ "./lib/plainList")
    .then(x => {
        var mainList: Abstracts.ItemList<string> = new x.default(
            document.getElementById('main_list') as HTMLElement);
        var addButton =
            document.getElementById('main_add') as HTMLElement;
        var addInput =
            document.getElementById('main_input') as HTMLElement;

        var mainGrid = new MyULAppendGrid(mainList, addButton,
            "li", addInput);
    })
```

```
        .catch(reason => {
            alert("an error occurred");
        });
```

Now run the project. The to-do list works properly and a new chunk, named
`common~fake~plainList.chunk.js`, is created. It contains just the `plainList` module
that has been factored out between the dynamic import entry named `plainList` and the
fake entry that references the same module.

Production and development configurations

In the `DOMManipulation` project used throughout this chapter, `webpack.config.js`
specifies a development profile through the `mode: "development"` setting, while the
library bundle is built with a production profile since `webpack.config.vendor.js`
specifies no `mode` setting. As a consequence, just the library bundle is minimized, while all
other chunks and bundles are not minimized. Information about the profile may be passed
either through WebPack middleware or as a WebPack parameter. In turn, the WebPack
command may be invoked with the desired parameter when the Visual Studio project is
published by hooking the publish event within the `.csproj` Visual Studio project file.

Let's use the `DOMManipulation` project we've been using. As a first step, let's modify
`webpack.config.js`. Find the following code:

```
    module.exports = {
        // WebPack settings
    };
```

Replace the preceding code with this:

```
    module.exports = (env) => {
        return {
            // the same WebPack settings as before
        }
    }
```

That is, now the configuration object, which must contain the same settings as before, is
returned by an arrow function whose unique parameter is `env`.

`env` is bound to the environment object passed in the WebPack middleware options:

```
    app.UseWebpackDevMiddleware(new WebpackDevMiddlewareOptions
    {
        HotModuleReplacement = false,
        EnvParam = new
```

```
        {
            prod = true
        }
    });
```

With the preceding WebPack middleware settings, `env` will be bound to the JavaScript object:

```
    {
        prod = true
    }
```

It may be used to select the mode:

```
    mode: env && env.prod ? "production" : "development"
```

If the project is run, all files are minimized since the WebPack `mode` has been set to `production`.

Let's reset `prod` to `false` in the WebPack middleware `EnvParam` option and run the project again to restore the development version of the whole WebPack output.

Now let's modify `DOMManipulation.csproj` in such a way that, whenever the project is published, it invokes WebPack with `env.prod` set to `true`.

Right-click on the project node in the solution explorer and choose **Edit DOMManipulation.csproj**, then add the following XML under the XML root:

```
    <Target Name="PublishRunWebpack" AfterTargets="ComputeFilesToPublish">
        <Exec Command="node node_modules/webpack/bin/webpack.js --env.prod" />
    </Target>
```

Save and close `DOMManipulation.csproj`, then select **Build | Publish DOMManipulation** and choose to publish the website in a folder. The published folder should contain the production version of all bundles.

Since JavaScript maps should not be published, the plugins WepPack setting may be replaced by:

```
    plugins: [
            new webpack.DllReferencePlugin({
                context: __dirname,
                manifest: require('./wwwroot/dist/vendor-manifest.json')
            })
        ].concat(env && env.prod ?
            [
            ] :
```

```
[
    new SourceMapDevToolPlugin({
        filename: '[file].map',
        moduleFilenameTemplate:
            path.relative(bundleOutputDir, '[resourcePath]')
    })
])
```

This way, JavaScript maps-generation is applied just during development.

 In an actual production project, one should avoid publishing in production TypeScript sources, but one should publish only the files created by WebPack. Accordingly, just the `dist` folder should be placed under `wwwroot`, since the whole content of `wwwroot` is published by visual studio.

Bundling CSS, images, and HTML

Images may be bundled with `"url-loader"`, HTML requires `"raw-loader"`, while `.css` files require `"style-loader"` and `"css-loader"` in development, but `MiniCssExtractPlugin` and `"css-loader"` in production. Moreover, CSS minimization requires `OptimizeCSSAssetsPlugin`.

Let's add all the necessary `npm` packages to `package.json` of the `DOMManipulation` project so all loaders and plugins are available in all the examples that follow:

```
{
    ...,
    "devDependencies": {
        ...
        "url-loader": "^1.0.1",
        "raw-loader": "^0.5.1",
        "css-loader": "^1.0.0",
        "style-loader": "^0.21.0",
        "mini-css-extract-plugin": "^0.4.1",
        "optimize-css-assets-webpack-plugin": "^5.0.0",
        "uglifyjs-webpack-plugin": "^1.2.7"
    },
    ...
}
```

`"uglifyjs-webpack-plugin"` has been added since the addition of the CSS minimizer resets WebPack default minimization settings, so it is necessary to manually add a JavaScript minimizer plugin too.

The subsection that follows analyzes how to use all the preceding loaders and plugins through simple examples based on the DOMManipulation project.

Bundling images

url-loader bundles images and returns their URL as a result of importing them. If the image size exceeds the limit parameter of the loader, it is bundled and put in the WebPack output directory; otherwise, the image is inserted online in the URL. Let's bundle and use the "wwroot/images/Banner2.svg" image of the project.

As a first step, let's declare that images must be processed with url-loader in the WebPack configuration file by adding the following declaration in the modulle.rules array of both webpack.config.js and webpack.config.vendor.js:

```
{
    test: /\.(png|woff|woff2|eot|ttf|jpg|jpeg|gif|svg)$/,
    use: 'url-loader?limit=10000'
}
```

url-loader has also been added to the library WebPack configuration file since it is needed to process CSS files that contain references to images/fonts, and a further subsection will move library CSS into the library WebPack configuration.

Next, let's import the "wwroot/images/Banner2.svg" image in the "modularToDoList.ts" module:

```
...
import 'bootstrap';
var banner = require("../images/banner2.svg");
...
```

The image must be imported with Node.js require instead of import, otherwise TypeScript complains that "../images/banner2.svg" is not a module.

Next, add the following code just before the dynamic import instruction:

```
...
(document.getElementById("banner") as HTMLImageElement).src = banner as
string;
import(/* webpackChunkName: "plainList" */ "./lib/plainList")
...
```

Finally, let's add an image tag in the `"Views/Home/Index.cshtml"` View, just after the page header:

```
...
<h1>@ViewData["Title"]</h1>
<img src="" id="banner"/>
...
```

When you run the project, the image appears. Since there are no new chunks, the image has been converted into an in-line URL format.

Bundling HTML

`raw-loader` imports HTML or any of the text file as a string. Let's declare HTML files must be processed with `raw-loader` in the WebPack configuration file by adding the declaration in the following `modulle.rules` array in `webpack.config.js`:

```
{ test: /\.html$/, use: 'raw-loader' }
```

Then let's create a folder named `"html"` under `"wwwroot"` and add an HTML file named `"item_template.html"` under this new folder. Open `"item_template.html"`, clear its default content, and place the following code inside of it:

```
<li class="list-group-item">
    <button type="button" class="btn btn-sm" title="remove">
        <span class="glyphicon glyphicon-minus" aria-hidden="true">
        </span>
    </button>
    <span>-par0-</span>
</li>
```

`"item_template.html"` will be used as the HTML template for creating new to-do items.

Finally, open `"modularToDoList.ts"` and import the new HTML file:

```
var banner = require("../images/banner2.svg");
var template = require("../html/item_template.html");
```

Then replace the `itemTemplate` method of `MyULAppendGrid` with the following code:

```
itemTemplate(str: string): HTMLElement {
    let toAdd =
        (template as string).replace("-par0-", str);
    let temp = document.createElement('ul');
    temp.innerHTML = toAdd;
```

```
        return temp.firstChild as HTMLElement;
}
```

When the project is run, no new chunk appears since the HTML page is bundled within `main.bundle.js`.

Bundling CSS

The `css-loader` property is similar to `raw-loader` since it imports a CSS file as a string, but it does something more: it parses the file to resolve all references to other files (such as `@import` statements), thus returning a unique string containing all style information. It may be used as it is if the application needs to process manually, but usually it is chained with other loaders to get the CSS directly in the web page. There are two options:

- Inserting automatically all styles within a `style` tag in the web page that includes the JavaScript file importing the CSS. The style-loader does this job. This is the recommended option in development mode, since it supports Hot Module Replacement, so if HMR is on, then changes to CSS files are applied immediately to the web page being rendered by the browser.
- Outputting the CSS in one ore more files (according to the `splitChunks` settings). This is the recommended option for production, and starting from WebPack 4, the recommended tool for this option is `MiniCssExtractPlugin`.

The preceding tools and options will be described by applying them to the our `DOMManipulation` project.

As a first step, let's bundle all CSS contained in the library packages. The only CSS needed by the project is Bootstrap CSS. Let's open `webpack.config.vendor.js` and add Bootstrap CSS to all entries:

```
entry: {
        vendor: ['bootstrap', 'jquery',
            'bootstrap/dist/css/bootstrap.css'],
}
```

Since all library files are needed just in the production version, the right option is the second option with `MiniCssExtractPlugin`. So let's require it just after the instruction that requires the `webapack` module, as shown in the following code:

```
const webpack = require('webpack');
const MiniCssExtractPlugin = require("mini-css-extract-plugin");
```

Let's also require JavaScript and the CSS minifier, which are needed to configure minification:

```
const MiniCssExtractPlugin = require("mini-css-extract-plugin");
const OptimizeCSSAssetsPlugin = require("optimize-css-assets-webpack-plugin");
const UglifyJsPlugin = require("uglifyjs-webpack-plugin");
```

Now let's add the `MiniCssExtractPlugin` plugin to the already existing `plugins` array in the configuration object:

```
new MiniCssExtractPlugin({
    filename: "[name].css",
    chunkFilename: "[id].css",
    publicPath:"./"
 })
```

Both `filename` and `chunkFilename` must be specified. They have the same meaning as the analogous properties of the `output` main configuration setting, but applied to all CSS files.

Now it is time to add all the loaders that must process CSS files to the `module.rules` array. The object to append to the existing array is:

```
{
    test: /\.css$/,
    use: [
        {
            loader: MiniCssExtractPlugin.loader,
            options: {
                publicPath: './'
            }
        },
        "css-loader"
    ]
}
```

CSS files are loaded by `css-loader` and then processed by `MiniCssExtractPlugin.loader`, which is part of the the `MiniCssExtractPlugin` package.

The `publicPath` option specifies the relative path (relative to the created CSS bundle) where to look for external assets (images and fonts). Since assets are processed by the `url-loader` plugin and inserted in the same directory of all CSS bundles, this relative path must be `./`.

Finally, let's add minimization settings. In WebPack 4, the minimization plugins must be placed in the dedicated `optimization.minimizer` array, as shown in the following:

```
optimization: {
    minimizer: [
        new UglifyJsPlugin(),
        new OptimizeCSSAssetsPlugin({})
    ]
}
```

JavaScript is minimized as a default in production mode, but if the `optimization.minimizer` array is redefined then this default setting is lost, so a JavaScript minimizer must also be added.

Now everything is ready for rebuilding the library bundles. Let's ensure that the project root is the current directory and launch `npm run-script build_vendor`. A new `vendor.css` file appears in the "`dist`" folder together with some fonts references by the processed CSS.

Let's replace the old CSS library settings in the `_Layout` View with this new file:

```
<environment include="Development">
    <link rel="stylesheet" href="~/lib/bootstrap/dist/css/bootstrap.css" />
    <link rel="stylesheet" href="~/css/site.css" />
</environment>
<environment exclude="Development">
    ...
</environment>
```

Replace the preceding code with this:

```
<link href="~/dist/vendor.css" rel="stylesheet" />
<link rel="stylesheet" href="~/css/site.css" />
```

Everything should work properly.

Let's do the same job with the main WebPack configuration file. However, in this case, the configuration file must handle both development and production mode. The production settings are completely analogous to the ones of `webpack.config.vendor.js`, but in development mode there are some differences:

- The `optimization.minimizer` array must be empty
- `MiniCssExtractPlugin` must not be included in the `plugins` array
- CSS loaders are now `['style-loader', 'css-loader']`

The overall WebPack configuration follows:

```
const path = require("path");
const webpack = require('webpack');
const SourceMapDevToolPlugin = webpack.SourceMapDevToolPlugin;
const bundleOutputDir = "./wwwroot/dist";
const baseUrl = path.join(__dirname, "wwwroot");
const MiniCssExtractPlugin = require("mini-css-extract-plugin");
const OptimizeCSSAssetsPlugin = require("optimize-css-assets-webpack-
plugin");
const UglifyJsPlugin = require("uglifyjs-webpack-plugin");
module.exports = (env) => {
    return {
        entry: {
            main: "./wwwroot/ts/modularToDoList",
            fake: "./wwwroot/ts/fake"
        },
        output: {
            filename: "[name].bundle.js",
            chunkFilename: "[name].chunk.js",
            path: path.join(__dirname, bundleOutputDir),
            publicPath: 'dist/'
        },
        resolve: {
            extensions: ['.js', '.ts']
        },
        optimization: {
            minimizer: env && env.prod ? [
                new UglifyJsPlugin(),
                new OptimizeCSSAssetsPlugin({})
            ] : [],
            splitChunks: {
                chunks: 'all',
                cacheGroups: {
                    common: {
                        minChunks: 2,
                        minSize: 0
                    }
                }
            }
        },
        mode: env && env.prod ? "production" : "development",
        //devtool: "source-map"
        module: {
            rules: [
                { test: /\.ts$/, use: 'awesome-typescript-loader' },
                { test: /\.html$/, use: 'raw-loader' },
                {
```

```
                    test: /\.(png|woff|woff2|eot|ttf|jpg|jpeg|gif|svg)$/,
                    use: 'url-loader?limit=10000'
                },
                {
                    test: /\.css$/,
                    sideEffects: true,
                    use: env && env.prod ? [
                        {
                            loader: MiniCssExtractPlugin.loader,
                            options: {
                                publicPath: './'
                            }
                        },
                        "css-loader"
                    ] : ['style-loader', 'css-loader']
                }
            ]
        },
        plugins: [

            new webpack.DllReferencePlugin({
                context: __dirname,
                manifest: require('./wwwroot/dist/vendor-manifest.json')
            })
        ].concat(env && env.prod ?
            [
                new MiniCssExtractPlugin({
                    filename: "[name].css",
                    chunkFilename: "[id].css"
                })
            ] :
            [

                new SourceMapDevToolPlugin({
                    // Remove the line below if you prefer inline source
maps
                    filename: '[file].map',
                    // Point sourcemap entries to the original file
locations on disk
                    moduleFilenameTemplate: path.relative(bundleOutputDir,
'[resourcePath]')
                })
            ])
    };
};
```

`site.css` must be imported in `modularToDoList.ts` in order to be processed by WebPack:

```
import "../css/site.css";
```

When assets are bundled in production mode, a new file named `main.css` is created, while in development mode the style settings are inserted directly in the web page. Thus, the _Layout View must reference `main.css` when in production mode:

```
<link rel="stylesheet" href="~/css/site.css" />
```

Replace the preceding code with the following:

```
<environment exclude="Development">
        <link rel="stylesheet" href="~/dist/main.css"
              asp-append-version="true" />
</environment>
```

Now let's run the project with the following WebPack middleware settings:

```
app.UseWebpackDevMiddleware(new WebpackDevMiddlewareOptions
{
    HotModuleReplacement = true,
    EnvParam = new
    {
        prod = false
    }
});
```

The program doesn't run since the bundling process creates the new `vendors~main.chunk.js` that has not been referenced.

Why? Simple: WebPack added some code to support Hot Module Replacement and the automatic addition of processed styles to the web page in the `main` bundle, and since this code is part of the `npm` packages it triggers `vendor cacheGroup`, which factors this library code out into this new chunk.

This chunk appears just in development mode, so it is enough to modify the scripts called by `Views/Home/Index.csstml`:

```
@section Scripts{
    <script src="~/dist/common~fake~main.chunk.js"></script>
    <environment include="Development">
        <script src="~/dist/vendors~main.chunk.js"
                asp-append-version="true"></script>
    </environment>
    <script type="text/javascript" src="~/dist/main.bundle.js"></script>
}
```

At this point, everything should work properly. Run the project, open `wwwroot/css/site.css`, and add this CSS rule:

```
input{
    background-color: yellow !important;
}
```

As soon as the file is saved, the input field to add a new to-do item becomes immediately yellow, thanks to Hot Module Replacement!

Summary

WebPack is able to to bundle several JavaScript files together with their dependencies in a single JavaScript file called a bundle. Each entry can specify one or more root files that are bundled together with all their dependencies. It is compatible with most browsers, supports all module systems, and uses the various import and dynamic import statements. ASP.NET Core provides the `Microsoft.AspNetCore.SpaServices` Nuget package, which contains a WebPack middleware that can be used to automatically invoke a WebPack build when the program starts, and to start/enable/configure various WebPack features.

Non-JavaScript files are supported through loaders that transform them into JavaScript code before passing them to the WebPack bundling algorithm. Loaders also allow the processing of HTML files that may be imported as strings into any JavaScript/TypeScript file, and images that are imported as URLs while simultaneously WebPack move the images in its output directory. If the image size is below a configurable size limit, they are converted into a URL format and no image is added to the WebPack output. Loaders are also able to bundle and minify interconnected CSS files.

WebPack plugins hook and modify the WebPack bundling process. They may be used to modify the way source maps are generated (needed to ensure compatibility with Visual Studio debugger) and to perform file-minification and bundle-optimization. `DllPlugin` allows library files to be bundled in a separate build whose result may be recalled by the main build. `SplitChunksPlugin` instead factors out modules that are common to various bundles into separate chunks.

WebPack may be informed whether it was invoked for development or production either by WebPack middleware or with a parameter on the command line. This information is used to set WebPack mode and to choose between alternative loaders or plugins. For instance, usually minification is applied just in production mode, while source maps are generated just in development mode. WebPack may be invoked automatically in production mode when a web application is published by hooking a WebPack build on the publish event in the Visual Studio project file.

Questions

1. How many entries are needed in `Webpack.Config.js` to get three separate bundles that reference a total of 30 dependencies?
2. Is it possible to use dynamic `import()` on target browsers that do not support it by using WebPack? Why? If yes, are there limitations?
3. How does one configure `Webpack.Config.js` to receive information on the environment it was called in (production or development)?
4. Is it possible to bundle completely independent files?
5. How does one enable Hot Module Replacement in ASP.NET Core projects?
6. Which plugins may be used to optimize bundles with WebPack 4?
7. Why is the style-loader recommended during development?
8. How does one automatically invoke WebPack in production mode when an ASP.NET Core application is published?
9. What is needed to make WebPack-created source maps compatible with the Visual Studio debugger?
10. Which configuration property must be customized to ensure modules are factored out in separated chunks only if they are common to at least three entries (in other words, to three main bundles)? What is the default name of a chunk factored out from three entries called: `bundle1`, `bundle2`, or `bundle3`?

Further reading

While this chapter provided a comprehensive description of WebPack that enables the reader to use WebPack in the most common situations, not all WebPack options, plugins, and loaders were analyzed. However, the comprehension acquired by the readers should enable them to easily find and understand other options, plugins, and loaders they might need in WebPack's official documentation: `https://webpack.js.org/concepts/`. All official plugins are listed and documented at `https://webpack.js.org/plugins/`, while all official loaders are listed at `https://webpack.js.org/loaders/`.

This chapter discusses how to enable Hot Module Replacement through ASP.NET Core WebPack middleware. Hot Module Replacement may be used without the help of ASP.NET Core and Visual Studio, as discussed in this guide: `https://webpack.js.org/guides/hot-module-replacement/`.

8
Building TypeScript Libraries

This chapter explains how to build and test a TypeScript library that may be reused in several projects. This chapter also introduces **Visual Studio Code** (**VS Code**), which is an advanced code editor powered with IntelliSense and debugging. VS Code is more flexible than the predefined Visual Studio project templates when working with TypeScript/JavaScript projects. Finally, the chapter shows how to use a well-known TypeScript/JavaScript testing framework—Jasmine.

More specifically, the following topics will be covered in the chapter:

- How to use VS Code
- How to write and package a TypeScript library with VS Code
- How to set up a testing environment based on Jasmine
- How to organize, write, and launch tests based on Jasmine

Technical requirements

We need the following tools and packages in this chapter:

- Node.js and `npm` package manager
- VS Code

Node.js and `npm` are both contained in Node.js installation packages, which you may find at `https://nodejs.org/en/`. Please select the recommended version and follow the simple steps contained at the beginning of the *Installation of Node.js-based TypeScript compiler* subsection of `Chapter 1`, *Introduction to TypeScript*, in order to verify that both Node.js and `npm` were properly installed.

The VS Code installer may be found at `https://code.visualstudio.com/`. Please download it, run the installer, and follow the simple installation instructions.

All the code used in this chapter can be downloaded from the following GitHub link: `https://github.com/PacktPublishing/Hands-On-TypeScript-for-CSharp-and-.NET-Core-Developers`.

Check out the following video to see the Code in Action: `http://bit.ly/2qql5HL`.

Using VS Code

VS Code is a light and powerful code editor that offers IntelliSense, debugging, source control, task definitions, and other useful features. Different from Visual Studio, VS Code projects do not need a project file to organize all project files or decide how to process the whole project. A VS Code project just consists of all files contained in a folder, and the developers may choose themselves which tools to use to process all the project files and how to configure them. This feature offers great flexibility when developing projects based entirely on TypeScript/JavaScript, since the developer is not constrained by a specific project template but instead may choose the most adequate JavaScript tools for their projects from the thousands of tools available as open source.

This section explores VS Code basics. More specific VS code features will be analyzed in the subsequent sections that cover the various steps involved in the implementation of a TypeScript library.

Let's create a new folder named `domlist` that contains another folder called `sources`. Then add the `AbstractLists.ts`, `plainList.ts`, and `jQueryList.ts` files from the `DOMManipulation` project used throughout Chapter 7, *Bundling with WebPack*, to the recently created `sources` folder. The idea is to group these files in a DOM manipulation library that may be reused in several projects. Since a lot of projects will depend on this library, it is worth submitting it to exhaustive testing. Therefore, later in this chapter, a testing framework will be added to the project.

The `domlist` folder defines the boundary of the VS Code project. Right-click on the `domlist` folder and select **Open with Code**. VS Code will open, and after clicking on the `AbstractLists.ts` file on the left pane, the editor should look like the following screenshot:

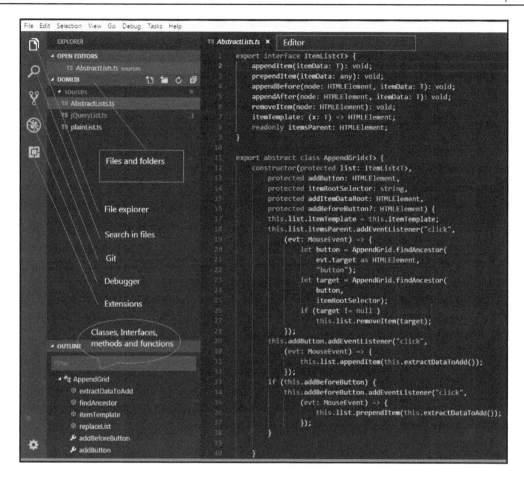

The right pane contains the currently opened files, while the left pane shows all files and folders in the project. The right pane contains a tab for each opened file that may be used to select the one displayed in the editor.

On the left pane under **OPEN EDITORS**, there is a list of all opened files. DOMLIB is the project folder. All project files are shown under the DOMLIB name. Next to the DOMLIB name, there are four buttons:

- One for creating a new file
- Another for creating a new folder
- Then a button for refreshing the file tree
- Finally, a button for collapsing all opened folders of the file tree

Files and folders are created under the currently selected folder, or, if no folder is selected, on the project root. Right-clicking on each filename opens a menu that allows all usual file operations, such as renaming and deleting.

Under **OUTLINE** there is an outline of what is shown in the editor. In the case of TypeScript files, these are classes, methods, and functions defined in the file. Clicking each item in the outline takes the cursor to the editor area where the item is defined.

The left pane contains five tabs that select the content of the left pane itself. As a default the first tab, which displays all files, is selected. The fifth tab displays a list of VS Code extensions that it is possible to install. The fourth tab opens a debug window, while the third pane allows source control operations in case the project folder has been put under Git source control.

Finally, clicking the second tab opens a search in files content. The same content may be selected with the edit item in the topmost menu. The topmost menu also contains a file menu that allows various file operations, and that also contains the **Preferences** sub-item that allows the customization of both user-level preferences and project-level preferences. Later on, preferences will be modified to change the TypeScript version VS Code uses for IntelliSense.

The **Go** item allows navigation among lines, opened windows, symbol definitions, and so on.

The **Debug** item contains all the usual debugger commands that are typically invoked through the equivalent keyboard commands (F10, F11, and so on).

The **Task** menu allows the definition and invocation of VS Code tasks. Later on in this chapter, some tasks will be defined for debugging and testing the code.

Finally the **Help** item, as usual, allows access to product information, documentation, community links, and issue reporting.

The upper-right corner of the right pane contains the split button.

Clicking this button splits the editor area into two editors, so two opened files may be displayed simultaneously.

Going to the **View** menu and selecting either **Integrated Terminal**, **Debug Console**, **Problems**, or **Output** opens the following new pane, at the bottom of the right pane:

The new pane contains four tabs that select four functionalities. The rightmost tab selects an integrated window console that is typically used to issue npm and Node.js commands. On the left is the tab that selects the debugger console, then a generic output window. Finally, the **PROBLEMS** tab lists all current problems/errors discovered in the project. In our case, no definitions were found for the jQuery module referenced by the jQueryList.ts. This is a TypeScript error message since the code has not yet been run. Thus, what is actually missing is the jQuery TypeScript declaration file.

The error may be fixed by installing the @types/jquery NPM package containing all jQuery TypeScript declarations. As a first step, let's add a package.json file in the project root by clicking the **Add New File** button, writing package.json in the textbox that opens, and then hitting the return key in package.json adds the following packages:

```
{
  "private": true,
  "devDependencies": {
  "@types/jquery": "^3.3.5",
  "jquery": "^3.3.1",
  "typescript": "^3.0.1"
  },
  "scripts": {
  "compile": "tsc"
  }
}
```

Together with `jquery` declarations, jQuery implementation and TypeScript compiler were also added. The jQuery implementation was added because it is needed to test the library, but it was included among `devDependencies` instead of `dependencies` because the library may also work without jQuery, so it is not obligatory for any project that uses the library to install jQuery.

TypeScript compiler must be installed because VS Code natively contains just TypeScript IntelliSense and not a whole TypeScript compiler. The compile script has been defined because VS Code natively doesn't automatically invoke the TypeScript compiler, either on each file save or on any other event.

Let's save all pending changes by choosing **Save All** from the **Files** menu. Commands can also be launched using a shortcut that depends on the operating system. The right shortcut for each menu item is shown in the menu item itself. The shortcut for the **Save All** command under Windows is *Ctrl + S*.

Installation of all packages is not performed automatically when saving `package.json`, but must be invoked manually by hitting the `npm install` command in the VS Code internal terminal.

Packages can be also installed by issuing the following command for each of them from a command console rooted in the project folder:

```
npm install <package name>@<package version>
```

Packages installed this way are automatically added to the `dependencies` section of the project `package.json`. If you want to add a package to the `devDependencies` section, you must add the `-D` option:

```
npm install <package name>@<package version> -D
```

Building your library

Before compiling the library, we must decide which files to distribute, where to place them, and then we must define an adequate `tsconfig.json`. TypeScript libraries usually don't distribute TypeScript sources, but distribute the transpiled JavaScript together with TypeScript declaration files.

The main reasons for directly publishing the JavaScript files are as follows:

- The original TypeScript usually needs different `tsconfig.json` settings (possibly different compiler settings or possibly a different TypeScript compiler version)
- Libraries might need to be processed by processors such as Webpack before being ready for an easy usage

Usually, all files to be distributed are placed in a directory called `dist`. A TypeScript configuration file such as the following should do the job:

```
{
    "compilerOptions": {
        "noImplicitAny": true,
        "strictNullChecks": true,
        "noEmitOnError": true,
        "removeComments": false,
        "sourceMap": true,
        "target": "es5",
        "module": "es6",
        "rootDir":"sources",
        "outDir": "dist",
        "declaration": true,
        "moduleResolution": "Node"
    },
    "include": [
        "sources/**/*.ts"
    ]
}
```

Let's create a `tsconfig.ts` file in the project root and place the proceeding code into it. Save the file and then launch compilation by issuing the `npm run-script compile` command in the VS Code internal console. All output files should be created properly.

However, before continuing there is a small issue to fix. If a TypeScript file is opened, the bottom-right corner of the editor shows the TypeScript version used by VS Code IntelliSense:

It is not the same version used to actually compile all TypeScript files! We should fix this to avoid inconsistency. Let's go to **File** | **Preferences** | **Settings**. Two windows open in the right pane. The left window contains default settings while the right window contains two tabs, one for user settings and the other for project (workspace) preferences.

User preferences override default preferences and apply to all user projects, while project (workspace) preferences override user settings and apply only to the current project. Workspace preferences are saved in a `settings.json` file that is automatically created under a `.vscode` folder.

We need to change the VS Code IntelliSense version to match the TypeScript version installed in the project. The place to change this setting is **workspace settings**. Add the following setting that defines the location of all TypeScript libraries of the TypeScript compiler installed in the project:

```
{
    "typescript.tsdk": "./node_modules/typescript/lib"
}
```

Then open any TypeScript file and click on the old TypeScript version number in the bottom right of the editor. A textbox with a list of TypeScript libraries under it opens. Click on `./node_modules/typescript/lib`. The version in the bottom-right corner should update. Recompile all files. Now a first version of the library is ready.

Packaging your library as an npm package

Libraries may be organized as `npm` packages. More fields can be added to `package.json`. However, `npm` packages usually export a unique module that allows access to the whole library. It is easy to fulfill this constraint by adding an `index.ts` module that re-exports all other modules, in the `sources` folder:

```
//index.ts
export * from "./AbstractLists";
export { default as jQueryList} from "./jQueryList";
export { default as plainList} from "./plainList";
```

Save the file and recompile the library with `npm run-script compile`.

Now five more fields can be added in `package.json`, namely, the following:

- `name`: The library name, which should be the same name as the project folder.
- `description`: A description of the library. It is displayed by IntelliSense when the library is added to `package.json` of any project.
- `version`: A version number in the `x.y.z` format. Version numbers should conform to the so-called **semantic versioning** (see `https://semver.org/`). A version change involves a `z` increment if only backward-compatible bug fixes are introduced. A version change involves a `y` increment if some new, backward-compatible functionality is introduced to the public API. Backward-incompatible changes must cause an `x` increment. In the package references, if a library is referred to as `"jquery": "3.3.1"`, then exactly that version is installed, and if that version is not compatible with other packages, a failure is reported. If a library is referred to as `"jquery": "^3.3.1"` instead, the reference matches any 3.x.y version different from 3.0.0. Finally, if a library is referred to as `"jquery": "~3.3.1"`, the reference matches any 3.3.y version different from 3.3.0.
- `main`: The path of the package's main module (in our case `dist/index.js`).
- `types`: The path to the declaration file associated with the package's main module (in our case `dist/index.d.ts`).

After adding these fields, `package.json` becomes:

```
{
    "name": "domlist",
    "description": "DOM list manipulation",
    "version": "1.0.0",
    "main": "dist/index.js",
    "types":"dist/index.d.ts",
    "devDependencies": {
        "@types/jquery": "^3.3.5",
        "typescript": "^3.0.1",
        "jquery": "^3.3.1"
    },
    "scripts": {
        "compile": "tsc"
    }
}
```

After these modifications, the package may be published in the public npm repository, or used in a private network/computer by referring to it through its filename in other package.json files, as shown in the following code:

```
{
  ...
  dependencies{
  ...
  "domlist": "file:../libraries/domlist"
  ...
  }
  ...
}
```

A package can be published on the public npm repository by first creating an account on the npm directory (https://www.npmjs.com/) and then launching the npm publish command from a console window rooted in the package folder. The first time you do it from a computer you will be asked for your credentials, then these credentials are stored for future use.

Installing a test framework – Jasmine

The simplest way to test a TypeScript library is by running all tests in Node.js, since it may work without a web server and a browser. Another advantage of running tests in Node.js is that library packages installed with npm, such as jQuery, may work as they are, while browser-based testing would require the use of a bundler since browsers do not support the Node.js-based module resolution algorithm required by npm packages.

On the other hand, tests that succeed under Node.js might fail on some browsers due to compatibility problems, so when Node.js testing is chosen, some browser-based compatibility tests on all dangerous features that might not be supported by all browsers are required.

Browser-based testing will be applied to Angular projects as described in the *Testing* section of Chapter 13, *Navigation and Services*. This and the next sections are dedicated to Node.js-based testing and debugging.

Since Node.js has no DOM, a library that mocks the DOM, such as `jsdom`, must be installed together with the chosen testing framework, that is, Jasmine, and together with all respective TypeScript type definitions. Some more `npm` commands for compiling and running the test must be added:

```
{
    ...
    "devDependencies": {
        ...
        "jasmine": "^3.2.0",
        "@types/jasmine": "^2.8.8",
        "jsdom": "^11.12.0",
        "@types/jsdom": "11.0.6"
    },
    "scripts": {
        "compile": "tsc",
        "compile_tests": "tsc --project tsconfig.tests.json",
        "init_tests": "jasmine init",
        "tests": "jasmine"
    }
}
```

Save `package.json`, and run `npm install` to install all new packages. Now, `compile_test` will compile all tests with a different TypeScript configuration file. The `init_test` command is to be run just once to prepare the project for the use of Jasmine, and, finally, `test` runs all tests using the information contained in a Jasmine configuration file.

Let's launch `npm run-script init_tests` to scaffold Jasmine files and folders. A `spec` folder to include all tests is created. This folder also contains the Jasmine configuration file:

```
{
  "spec_dir": "spec",
  "spec_files": [
    "**/*[sS]pec.js"
  ],
  "helpers": [
    "helpers/**/*.js"
  ],
  "stopSpecOnExpectationFailure": false,
  "random": true
}
```

It defines the directory containing all tests and the type of file to be considered a test (all of those ending with Spec.js). Then, all possible helper JavaScript files must be loaded before running the tests (as a default all of those contained in the helpers folder under the spec folder). Finally, setting stopSpecOnExpectationFailure to false prevents tests from stopping at the first failure, and random set to true forces tests to be chosen at random to prevent any interference among the various tests.

Let's also define a specSources folder for the TypeScript sources of all tests and the tsconfig.tests.json TypeScript configuration file for the compilation of all tests:

```
{
    "compilerOptions": {
        "noImplicitAny": true,
        "strictNullChecks": true,
        "noEmitOnError": true,
        "removeComments": false,
        "sourceMap": true,
        "target": "es5",
        "module": "commonjs",
        "rootDir":"specSources",
        "outDir": "spec",
        "moduleResolution": "Node"
    },
    "include": [
        "specSources/**/*.ts"
    ]
}
```

The preceding file compiles specSources into spec. It has "module" set to "commonjs", because Node.js doesn't support ES6 modules. The same setting must be changed also in tsconfig.json, in order to test the library under Node.js. Then, before the library release, the setting may be reset to es6.

It is also worth defining VS Code commands that launch both the compilation of the library files and the compilation of all test files. This can be done as follows:

- Defining a VS Code task that launches library compilation
- Defining a VS Code task that launches test compilation
- Defining a task that invokes all previous tasks

Let's go to **Terminal** | **Configure Tasks**. A textbox with a list opens on the top of the edit pane. Select `npm: compilation`. A VS Code task for invoking library compilation is created. Let's give it the label `"library compilation"`:

```
{
    "label": "library compilation",
    "type": "npm",
    "script": "compile",
    "problemMatcher": []
}
```

Let's define two more tasks in `"tasks.json"`, to get the following:

```
"tasks": [
    {
        "label": "library compilation",
        "type": "npm",
        "script": "compile",
        "problemMatcher": []
    },
    {
        "label": "test ompilation",
        "type": "npm",
        "script": "compile_tests",
        "problemMatcher": []
    },
    {
        "label": "Build",
        "dependsOn": ["library compilation", "test ompilation"]
    }
]
```

The `"Build"` task invokes both compilations. We may invoke it by selecting **Task** | **Run Task** and by selecting **Build** in the list under the textbox.

Now we are ready to cope with library tests.

Testing your library with Jasmine

In Jasmine, tests are organized into test suites. Each test suite is defined with a call to the `describe` function that accepts two arguments, a string containing a description of the suite, and an arrow function whose body contains all tests of the suite.

In turn, each test is defined by calling the `it` function that accepts two arguments, a string containing a description of the test, and an arrow function whose body contains the code that defines the test. Thus, each test suite looks like the following:

```
describe("this is a test suite", () =>{
    it("this is test 1", () =>{
        //test code
        ...
        //test assertion
        expect(<an expression here).toBe(5);
    });
    ...
    it("this is test n", () =>{
        ....
    });
});
```

Each test contains at least one call to `expect` that compares an actual value obtained by using the library to test (`expect` unique argument) with an expected value (in the preceding example the argument of the `toBe` function). The `toBe` function tests for equality, but there are other functions that perform a lot of useful comparisons. The body of the `describe` function may also contain a call to four different functions, each accepting an arrow function with no arguments. They help to set up the environment before the execution of the tests and clearing it after tests are executed, which are the following:

- `beforeEach`: The arrow function it defines is called before executing each test
- `afterEach`: The arrow function it defines is called after executing each test
- `beforeAll`: The arrow function it defines is called before executing the whole test suite
- `afterAll`: The arrow function it defines is called after executing the whole test suite

 Tests that contain asynchronous calls are supported by a different overload of the `it` function whose arrow function accepts a `done` callback to be invoked with no arguments, when the asynchronous calls return. The same overload also accepts a timeout as its third argument. There are analogous overloads for the `beforeEach`, `afterEach`, `beforeAll`, and `afterAll` functions.

At this point, we should be ready to write tests for the `domlist` library.

Writing domlist library tests

Let's create a file named `plainDomSpec.ts` under the `specSources` folder. It will contain tests of the plain TypeScript implementation of the `ItemList<T>` interface. As a first step, let's import the `domlist` library and the DOM mock previously installed through npm:

```
import * as DOMLIST from "../dist/index"
import * as VDOM from "jsdom"
```

It is worth pointing out that the `domlist` library must be imported from the `dist` distribution folder that contains all target files, and not from the folder containing all library sources since we are simulating a normal usage of the library. For the same reason, we must import the `index` library root module.

Then we must define all preparation code contained in the `beforeEach`, `afterEach`, `beforeAll`, and `afterAll` functions:

```
describe("plain list specifications", () =>{
    let dom: VDOM.JSDOM;
    let listRoot: HTMLElement;
    let list: DOMLIST.plainList<string>;
    let childId: string|null;

    beforeAll(()=>{
        dom = new VDOM.JSDOM("<div id='me'></div>");
        listRoot = dom.window.document.getElementById('me') as HTMLElement;
        list = new DOMLIST.plainList<string>(listRoot);
        list.itemTemplate = s => {
            var res = dom.window.document.createElement("div");
            if(childId != null) res.setAttribute("id", childId);
            res.appendChild(dom.window.document.createTextNode(s));
            return res;
        };
    });
    beforeEach(()=>{
        listRoot.innerHTML="";
    });
});
```

All variables used to share objects between `beforeAll` and `beforeEach`, and the tests must be placed at the beginning of the `describe` function body. The `beforeAll` function creates a mock DOM and places it in the `dom` variable, then extracts the node that will be the root of the list and places it in `listRoot`. Then it creates an implementation of `ItemList<T>` and attaches it to an item template function to enable all `ItemList<T>` operations. The`beforeEach` function clears the list before a new test starts.

Finally, we may add two tests. The first tests the addition operation, and the second tests a delete operation executed immediately after an addition:

```
it("addition", () =>{
  childId="child1";
  list.appendItem("test");
  var added = dom.window.document
  .getElementById(childId) as HTMLElement;

  expect(added).not.toBeNull();
  expect(added.innerHTML).toBe("test");
  expect(listRoot.childNodes.length).toBe(1);

});
it("addition and delete", () =>{
  childId="child1";
  list.appendItem("test");
  var added = dom.window.document
  .getElementById(childId) as HTMLElement;

  list.removeItem(added);
  expect(listRoot.childNodes.length).toBe(0);

});
```

The `not` property of `expect` executes a JavaScript negation of the `expect` argument, so `expect(added).not.toBeNull()` is a not null test. The remainder of the code should be self-explanatory.

Let's run the `Build` task and then launch all tests with the `npm run-script test` command in the internal terminal.

All tests succeed! However, if some tests fail, we need to debug the code, as explained in the next section.

There is also a VS Code extension called *Jasmine Test Explorer for VS Code* (`https://marketplace.visualstudio.com/items?itemName=hbenl.vscode-jasmine-test-adapter`), which furnishes a helpful user interface for running Jasmine tests and for listing their results. From there, a single test may be launched and debugged.

Debugging tests

Let's click the debugger tab in the left pane. Next to the play button, there is a select box complaining that no debugger configuration has been defined. Click the select box and choose **Add Configuration...**:

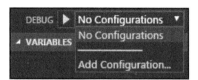

In the page that opens in the editor, replace the proposed configuration with the following:

```
{
            "type": "node",
            "request": "launch",
            "name": "Debug tests",
            "program":
"${workspaceFolder}/node_modules/jasmine/bin/jasmine.js",
            "preLaunchTask": "Build",
            "outFiles": [
                "${workspaceFolder}/dist/**/*.js",
                "${workspaceFolder}/spec/**/*.js"
            ]
        }
```

The first two properties simply say that debugger is required to launch a JavaScript file in Node.js. Now, `name` is the name of the configuration. The `program` keyword specifies the path to the JavaScript file to launch, in our case Jasmine. The `preLaunchTask` function specifies a task to execute before launching the debugger. In our case, we launch the `Build` task that compiles both the library and all tests.

Finally, `outFiles` contains the path of all folders containing JavaScript files that might be involved in the debugging. We must specify the final target files that are actually executed, not the TypeScript sources or other intermediary files. In fact, the debugger may reach the sources from the targets through the map files, but it can't do the reverse operation.

Now debugger is ready to run, so let's open the `plainList.ts` file and place a breakpoint in the `appendItem` method. Then launch the debugger. After a little time, the breakpoint is actually hit!

Summary

VS Code gives more flexibility than Visual Studio in organizing pure TypeScript/JavaScript projects. VS Code supports natively TypeScript IntelliSense, but the TypeScript compiler must be installed with npm. TypeScript IntelliSense must be configured to match the same version of the installed TypeScript compiler. All build tasks may be organized both with the help of npm scripts defined in the package.json file and with VS Code tasks. Debugger must be configured by specifying the hosting environment (Node.js), the JavaScript file to launch, and all folders containing JavaScript files that might be involved in the program execution. It is also possible to define some tasks to launch before starting the debug (usually a complete build).

TypeScript libraries must have a distribution folder containing both the JavaScript distribution together with the associated TypeScript declaration files that may be generated automatically by the TypeScript compiler by setting "declaration": true in the TypeScript configuration file. Libraries may be organized as npm packages by filling all the required fields in the package.json file and by organizing all their modules in such a way that they may be accessed by a unique root module. Then the package may be distributed in a public repository or used privately by referencing it from the filesystem.

Library testing may be organized either by referencing the library from a web project that has a JavaScript framework installed on it or by running all tests in Node.js with the help of a DOM mock such as jsdom. Test files must be organized in different folders, and their target files must not be included in the distribution folder. Accordingly, the best option is to compile them separately with a different TypeScript configuration file.

Questions

1. How do you configure VS Code so that IntelliSense matches the version of the installed compiler?
2. How do you enter the VS Code debug configuration?
3. How do you enter the VS Code task configuration?
4. What is the purpose of the types field in the package.json file of a TypeScript library?
5. Why is jsdom needed to perform tests in Node.js?
6. How do you inform VS Code to debug tests instead of launching a library file?

7. For what are `beforeAll` and `beforeEach` needed?

8. What is the Jasmine function that compares the expected results with the actual results returned by the library under the test?

Further reading

While this chapter describes all VS Code functionalities that are needed for building and running TypeScript/JavaScript projects, it is not exhaustive. You may look for other features you might need (such as sources control) in the official VS Code documentation: `https://code.visualstudio.com/docs`.

All builds in the chapter were implemented with `npm` scripts and VS Code tasks. Large library projects that involve several more build steps (for instance, JavaScript files minimization) typically use specialized build tools such as **Gulp** (`https://gulpjs.com/`) and **Grunt** (`https://gruntjs.com/`). Sometimes large projects are also bundled with WebPack, by configuring the bundle as a library. Please refer to `Chapter 7`, *Bundling with WebPack*, for a WebPack primer and to the official WebPack documentation on how to configure WebPack bundles as libraries: `https://webpack.js.org/guides/author-libraries/`.

A detailed description of all Jasmine features may be found on Jasmine's official website: `https://jasmine.github.io/`.

Decorators and Advanced ES6 Features

9

This chapter introduces the TypeScript equivalent of C# attributes and metadata, namely, TypeScript decorators and metadata. It also introduces advanced ES6-7 features available in TypeScript that might still be unfamiliar to the average JavaScript developer, such as symbols, iterators, generators, promises, and their associated C#-like async/await notation.

More specifically, the following topics will be covered in this chapter:

- How to use ECMAScript 6 symbols in TypeScript?
- How to define and use the ECMAScript 6 equivalent of C# IEnumerables, in other words, iterators, iterables, and generators, and how to use ECMAScript 6 built-in iterables (maps, sets, and so on)?
- How to handle asynchronous operation with ECMAScript 6 promises, and with C#-like async/await notation?
- How to use the TypeScript equivalent of C# attributes, in other words, decorators? Decorators are a stage 2 ECMAScript proposal, and are widely used in the Angular framework which is the subject of the final part of this book
- How to use decorators to define C#-like JavaScript metadata, available at runtime?

Technical requirements

The technical requirements for this chapter are minimal:

- Visual Studio 2017, with the latest ASP.NET Core tools
- Visual Studio TypeScript SDK

Let's create an ASP.NET Core MVC project called `AdvancedFeatures` without
authentication, and add a `.ts` folder. Also, add the following standard `tsconfig.json`
configuration file to the project root:

```
{
    "compileOnSave": true,
    "compilerOptions": {
        "noImplicitAny": true,
        "strictNullChecks": true,
        "noEmitOnError": true,
        "removeComments": false,
        "sourceMap": true,
        "target": "es5",
        "lib": ["dom", "es5"],
        "outDir": "wwwroot/js"
    },
    "include": [
        "wwwroot/ts/**/*.ts"
    ]
}
```

The `AdvancedFeatures` project in the code repository will be used throughout the entire
chapter.

All the code used in this chapter can be downloaded from the following GitHub
link: `https://github.com/PacktPublishing/Hands-On-TypeScript-for-CSharp-and-.
NET-Core-Developers`.

Check out the following video to see the Code in Action: `http://bit.ly/2ESHV4G`.

Symbols

`symbol` is a new data type introduced in ECMAScript 6. Symbols are the foundation for
adding any metadata support and customizing built-in behaviors in JavaScript. TypeScript
supports the `symbol` type, but it doesn't create equivalent code if the target environment
doesn't support it. This is because no equivalent code can be easily produced. Moreover, it
is not possible to create a polyfill that can be relied upon to always behave like
the `symbol` type. Some polyfills try to simulate symbols with strings, but they might fail in
very unlikely situations. Luckily, symbols are supported by all mainstream browsers, the
sole exception being Internet Explorer (just Internet Explorer; Edge does support `symbol`).

Since `symbol` is not included in ES5, in order to use it in TypeScript, either we change the TypeScript target to ES6, or we manually add the symbol library to the `"lib"` compiler options in `tsconfig.json`:

```
"lib": ["dom", "es5", "es2015.symbol"]
```

After adding symbol support to the TypeScript compiler, the `AdvancedFeatures` project is ready for testing a number of symbol features. Let's add a `SymbolExamples.ts` file under the `.ts` folder, and append the following code to the `Views/Home/Index.cshtml` view, so that the `SymbolExamples.ts` code is executed as soon as the project is run:

```
@section Scripts{
    <script src="~/js/SymbolExamples.js"></script>
}
```

All code snippets in this section should be added to `SymbolExamples.ts` by enclosing them in a namespace called `SymbolExample`:

```
namespace SymbolExample {
    //code snippets here
}
```

Symbols are created by calling the `Symbol()` function which accepts an optional string argument that specifies a description, as shown in the following examples:

```
//symbol without a description
let unNamedSymbol = Symbol();

//symbol with a description
let namedSymbol = Symbol("I am a named symbol"); //symbol with a
description
```

The description doesn't change the symbol behavior, only appearing when the symbol is logged or displayed somehow. In other words, it is just an aid for documentation, maintenance, and debugging.

Symbols are useful on account of the following properties they possess:

- Symbols are unique. In other words, any equality test between symbols created by two calls of the `Symbol` function always fails.
- Symbols may be used as identifiers for object and class members. In other words, symbols may replace string identifiers in the definition of methods and properties.

When symbols replace string identifiers, they must be surrounded by square brackets. The following are a number of examples that show the preceding concepts and clarify all syntactic details:

```
let s1 = Symbol("s");
let s2 = Symbol("s");
alert(s1 == s2); //display false

//symbol used as object property
let o1: any = {};
o1[s1] = 1;
alert(o1[s1]);

export let className = Symbol("className");
export let toString = Symbol("toString");
export class Person {
    constructor(public name: string, public surname: string) {
    }
    //symbol used as method name
    [toString]() {
        return this.name + " " + this.surname;
    }
    //symbol used as computed property name
    get [className]() {
        return "Person";
    }
}

let anObject: any = new Person("Francesco", "Abbruzzese");

alert(anObject[toString]());
alert(anObject[className]);
```

Why are symbols so useful?

First of all, no other JavaScript entity has both property 1 and property 2 of symbols. Any JavaScript object is unique, since object comparisons are done by comparing their pointers, and pointers are unique, but an object can't be used to define properties and methods. At the other end, strings may be used to define a property and methods, as shown in the following:

```
//string defines members
let string1 = "aProperty";
let objectWithStrings: any =
    {
        [string1] : 1
    };
```

With strings, however, the same property may be accessed by both `string1` and by any other string having exactly the same characters in the same order:

```
let string2 = "aProperty";

//both display 1
alert(objectWithStrings[string1])
alert(objectWithStrings[string2])
```

If, in the same example, symbols are used, then the property may be successfully accessed by just the original symbol, demonstrated as follows:

```
//symbol defining member
let symbol1 = Symbol("aProperty");
let objectWithSymbols: any =
    {
        [symbol1]: 1
    };
let symbol2 = Symbol("aProperty");

//displays 1
alert(objectWithStrings[symbol1])
//displays undefined
alert(objectWithStrings[symbol2])
```

The peculiarity of symbols is that they define places inside objects/class instances that may be accessed just through the original symbols used to define them! In other words, they define standard places where procedures that process various objects/classes may store and retrieve information. Such places are only visible to procedures that know the original symbols, and are completely hidden to the remainder of the code, so there is no risk of collisions among procedures that manipulate members defined by different symbols.

Hence, for instance, the `className` symbol used in the previous `Person` class defines a standard place as to where to place the class name so that it is accessible at runtime. If the `className` symbol is accessible just to the few procedures that manipulate class names, then there is no risk that that class name might be broken or overridden by other procedures that use symbols to store different information.

Such standard places are the foundation for adding metadata to JavaScript objects. ES6 comes with built-in symbols called **well-known symbols**, which are accessible as properties of the `Symbol` function. As detailed in the next subsection, these symbols define standard places inside objects where the developer can place code that customizes built-in operations.

Well-known symbols

If the TypeScript target is `"es5"`, another library must be added to the `"lib"` compiler option in order to use well-known symbols:

```
"lib": ["dom", "es5", "es2015.symbol", "es2015.symbol.wellknown"]
```

The most useful well-known symbols are described in the following subsections.

Symbol.toStringTag

When an object is converted to a string, it displays in a standard way as either `'[object Object]'`, or `'[object Array]'` if it is an array. The `[Symbol.toStringTag]` computed property customizes the string shown after `object`, so that the object converted to string displays as `'[object <customized string>]'`. For instance, it is possible to customize the `Person` class so that it displays as `'[object Person]'`:

```
export class Person {
    ...
    get [Symbol.toStringTag]() {
     return "Person";
    }
    ...
}
let anObject: any = new Person("Francesco", "Abbruzzese");
// shows [object Person]
alert(anObject);
```

Symbol.toPrimitive

The `[Symbol.toPrimitive](hint: string)` method customizes how an object is converted to a primitive type. When a conversion is required, this method is invoked, passing the name of the primitive type in the `hint` argument. For instance, the `Person` class may be customized to display the full name of the `Person` instance instead of displaying as `'[object x]'` when it is converted to a string:

```
export class Person {
    ...
    [Symbol.toPrimitive](hint: string) {
        if (hint == 'string') {
            return this.name + " " + this.surname;
        }
        else return null;
```

```
        }
        ...
    }
    let anObject: any = new Person("Francesco", "Abbruzzese");
    // shows "Francesco Abbruzzese"
    alert(anObject);
```

Symbol.search, Symbol.match, and Symbol.replace

The `search` string method searches a string in another string. If any object defines
the `[Symbol.search](stringTosearch: string)` method, then it may be searched in a
string as if it were a string itself; for example, a `Person` instance may be searched in a string
by looking for occurrences of its full name:

```
export class Person {
    ...
    [Symbol.search](stringTosearch: string) {
        return stringTosearch
            .indexOf(this.name + " "
                + this.surname)
    }
    ...
}
let anObject: any = new Person("Francesco", "Abbruzzese");
let toSearch =
    "This book was written by Francesco Abbruzzese";
//should display 25
alert(toSearch.search(anObject));
```

An object that defines the `[Symbol.match](stringTosearch: string)` method
replaces a regular expression in a string search based on the string `match` method. Finally,
an object that defines the `[Symbol.replace](stringTosearch,replacer )` method
may replace a regular expression in a string search-and-replace operation based on the
string's `replace` method. Let's perform an example by enabling `replace` on the `Person`
class:

```
export class Person {
    ...
    [Symbol.replace](stringTosearch: string, replacer: any) {
        var fullName = this.name + " " + this.surname;
        var index = stringTosearch.indexOf(fullName);
        if (index === -1) {
            return stringTosearch;
        }
        if (typeof replacer === 'function') {
```

```
        replacer = replacer.call(undefined,
            fullName, stringTosearch);
    }
    return stringTosearch.slice(0, index)+
        replacer +
        stringTosearch.slice(index + fullName.length);
}
...
}
let anObject: any = new Person("Francesco", "Abbruzzese");
let toSearch =
    "This book was written by Francesco Abbruzzese";
//should display: This book was written by its author
alert(toSearch.replace(anObject, "its author"));
```

Symbol.split

An object that defines the [Symbol.split](x: string) method can replace the split
string parameter in the split string method. For instance, a Person instance may be used
to split a string in all occurrences of its full name, as can be seen in the following:

```
export class Person {
    ...
    [Symbol.split](string: string) {
        var fullName = this.name + " " + this.surname;
        var index = string.indexOf(fullName);
        if (index === -1) {
            return string;
        }
        return [string.substr(0, index),
            string.substr(index + fullName.length)];
    }
    ...
}
let anObject: any = new Person("Francesco", "Abbruzzese");
let toSplit =
    "This string will be split in two parts" +
    " by Francesco Abbruzzese, isn't it?";
//should display 2
alert(toSplit.split(anObject).length);
```

Symbol.iterator and Symbol.isConcatSpreadable, which are useful for defining
iterables (the JavaScript equivalent of C# IEnumerables), are described in the next section,
which is dedicated to iterables. A link to the documentation of the full list of well-known
ECMAScript symbols is provided in the *Further reading* section (this chapter describes
almost all of them).

Iterators, iterables, and generators

As is the case with C# IEnumerables, JavaScript iterables are also based on the idea of suspending a computation and resuming it when a new value is required. More specifically, iterators and generator functions are the foundation of JavaScript iterables.

Iterators and iterables

Iterators are interfaces (`Iterator<T>`) that support a `next()` operation, which, in turn, returns the following generic interface:

```
interface IteratorResult<T>
{
    done : boolean;
    value : T
}
```

Where the `done` property must return `true` if, and only if, no more values are available in the iteration, and where the `value` property must contain the current element of the iteration. Being an interface, we are free to implement `Iterator<T>` in the way we prefer. The following is an implementation that lists all integers up to a given value:

```
function getNumberIterator(x: number): Iterator<number> {
    let i = 0;
    let iterator = {
        next: function (): IteratorResult<number> {
            return {
                done: i > x,
                value: i++
            }
        }
    };
    return iterator;
}
let iterator5 = getNumberIterator(5);
```

The `getNumberIterator` function returns an iterator that iterates until the value passed in its x parameter. In order to test iterables, we need to add two more declaration libraries to the `"lib"` TypeScript compiler option, since we are targeting `"es5"`, and not `"es6"`. For the same reason, we need to set the `downlevelIteration` compiler option to true in order to make that TypeScript compiler translate a `for ...of` ES6 loop into ES5-equivalent code:

```
...
"lib": ["dom", "es5",
```

```
        "es2015.symbol","es2015.symbol.wellknown",
        "es2015.generator","es2015.iterable"],
    "downlevelIteration": true,
    ...
```

The `getNumberIterator` function snippet must be inserted inside an `Iterables` namespace into an `Iterables.ts` file under the `.ts` folder:

```
namespace Iterables {
    //iterables examples here
}
```

Then, in order to execute the TypeScript code, replace the previous `Scripts` section in `Views/Home/index.cshtml` with the following:

```
@section Scripts{
<script src="~/js/Iterables.js"></script>
}
```

Now the `iterator5` iterator can be used with a `while` loop:

```
let curr: IteratorResult<number>;
while (!(curr = iterator5.next()).done) alert(curr.value);
```

Typically, however, functions such as `getNumberIterator` are not used alone, but as building blocks for defining iterables that are the JavaScript equivalent of C# IEnumerables. Iterables are objects that implement the `Iterable<T>` interface, which, in TypeScript built-in declaration libraries, is defined as follows:

```
interface Iterable<T> {
    [Symbol.iterator](): Iterator<T>;
}
```

That is, iterables are objects containing a `[Symbol.iterator]()` method that returns an iterator. It is worth pointing out that `Symbol.iterator` is a well-known symbol. The previous example may be redefined as follows:

```
class NumberIterable implements Iterable<number>
{
    constructor(readonly x: number) { }
    [Symbol.iterator] = () => {
        let i = 0;
        return {
            next: () => {
                return {
                    done: i > this.x,
                    value: i++
```

```
                }

            }
        };
    };
}
let iterable5 = new NumberIterable(5);
```

Iterables may be processed by the `for...of` loop, which is the TypeScript equivalent of a C# `foreach...in` loop:

```
for (let item of iterable5){
    alert(item);
}
```

The whole technique for defining an iterable through the explicit creation of an iterator and its `next()` method appears quite cumbersome. The definition of the `[Symbol.iterator]` method is also quite evolved from the simple `NumberIterable` example that simply iterates over integers. There are a lot of nested functions and objects; for instance, a function that returns an iterator whose `next` method returns another object. The next subsection analyzes a technique that simplifies the definition of iterables by avoiding the explicit definition of iterators.

Generator functions and iterables

The source of the whole complexity of the iterator-next-method technique for defining an iterable is the demand to decouple the code of the iterable from the code that uses all the values produced by the iterable. Without this demand, the entire code of the `NumberIterable` example would collapse into trivial code:

```
for(let i=0; i<=x; i++) alert(i);
```

The complication of using a `next` method is necessary to carry out this code decoupling. The `next` method call is the way in which producer and consumer of values synchronize, the producer remains in a waiting state until the consumer requires a new value by calling the `next` method, then it resumes running in order to produce the new value, and then it goes back to a waiting state again.

Notwithstanding the complications associated with the next level iterator, simple examples such as NumberIterable are quite easy to code, but what if you require a more complex enumeration; for example, an iterable that enumerates all descendants of a DOM node, in other words, the entire subtree of DOM elements that are under a given node. Processing all the nodes of a tree can be executed by means of a simple recursive procedure, but what about implementing it with the iterator? It would be quite hard because you should transform recursion into iteration and then encode nested iterations with the iterator. This can be quite complex, likelihood of errors.

Luckily, generator functions solve the problem of synchronizing producers and consumers in a smart way. The producer code is written as if the producer and consumer were not decoupled, that is, with loops and/or recursive calls. However, whenever a new item x is computed, they execute the special instruction yield x. This instruction makes the new value available to the consumer and then it automatically freezes the producer code execution. Execution is resumed when the consumer requires a new item, and continues until the next yield instruction is encountered. At that point, the new value is returned to the consumer, and producer execution is frozen again.

With this technique, the core code of the generator function for the NumberIterable example becomes something very simple:

```
for(let i=0; i<=x; i++) yield i;
```

This is almost identical to the code needed when there is no producer-consumer decoupling!

A function is declared to be a generator function by appending an asterisk to the function keyword, as can be seen in the following:

```
function* thisIsAGenerator(....){
    ...
    yield...;
    ...
}
```

In case the function keyword is not required, as in the example of class methods, it is sufficient to precede the method definition with an asterisk:

```
* thisIsAGeneratorMethod(...){
    //method code
}
```

When a generator function/method is invoked, the JavaScript runtime creates an `Iterator<T>` wrapper around its code and its activation record (the copy of the whole function state that is created each time a function is invoked), and this iterator is returned as the function value. The `Iterator<T>` wrapper takes care of resuming and suspending code execution as required, when the consumer code calls the `next` method of the `Iterator<T>` wrapper. By way of clarification, let's create a generator function-based implementation of the `NumberIterable` iterable:

```
class NumberIterable implements Iterable<number>
{
    constructor(readonly x: number) { }
    * [Symbol.iterator](){
        for (let i = 0; i <= this.x; i++) yield i;
    };
}
```

After this definition, the consumer code may process all the values returned by the iterable in the exact same way as with the previous implementation:

```
for (let item of new NumberIterable(5)){
    alert(item);
}
```

Generator functions can also use a `yield*` instruction that, instead of returning a single value, moves the computation path to the values produced by another iterable. The `yield*` instruction allows the transformation of recursion-based visits into generator functions. Let's see how `yield*` works with the previously mentioned DOM tree iterable that enumerates the DOM subtree rooted in a given node:

```
export class DOMTreeIterable implements Iterable<Element>
{
    constructor(readonly root: Element) { }
    *[Symbol.iterator](): Iterator<Element> {
        yield this.root;
        for (let child of this.root.children) {
            yield* new DOMTreeIterable(child);
        };
    }
}
```

`DOMTreeIterable` returns the root node, and then recalls itself on each child element with `yield*`. The collection of child elements is iterated with a `for ...of..` loop, since all DOM collections are iterables themselves. However, in order to enable TypeScript to accept `for ...of..` loops for DOM collections, the `"dom.iterable"` library must be added to the `"lib"` compiler option as follows:

```
"lib": ["dom", "es5",
        "es2015.symbol","es2015.symbol.wellknown",
        "es2015.generator","es2015.iterable",
        "dom.iterable"]
```

After that, the `DOMTreeIterable` instance is ready to be tested, for example, by logging the tag names of all the elements contained in the document body in the JavaScript console:

```
for (let item of new DOMTreeIterable(document.body)) {
    console.log(item.tagName);
}
```

Inheriting from Array<T>

The simplest way to define an iterable is to inherit from a built-in iterable. If a browser supports iterables, then all built-in collections are implemented as iterables. In particular, it is often very useful to inherit from arrays because JavaScript has a lot of built-in operations to process arrays that will be automatically inherited by all array subclasses.

For instance, it is possible to define a subclass of `Array<T>` that has one more constructor accepting an iterable as its unique argument:

```
export class EnhancedArray<T> extends Array<T>
{
    constructor(x: number);
    constructor(...items: T[])
    constructor(x: Iterable<T>);
    constructor(x?: number | Array<T> | Iterable<T>) {
        if (typeof x === "undefined") super();
        else if (x instanceof Array) super(...x);
        else if (typeof x == "number") super(x)
        else {
            super();
            for (let item of x) this.push(item);
        }
    }
}
```

The `EnhancedArray<T>` subclass provides the same two standard constructors of `Array<T>` and then adds the new one. The elements of the iterable passed as arguments are pushed to the subclass one after the other.

Subclasses of `Array<T>` may define the `[Symbol.isConcatSpreadable]` computed Boolean property. If it returns `true`, the elements of any instance of the subclass are flattened with all elements of other arrays when the subclass is involved in an array `concat` operation. If `[Symbol.isConcatSpreadable]` returns `false`, the entire subclass is considered a single non-array element and its elements are not flattened during array `concat` operations. Thus, for instance, if you add the following code to the `EnhancedArray<T>` class, then instances of `EnhancedArray<T>` will never have their elements flattened in array `concat` operations:

```
...
get [Symbol.isConcatSpreadable]() {
    return false;
}
...
```

The next subsection describes new collections introduced by ECMAScript 2015.

ECMAScript 2015 built-in iterables

ECMASCript 2015 has built-in iterables that implement the abstract dictionaries and set data structures. In order to use them in TypeScript, the `"es2015.collection"` declarations library must be added to the `"lib"` compiler option:

```
"lib": ["dom", "es5",
        "es2015.symbol","es2015.symbol.wellknown",
        "es2015.generator","es2015.iterable",
        "dom.iterable", "es2015.collection"]
```

Built-in iterables are supported by all mainstream browsers with the exception of Internet Explorer (just Internet Explorer, not Edge), which offers partial support for `Map`, `Set`, and `WeakMap`, and doesn't support `WeakSet` at all. Partial support refers to the absence of all iterable-related features, since, as has already been pointed out, Internet Explorer doesn't support iterables. All built-in iterables have a constructor that either accepts no argument, an array, or an iterable (Internet Explorer only accepts an array). In the case of `Set` and `WeakSet`, the iterable contains all the elements to insert initially into the `Set` (`WeakSet`), while, in the case of `Map` and `WeakMap`, the iterable is composed of two-element tuples whose first element is the dictionary key and whose second element is the corresponding value.

A review of each ECMAScript 2015 built-in iterable follows. As regards the examples used in this subsection, please create a new TypeScript file named `BuiltInIterables.ts` under the `.ts` folder.

Map<K, V> and WeakMap<K, V>

`Map<K, V>` is a key-value pair dictionary. For example, you may use it to create a book of friends that associates a `Person` object with each friend's name that represents them and contains all their data:

```
namespace BuiltInIterables {
    import Person = SymbolExample.Person;
    let friendBook = new Map<string, Person>();
}
```

New key-value pairs are added using the `set` method:

```
friendBook.set("John", new Person("John", "Smith"));
```

Values are then retrieved through their associated keys using the `get` method:

```
let found = friendBook.get("John");
if (typeof found !== "undefined")
    alert(found.name + " " + found.surname);
```

The `size` property returns the number of key-value pairs stored in `Map`:

```
 alert(friendBook.size);
```

The `forEach` method invokes a callback on each pair contained in `Map`:

```
friendBook
    .forEach((value, key, dict) =>
        { alert(value.surname) })
```

The callback is passed, along with the value, the key, and the whole `Map`.

The `delete` method deletes a pair from `Map` through its key:

```
friendBook
    .delete("John")
alert(friendBook.size);
```

The `clear` method deletes all pairs (though it is, usually, more efficient to create a new empty `Map`). The `entries` property contains an iterable with all key-value pairs represented as two-element tuples. The `keys` property contains an iterable that enumerates all keys, while the `values` property contains an iterable that enumerates all values.

`WeakMap<K, V>` works as `Map<K, V>`, the only difference being the manner in which the key-value pairs are garbage-collected by JavaScript (garbage collection is the process that removes all unused objects to free up memory). More specifically, if during the evolution of the process, a key of a key-value pair is used just by a `WeakMap` instance, while no other object has a pointer to it, then the whole key-value pair is removed from that `WeakMap` instance. This way, the value referenced in the key-value pair remains completely unreferenced and is garbage collected by JavaScript. In other words, the references of all `WeakMaps` to all their key objects are not taken into account by the garbage-collector in deciding whether an object is used or not. `WeakMaps` are useful for encoding temporary associations between objects used in a computation, so that when that computation ends and some of those objects are no longer used, they must also be removed from all the maps they are in so that the garbage collector may free up their memory.

Set<T> and WeakSet<T>

`Set<T>` is an implementation of a mathematical finite set. Accordingly, it is a collection with no repetitions, so if the same value is added several times, only the first occurrence is taken.

Values are added using the `add` method:

```
let mySet = new Set<number>([1, 5, 7, 9]);
mySet.add(10);
```

The `has` Boolean method tests whether a value is contained in `Set`:

```
alert(mySet.has(10));//it  returns true;
alert(mySet.has(9));//it returns true;
alert(mySet.has(8));//it returns false;
```

The `size` property returns the number of values contained in `Set`:

```
alert(mySet.size);//it returns 5;
```

The `forEach` method invokes a callback on each value contained in `Set`:

```
mySet.forEach((value) => {
    alert(value)
});
```

A `value` may be removed from a set using the `delete` method:

```
mySet.delete(9);
alert(mySet.has(9));//it returns false;
```

The `clear` method deletes all values from a set (though it is, usually, more efficient to create a new empty set). Finally the `values` property contains an iterable that enumerates all values.

The difference between `WeakSet<T>` and `Set<T>` is the same as the difference between `WeakMap<K, V>` and `Map<K, V>`. That is, if, during the process evolution, a value is used just by `WeakSet` instances, while no other object has a pointer to it, that value is removed from that `WeakSet` so that it remains completely unused and may be garbage-collected by the JavaScript garbage collector.

Promises and async/await notation

Promises are ECMAScript 2015's way of handling asynchronous operations. They have extensive support across all mainstream browsers, with the exception of Internet Explorer. In any case, polyfills are available. With an ES5 target, the use of promises in TypeScript requires the addition of the `"es2015.promise"` and `"es2018.promise"` declaration libraries to the `"lib"` compiler option:

```
"lib": ["dom", "es5",
        "es2015.symbol","es2015.symbol.wellknown",
        "es2015.generator","es2015.iterable",
        "dom.iterable", "es2015.collection",
        "es2015.promise", "es2018.promise"
        ]
```

With the `Promise` pattern, functions that execute asynchronous operations, instead of accepting a callback that is invoked when the asynchronous operation ends, return a `Promise` instance. The code to execute when the asynchronous operation succeeds or fails is specified by means of the `then`, `catch`, and `finally` methods of `Promise`:

```
IReturnAPromiseOfT.
    then(function(returnvalue: T){
```

```
        //code executed when operation succeeds
    })
    .catch(function(reasonOfFailure: any){
        //code executed when operation fails
    })
    .finally(function(){
        //code to execute when operation ends
        //that is when it either succeeds or fails
    })
```

The function passed in the `then` method is invoked using the value returned by the asynchronous operation, while the function passed in the `catch` method is invoked with an error object or string that should explain the reason for the failure. The `finally` method is invoked in all cases when the asynchronous operation ends, and may be used to encode some clean-up logic, such as removing a loading animation or a block from the area of the page that should update because of the asynchronous operation.

`finally` was added in ECMAScript 2018, which is why `"es2018.promise"` was also added to the `"lib"` compiler option.

Promises were used in the *Dynamic module loading* section in Chapter 6, *Namespaces and Modules*, to dynamically load JavaScript code modules with the `import` function that returns a `Promise`:

```
import("./lib/plainList.js")
    .then(x => {
        var mainList = new x.default(
            document.getElementById('main_list') as HTMLElement);
        ...
    })
    .catch(reason => {
        alert("an error occurred");
    });
```

Promises are created as follows:

```
new Promise<T>(succeeds, fails) => {
    //code that launches the asynchronous operation
    //and calls "succeeds" callback on success
    //and "fails" callback on failure
});
```

By way of an example, we define a promise-based function that retrieves data from the server:

```
namespace ApiCall {
    function ServerGet(url: string): Promise<string>
```

```
    {
        return new Promise<string>((resolve, reject) => {
            const xhr = new XMLHttpRequest();
            xhr.open("GET", url);
            xhr.onload = () => resolve(xhr.responseText);
            xhr.onerror = () => reject(new Error(xhr.statusText));
            xhr.send();
        });
    }

    ServerGet("https://localhost:44353/Home/ApiEndpoint")
        .then(bodyText => {
            let json = JSON.parse(bodyText);
            alert(json);
        })
        .catch(error => {
            alert("an error occurred: " + error);
        })
        .finally(() => { alert("call ended"); })
}
```

The preceding code may be tested by inserting it in an `ApiCall.ts` file placed under the `.ts` folder, and then replacing the scripts at the bottom of the `Views/Home/Index.cshtml` view with the following:

```
@section Scripts{
<script src="~/js/ApiCall.js"></script>
}
```

A new action method that answers the client call must be added, too. Place the following action method code in the `HomeController` controller (`Controllers/HomeController.cs`):

```
[HttpGet]
public IActionResult ApiEndpoint()
{
    return Json(new int[] { 10, 20, 30 });
}
```

Since `then`, `catch`, and `finally` return promises, several `then` and `catch` calls may be chained (it makes no sense to chain several `finally` calls). The callback in the first `then` call receives the result of the asynchronous operation as its argument, while every other `then` receives the result returned in by the callback in the previous `then` as its argument. The same happens with chained `catch` calls. Moreover, an exception thrown in any `then` callback is intercepted by the first catch that follows it, and the exception is passed as an argument to the callback contained in this `catch`.

By way of an example of chaining and exception interception, let's improve the code that invokes the `ServerGet` function:

```
ServerGet ("https://localhost:44353/Home/ApiEndpoint")
    .then (bodyText => {
        try {
            return JSON.parse(bodyText);
        }
        catch{
            throw "wrong json returned by server: ";
        }
    })
    .catch(error => {
        alert("an error occurred:" + error);
    })
    .then((json) => alert(json))
    .finally(() => { alert("call ended"); })
```

The first `then` just tries to decode the JSON returned by the server, and returns the result of the decoding operation, if the JSON is correct, otherwise it throws an exception if the JSON is hill-formed. The following `catch` intercepts any HTTP and network error, plus the exception possibly thrown by the first `then`. The actual client code is contained in the second `then` which receives directly the data structure created in the first `then`.

When several `then` are chained, the callback of each intermediary `then` may return a promise instead of an immediate value. In this case, the next `then` is invoked when this promise succeeds. If, instead, the intermediate promise fails, the closest following `catch` is invoked and its callback is passed as the reason for the failure.

When several asynchronous operations, each returning a promise, have to be launched in parallel, the `Promise.all` method is used to create an overall `Promise` that succeeds after all promises succeed, and fails as soon as any `Promise` fails:

```
Promise.all([firstPromise, ...<other Promises])
    .then([firstresult, ...<other results>] =>{
        //code that processes all Promise results
    })
    .catch((reasonOfFailure: any) =>{
        // code that processes the
        //failed Promise
    });
```

All promises are passed either in an array or in any iterable. The `then` callback receives an array with all results of promises, while the `catch` callback receives the reason for the first failed promise, assuming there is one.

Let's use `Promise.all` in the previous example by adding another action method and another server call:

```
public IActionResult AnotherApiEndpoint()
{
    return Json("this call succeeded");
}
```

On the client side, `ServerGet` is now invoked twice:

```
Promise.all([
    ServerGet("https://localhost:44353/Home/ApiEndpoint"),
    ServerGet("https://localhost:44353/Home/AnotherApiEndpoint")])
    .then(([res1, res2]) => {
        try {
            return [
                JSON.parse(res1),
                JSON.parse(res2)];
        }
        catch{
            throw "wrong json returned by server: ";
        }
    })
    .catch(error => {
        alert("an error occurred:" + error);
    })
    .then(([json1, json2]) => {
        alert(json1);
        alert(json2);
    })
    .finally(() => {
        alert("call ended");
    });
```

A `Promise.race` method is also available which succeeds as soon as any of the several `Promise` instances succeeds. In this case, the callback in the first `then` receives just one result. It is useful for trying to download a resource from several alternative sources.

The `Promise.resolve(<result>)` and `Promise.reject(<failure reason>)` methods return, respectively, a promise that succeeds immediately, with the result passed as argument, and a promise that fails immediately, with the reason passed as an argument. They are very useful for code testing.

fetch API

Actually, there is no need to write a `ServerGet` function, since ECMAScript introduced the `fetch` API to communicate with a server. Unluckily, it is not supported by all browsers, so a `fetch` polyfill must be included for the browsers that do not support it yet. With the `fetch` API, the previous example becomes the following:

```
Promise.all([
    fetch("https://localhost:44353/Home/ApiEndpoint"),
    fetch("https://localhost:44353/Home/AnotherApiEndpoint")])
    .then(([res1, res2]) => {
        if (!res1.ok) throw (res1.statusText);
        if (!res2.ok) throw (res2.statusText);
        return Promise.all([
            res1.json(),
            res2.json()]);
    })
    //unchanged code
    ...
```

The `fetch` function returns a `Response` object, so the code changes a little. The `ok` property is `true` if no HTTP error is received, and the `statustext` property contains the status text returned by the server. There is also a `status` property that contains the numeric status code. The `headers` property contains a `Map<string, string>` iterable, with all response headers represented as key-value pairs.

The `json()` method decodes the response body as `json`, but doesn't directly return a data structure but a promise, which is why the code combines the two results with `Promise.all` before returning them.

There is also a `text()` method that returns the body content as text (this is useful when the response body contains HTML or simple text). Like the `json()` method, the `text()` method also returns a promise. Both methods must return promises because the `fetch` promise ends as soon as the client receives the response header, before extracting the whole body from the stream.

`fetch` also has another options argument that is used to add request headers, credentials, and so on. The following are a number of fields with the values they may take:

```
{
    method: "GET",// or POST, or...,
    body: "any object or string to send as body",
    credentials: "include", //or "same-origin", "omit"
    cache: "default", //no-store, reload, no-cache,
        //force-cache, or only-if-cached.
```

```
    headers: //Headers instance with headers
            //added as key-value pair,
}
```

`credentials` specifies when to send cookies and credentials. If not specified, neither of them is ever sent to the server. `body`, when included, specifies the content of the request body. It is useful for sending data structures (JSON), or files, to the server. `cache` specifies the caching policy, while `headers` may contain an object created with `new Header()`, where the developer may append several request headers as key-value pairs. There are a number of other options, but they will not be discussed here since a discussion of their meaning and details would lead us far beyond the subject of the book. A link to the whole `fetch` documentation will be provided in the *Further reading* section.

async/await notation

Asynchronous operations that don't use promises have their own custom callbacks that are invoked upon termination of the operation. This way, asynchronous operations may be chained only by nesting the next asynchronous operations inside the callback of the previous asynchronous operation, so that each callback uses other callbacks, which, in turn, use other callbacks, and so on. In this way, asynchronous code, instead of being a sequence of statements, becomes an unmodular tree of nested callbacks:

```
myAsyncOp(url, () =>{
    nestedAsyncOperation(url1, () => {
        nestedNestedAsyncOperation(url2, () => {
            //and so on
        });
    });
});
```

Promises improve code modularity, and readability, by standardizing callbacks, and by offering a better way to chain several asynchronous operations. In fact, when a `then` callback invokes another asynchronous operation, it can return directly the promise of this nested asynchronous operation, instead of waiting for its completion in a nested `then` statement. This way, a sequence of asynchronous operations is encoded with a sequence of `then` calls that are more modular and readable than nested callbacks:

```
myAsyncOp(url)
    .then((x) =>{
        ...
        return
          nestedAsyncOperation(url1);
    })
```

```
    .then((x) =>{
        ...
        return
            nestedNestedAsyncOperation(url2);
    })
    //and so on
```

Thus, with promises, sequences of operations are encoded with more readable sequences of `then` calls.

The async/await pattern allows a further improvement. In fact, with the async/await pattern, the preceding snippets are encoded as follows:

```
let res1 = await myAsyncOp(url);
...
let res1 = await nestedAsyncOperation(url1)(url);
...
let res1 = await nestedNestedAsyncOperation(url2);
```

When the `await` keyword is placed before a method that returns a promise, execution is frozen until the promise is completed. After that, the return value that would be passed to the `then` callback is returned directly as if it were the return value of a non-asynchronous call. If the promise fails, the object that should be passed to the `catch` callback is thrown as an exception.

The `await` keyword recovers full readability of asynchronous code, since a sequence of asynchronous instructions is encoded in the same way as a sequence of non-asynchronous instructions.

In order for a method or function to use the `await` operator, it must be marked as `async` by placing the `async` keyword before its definition, as follows:

```
//async function
async function IAmAnAsyncFunction(....){
    ...
    let myAsyncRes = await myAsyncCall(...);
    ...
}

//async method
async IAmAnAsyncMethod(....){
    ...
    let myAsyncRes = await myAsyncCall(...);
    ...
}
```

Let's encode the previous `fetch` API example with the async/await pattern:

```
async function getData(): Promise<void> {
    try {
        var response =
            await fetch("https://localhost:44353/Home/ApiEndpoint");
        if (!response.ok) throw (response.statusText);
        alert(await response.json());
        response =
            await
fetch("https://localhost:44353/Home/AnotherApiEndpoint");
        if (!response.ok) throw (response.statusText);
        alert(await response.json());
    }
    catch (error) {
        alert("an error occurred: " + error);
    }
    alert("call ended");
}

getData();
```

The code is simplified significantly and becomes more readable. The final call to `getData` executes in non-blocking mode since it is not preceded by the `await` operator, but this is the only option since `await` may be used only within functions/methods that have been marked as `async`. It is worth to give a look to the transpiled code in the "wwwroot/js/ApiCall.js" file to verify how async/await is translated into `Promise` based code.

The async/await operator is part of the ECMAScript 2017 standard, but, if the TypeScript target is lower, the TypeScript compiler creates equivalent code based on promises. Therefore, async/await requires the `"es2015.promise"` declaration library, along with a `promise` polyfill in the event that Internet Explorer has to be supported.

Decorators and metadata

Decorators are custom modifiers that are applied to classes, methods, properties, computed properties, and method parameters. Each decorator consists of an @ symbol, followed by a TypeScript expression, which evaluates to a function. Decorators can add metadata to classes, can modify class behavior, and can specify the role of a class in a client framework. They play a fundamental role in the Angular framework, described in the final part of this book, that uses them to specify the roles of special classes in the framework (components, modules, directives, and so on), to constrain the roles of some class properties (input or output), to assign special roles to certain methods (such as the event handler role), and to specify that some parameters must be injected automatically in a method call with a technique called dependency injection (@Inject).

The following is a class definition that shows the various types of decorators:

```
@IAmAClassDecorator @IamAnotherClassDecorator
class Person {
    constructor(public name: string, public surname: string) {
    }
    @IAmAnAccessorDecorator
    get fullname() {
        return this.name+' '+this.surname;
    }
    @IAmAPropertyDecorator
    address: string;
    @IAmAMethodDecorator
    Show(@IAmAParameterDecorator includeAddress: bool): string
    {
        ...
    }
}
```

All decorators in the preceding example are constant expressions, that is, each decorator is the name of a function. Several decorators can be applied to a class, method, property, computed property, and method parameter.

At runtime, when the definition of a class containing decorators is processed, the function each decorator evaluates to is executed and is passed as a list of arguments that are dependent on where the decorator was applied. Since these arguments are pointers and/or names of parts of the class, each decorator, when executed, has the opportunity to modify the class definition and/or to attach data either to the class constructor function or to the class prototype (these are the only parts that compose a class at runtime).

The order of execution of decorators is as follows:

1. When several decorators are applied to the same entity, all expressions are evaluated from left to right. Once a function has been computed for each decorator, these functions are executed in reverse order, that is, from right to left.
2. Parameter decorators, followed by method, accessor, or property decorators, are applied for each instance member. Then parameter decorators, followed by method, accessor, or property decorators, are applied for each static member. Parameter decorators are then applied for the constructor. Finally, class decorators are applied for the class.

Data that is attached to either the constructor function or to the class prototype by decorators is called metadata. In order to attach metadata in safe places that cannot be accessed by other code, decorators define members named by symbols that are kept hidden inside the code that manipulate the metadata. This way, due to symbol unicity, other chunks of code that have no references to these symbols are unable to access the metadata-storing members.

While each developer is free to build their own metadata manipulation functions, there is an ECMAScript proposal to standardize them, and the `reflect-metadata` NPM package contains a polyfill that implements the specifications of this proposal. Therefore, it make sense to use this `reflect-metadata` library, instead of custom code. As will be explained at the end of this section, the TypeScript compiler itself relies on this library for some experimental features. Thus, let's add a `package.json` package to the `AdvancedFeatures` project root, and then add the `reflect-metadata` package to it:

```
{
  "version": "1.0.0",
  "name": "asp.net",
  "private": true,
    "devDependencies": {
        "reflect-metadata": "^0.1.12"
    }
}
```

Decorators are a stage 2 ECMAScript proposal, but TypeScript produces equivalent code if the chosen target JavaScript doesn't support them. Decorator support must be enabled by setting the `experimentalDecorators` compiler option to `true` in `tsconfig.json`.

 Decorators may only be applied to implementation code, not to declarations, since they are themselves implementations. In particular, they can't be applied to the declaration of classes contained in TypeScript declaration files.

Class decorators

The function that each class decorator evaluates to is invoked with the class constructor function as its only argument. If this function returns a value, that value is interpreted as a new constructor function that will replace the original constructor function.

As an example, let's write a class decorator that writes a log message each time a new instance of the class is created. Basically, the function that implements the decorator must replace the original constructor function with a new constructor function that prints the log message and then invokes the original constructor. Let's add the decorator definition to a new file named `Decorators.ts`, under the `.ts` folder:

```
namespace Decorators {
    export function logClass(target: any) {
        //store original constructor
        var original = target;

        // new constructor that
        //will replace original constructor
        let newConstructor: any = function (...args:any[]) {
            console.log("New: " + original.name + " " + args);
            //wrap apply-call of original constructor
            //inside a function, because apply
            // can't be invoked with new
            var caller: any = function () {
                original.apply(this, args);
            }
            // copy old prototype
            caller.prototype = original.prototype;
            return new caller();
        }
        // copy old prototype
        newConstructor.prototype = original.prototype;
        // return new constructor
        return newConstructor;
    }
}
```

Since the original constructor must be called with `apply`, and `apply` can't be invoked with `new`, the `apply` call to the original constructor is wrapped inside the `caller` constructor function that, instead, can be invoked with `new`. The original prototype is copied in both the intermediary `caller` constructor and in the new `newConstructor` constructor, to ensure that inheritance and all object-oriented stuff works properly.

The decorator can be tested by creating a TypeScript test file called `DecoratorsTests.ts` and then replacing the scripts at the bottom of `/Views/Home/Index.cshtml` with the following:

```
@section Scripts{
<script src="~/js/Decorators.js"></script>
<script src="~/js/DecoratorsTests.js"></script>
}
```

The following test code in `DecoratorsTests.ts` does the job:

```
namespace DecoratorsTests {
    @Decorators.logClass
    class Product {
        constructor(readonly name: string, readonly model: string)
        { }
        quantity: number=0;
        get fullname(): string {
            return this.name + ' ' +
                this.model + ' ';
        }
        add(x: number): void {
            this.quantity += x;
        }
    }

    let prod = new Product("computer", "32G-1T");
    alert(prod.fullname);
}
```

Running the project shows an alert box with the name of the product. However, by opening the browser console, the following message appears—`New: Product computer, 32G-1T`.

Unluckily, a class logger is useful if it may only be turned on in debug mode, since, in production, the whole execution of several class loggers would slow down the computation. Something like `@Decorators.logClass(production)`, which executes the decorator code only if `production` is `false`, would solve the problem if production is a global variable that the developer may turn on/off in a single place.

However, the parameters passed to a class decorator function aren't decided by the developer, since a class decorator is automatically passed the class constructor function as its unique parameter. Thus, if we would like to improve the code, we can no longer use a constant function as a decorator. The decorator must be a more complex expression that may accept parameters, and that, once executed, returns the function that implements the decorator.

Decorator factories

The standard solution used for decorators that need parameters is a decorator factory, that is, a function that accepts all the requisite parameters, and that returns the actual decorator code as an unnamed function defined in its body. This way, parameters received by the decorator factory are also visible to the unnamed function that shares its same lexical scope:

```
function IAmADecoratorFactory(par1, par2, ...){
    ...
    return function(target: any){
     //par1 is visible also here
    if(par1)....
        ...
        //also par2 is visible inside
        //the unnamed function
        ...par2 + "...."...
    };
}
```

Let's turn `logClass` into a decorator factory:

```
export function logClass(production?: any) {
        if (production) return () => { };
        return function(target: any) {
            //store original constructor
            var original = target;
            //code below is unchanged
            ...
        }
    }
```

If `production` is `true`, the decorator factory returns a decorator processor that does nothing, otherwise it returns the same decorator seen in the previous subsection.

The test code must be changed as follows:

```
(window as any)["_DEBUG"] = true;

@Decorators.logClass(!(window as any)["_DEBUG"])
class Product {
    ...
}
...
```

Instead of using a `production` global variable, the code uses a global `_DEBUG` variable as this is more useful. If the decorator is called with no parameters (`@Decorators.logClass()`), then `production` is `undefined` and is assumed to be false, so class instance creations are logged.

JavaScript built-in metadata – PropertyDescriptor

ECMAScript 5 also has a number of embryonic metadata features. Namely, object and class member features may be changed at runtime by configuring a `PropertyDescriptor` interface:

```
interface PropertyDescriptor {
    configurable?: boolean;
    enumerable?: boolean;
    value?: any;
    writable?: boolean;
    get?(): any;
    set?(v: any): void;
}
```

`PropertyDescriptor` instances are passed to method and accessor decorator functions, so they may read/modify all member features.

`PropertyDescriptor` instances are retrieved and set with the following built-in static methods of the `Object` class:

```
Object.getOwnPropertyDescriptor(object: any, memberName: string|symbol)
    : PropertyDescriptor
Object.defineProperty(object: any, memberName: string,
    settings: PropertyDescriptor ) : void;
```

Where `object` is the object(or object prototype) you want to set/get the `PropertyDescriptor` property, and `memberName` is the name of the member e whose `PropertyDescriptor` must be set/get. `memberName` may be either a string or a symbol.

The following is a description of all `PropertyDescriptor` members:

- `value`: The property default value, before any assignment modifies it
- `writable`: Defaults to `true`, but, if set to false, the member becomes read-only

- enumerable: Defaults to `true`, but if it is set to `false`, the member is not enumerated in any instruction/method that enumerates members, such as a `for...in` loop
- configurable: Defaults to `true`, but, once set to `false`, it freezes the `PropertyDescriptor`, and no `PropertyDescriptor` option can be changed anymore
- get, and set: Getter and setter functions in case the member is an accessor (computed property)

Examples of how `Propertydescriptor` is utilized are shown in the following subsection, which describes method and accessor decorators.

Method and accessor decorators

Method and accessor decorator functions are passed three arguments:

- The `"target"` decorator. This is the constructor function of the class for static members, and is the prototype of the class for instance members. The `"target"` is where metadata possibly created by the decorator is stored (typically in symbol-named properties). Thus, for static members, they are stored in the static part of the class that is its constructor, while for instance members, they are stored in the instance part of the class that is the class prototype. Please refer to the *Static members and static part of a class* section under `Chapter 4`, *Using Classes and Interfaces*, to review the definition of static part of a class.
- The name of the member. This may either be a string or a symbol.
- The `PropertyDescriptor` property of the member.

If a method or accessor decorator returns a value, it is expected to be a `PropertyDescriptor` that will replace the original one. Usually, however, the `PropertyDescriptor` passed as an argument is modified instead of being completely replaced.

As an example of a method decorator, let's define a method logger analogous to the class logger by using a decorator factory to turn logging on/off. Let's add the following code to the `Decorators.ts` file:

```
export function logMethod(production?: any) {
    if (production) return () => { };
    return function (target: any, propertyKey: string | symbol,
        descriptor: PropertyDescriptor) {
        //store original method
```

```
        var original = descriptor.value;

        // new method that
        //will replace original method
        let newMethod: any = function (...args: any[]) {
            console.log(propertyKey as any + " " + args);
            return original.apply(this, args);
        }
        descriptor.value = newMethod;
    }
}
```

The code for a `logAccessor` decorator is similar to the preceding code, the only difference being that instead of replacing the function defined in the `value` property of the `PropertyDescriptor`, you must replace the function contained in its `set` property.

The preceding code may be tested by applying the `@Decorators.logMethod(!(window as any)["_DEBUG"])` decorator to the `add` method, and the following few lines at the end of `DecoratorsTests.js`:

```
prod.add(1);
alert(prod.quantity);
```

Handling metadata with the reflect-metadata polyfill

The `reflect-metadata` metadata handling library is designed to be imported as a module. Moreover, since it is a polyfill, it acts by defining global identifiers, so it must be imported for its side effects only with the following `import` statement:

```
import "reflect-metadata";
```

Moreover, since the `node_modules` folder is not accessible from the web, and is not copied when the project is deployed, modules must be bundled with WebPack (or any other bundler), otherwise the module load operation will also fail in browsers that support ES6 modules (please refer to Chapter 7, *Bundling with WebPack*, to learn how to use WebPack).

The `reflect-metadata` library may also be used with namespaces, but, in this case, an ad-hoc declaration file must be imported manually in each TypeScript file that uses the library with the following triple-slash declaration at the top of the TypeScript file:

```
///<reference path="../../node_modules/reflect-metadata/standalone.d.ts" />
```

Moreover, the `/node_modules/reflect-metadata/Reflect.js` file must be copied somewhere inside the `wwwroot` folder, so that it may be accessed from the web, and a reference to it must be added in all views that use metadata and reflection.

The following are all the functions exposed by the `reflect-metadata` library (taken from NPM documentation):

```
// define metadata on an object or property
Reflect.defineMetadata(metadataKey, metadataValue, target);
Reflect.defineMetadata(metadataKey, metadataValue, target, propertyKey);

// check for presence of a metadata key on the prototype chain of an object
or property
let result = Reflect.hasMetadata(metadataKey, target);
let result = Reflect.hasMetadata(metadataKey, target, propertyKey);

// check for presence of an own metadata key of an object or property
let result = Reflect.hasOwnMetadata(metadataKey, target);
let result = Reflect.hasOwnMetadata(metadataKey, target, propertyKey);

// get metadata value of a metadata key on the prototype chain of an object
or property
let result = Reflect.getMetadata(metadataKey, target);
let result = Reflect.getMetadata(metadataKey, target, propertyKey);

// get metadata value of an own metadata key of an object or property
let result = Reflect.getOwnMetadata(metadataKey, target);
let result = Reflect.getOwnMetadata(metadataKey, target, propertyKey);

// get all metadata keys on the prototype chain of an object or property
let result = Reflect.getMetadataKeys(target);
let result = Reflect.getMetadataKeys(target, propertyKey);

// get all own metadata keys of an object or property
let result = Reflect.getOwnMetadataKeys(target);
let result = Reflect.getOwnMetadataKeys(target, propertyKey);

// delete metadata from an object or property
let result = Reflect.deleteMetadata(metadataKey, target);
let result = Reflect.deleteMetadata(metadataKey, target, propertyKey);

// apply metadata via a decorator to a class
@Reflect.metadata(metadataKey, metadataValue)
class C {
  // apply metadata via a decorator to a method (property)
  @Reflect.metadata(metadataKey, metadataValue)
  method() {
```

```
        }
    }
```

An example of usage of the `reflect-metadata` library is contained in the next subsection, which describes parameter decorators.

Parameter decorators

Parameter decorators are passed in the following arguments:

- The decorator target. This is the constructor function of the class for static members, and is the prototype of the class for instance members.
- The name of the member. This may be either a string or a symbol.
- The ordinal index of the parameter in the function's parameter list.

Since they lack a `PropertyDescriptor`, parameter decorators may only store metadata. Such metadata can be used directly by the client code, or by some method decorator that uses it to modify the whole method behavior. The following is an example of a parameter decorator that adds a maximum-length constraint to string parameters. The constraint is added to the class metadata and can be used either by the method code, by the caller of the method, or by some validation method decorators. The code to add to the `Decorators.ts` file is as follows:

```
interface stringLengthConstraint {
    index: number,
    limit: number
}
const maxStringLengthMetadataKey = Symbol("maxStringLength");
export function maxStringLength(limit: number) {
    return function (target: any, propertyKey: string | symbol,
        parameterIndex: number ) {
        //retrieve existing constraints if any
        let previousConstraints: stringLengthConstraint[] =
            Reflect.getOwnMetadata(
                maxStringLengthMetadataKey,
                target, propertyKey) || [];
        //add new constraints
        previousConstraints.push({
            index: parameterIndex,
            limit: limit
        });
        //save updated constraints
        Reflect.defineMetadata(
            maxStringLengthMetadataKey,
```

```
                previousConstraints, target, propertyKey);
        }
    }
```

Since we are using the `reflect-metadata` library, with namespaces instead of modules, we must manually add a reference to the associated declaration file by adding the following code at the top of the `Decorators.ts` file, as discussed in the previous subsection:

```
///<reference path="../../node_modules/reflect-metadata/standalone.d.ts" />
```

The constraints stored in the metadata by the `maxStringLength` decorator can be enforced by a `normalizeStrings` method decorator defined as follows:

```
export function normalizeStrings(production?: any) {
    if (production) return () => { };
    return function (target: any, propertyKey: string | symbol,
        descriptor: PropertyDescriptor) {
        //store original method
        var original = descriptor.value;
        // new method that
        //will replace original one
        let newMethod: any = function (...args: any[]) {
            let constraints: stringLengthConstraint[] =
                Reflect.getOwnMetadata(
                    maxStringLengthMetadataKey,
                    target, propertyKey) || [];
            for (let item of constraints) {
                let par = args[item.index];
                if (typeof par === "string" &&
                    par.length > item.limit)
                    args[item.index] =
                        par.substr(0, item.limit);
            }
            return original.apply(this, args);
        }
        descriptor.value = newMethod;
    }
}
```

In order to test the code, as a first step, we must copy the `/node_modules/reflect-metadata/Reflect.js` file into the `wwwroot/js` folder, since the `node_modules` folder is not accessible from the web. Then, we must add a reference to it in the `/Views/Home/index.cshtml` view:

```
@section Scripts{
<script src="~/js/Reflect.js"></script>
<script src="~/js/Decorators.js"></script>
```

```
<script src="~/js/DecoratorsTests.js"></script>
}
```

Finally, we must add a new property `description` property and a new `addDescription` method to the `Product` class:

```
@Decorators.logClass(!(window as any)["_DEBUG"])
class Product {
    constructor(readonly name: string, readonly model: string)
    { }
    private description: string | null = null;
    @Decorators.normalizeStrings()
    addDescription(
        @Decorators.maxStringLength(20) newName: string) {
        this.description = newName;
    }
    quantity: number=0;
    get fullname(): string {
        return (this.description != null ?
            this.description : this.name) + ' ' +
            this.model + ' ';
    }
    @Decorators.logMethod(!(window as any)["_DEBUG"])
    add(x: number): void {
        this.quantity += x;
    }
}
let prod = new Product("computer", "32G-1T");
prod.addDescription(
    "this is a very long, too long description");
alert(prod.fullname);
```

When running the project, the `description` strings appear truncated in the alert box.

Property decorators

Property decorators are passed by only two arguments, namely, the target, and the property name; in other words, the same arguments of the method and accessor decorators, but the `PropertyDescriptor` argument as well. This limitation stems from a technical difficulty and not from specification needs. The lack of a `PropertyDescriptor` enables property decorators to store metadata, but not to modify the property behavior. Therefore, applications that need to modify property behaviors must define these properties as accessors, instead of simple properties.

The technique used to store metadata is completely analogous to the one shown in the *Parameter decorators* section example, so no further example is presented in this subsection.

Automatic generation of metadata

If the `reflect-metadata` library is added to the project, and if the `emitDecoratorMetadata` compiler option is set to `true`, in `tsconfig.ts`, the TypeScript compiler will automatically add some metadata. More specifically, it will add a metadata entry containing the design-time type of each class property. Class types are represented by a pointer to the class constructor function, while all other types are represented by their string names. The metadata entry containing design-time type information is named `design:type`. Thus, automatic metadata generation is equivalent to applying a decorator like the following to all properties:

```
@Reflect.metadata("design:type", <class constructor pointer or name of
type>)
```

For a property whose type is, for instance, the `Product` class, the preceding statement becomes the following:

```
@Reflect.metadata("design:type", Product)
```

Summary

We started off the chapter with symbols. Symbols, due to their unicity, solve the problem of defining standard places inside objects/prototypes, thereby eliminating the risk of collisions with other properties defined in other software modules. For this reason, they are the foundation of JavaScript metadata programming.

We then moved on to iterables. The concept of iterable is a powerful abstraction that allows quite different data structures to be processed by the same functions and instructions, such as the `for..of` loop. Moreover, they delay the computation of each item of an enumeration until the time it is actually needed, thereby saving time when the enumeration happens to be incomplete. Generator functions are a powerful tool designed to simplify the definition of iterables, since they overcome the communication problem generated by the demand to decouple the code of the iterable from the code that uses all values produced by the iterable.

ES6 built-in iterables bring JavaScript to the level of advanced languages, such as C++, C#, and Java, by providing implementation of abstract data types as sets and generic dictionaries whose keys are not limited to strings and integers. They are supported by all mainstream browsers.

Promises improve the quality of asynchronous code from a spaghetti-code-like tree of nested callbacks to a sequence of `then` method invocations. The async/await pattern improves further the Promise model, since a sequence of asynchronous instructions is encoded in the same way as a sequence of non-asynchronous instructions, thereby recovering the same readability of non-asynchronous code.

Decorators are a powerful tool to easily add metadata to all class parts, and a way of adding features defined by unique chunks of code to all possible classes and/or parts of classes. They are fundamental building blocks for various client-side frameworks, such as Angular, which, with their help, can factor out the code that is specific for each role required by the framework. Decorators are more effective than simple class inheritance in this factoring-out operation since they don't constrain each class to a unique inheritance hierarchy, but several decorators applied to different parts of a class add new behaviors in an additive and incremental way.

Questions

1. Why are symbols so useful for metadata handling?
2. What is a well-known symbol?
3. What is `Symbol.Iterator` needed for?
4. What TypeScript instruction is specific to iterables?
5. What is the advantage of generator functions over defining iterators directly?
6. Can TypeScript generate equivalent code for browsers that do not support iterables?
7. What is the advantage of `Map<T>` over indexable types (please refer to the *Indexable types* subsection of `Chapter 2`, *Complex Types and Functions*)?
8. How do Promises improve the classic callback pattern for handling asynchronous operations? In turn, how do the async/await patterns improve the standard usage of Promises?
9. What is the purpose of decorators, and what entities may they be applied to? What is the relation between decorators and metadata?
10. What is the standard technique for defining decorators that accept parameters?

Further reading

This chapter offers a quite exhaustive description of symbols; just a few, less frequently used and less well-known symbols have been omitted. The complete list of all well-known symbols is available in Mozilla documentation here: `https://developer.mozilla.org/en-US/docs/Web/JavaScript/Reference/Global_Objects/Symbol`.

In case a Promise polyfill is needed because promises must also be used in old browsers, the `es6-promise` NPM package is a good choice. More information regarding the `npm` directory can be found here: `https://www.npmjs.com/package/es6-promise`.

This chapter describes the more common applications of the `fetch` API. An exhaustive description of all available options can be found in Mozilla documentation here: `https://developer.mozilla.org/en-US/docs/Web/API/Fetch_API`. Since `fetch` doesn't have complete support in all browsers, a polyfill is usually added. The `isomorphic-fetch` NPM package is a good choice. More information on this can be found in the NPM documentation at `https://www.npmjs.com/package/isomorphic-fetch`.

This chapter describes the static methods of the `Object` class used to manipulate `PropertyDescriptor` instances. However the `Object` class also contains other useful metadata manipulation methods. They are listed in the Mozilla documentation here: `https://developer.mozilla.org/en-US/docs/Web/JavaScript/Reference/Global_Objects/Object`.

The *Handling metadata with the reflect-metadata polyfill* subsection uses a triple-slash TypeScript directive to declare that a specific declaration file must be used. The book doesn't go into detail on triple-slash directives since they increasingly became less important with every updated TypeScript version. However, in some rare situations, such as the one in the *Handling metadata with the reflect-metadata polyfill* subsection, they are necessary. An exhaustive discussion of the topic can be found in TypeScript's official documentation at `https://www.typescriptlang.org/docs/handbook/triple-slash-directives.html`.

TypeScript's official documentation also contains a complete list of all TypeScript compiler options here: `https://www.typescriptlang.org/docs/handbook/compiler-options.html`. This book describes most of them, but some minor, or less frequently used options, were omitted.

10
Angular ASP.NET Core Project Template

This is the first of four chapters on the Angular Client framework that utilizes most of the more advanced topics we learned throughout the book, including await/async pattern, decorators, modules, and bundling. Angular is a **Single Page Application** (**SPA**) framework; in other words, the entire application is implemented in a single HTML page. There is no server-side HTML rendering, but the HTML needed to change the content of the single HTML page is generated on the client side itself by JavaScript code. The interaction between client and server is limited to the exchange of data in JSON format, in other words, to the invocation of API controller methods.

Angular follows a **Model-View-View Model** (**MVVM**) pattern that keeps logic separated from graphics. For those who have experience of desktop and native mobile development, MVVM is the pattern behind a number of Windows technologies, such as WPF and Universal Windows applications, as well as Xamarin presentation layer. According to MVVM, presentation layer data is written in **ViewModels** whose properties and methods are bound to graphic elements of Views in such a way that changes in ViewModels cause automatic changes to graphics, and vice versa. MVVC is similar to the MVC pattern, used by ASP.NET Core MVC, the only difference being the way ViewModels are bound to Views. While, in MVC, form fields are bound to a server-side ViewModel after a form is sent to the server with an HTTP Verb (usually POST), in MVVC everything takes place on the client side and bindings propagate changes instantaneously. As explained in detail in this chapter, Angular, like most of modern frontend libraries, follows also a component oriented architecture.

This first chapter introduces the Visual Studio project template for building applications based on ASP.NET Core and Angular, which, as far as Angular is concerned, is based essentially on the standard Angular **Command-Line Interface** (**CLI**). In other words, Visual Studio operates on the Angular part of the project by issuing Angular CLI commands. The Visual Studio project template will be used in all four chapters concerned with the Angular learning path. This chapter, then, discusses Angular architecture and the basics of Angular. More specifically, the reader will learn about the following topics:

- How to start an Angular project using the Visual Studio Angular project template
- The Angular project structure
- How Angular works and updates HTML
- How to define modules and components and how to bind data to component templates
- Configuring, building, and publishing an Angular application

Technical requirements

The requirements for this chapter are as follows:

- Visual Studio 2017, with the latest ASP.NET Core tools
- Visual Studio TypeScript SDK
- A version of Angular CLI installed globally (version 6 or above)
- Angular 6 CLI requires Node 8.9 or higher, together with npm 5.5.1 or higher

Angular CLI global installation is needed to update Angular to its latest version if the Visual Studio Angular template is not updated to the latest version of Angular. This is likely to occur since Angular versions are released more frequently than Visual Studio project templates.

Angular CLI is an NPM package. In order to install it globally, as a first step, let's verify the Node and npm versions by typing the following:

```
>node -v
```

The following also needs to be typed:

```
>npm -v
```

If the versions are below what is required, please install the latest recommended Node version. Then, open a Windows console and type the following:

```
>npm install –g @angular/cli
```

After that, Angular CLI commands may be issued in any Windows console as follows:

```
ng <command with options>
```

All the code used in this chapter can be downloaded from the following GitHub link: `https://github.com/PacktPublishing/Hands-On-TypeScript-for-CSharp-and-.NET-Core-Developers`.

Check out the following video to see the Code in Action: `http://bit.ly/2qgopVC`.

Creating an Angular project

Open Visual Studio and create a new project by going to **File** | **New** | **Project**, selecting **ASP.NET Core Web Application**, and then naming it `AngularQuickStart`. Press **OK**, and, in the window that opens, choose an **Angular** application.

The whole Angular Client application is contained in the `ClientApp` folder. Let's open this folder and take a look at the Angular `package.json` to verify whether the version used in the Visual Studio template is sufficiently recent. At the time this book was written, the Visual Studio template was based on Angular 5.2, while the most recent Angular release was 6.1.

The simplest way to move to the test Angular version is to delete the whole `ClientApp` folder and to create a new Angular application with the latest version of Angular CLI installed in the *Technical requirements* section, as follows:

1. Delete the `ClientApp` folder.
2. In Windows File Explorer, right-click on the project folder (the project folder, not the solution folder) while pressing the *Shift* key.
3. The file menu contains options to open a Windows console in that folder. Select that option, and then issue the following command:

```
>ng new ClientApp
```

4. After the new application has been scaffolded by Angular CLI, let's open the new `package.json` and, in its `scripts` section, replace the following command:

```
build": "ng build",
```

With the following new commands:

```
"build": "ng build --extract-css",
"build:ssr": "npm run build -- --app=ssr --output-hashing=media",
```

5. The first command empowers the original build command with the option to automatically collect all styles mixed in the HTML and to add them to the bundled CSS files, while the second command builds a version of the application for execution on Node.js on the server side. This is required if the developer decides to pre-render the initial page on the server side in order to speed up application loading. It is worth pointing out that server-side pre-rendering requires further changes to the project as a whole.

After the project is run, the browser shows the default page of an empty Angular application that contains just the Angular logo and some links to external documentation. If the purpose is to start a new Angular application from scratch, the preceding method is the best option.

However, for didactic purposes, it is more appropriate to upgrade the Angular application scaffolded by Visual Studio to the new Angular version, since this non-trivial application immediately shows most of the main Angular building blocks. The Visual Studio project can be upgraded as follows:

1. Create a new Angular project called AngularVSTemplate.
2. Open a Windows console in the ClientApp folder.
3. In order to run the upgrade procedure, the Angular CLI version installed locally in the ClientApp folder must be upgraded to the latest version. This is easily achieved by issuing the following command:

   >npm install @angular/cli

4. At this point, the format of the Angular application must be upgraded to match one of the latest versions with ng update @angular/cli. The update command was introduced in Angular 6, to upgrade automatically all packages to their last releases. After this upgrade, if the original Angular version was older than version 6, the angular-cli.json Angular configuration file should be replaced by the newer angular.json configuration file. However, this operation may fail the first time. If this is the case, and the new angular.json configuration file doesn't replace the old one, please repeat the same command. This operation will be successful the second time.

5. Upgrade the Angular core modules with `ng update @angular/core`.

6. Open `package.json`, and, if the `scripts` section contains the following command:

   ```
   "start": "ng serve --extract-css"
   ```

   You will need to replace it with the following command:

   ```
   "start": "ng serve"
   ```

   Since Angular version 6 appeared on the market, the `--extract-css` option is only possible in the `build` command.

7. Remove the `typings.d.ts` file from the `ClientApp/src` folder since it is not used by the latest Angular versions that use WebPack instead of the old SystemJS.

8. Run the project.

A non-trivial application with a menu and three pages appears! Play with it to get a feeling of what can be done with Angular. The next section analyzes the various component parts of the project.

 Since Angular automatically handles WebPack configurations, it is not possible to add the `SourceMapDevToolPlugin` plugin to configure WebPack in such a way that TypeScript sources can be debugged in Visual Studio, as explained in the *WebPack plugins – recovering Visual Studio debugger* section in `Chapter 7`, *Bundling with WebPack*. However, the browser debugger shows Typescript sources so that code can be debugged in the browser. For instance, Chrome shows TypeScript sources in the `<folder with no name>/src` path under the `webpack://` folder. As soon as the code hits the first browser breakpoint, the browser understands the location of source maps on the server and triggers Visual Studio debugger. From then on, debugging can continue in Visual Studio.

Project structure

The whole Angular Client application is contained in the `ClientApp` folder. This folder contains various configuration files and two folders that define two Angular applications:

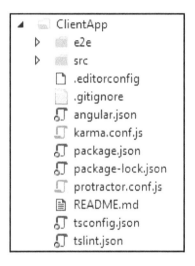

The `src` folder contains the main application to publish, while the `e2e` folder contains an application whose only purpose is the execution of end-to-end tests on the main applications. End-to-end tests are integration tests that also simulate actual user interaction with the application. Ends-to-end tests are based on the Protractor framework which will be described in the *Testing* section of `Chapter 13`, *Navigation and Services*.

The following is a descriptions of all configuration files contained in the `ClientApp` folder:

- `Angular.json`: This is the main Angular configuration file. Here, the developer may configure how the application is built, and how WebPack bundles all application assets. In fact, Angular CLI takes on the burden of invoking WebPack and defining its correct configuration to fulfill all requirements contained in `Angular.json`. `Angular.json` is used by various Angular CLI commands, such as `serve` and `build`, for example.

- `tsconfig.json`: This is a TypeScript configuration file. The developer can't change it too much, because some changes might break the application. Developers should confine themselves to adding other declaration libraries to the `"lib"` compiler option.
- `tslint.json`: TSLint is a software engineering tool that the Angular project uses to check TypeScript code for readability, maintainability, and functionality errors. `tslint.json` lets developers configure which checks are enabled. There is no need to change the scaffolded settings, but developers that are proficient in TSLint can change them with no risk of breaking the application.
- `package.json`: This is a Node.js configuration file. As usual, developers may add further libraries here to use in the project, or they may upgrade the existing libraries to newer versions. However, existing Angular packages must be updated with the Angular CLI `ng update...` command, which we already used in the *Creating an Angular project* section in order to upgrade Angular core to its latest version.
- `karma.conf.js`: Karma is a wrapper that enables the Jasmine unit test framework to run in a browser, while also facilitating automatic generation of unit test skeleton classes. Jasmine is described in the *Testing your library with Jasmine* section of `Chapter 8`, *Building TypeScript Libraries*. Unit testing in Angular is described in the *Testing* section in `Chapter 13`, *Navigation and Services*. `karma.conf.js` is the Karma tests configuration file. Since unit tests are scaffolded and automatically handled by Angular CLI, usually, there is no need to change this file.
- `protractor.conf.js`: This is a protractor configuration file that configures end-to-end test to perform with Protractor. Protractor tests are based on Jasmine, augmented by functions that simulate user behavior in the application. Protractor is described in the *Testing* section of `Chapter 13`, *Navigation and Services*.

The main application folder

The `ClientApp/src` application folder contains various files and folders, as demonstrated in the following screenshot:

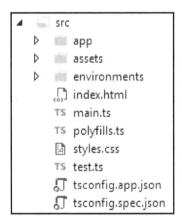

The `tsconfig.app.json` and `tsconfig.spec.json` files are specializations of the main `tsconfig.json` folder for the main application TypeScript files, and for the main application Karma-based test files. They use the `"extends": "../tsconfig.json"` option to import all settings in `tsconfig.json`. They just add source and target folder/files settings that are specific to the main application. In fact, each Angular workspace may contain several Angular applications, and the basic project scaffolded by Angular CLI contains a second test application based on Protractor (the one contained in the `e2e` folder).

`index.html` is the unique page that will host the entire SPA:

```
<!doctype html>
<html lang="en">
<head>
  <meta charset="utf-8">
  <title>ClientApp</title>
  <base href="/">

  <meta name="viewport" content="width=device-width, initial-scale=1">
  <link rel="icon" type="image/x-icon" href="favicon.ico">
</head>
<body>
  <app-root></app-root>
</body>
</html>
```

The developer is only allowed to change a number of headers, including title, description, and favicon, since the entire document body is contained inside the `app-root` component (see the following). However, developers may not add CSS or JavaScript files there, since they are automatically handled by Angular CLI through WebPack.

`<base href="/">` specifies the path all relative URLs are referred to, in other words, asset URLs (such as, for example, image URLs), but also API calls to the server. Usually, it is the domain root, but an application may also be deployed to an inner path of a domain.

The entire document body is specified by an Angular root component called `app-root`, so the developer must change this component in order to modify the application layout. In fact, as explained in the *General Angular architecture* section, each Angular application is organized as a hierarchy of modules called **components**, each composed of a TypeScript class and an HTML template.

Angular uses Typescript modules, so the entire TypeScript code is a tree of modules rooted into a unique entry-point module. `main.ts` is the main application entry point, while `test.js` is the Karma test entry point. Developers should not modify any of theses two files.

The `style.css` file contains style settings that are applied to the whole application. Each component can also specify its specific CSS settings file that is applied to that component only. WebPack takes care of handling all CSS files adequately. Developers' overall custom CSS settings can be added to `style.css`, or to further CSS files added to `Angular.json`, as detailed in the *Configuring and building an Angular application* section of this chapter.

`polyfill.ts` is a module that just collects all imports of polyfill modules. Polyfills are imported for side effects only, since they simulate non-supported features with symbols defined globally. Putting all polyfills in this module is a simple way to bundle them in the application, while keeping the symbols they define as global. `polyfill.ts` already contains some common polyfills, and most of them are commented out. Each polyfill import statement is preceded by a short explanation of when it must be added. Developers can also add polyfills after having installed them in `package.json`.

The `assets` folder is where images, audio, and video are placed to be bundled with the application. Developers may organize their assets in a hierarchy of subfolders. It is sufficient to reference assets in this folder from any HTML for causing the asset to be bundled with the application. In fact, since HTML templates are processed by WebPack, WebPack discovers all references and processes them adequately. The following is an example of an image reference:

```
<img src="assets/img/myImage.png">
```

The `environment` folder contains various TypeScript files, each included in a different build environment. Environments are defined in `Angular.json` and each environment specifies which file under `environment` must be included in its build. As a default option, there are just two environments: production and development. However, the developer may further define build types and build environments. The following is the content of the two default environment files:

```
//environment.ts
//included in the development build

export const environment = {
  production: false
};

//environment.prod.ts
//included in the production build

export const environment = {
  production: false
};
```

Each developer module that behaves differently in production and development must include the following import statement:

```
import { environment } from './environments/environment';
```

Then, it can test the `environment.production` property to adapt its behavior to the environment it was built in. `'./environments/environment'` is bundled as `./environments/environment.ts` or as `./environments/environment.prod.ts`, depending on which build environment is selected by the Angular CLI `build` command.

If more than two default build environment files are defined, the developer should add further properties to the `environment` constant object in order to trigger different behaviors in each different build environment.

Finally, the `app` folder contains the actual application code, that is, components and other Angular building blocks required by the application:

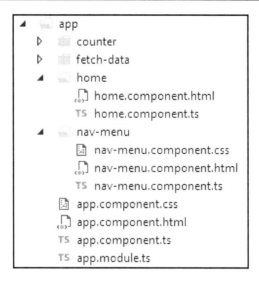

More specifically, the folder root contains the root component of the whole application, app.component.ts, in other words, the one associated with the <app-root></app-root> tags in index.html:

```
import { Component } from '@angular/core';

@Component({
    selector: 'app-root',
    templateUrl: './app.component.html',
    styleUrls: ['./app.component.css']
})
export class AppComponent {
    title = 'app';
}
```

Each component is defined by a public TypeScript class decorated with the @Component decorator. The decorator properties define the parts the component is made of. In the preceding case, these parts are its tag name app-root, an HTML template that defines its layout, and private CSS styles that apply just to its HTML. In general, the TypeScript class that defines a component may contain various properties and methods that encode its behavior. Each component may have other components nested inside its HTML template:

```
<div class='container-fluid'>
  <div class='row'>
    <div class='col-sm-3'>
      <app-nav-menu></app-nav-menu>
    </div>
    <div class='col-sm-9 body-content'>
```

```
        <router-outlet></router-outlet>
      </div>
    </div>
  </div>
```

<app-nav-menu> is the application menu on the left-hand of the page that is defined inside the nav-menu folder, while <router-outlet> is a kind of placeholder that is replaced by the component selected with the <app-nav-menu> menu. In fact, as explained in the *Angular architecture* section, links in the left-hand menu are mapped into components, and component parameters, so that, when a link is clicked, an instance of the corresponding component is created and placed in <router-outlet>.

The app folder also contains four subfolders with further components defined inside them: the left-hand menu, and the three different contents the user may select with this menu. Finally, the app folder contains a module named app.module.ts. Modules are described in the next section together with all the building blocks that comprise an Angular application.

Angular architecture

Angular is a framework, that is, it is not a library for handling a single application exigency, but it is a comprehensive library, like jQuery, that supplies everything that is needed to build a complete client application based on TypeScript (or JavaScript). However, unlike jQuery, it is an opinionated framework, that is, it is not just a collection of utilities, but it also enforces the whole application architecture. In short, Angular supplies both a comprehensive set of utilities and a pre-organized application architecture.

An Angular application is comprised of the following building blocks: components, directives, bindings, pipes, services, modules, and routers.

Components were described briefly in the previous section and will be studied in detail in the *Modules, components, and data binding* section of this chapter. They extend the usual HTML tags, with further tags defined by the developer. Just like the standard HTML tags, components may also have properties and methods associated with them. While the component layout and graphics are defined by the component HTML template and CSS files, component properties, methods, and behavior are defined in the component TypeScript class.

Directives are modifiers that may be applied to HTML tags, and to components, in order to modify their standard behavior. Angular comes with a comprehensive set of useful directives, but the developer may define custom directives through TypeScript classes decorated with the `@Directive` decorator. The behavior of the standard HTML anchors in the `nav-menu` is modified by the Angular Core `routerLink` directive that changes its behavior from moving to an external page to loading a new component in `<router-outlet>` of the root component:

```
<a [routerLink]='["/counter"]' (click)='collapse()'>
```

Bindings are means whereby Angular can connect component class properties and methods to the component HTML template. They are the way in which values are written in an input field or moved to class properties, and vice versa, and the way in which property values are inserted into various parts of each component HTML template. The `currentCount` property of the TypeScript class that defines the `counter` component is bound to the component HTML template, so that whenever the property value changes, the appearance of the template changes to show the new value:

```
<p>Current count: <strong>{{ currentCount }}</strong></p>
```

The `counter` component also shows how the `incrementCounter` class method, which increments the `currentCount` property, can be bound to events such as the click event:

```
<button (click)="incrementCounter()">Increment</button>
```

Running the application and going to the counter page shows how both the preceding bindings work. Bindings are described in the *Modules, components, and data binding* section of this chapter.

Pipes modify the standard behavior of bindings by transforming values while they move from class properties to templates. Several pipes may be stacked one after the other in the same binding. The predefined currency pipe adds a currency sign to the value displayed by the `counter` component, as follows:

```
<p>Current count: <strong>{{ currentCount|currency}}</strong></p>
```

Further pipes may be added by stacking further | symbols with the pipe name after them. Pipes are described in detail in the *Pipes* section of `Chapter 11`, *Input and Interactions*.

Services are business elements that help components and directives to do their job. In Angular, they are automatically injected by the Angular framework into the constructors of the classes that use them. For instance, the `fetch-data` component uses the `HttpClient` service class to communicate with the server. An instance of this class is automatically injected by the framework as follows:

```
constructor(http: HttpClient, @Inject('BASE_URL') baseUrl: string) {
    http.get<WeatherForecast[]>(baseUrl +
'api/SampleData/WeatherForecasts')
        .subscribe(result => {
          this.forecasts = result;
        }
```

Services are described in detail in the *Services and Dependency Injection* section of `Chapter 13`, *Navigation and Services*.

Angular modules are higher-level groupings of code comprised of several TypeScript modules that help to organize Angular applications hierarchically. Angular modules are implemented with TypeScript classes decorated with the `@NgModule` decorator. Angular module classes are usually empty, since all information is provided in the `@NgModule` decorator. The `declaration` property of the decorators lists all components, pipes, and decorators considered part of the module, while the `providers` property lists all services that are considered part of the module. Each entity that is part of a module may use all other entities defined in the same module, plus the one contained in all other modules imported by their module. Imported modules are declared in the `@NgModule imports` property. Only entities exported by listing them in the `@NgModule exports` property are visible outside each module and can be used when that module is imported. Each application has a main module that specifies the bootstrap main component, which, in the case of `AngularVSTemplate`, is `AppComponent`. A definition of the unique `AngularVSTemplate` module is as follows:

```
@NgModule({
  declarations: [
    AppComponent,
    NavMenuComponent,
    HomeComponent,
    CounterComponent,
    FetchDataComponent
  ],
  imports: [
    BrowserModule.withServerTransition({ appId: 'ng-cli-universal' }),
    HttpClientModule,
    FormsModule,
    RouterModule.forRoot([
      { path: '', component: HomeComponent, pathMatch: 'full' },
```

```
        { path: 'counter', component: CounterComponent },
        { path: 'fetch-data', component: FetchDataComponent },
      ])
  ],
  providers: [],
  bootstrap: [AppComponent]
})
export class AppModule { }
```

The `delarations` property contains all five application components, while the `imports` property contains a lot of Angular predefined modules:

- `BrowserModule` contains all Angular stuff that is specific for running Angular in a browser. In turn, `BrowserModule` imports and re-exports `CommonModule` which contains all the principal Angular directives, components, and pipes. Applications that run in Node.js, instead of a browser or other modules that do not bootstrap the application, must import just `CommonModule`. The call to the static `withServerTransition` method returns an Angular module that is specific to bootstrapping an application that has been pre-rendered on the server side. Removing `withServerTransition` has no effect if the project has not been configured for pre-rendering. Pre-rendering will not be discussed in this book since it has too many drawbacks to actually be useful.

- `HttpClientModule` contains services useful for communicating with the server, such as an HTTP Client. They are used by the `fetch-data` component.

- `FormsModule` contains directives and services for handling HTML forms and their inputs. `AngularVSTemplate`, in its present form, doesn't use forms, so this module import may be removed (try it). However, later on in this chapter, form-related stuff will be added to the application.

- `RouterModule` contains directives and services for handling routing, in other words, for turning URLs specified in `[routerLink]` into component instances to be loaded in `<router-outlet>` tags. The call to the `forRoot` static method returns a module with all the rules for turning URLs into components and component parameters.

More details and examples on Angular modules are given in the *Modules, components, and data binding* section.

Routers are configured in the module definition, and each configuration is a set of objects, each specifying a routing rule that translates URLs into instances of components to load in `<router-outlet>`. The rules for the `AngularVSTemplate` application are very simple; just path/component pairs. Usually, a rule is fired when the string specified in the path matches the start of the URL, but a complete match may be required by setting the `pathMatch` property to `full`:

```
[
    { path: '', component: HomeComponent, pathMatch: 'full' },
    { path: 'counter', component: CounterComponent },
    { path: 'fetch-data', component: FetchDataComponent },
]
```

Rules are tried sequentially until a matching rule is found.

The `AngularVSTemplate` project contains just a single `<router-outlet>`, but HTML templates may also have several `<router-outlet>`, in which case they must be named, so link-mapping rules may specify which component must be placed in each `<router-outlet>`.

Routers are described in detail in the *Routing and navigation* section of `Chapter 13`, *Navigation and Services*.

How Angular updates the HTML rendered by component templates

Since templates are bound to class instance properties, each property change might require the re-rendering of the component HTML template to adapt it to the new property value. However, how does Angular Engine come to know that a property change took place? It can't, because object property changes do not trigger any event that might be used to execute an HTML update routine. Moreover, if a similar event were to exist, it wouldn't be convenient to use it because each user interaction typically causes several simultaneous property changes that would trigger too many redundant calls to the HTML update routine.

Angular does something simpler; it detects all causes that may provide changes in the application, namely, JavaScript events, delayed executions (`setTimeout`, and so on), and AJAX operations by hooking all JavaScript functions connected with them (such as `addEventListener`). Moreover, Angular executes each component in the scope of a function, so it may provide hooks that are specific for each component instance in the various function execution contexts. This way, it is able to recognize the component where the event took place by means of the specific hook that was called.

When a JavaScript event takes place inside a component with a template x, Angular checks which of the properties bound to that template changed their values. Now, an event occurring in a template x may cause **direct changes** only to properties bound to x, or to any template x is in, in other words, to properties bound to x or to any ancestor template of x that intercepts an event triggered by x. In fact, properties of objects contained in children components of x and in children components of any ancestor of x may change their values only if a property bound to x or to any ancestor of x is **explicitly passed** to them because of component encapsulation.

Thus, when an event is triggered in a component x, Angular does the following:

- It checks which of the properties bound to x, or to any ancestor of x, changed
- If any of the changed properties are passed to other children components, their templates are also checked for property changes
- For each changed property, all leaf templates that must change their HTML because of the property change are added to a list of templates that must be re-rendered
- All templates in the list of templates to re-render are re-rendered

The preceding algorithm discovers all templates that need to be re-rendered, with this entailing just the extra cost of checking for property changes within all ancestor templates of the template x that originated the JavaScript event.

Modules, components, and data binding

Previous sections, *Project structure* and *Angular architecture*, already described the basic structure of components. This section provides a few missing details and focuses on bindings and how to pass input to components.

As already discussed, components are made up of three parts: a TypeScript class decorated with the `@Component` decorator, an HTML template, and CSS styles. The TypeScript class has a leading role since the other two parts are specified as properties of the `@Component` class decorator together with the component tag name:

```
@Component({
   selector: 'app-nav-menu',
   templateUrl: './nav-menu.component.html',
   styleUrls: ['./nav-menu.component.css']
})
export class NavMenuComponent {
   isExpanded = false;

   collapse() {
      this.isExpanded = false;
   }

   toggle() {
      this.isExpanded = !this.isExpanded;
   }
}
```

`styleUrls` is an array, since several CSS files may be used by the same component. Both template and styles may be provided in-line for simple components instead of being defined in external files. In-line definitions are placed in the `styles` and `template` properties, as the following example demonstrates:

```
@Component({
   selector: 'app-smart-date',
   template:'<span>{{roughDate|date}}</span>',
   styles: ['span {color: red ;}']
})
```

All components scaffolded in `AngularVSTemplate` do not receive input parameters. Let's create a new, very simple component to show how components may be passed parameters. Let's call it `SmartDate`, since it will render an input `Date` object in a pretty red format.

All Angular elements are easily scaffolded with the Angular CLI `ng generate...` command. Let's open a Windows console rooted in the `ClientApp` folder, and type the following:

ng generate component SmartDate

The command above can be also shortened as:

ng g c SmartDate

A new folder named `smart-date` with the CSS component, HTML template, and Typescript class files is created. The folder also contains a `.spec` file for testing the component. The new component is automatically added to the declarations of the `app.module.ts` Angular module. In the event that the application contains several modules, the module name may be specified with the `-m` parameter:

```
ng generate component SmartDate -m App
```

 While developing Angular applications with Visual Studio, always keep a Windows console open in the `ClientApp` folder so as to speed up Angular CLI usage.

Since, for this simple component, it is easier to use in-line styles and templates, let's replace `templateUrl` and `styleUrls` with the following:

```
template:'<span>{{roughDate|date}}</span>',
styles: ['span {color: red ;}']
```

`roughDate` is a property defined in the `SmartDateComponent` class, and `date` is a predefined Angular pipe that transforms the date object into a string containing the date in a pretty format:

```
roughDate: Date;
```

Component input properties may be set in the component tag in a way similar to attributes of HTML tags. Hence, the idea is to render a date in a pretty format in a template by referencing the `SmartDate` component with something like the following:

```
<app-smart-date [date]='todayDate'></app-smart-date>
```

Here, `todayDate` is a property or a variable containing the date to render, and `date` is an alias for the `SmartDateComponent` `roughDate` property.

`roughDate` may be declared an input property by preceding it with the `@Input` decorator:

```
@Input('date') roughDate: Date;
```

The string passed to the decorator defines the alias to use in the component tag. If no alias is provided, the property name is used.

The `Input` symbol must be imported from `@angular/core` by adding it to the import statement the top of the `SmartDateComponent.ts` file:

```
import { Component, OnInit, Input } from '@angular/core';
```

The final component code is as follows:

```
import { Component, OnInit, Input } from '@angular/core';

@Component({
  selector: 'app-smart-date',
  template:'<span>{{roughDate|date}}</span>',
  styles: ['span {color: red ;}']
})
export class SmartDateComponent implements OnInit {
  constructor() { }
  @Input('date') roughDate: Date;
  ngOnInit() {
  }
}
```

ngOnInit is called after the component has been added to the DOM, so it is a good location for placing some initialization code. More details on Angular life cycle hooks are given in the *Templates life cycle hooks* section of Chapter 11, *Input and Interactions*.

Component input properties may also be declared by adding their names to the inputs array property of the @Component decorator, instead of using the @Input decorator:

```
@Component({
  selector: 'app-smart-date',
  template:'<span>{{roughDate|date}}</span>',
  styles: ['span {color: red ;}'],
  inputs: ['roughDate:date']
})
```

Again, if the colon followed by an alias is omitted, the property name is taken as a tag attribute. The use of inputs is not recommended, since property names are passed as strings and, consequently, they don't receive any TypeScript compile-time check.

Components may also have output properties, but they are dealt with as events that must be handled by event-handling methods defined in the surrounding components. Events are covered in the *Components interaction* section of Chapter 11, *Input and Interactions*.

We may use the SmartDateComponent instance in the home.component. By way of a first step, let's add a todayDate property to the home.component class:

```
import { Component, OnInit } from '@angular/core';
@Component({
  selector: 'app-home',
  templateUrl: './home.component.html',
})
export class HomeComponent implements OnInit {
```

```
  todayDate: Date;
  ngOnInit() {
    this.todayDate = new Date();
  }
}
```

The component has been modified to import the `OnInit` interface and to implement it. Assigning the `now` date to `todayDate` allows this date to be refreshed each time the component is instantiated, that is, each time the user selects the home page in the menu. Placing the assignment in the constructor doesn't work properly because component instances might be cached by the framework.

Now, the component may be added to the home component template:

```
<h1>Hello, world!</h1>
<p> <app-smart-date date='{{todayDate}}'></app-smart-date> Welcome to.....
```

`{{...}}` is the interpolator operator that inserts the result of a JavaScript expression inside a template. There will be more on bindings in the next subsection.

Template bindings

Each component template may contain various syntactic constructs that are bound to JavaScript expressions. The simplest of such syntactic constructs is the interpolation operator: `{{<expressions here>}}`. The interpolation operator may be mixed in the text of text nodes, as in the following examples:

```
<!-- Taken from the counter component template -->
<p>Current count: <strong>{{ currentCount}}</strong></p>
<!-- works also without the strong tag -->
<p>Current count: {{ currentCount}}</p>
```

Whatever value is returned by the interpolation operator is cast to a string before being replaced in the HTML. Interpolation operators can also be placed within an HTML property value:

```
<p>Current count: <input type = 'text' value='{{ currentCount}}'
name='myInput'/></p>
```

It may also be used within an input property of a component:

```
<h1>Hello, world!</h1>
<p> <app-smart-date date='{{todayDate}}'></app-smart-date> Welcome to.....
```

Also in this case, the expression result is cast to a string before the replacement, and then the string is cast again to the type of the input property before being assigned to that property. In the case of the `Date` type, the double cast operation always returns the original date object and everything works fine. However, in the case of generic object types, the double cast is not able to return the original object, so the `{{...}}` operator can't be used. When an expression has to be bound to a component input property or to an HTML element DOM property, the double cast may be avoided by replacing `<property>='{{<expression>}}'` with `[<property>]='<expression>'`:

```
<h1>Hello, world!</h1>
<p> <app-smart-date [date]='todayDate'></app-smart-date> Welcome to.....
```

Bindings may also be applied to directives that accept inputs. For example, the `routerLink` directive used in the anchors of the `nav-menu` component is bound to arrays of strings where each string specifies a URL segment:

```
<a [routerLink]='["/counter"]' (click)='collapse()'>
    <span class='glyphicon glyphicon-education'></span>
    Counter
</a>
```

The expressions inside the interpolation operator, and to the right of the `[]` operator, are called **binding expressions**, and usually contain properties of the class that defines the component the template is part of, but they may also contain variables defined in the template itself, as in the `fetch-data` component:

```
    ...
<tr *ngFor="let forecast of forecasts">
  <td>{{forecast.dateFormatted }}</td>
    ...
```

The `*ngFor` directive iterates over all objects of the `forecast` array that is a component property. In each iteration, it defines a new `forecast` variable that may be used in the whole block that is iterated, that is, within the content of the `tr` tag. Also, nested properties of a variable/properties, such as `forecast.dateFormatted`, may be used in binding expressions. More details on structural directives, such as `*ngFor`, are given in the *Structural directives* section of `Chapter 12`, *Angular Advanced Features*.

Binding expressions may also contain variables defined with the so-called template references:

```
<p>The text mirrors the input content:<input #toMirror/>
    <span>{{toMirror.value}}</span>
</p>
```

`#toMirror` inside the input tag defines the `toMirror` variable that contains a reference to the input field, so the remainder of the template may refer to all input field properties through this variable. The preceding code may be tested by inserting it at the bottom of the `counter` component. Each time the counter button is clicked, the content of the input element is mirrored in the span. The code is not mirrored immediately, since the input field is not bound to any property/method, and, as explained at the end of the previous section, Angular only updates templates when a bound event is triggered. Later on in this subsection, we will bind a property to this input field, and the update will be immediate.

Interpolation expressions may be more complex than simple property accessors. They may contain mathematical operators and string operations. However, they can't contain any `new` operation and, in general, no operation that has side effects (that is, effects other than returning a result). For instance, the counter interpolation expression can compute the square of the counter value as follows:

```
<p>Current count:
<strong>{{currentCount*currentCount|currency}}</strong></p>
```

Complex expressions should be avoided since they have a high performance cost. They should somehow be moved inside the class code (for instance, by using computed properties), or handled with pipes.

HTML elements have both properties and attributes. Most element properties have attributes with the same name, such as, for example, the value property, in which case the attribute specifies the initial value for the property with the same name, but changes to the property are not reflected back to the corresponding attribute. For instance, if an HTML document contains the following:

```
<input name="myName" value="Francesco" />
```

Then the `value` attribute is set to `"Francesco"`, which, in turn, also causes the `value` property to be set to `"Francesco"`. However, if the `value` property is then changed from JavaScript with something like `myNode.value="John"`, the `value` attribute remains unchanged and set to `"Francesco"`. The `value` attribute can only be changed by `myNode.setAttribute("value", "John")`.

If the same `<input name="myName" value="Francesco" />` HTML is placed in a component template, the `value` attribute is set to `"Francesco"`, as in any standard HTML document. However, if `value` is bound to an expression, as in the following code snippet:

```
<input name="myName" value="{{Name}}" />
<input name="myName" [value]="Name" />
```

Then, the content of the `Name` property is inserted into the `value` property and the `value` attribute remains empty! Thus, as a default, Angular bindings operate on properties, not on attributes. Accordingly, writing the following code throws an exception:

```
<button [aria-label]="currentLabel">{{currentLabel}}</button>
```

In fact, the `aria-label` attribute has no corresponding property, so the binding target doesn't exist. The right way to bind attributes is by preceding them with the `attr.` prefix, as follows:

```
<button [attr.aria-label]="currentLabel">{{currentLabel}}</button>
```

Style and class bindings

CSS classes may be bound in the same way as all other properties with an expression that returns a string with all CSS classes to apply:

```
<!-- overallClassesProperty contains the string "btn btn-primary" -->
<button [class]="overallClassesProperty"
(click)="incrementCounter()">Increment</button>
```

However, each single class may be turned on/off by a Boolean expression with a syntax similar to the following:

```
<button class="btn" [class.btn-primary]="currentCount>4"
        (click)="incrementCounter()">Increment
</button>
```

The disadvantage of this solution is that you have to add as many [class] bindings as there are classes to turn on/off. The `ngClass` directive allows a simultaneous binding of several CSS classes:

```
<button [ngClass]="{'btn': true, 'btn-primary': currentCount>4,
                    'btn-info':currentCount<=4}"
        (click)="incrementCounter()">Increment
</button>
```

It is also possible to directly set the element style with an expression such as `[style.<property-name>]='value'` or `[style.<property-name>.<unit of measure>]='value'` when the style property needs a unit of measure:

```
<p>Current count:
  <strong [style.color]="currentCount>4? 'red' : black"
          [style.font-size.%]="currentCount>4? 150 : 100">
  {{ currentCount|currency}}
```

```
    </strong>
  </p>
```

An `ngStyle` directive is also available to simultaneously specify several style properties:

```
<p>
  Current count:
  <strong [ngStyle]="currentCount>4 ?
                    {'color': 'red', 'font-size': '150%'}:
                    {'color': 'black', 'font-size': '100%'}">
    {{ currentCount|currency}}
  </strong>
</p>
```

Events and two-way bindings

HTML elements and Angular components communicate with other elements or components that they are in by issuing events that can be intercepted by the ancestors they are in. Thus, while input properties are the way components receive input from their ancestors, events are the way components communicate the output to their ancestors. Code may be associated with an event by adding to the component/HTML element a syntax such as (<event name>)='code to execute'. Code may contain properties and methods of the component class, plus template variables and element references, unlike the code of input binding expressions, the code bound to events may have, and usually have, side effects. The following are two examples of event bindings:

```
<!-- Taken from nav-menu component -->
<a [routerLink]='["/counter"]' (click)='collapse()'>....

<!-- Taken from counter component -->
<button (click)="incrementCounter()">Increment</button>
```

Both the code snippets listed involve a component method. This is the usual way to handle events, but more complex statements may be bound to events. The reader is encouraged to look at the definitions of the methods used in the preceding examples to get a better feel for how events work.

HTML events, as well as custom-defined component events, have an event object associated with them that contains information regarding the event. This object is created when the event is issued and it is passed in the $event variable that is accessible in the context of each code snippet bound to an event:

```
<button (click)="incrementCounter($event)">Increment</button>
```

The preceding code may be tested by modifying the `incrementCounter` method as follows, and then by inspecting the event object in the debugger:

```
public incrementCounter(evt: any) {
    this.currentCount++;
}
```

In the case of HTML events, `$event` is bound to the original browser event, while custom events triggered by components define their custom event objects. Component events are discussed in detail in the *Components interaction* section of `Chapter 11`, *Input and Interactions*.

Form inputs may also have two-ways bindings that bind their values to property elements, in which case information not only moves from a component property to the input value, but also from the input value to the bound component property. Input from two-way bindings have the following format: `[(ngModel)]='<expression representing an object property or a variable>'`. Use of the `ngModel` directive requires that the Angular core module `FormsModule` be imported by the module the component is in:

```
@NgModule({
...
imports: [
    ...
    FormsModule,
    ...
    ])
...
})
```

In order to test them, let's add a new property to the `counter` component:

```
public currentCount = 0;
```

Then, add a two-way binding to the `#toMirror` input we added in the `counter` template, plus another span to mirror the input value from the new `currentCount` property:

```
<p>
    The text mirrors the input content:<input [(ngModel)]="testInput"
#toMirror /><br />
    direct mirror: <span>{{toMirror.value}}</span><br />
    property mirror: <span>{{testInput}}</span><br />
</p>
```

Each time the input value is changed, both mirrors are updated to reflect the input value.

Behind the scenes, two-way bindings are implemented with a standard one-way binding plus an event. More specifically, the two-way binding shown in the preceding example is equivalent to the following:

```
<input [ngModel]="testInput" [ngModelChange]='testInput=$event' #toMirror
/>
```

The *Components interaction* section of `Chapter 11`, *Input and Interactions*, explains how to define two-way bindings for all HTML element properties as well as for components.

Angular modules

The structure of modules was already explained in the *Angular architecture* section of this chapter. This section shows an example of how to create an additional Angular module in an existing application. The *Routing and navigation* section in `Chapter 13`, *Navigation and Services*, explains how to lazy load extra modules only when they are needed.

A new Angular module is easily created with Angular CLI. Let's open a Windows console rooted in the `ClientApp` folder and issue the following command:

```
>ng generate module ExtraFeatures
```

A new module, with a test file, is created in a new `extra-features` folder in the `src\app` path. It imports just the `CommonModule`, which contains Angular core definitions, since the wider `BrowserModule` must be imported just by the main module that takes care of browser interaction. We will put a new SPA page in the `extra-features` module. Hence, we must add in some routing capabilities with `RouterModule.forChild` that do not define a new router, since each application must have a single router, but just new routes that will be merged with the main router routes defined with `RouterModule.forRoot` in the main application module.

A new component may be added to the `extra-features` module as follows:

```
>cd src/app/extra-features
>ng generate component TestComponent1 -m extra-features
```

The -m parameter specifies the module in which to place the component. The command requires the module filename without the `.module.ts` postfix.

Also possible to write simply:

```
>ng generate component extra-features/TestComponent1
```

The component is automatically added to its module declarations. However, a router for this component must be added, too, as follows:

```
...
import { RouterModule } from '@angular/router';
@NgModule({
  imports: [
    CommonModule,
    RouterModule.forChild([
      { path: 'test', component: TestComponentComponent },
    ])
  ],
  declarations: [TestComponentComponent],
  exports: [/*TestComponentComponent*/]
})
export class ExtraFeaturesModule { }
```

If `TestComponentComponent` is used only in routes defined in `ExtraFeaturesModule` it doesn't need to be exported. However, if it is also a utility component that can be used inside the template of other components, it must be included in the module exports.

Now, the new module must be imported in the main application module. As a first step, let's add the following import statement at the top of the `app.module.ts` file:

```
import {ExtraFeaturesModule} from './extra-features/extra-features.module'
```

Then add the new module to the `imports` property of the `@Module` decorator:

```
imports: [
    ...
    ExtraFeaturesModule,
    ...
    ])
```

At this point, let's add some HTML to the new `test-component.component.html` component template file:

```
<p>
  extra module test-component works!
</p>
```

Now, the new module and its component are ready to be tested. Let's add the new link for the new route in `nav-menu.component.html`:

```
....
  <li [routerLinkActive]='["link-active"]'>
    <a [routerLink]='["/test"]' (click)='collapse()'>
```

```
      <span class='glyphicon glyphicon-th-list'></span> external page
    </a>
  </li>
</ul>
```

When the application is run, the component defined in the new module is rendered properly!

Configuring and building an Angular application

The `Angular.json` file contains various configurations used by Angular CLI. Let's open it and take a look at it:

```
{
    "$schema": "./node_modules/@angular/cli/lib/config/schema.json",
    "version": 1,
    "newProjectRoot": "projects",
    "projects": {
      "AngularVSTemplate": [...],
      "AngularVSTemplate-e2e": [...]
    },
    "defaultProject": "AngularVSTemplate",
    "schematics": {
      "@schematics/angular:component": {
        "prefix": "app",
        "styleext": "css"
      },
      "@schematics/angular:directive": {
        "prefix": "app"
      }
    }
}
```

At the top level, the configuration `.json` file contains the workspace version (`version`), the two projects contained in the workspace (`projects`), the path (`newProjectRoot`) where new projects, when created with the CLI, will be added, and the default project (`defaultProject`) that is launched when the workspace is run, and that is built for deployment. Finally, it contains some defaults for the various types of entities that can be created with the CLI, namely, components, directives, pipes, modules, services, and classes. All these defaults can be overridden with Angular CLI command parameters. The `AngularVSTemplate` project contains the actual application, while `AngularVSTemplate-e2e` contains an application based on Protractor that performs end-to-end tests by simulating user behavior.

When opened, the `AngularVSTemplate` node contains configuration options that are specific to the project:

```
"AngularVSTemplate": {
    "root": "",
    "sourceRoot": "src",
    "projectType": "application",
    "architect": {
        "build": ...,
        "serve": ...,
        "extract-i18n": ...,
        "test": ...,
        "lint": ...
    }
},
```

We have the following:

- The project root folder (`root`), whose value is the `ClientApp` folder itself
- The folder containing all sources (`sourceRoot`)
- The type of project (`projectType`), that may be either application or library
- Options that specify how to build the application (`build`)
- Options that specify how to build and run the application in development mode (`serve`)
- Options for the application localization (`extract-i18n`)
- Karma test configuration (`test`)
- The lint software engineering tool configuration (`lint`)

Localization settings will be discussed in the *Pipes* section of `Chapter 11`, *Input and Interactions*. The only other options that the developer might need to change manually are the ones in the build node that contain some general options, and then option overrides for each configuration. Configurations are just names that are passed in the Angular CLI build command to select slightly different configurations for different target environments. As a default, Angular workspaces are created with just a production configuration that overrides development options to adapt them to a production environment. However, more configurations may be added, for instance, to configure the application for a staging environment.

The general options are as follows:

```
"options": {
  "outputPath": "dist",
  "index": "src/index.html",
  "main": "src/main.ts",
  "tsConfig": "src/tsconfig.app.json",
  "progress": true,
  "polyfills": "src/polyfills.ts",
  "assets": [
    "src/assets"
  ],
  "styles": [
    "src/styles.css",
    "node_modules/bootstrap/dist/css/bootstrap.min.css"
  ],
  "scripts": []
},
```

`outputPath` is the folder where all files bundled by WebPack are placed. `index` is the single HTML page where the application will run. `main` is the application entry point. `tsConfig` contains the path to the application TypeScript configuration file. `process` specifies whether information needs to be logged while `build` proceeds. `polyfills` specifies the files that include all the polyfills required. `assets` specifies the list of all folders that may contain assets (images, media, and so on) that must be bundled with the application. `styles` specifies a list of CSS files whose rules must be applied globally to the whole application. Finally, `scripts` specifies a list of JavaScript files whose global symbols must be available throughout the application, with no need to include them as modules. `scripts` is a good place to place the jQuery library, if jQuery has to be used throughout the application.

The `configuration` node contains just a single configuration named `prodution`:

```
"configurations": {
  "production": {
    "optimization": true,
    "outputHashing": "all",
    "sourceMap": false,
    "extractCss": true,
    "namedChunks": false,
    "aot": true,
    "extractLicenses": true,
    "vendorChunk": false,
    "buildOptimizer": true,
    "fileReplacements": [
      {
        "replace": "src/environments/environment.ts",
        "with": "src/environments/environment.prod.ts"
      }
    ]
  }
}
```

`optimization` set to `true` turns on all WebPack optimizations (JavaScript and CSS minification). `outputHashing` specifies whether to append a hash to the end of files to prevent caching when they change. Possible values are: `none`, `all`, `media`, and `bundles`. `sourceMap` specifies whether to generate source maps. Sometimes, it is useful to set this option to `true` in production as well in order to process hard-to-find bugs. `extractCss` set to `true` enables automatic collection of styles contained in HTML files, to bundle them in separate CSS files. `namedChunks` specifies whether to use original filenames or automatically created IDs for Angular modules that are lazy loaded. `aot` enables ahead-of-time component compilation, otherwise components are compiled when first used. `buildOptimizer` turns on optimizations of `aot` compiler. `extractLicenses` set to `true` causes all software licenses to be placed into a unique file. When `vendorChunk` is set to `true`, all libraries are bundled in a separate bundle (see the *Bundles optimization* section of `Chapter 7`, *Bundling with WebPack*, to review why this might be useful).

Finally, `fileReplacements` causes `src/environments/environment.ts` be replaced by a configuration-specific file so that the application may check the configuration it was built in.

The complete description of all `Angular.json` options is documented here: `https://github.com/angular/angular-cli/wiki/angular-workspace`

Building and serving the application

The application may be run in development mode with the `ng serve` CLI command, or with `npm start`, since `package.json` contains various CLI commands with adequate parameters. CLI is automatically run when ASP.NET Core starts because of the Angular middleware placed in the `Startup.cs` file:

```
app.UseSpa(spa =>
{
    spa.Options.SourcePath = "ClientApp";
    if (env.IsDevelopment())
    {
        spa.UseAngularCliServer(npmScript: "start");
    }
});
```

However, triggering a complete Angular compilation each time the project is run might be very time-expansive when the developer has to perform several changes, with each immediately followed by a test, since the compilation process lasts more than 10 seconds. In similar cases it is better to launch `npm start` manually, and rely on the WebPack hot-module replacement to replace and recompile just the chunks that have been changed. Once compilation is complete, and the Angular development server has been launched, there is no need to recompile the whole application from scratch.

The entire procedure is as follows:

1. Issue the `npm start` command.
2. Change ASP.NET Core middleware so that it doesn't execute the `npm start` command:

   ```
   app.UseSpa(spa =>
   {
       spa.Options.SourcePath = "ClientApp";
       if (env.IsDevelopment())
       {
           spa.UseProxyToSpaDevelopmentServer("http://localhost:4200");
       }
   });
   ```

3. Keep the Windows console where the `npm start` command was issued open. If you need a Windows console to issue other commands, please open another Windows console.

4. Carry out all the modifications required and run the Visual Studio project as needed.

5. When you have finished, close the Angular development server with *Ctrl + C*.

Application files needed for deployment are generated by running `npm run build -- -- prod`. However, there is no need to issue this command manually, since it is automatically issued on the Visual Studio publish event, that is, when the whole Visual Studio project is published. This is easily verified by right-clicking on the project node and selecting `Edit AngularVSTemplate.csproj`:

```
<Target Name="PublishRunWebpack" AfterTargets="ComputeFilesToPublish">
   ...
    <Exec WorkingDirectory="$(SpaRoot)" Command="npm run build -- --prod"
/>
   ...
</Target>
```

If there are several configurations defined in `Angular.json`, the command must be replaced with `npm run build -- --prod -c <configuration name>`.

Let's add a staging configuration to `Angular.json` and modify `AngularVSTemplate.csproj` so that when the ASP.NET Core project is published with the debug configuration, the Angular project is built with the staging configuration. As a first step, let's add a staging configuration to `Angular.json` as follows:

1. Close the `production` node and copy it.
2. Paste a copy of the same node immediately after it.
3. Add a comma between the two configurations.
4. Change the name of the newly copied node to staging.
5. Change `sourceMap` from false to `true`, since in staging, we want the same production settings, but with source maps enabled to discover all bugs.
6. Then edit `AngularVSTemplate.csproj` and replace the following line:

```
<Exec WorkingDirectory="$(SpaRoot)" Command="npm run build -- --
prod" />
```

With the following lines:

```
<Exec WorkingDirectory="$(SpaRoot)"
    Command="npm run build -- --prod -c staging" Condition="
'$(Configuration)' == 'Debug' " />
<Exec WorkingDirectory="$(SpaRoot)"
    Command="npm run build -- --prod -c production" Condition="
'$(Configuration)' == 'Release' " />
```

Now, if the Visual Studio project is published in the debug configuration, Angular will use source maps that helps to locate bugs.

The complete list of all Angular CLI commands is documented here: `https://github.com/angular/angular-cli/wiki`.

Summary

Angular development is organized in workspaces that may contain several projects of different types: applications, libraries, and test projects. All Angular operations are easily achieved with Angular CLI commands, whose behavior is configured in the `Angular.json` configuration file. The same initial workspace can be scaffolded with Angular CLI. Visual Studio has an Angular project template that aids the development of Angular applications and their integration with ASP.NET Core. The Angular application scaffolded by Visual Studio can be easily adapted to the last version of Angular.

Angular applications are based on six types of building blocks: components, directives, pipes, services, modules, and routers. Modules are just groupings of the other types of building blocks that help keeping applications modular and that allow lazy loading of application parts. Components extend the set of HTML tags with new tags, while directives empower existing tags with further capabilities. Components are composed of an HTML/CSS part, and a TypeScript class part. TypeScript code is connected to the HTML part through bindings. Pipes transform JavaScript values as they move from code to HTML templates through bindings. Services are business elements that help all other building blocks to do their job. They are automatically injected into the constructors of other Angular entities. Finally, routers do the magic of allowing a whole Angular application to run in a single HTML page by taking care of translating URLs into component instantiations and placement into router-outlets.

The next chapter describes the use of input forms, and pipes, and how to localize Angular applications. It also describes how to customize Angular life cycle with life cycle hooks, thereby enabling, for instance, the utilization of jQuery widgets.

Questions

1. Where in the `@NgModule` decorator should a component that has to be exported to other modules be placed?
2. Is it possible to pass a `Person` class instance to a component input property with the interpolation operator? How is this done? If not, what is the correct way?
3. What Angular CLI command scaffolds a new component? What CLI command starts the application in development mode?
4. What is the right way to bind a property to a `colspan` of a `td` tag?
5. How is a two-sided binding with the `value` property created?
6. How can source maps be enabled in production mode?
7. Where are alternative application configurations defined? How is code made aware of the configuration it was built in?
8. What is the right way to add jQuery to a whole Angular application?
9. Where are polyfills configured?
10. What kind of properties/variables may be used in binding expressions?

11
Input and Interactions

This chapter explains how to take and validate user input, and how to customize standard data binding behavior with pipes and life cycle hooks. The user is required to practice these concepts by writing new components.

In this chapter, you will learn the following topics:

- Template life cycle events, adding non-Angular widgets
- Event and component interaction
- How to use and validate input fields with Angular forms
- How to customize data binding behavior with pipes and culture localization

Technical requirements

The requirements for this chapter are as follows:

- Visual Studio 2017 with the last ASP.NET Core tools
- Visual Studio TypeScript SDK
- Angular CLI version higher than the 6th version should be installed globally

For the installation of Angular CLI, please refer to the *Technical requirements* section of `Chapter 10`, *Angular ASP.NET Core Project Template*.

The whole chapter uses a copy of the `AngularQuickStart` project created in the *Creating an Angular project* section in `Chapter 10`, *Angular ASP.NET Core Project Template*. Make a copy of it and rename its root folder to `InputAndInteractions`.

All the code used in this chapter can be downloaded from the following GitHub link: `https://github.com/PacktPublishing/Hands-On-TypeScript-for-CSharp-and-.NET-Core-Developers`.

Check out the following video to see the Code in Action: `http://bit.ly/2yGnhiB`.

Template life cycle events

While each application runs, Angular automatically creates, modifies, and destroy components and their associated HTML. Since developer initialization and cleaning up the code must be synchronized with the preceding Angular processing stages, Angular exposes events all components and directives must use to run initialization, update, and cleanup at the right time.

There are lifetime events that are triggered just once in the life of each component/directive instance, and update events that are linked to the Angular change detection process (sketched in `Chapter 10`, *Angular ASP.NET Core Project Template*). Lifetime events are used by all developers the most, since they allow proper component/directive initialization and enable the developer to modify the HTML code generated by Angular, for instance, by adding non-Angular widgets. Update events are less used by developers since it is usually easier and more modular to react directly to user events than to the updates they indirectly cause.

Angular lifetime events

In the order they are triggered, Angular lifetime events are as follows:

- `ngOnInit`: Angular triggers this event after each component/directive has been initialized and its input properties have been bound to their initial values. This event is the right place to place component initialization code. The `app-smart-date` component described in the *Modules, components and data-binding* section in `Chapter 10`, *Angular ASP.NET Core Project Template,* is a good example of using the `ngOnInit` event. The user should place the component initialization code here instead of inserting it in the component constructor for the following reasons:
    - When this event is triggered, all input properties are available and can be used to initialize the component/directive properly.

- There is no way to prevent constructor code execution, so this code is also executed during the unit testing of all components. Instead, initialization code inserted in `ngOnInit` can be skipped during unit testing, and/or tested separately.
- Future versions of Angular might offer the option to cache some components. In this case, code placed in the constructor wouldn't be re-executed when cached components are reused.

- `ngAfterContentInit`: Similar to the `ngAfterViewInit` event discussed in the next point, but it concerns **content projection**, also called **transclusion**. This event is discussed in the *Structural directives and content projection* section in `Chapter 12`, *Angular Advanced Features*.
- `ngAfterViewInit`: Angular triggers this event after all child components have been loaded and initialized, and the HTML associated to the component/directive has been rendered. Since this event is triggered when the whole component instance HTML is available, this event is the right place to customize the component HTML, for instance, by adding non-Angular widgets.
- `ngOnDestroy`: Angular triggers this event immediately before destroying a component. This is the right place to execute some cleanup code and to destroy non-Angular widgets that were added with frameworks like jQuery. It is here where one should unregister handlers that were added manually (Angular events are cleaned up automatically by the framework).

How to handle Angular life cycle hooks

Each Angular life cycle has an associated interface defined in `'@angular/core'`. Each interface has a method with the event name as its unique member. The interface name is the name of the event without the `ng` prefix. Thus, for instance, the interface associated to the `ngOnInit` event is this:

```
interface OnInit{
    ngOnInit(): void;
}
```

The right procedure to hook a life cycle event is this:

1. Import the interface from `'@angular/core'`:

```
import { Component, OnInit } from '@angular/core';
```

2. Declare that the component implements the interface:

```
export class HomeComponent implements OnInit
```

3. Implement the unique interface method:

```
ngOnInit() {
  this.todayDate = new Date();
}
```

Using a Bootstrap modal in Angular

As an example of using Angular lifetime events, this section shows how to use a Bootstrap modal in Angular. As a first step, Bootstrap and jQuery must be installed in `package.json`. The `@types/...` packages that contain TypeScript declarations for them are also required:

```
{
  ...
  "dependencies": {
    ...
    "jquery": "^3.3.1",
    "bootstrap": "^4.1.3"
  },
  "devDependencies": {
    ...
    "@types/jquery": "^3.3.7",
    "@types/bootstrap": "^4.1.2",
    ...
  }
}
```

Please use a Bootstrap version greater than 4.0, since the remainder of the chapter assumes it.

Then, jQuery and Bootstrap JavaScript together with Bootsrap CSS must be declared as globally visible throughout the whole application by inserting them into the application styles and scripts sections of `Angular.json`:

```
"ClientApp": {
    . . .
    "architect": {
      "build": {
        . . .
        "options": {
          . . .
          "styles": [
            "src/styles.css",
            "node_modules/bootstrap/dist/css/bootstrap.min.css"
          ],
          "scripts": [
            "node_modules/jquery/dist/jquery.min.js",
            "node_modules/bootstrap/dist/js/bootstrap.js"
              . . .
```

As explained in `Chapter 10`, *Angular ASP.NET Core Project Template*, this is the usual way to add global dependencies to Angular. All symbols defined in the files added there are visible all over the whole application, with no need to import them. This global visibility must also be declared in `tsconfig.app.json`. In fact, the default `tsconfig.app.json` scaffolded by Angular contains a compiler option that overrides the default global visibility of all NPM `@types/...` packages with TypeScript definitions:

```
"types": []
```

The `types` compiler option explicitly declares which packages are globally visible to the TypeScript compiler. Angular sets it to an empty array since Angular is module-based and consequently, as a default, packages must be visible to the compiler only when they are explicitly imported with an `import` statement. Accordingly, Bootstrap and jQuery TypeScript declaration packages, and, in general, all globally visible TypeScript definition libraries, must be added to the `types` array:

```
"types": ["jquery", "bootstrap"]
```

The plan is as follows:

1. Create a component with the HTML for the modal.
2. On ngAfterViewInit, the Bootstrap modal widget is applied to this HTML with a typical jQuery syntax: $(...).modal(..). Normally, Bootstrap automatically recognizes widgets by their markup and automatically applies the right jQuery widget syntax to each of them on the document ready event. However, since Angular components are created dynamically, one can't rely on this mechanism, which only works at program start. That's why widgets are manually applied in the ngAfterViewInit event when one is sure all the component HTML has already been rendered. In order to prevent the same *modal* enhancement from being applied twice, the standard page-start Bootstrap widget enhancement must be prevented. This is easily achieved by removing the modal fade CSS classes that Bootstrap uses to recognize modals from the modal root. They will be re-added in the ngAfterViewInit event immediately before enhancing the HTML markup with the modal widget.
3. Bind modal opening/closing to some button click events.
4. Destroy the modal widget on the ngOnDestroy event.

Let's scaffold a new component called ModalTest with Angular CLI. Then, in the newly created modal-test folder, let's delete the CSS file since no custom styles will be provided for this component. Then, let's place the content of its HTML template with this:

```
<div #modalRoot tabindex="-1" role="dialog" aria-labelledby="modal_title">
  <div class="modal-dialog modal-lg" role="document">
    <div class="modal-content">
      <div class="modal-header">
        <h4 id="modal_title" class="modal-title">{{Title}}</h4>
        <button type="button" class="close" data-dismiss="modal" aria-
label="Close">
          <span aria-hidden="true">&times;</span>
        </button>
      </div>
      <div class="modal-body">
          This is a bootstrap modal
      </div>
    </div>
  </div>
</div>
```

The preceding example is a quite standard Bootstrap modal markup. The modal title is bound to a component property called Title, so that it can be supplied by the code that uses the ModalTest component.

The `#modalRoot` template reference (see the *Template bindings* subsection in `Chapter 10`, *Angular ASP.NET Core Project Template*) is a way to get a reference to the root template element in the `ModalTest` TypeScript class.

Consider the following `ModalTest` class skeleton (new syntax is explained, in the paragraph after the code):

```
import {
  Component, OnDestroy, AfterViewInit,
  Input, ViewChild, ElementRef
} from '@angular/core';

@Component({
  selector: 'app-modal-test',
  templateUrl: './modal-test.component.html'
})
export class ModalTestComponent
    implements OnDestroy, AfterViewInit {
  constructor() { }
  @ViewChild('modalRoot') root: ElementRef;
  @Input() Title: string;
  ...
}
```

`Title` contains the modal header string. It is accepted as an input parameter by the directive; therefore, `Title` is declared as an input property with the `@Input` decorator. The `@ViewChild` decorator causes the HTML element with the `modalRoot` template reference to be bound to the `root` property. The code needs it to apply the modal widget to the root of the component template.

When the `ViewChild` argument is the name of a template reference that is bound to an HTML element, `ViewChild` returns an `ElementRef` whose `nativeElement` property contains the `HTMLElement` referenced by the template reference. If the HTML element contains some directives, an instance of one of the directives may be obtained, instead of `ElementRef`, by writing `@ViewChild(myTemplateReference', {read: <Directive Class Type>})`.

When the `ViewChild` template reference string is bound to a component, `ViewChild` returns the current instance of the component. In this case, `ElementRef` with the root of the component may be obtained, instead, by writing `@ViewChild(myTemplateReference', {read: ElementRef})`.

The class declares the implementation of `OnDestroy`, `AfterViewInit`. All `OnDestroy`, `AfterViewInit`, `Input`, `ViewChild`, and `ElementRef` used in the class are imported from `'@angular/core'`.

`OnDestroy` and `AfterViewInit` implementations are straightforward:

```
ngAfterViewInit() {
    $(this.root.nativeElement)
      .addClass("modal fade")
      .modal({
      show: false,
      backdrop: "static"
    });
}
ngOnDestroy() {
    $(this.root.nativeElement).modal("dispose");
}
```

Furthermore, `ngAfterViewInit` applies the classes needed by the modal that were not included in the template to prevent Bootstrap's automatic widget enhancement. Immediately after this, it applies the modal widget with some options to the template root.

The `show` option set to `false` prevents the modal from immediately opening, while `backdrop` set to `"static"` prevents the modal from being closed when the user clicks outside of the modal. Basically, `ngOnDestroy` simply calls the modal's `dispose` method to destroy the widgets when the component is destroyed in order to prevent memory leaks.

The component also needs methods to open and close the modal:

```
Open() {
  $(this.root.nativeElement).modal("show");
}
Close() {
  $(this.root.nativeElement).modal("hide");
}
```

The component may be tested by adding the following code to the bottom of `app.component.html`:

```
<button (click)="modalToOpen.Open()" type="button" class="btn btn-success">
  Open modal
</button>
<app-modal-test #modalToOpen Title="This is the modal title"></app-modal-
test>
```

The *Structural directives and content projection* section in `Chapter 12`, *Angular Advanced Features* explains how to abstract the modal component to accept not only the modal title as input, but also the whole modal body.

Angular update events

In the order they are triggered, Angular update events are as follows:

- `ngOnChanges`: Triggered each time Angular detects changes in the input properties of the component. It receives a `SimpleChanges` interface as its unique parameter. The `SimpleChanges` interface is a map that associates a `SimpleChange` class instance to each string that represents a property name. In turn, each `SimpleChange` instance contains both the previous and new property values. When `ngOnInit` also fires, `ngOnChanges` fires before it, and the `SimpleChanges` map contains the initial input values of the component. Additionally `ngOnChanges` may be used to automatically update other properties that depend on the input properties. This event must be used very carefully since it may cause a waste of computational time for updating values that are not used each time they are updated. When possible, dependent properties should be updated immediately before being used to save processing time, for instance, when the user clicks the **save**, **confirm**, or **update** buttons. An alternative to the use of `ngOnChanges` is to define some input properties as setter/getter pairs, so they may automatically update other properties when they are set.

- `ngDoCheck`: Triggered by Angular each time an event that *might* change some property values in the component is fired. It is an opportunity for the user to detect manual changes that, for some reason, Angular is not able to detect automatically. When `ngOnChanges` is also fired, `ngDoCheck` is fired immediately after it. Use it only if `ngOnChanges` is not working for some property, and, as a first step in the event handling code, verify the properties have changed by keeping track of their previous values. If no value change is detected, immediately abort the method execution to save processing time, since `ngDoCheck` is triggered very frequently.

- `ngAfterContentChecked`: Triggered after `ngDoCheck` has been called on the content projected into the component. Content projection is explained in the *Structural directives and content projection* section in `Chapter 12`, *Angular Advanced Features*. Useful when `ngDoCheck` also fails to detect a change. It is able to detect more changes, since it is called more frequently than `ngDoCheck`, but it has also an higher performance impact. It is very rarely used.

- `ngAfterViewChecked`: Triggered after `ngDoCheck` has been called on all child components. Useful when `ngDoCheck` also fails to detect a change. It is able to detect more changes, since it is called more frequently than `ngDoCheck`, but it has also a higher performance impact. It is very rarely used.

Component interaction

Each HTML element interacts with the remainder of the DOM by receiving input values in its properties and by providing output by issuing events that are intercepted by handlers added to other HTML elements. Thus, the DOM uses properties to provide inputs, and events to send outputs. The *Modules, components, and data-binding* section in `Chapter 10`, *Angular ASP.NET Core Project Template*, discusses how HTML element properties and events are handled by Angular, and how analogously to HTML elements, Angular components may receive input through input properties. Angular goes on with the analogy between HTML elements and components by also defining custom events for components.

The following are the general steps to enhance a component with an event type:

1. Define a data type, say, `T`, that conveys the event information, and which information it must convey.
2. Define a property, say, `myEvent`, that represents the event type, decorate it with the `@Output()` decorator, and assign it an instance of `EventEmitter<T>`. The `@Output()` decorator accepts the event name as an optional argument. If the name is not provided, the property name is used as the event name.
3. Define when to emit the event and add the needed code to the component.
4. When needed, the event is issued by invoking the `emit` method of `myEvent`,and passing it an instance of `T`.
5. Subscription to the event is done by adding to the component tag a binding like this: `(<event name>)='<code to be executed when the event is captured>'`. Analogously to the case of native HTML events, the `$event` variable, bound to the class instance issued with the event, is available in the context of the code that is executed in the binding.

As an example, let's add an event that is issued when the modal is closed for the
`ModalTest` component. As a first step, the `Output` symbol must be imported
from `'@angular/core'`. Then, a new `ModalClosed` property is defined as follows:

```
@Output() ModalClosed =
    new EventEmitter<ModalTestComponent>();
```

The `ModalTestComponentclass` itself is used as a generic parameter of
the `EventEmitter` type, since the whole component instance will be issued by the event. A
jQuery event handler must be added to the component root to detect when the modal is
closed. The same event must be removed when the component is destroyed to prevent
memory leaks. Accordingly, the `ngAfterViewInit` and `ngOnDestroy` methods must be
modified as follows:

```
ngAfterViewInit() {
  $(this.root.nativeElement)
    .addClass("modal fade")
    .modal({
      show: false,
      backdrop: "static"
    })
    .on('hidden.bs.modal', e => {
      this.ModalClosed.emit(this);
    });
}
ngOnDestroy() {
  $(this.root.nativeElement)
    .off('hidden.bs.modal')
    .modal("dispose");
}
```

The newly defined event is easily tested by replacing the existing `app-modal-test` tag in
`app.component.html` with this:

```
<app-modal-test #modalToOpen
    Title="This is the modal title"
    (ModalClosed)="doAlert($event.Title+' was closed!')">
</app-modal-test>
```

And we define the `doAlert` method in `app.component.ts` as follows:

```
doAlert(x): void {
  alert(x);
}
```

Global variables such as $, jQuery, window, document, and more are not available in binding expressions, since they may use only template references, variables defined in the template, and properties of the component class. That's why the call to the alert method was enclosed within the doAlert method.

The *Events and two way bindings* section in Chapter 10, *Angular ASP.NET Core Project Template*, introduces two-way binding as a way to keep an input value and a property aligned through the ngModel binding. Two-way binding can be defined not only for input fields but also for generic components. The next subsection explains how to define custom two-way bindings.

Custom two-way bindings

A two-way binding may be added to a component if and only if that component has an input property named x and a corresponding event named x+'Changed', and if the type issued by the x+'Changed' event is the same as the type of x. When a property P is bound to x, whenever P changes, x reflects the value of P, while whenever an x+'Changed' event is issued, P takes the value conveyed by that event. As an example, let's define a FontSize component that can be used to modify the font size used in a page area. The component is very simple and consists of an input field bound to a Size input property with an associated SizeChange event. Let's scaffold it with Angular CLI.

Then, let's add the following style to the FontSize component CSS file:

```
input {
  max-width:400px;
  margin: 5px;
}
```

Then, let's also define its template as follows:

```
<div>
  <input type="number" class="form-control"
         [(ngModel)]='Size'/>
</div>
```

Since the component uses ngModule, the main app.module.ts application module must import FormsModule from '@angular/forms' and must declare it in its module imports:

```
import { FormsModule } from '@angular/forms';
...
@NgModule({
```

```
  ...
  imports: [
    BrowserModule,
    FormsModule
  ],
  ...
})
```

Finally, let's add the code for the component TypeScript class:

```
import { Component, Input, Output, EventEmitter }
  from '@angular/core';
...
export class FontSizeComponent{
  constructor() { }
  private _Size: number;
  @Input() set Size(x: number) {
    let changed = this._Size != x;
    this._Size = x;
    if (changed) this.SizeChange.emit(x);
  }
  get Size(): number {
    return this._Size;
  }
  @Output() SizeChange =
    new EventEmitter<number>();
}
```

The Size property is implemented with a setter/getter pair, so that when set, it can trigger the SizeChange event if appropriate.

The FontSize component can be used to control the font size of the App component template header. As a first step toward this target, let's add a template reference to the template header so that the AppComponent class may reference it:

```
<!-- app.component.html -->
....
<h1 #MainHeader>
    Welcome to {{ title }}!
</h1>

//in the AppComponent class

@ViewChild("MainHeader") header: ElementRef

//Where the ViewChild and ElementRef must be imported
```

Since the techniques to get and set a font size are quite different, it is appropriate to handle the header font size in the `AppComponent` class with a setter/getter pair that would perform the appropriate actions to set and get the font size:

```
get HeaderFontSize(): number {
    return parseFloat(window
        .getComputedStyle(this.header.nativeElement, null)
        .getPropertyValue('font-size'));
}
  set HeaderFontSize(x: number) {
    this.header.nativeElement.style.fontSize
        = x + "px";
}
```

The reason for the preceding complication is that the actual font size is determined by the overall style computed by the browser, while the font size must be changed by modifying the element style property.

Now, it is enough to add a `FontSize` component at the bottom of the `AppModule` template and to bind its `Size` property with the `HeaderFontSize` property of the `App` component through a two-way binding:

```
<app-font-size [(Size)]="HeaderFontSize" ></app-font-size>
```

As soon as the application is launched, the input of the `FontSize` component contains the original size of the header font in pixels, then each change to the input field is immediately reflected in the header font size.

Forms

Typically in **Single Page Frameworks** (**SPA**) such as Angular, forms are not used to automatically submit data to the server, because input fields are bound to properties of JavaScript objects that are sent in JSON format to the server through AJAX operations. However, forms still remain useful for the functionalities listed in the following points **1** and **2**. Input fields are validated in the context of all other input fields contained in the same form, and further processing of the form data may proceed only if the form is valid, that is, if all input fields contained in the form are valid.

HTML forms have three connected purposes:

1. Grouping input fields that contribute to the same update operation.
2. Providing a context for validation. In fact, in general, validation rules may involve several input fields belonging to the same logical update operation.
3. Triggering an automatic HTTP operation, which is usually `POST`.

Angular enhances HTML forms and input field functionalities with the following features:

- Provides the `ngModel` two-way binding.
- Enriches all input fields with a complete validation status that includes if it is valid (`valid` property) or not (`invalid` property), or if validity is being computed by an asynchronous operation (`pending` property), if it was changed by the user (`dirty` property) or not (`pristine` property), and if it was touched by the user (`touched` property) or not (`untouched` property). Moreover, in case the input field is invalid, the input field contains the list of names of all failed validation rules.
- Each of the validation status properties listed in the previous point has an associated CSS class that is automatically added to the input field when the corresponding property is `true`. The CSS class name is obtained by prefixing the property name with the `ng-` prefix. Thus, for instance, the CSS class associated to the `dirty` property is `ng-dirty` and it is added automatically to the input field when the `dirty` property is `true`. These CSS classes are very useful to give visual feedback on the input status to the user.
- Provides browser-independent implementations of all standard HTML 5 validation attributes: `required`, `min`, `max`, `step`, `minlength`, `maxlength`, and `patter`, which validate against a regular expression. `required` is allowed on all fields, including checkboxes, `min`, `max`, and `step` define a range of values and increment steps in date/time and numeric input types, while `minlength`, `maxlength`, and `pattern` work with string type inputs (`input` tag with `type` attribute `text`, `search`, `url`, `tel`, `email`, and `password`). Moreover, Angular automatically validates email format on all `input` with `type = "email"`. However, the `min` and `max` Angular validators work with numbers only. The `step` attribute is not considered a constraint; it may be added only programmatically, so the developer is responsible for writing their own directives to add them directly in the templates. As `step` is not considered a constraint, just an indication of a numeric input increment, no validator is associated to it. The *Attributes* section in `Chapter 12`, *Angular Advanced Features*, explains how to define the `min`, `max`, and `step` directives.

- Computes a validation status of the whole form (`form.valid` property) that is `true` only if all input fields in the form are valid. With a similar logic, all properties and CSS classes associated to input fields are extended to forms.
- Adds an `ngSubmit` event to the form that is used to trigger an adequate action when the form is submitted, such as sending the object bound to the input fields to the server in JSON fomat. An `ngReset` event is also available to intercept form resets too.

All Angular form features are provided by the `FormsModule`, which must be imported from `'@angular/forms'` and added to the imports of the module that uses Angular forms.

Let's see how all this works in practice. As a first step, let's scaffold a new TypeScript class in the `InputAndInteractions` project, issuing the following Angular CLI command in a Windows console rooted in the `ClientApp` folder:

```
ng generate class SimpleOrder
```

`Simple Order` is the business class filled with the input form. Let's add the following code to the scaffolded file:

```
export class SimpleOrder {
  Name: string;
  Quantity: number;
  Size: string;
}
```

The form will be inserted in a new component called `FormTest`. Let's scaffold it with Angular CLI. The CSS component can be used to define the user feedback on the input fields status:

```
.ng-dirty.ng-valid:not(form) {
  /*green border*/
  border: 4px solid #42A948 !important;
}

.ng-touched.ng-invalid:not(form),
.ng-dirty.ng-invalid:not(form),
.form-submitted .ng-invalid {
  /*red border*/
  border: 4px solid #a94442 !important;
}
```

A green border is added to all valid fields that are modified by the user to inform the user that its input is correct. Adding visual feedback for invalid fields is more subtle, since it is inappropriate to show an error on an empty required field before the user either touches it or submits the form. Accordingly, invalid fields are surrounded by a red border only if they are changed by the user, or if the user clicks on them and then leaves them (ng-touched), or if the form has the form-submitted CSS class, which will be added with custom code to the form when it is unsuccessfully submitted.

The template skeleton for the FormTest component is as follows:

```
<form (ngSubmit)="onSubmit()" #mainForm="ngForm"
      [ngClass]="{ 'form-submitted':errorSubmitted}">
      <!-- form fields here -->
  <button type="submit" class="btn btn-primary">
    Submit
  </button>
</form>
```

All properties provided by Angular to the form (valid, invalid, and more) are contained in an ngForm directive, that is automatically added by Angular to all forms. The preceding code adds the template reference #mainForm to refer to the ngForm instance from inside the template and from the component TypeScript class. Note that errorSubmitted is a property that is set to true when the form is unsuccessfully submitted, that is, submitted with errors. It triggers the addition of the form-submitted CSS class used in the .css component file. The ngSubmit event triggers the onSubmit method when the form is submitted with the submit button. The submit button and all input fields will be styled with Bootstrap 4 classes. This is advised but not obligatory, since Angular forms do not depend on any CSS framework.

The code for the component TypeScript class is as follows:

```
import { Component, ViewChild} from '@angular/core';
import { SimpleOrder} from '../simple-order'
import { NgForm } from '@angular/forms';
@Component({
  selector: 'app-form-test',
  templateUrl: './form-test.component.html',
  styleUrls: ['./form-test.component.css']
})
export class FormTestComponent {
  @ViewChild('mainForm') mainForm:NgForm;
  Model = new SimpleOrder();
  errorSubmitted: boolean;
  constructor() { }
  onSubmit(): void {
```

```
      if (!this.mainForm.form.valid) {
        this.errorSubmitted = true;
        return;
      }
      alert("form succesfully submitted: "
        + JSON.stringify(this.Model));
      this.mainForm.reset();
      this.errorSubmitted = false;
   }
 }
```

The `Model` property contains an instance of the business class to fill with the form. The `mainForm` property is filled with the `ngForm` template through the `ViewChild` decorator. It is used to verify the form is valid in the `onSubmit` method. If the form is invalid, `errorSubmitted` is set to `true` and causes the `form-submitted` CSS classes to be added to the form, so that the user's visual feedback is updated appropriately. If the form is valid, some business logic code should be called. This simple example just shows the content of the business class in JSON format in an alert box. After the business logic returns, the `errorSubmitted` property and the form are reset, so they can process other inputs. The form is reset by calling the `ngForm reset` method, which clears all input fields and resets the status of both the form and all input fields (all elements become `pristine` and `untouched`).

Let's add the first input field inside the form:

```
<div class="form-group">
    <label for="name">Name</label>
    <input type="text" class="form-control" [(ngModel)]="Model.Name"
           required minlength="5" maxlength="20"
           id="name" name="name" #name="ngModel" >
</div>
```

Basically, `ngModel` binds this field with the name property of the business class that is contained in the `Model` component property. Each input field must have an `id` to be referred to by its field label. The input field has three validation attributes, and the `#name` template reference is bound to the `ngModel` input, which contains all status information for the input field (`valid`, `pristine`, and more). In general, `#name` will be used to display adequate error messages. However, before going on let's verify that everything works properly by adding the `FormTest` component at the bottom of `app.component.html`:

```
<div class="row justify-content-center">
  <div class="col-6">
    <app-form-test></app-form-test>
  </div>
</div>
```

The preceding code also adds some Bootstrap to get a pretty appearance. Let's run the project and let's verify that the validation rule, validation feedback, and the successful submission alert box work properly.

Some smart logic may be added to show error messages when the input field shows an invalid appearance. It is enough to add the this `div` immediately after the input field:

```
<div *ngIf="name.invalid && (name.dirty || name.touched || errorSubmitted)"
        class="alert alert-danger">
    <div *ngIf="name.errors.required">
        Name is required.
    </div>
    <div *ngIf="name.errors.minlength || name.errors.maxlength">
        Name must have between 5 and 20 characters.
    </div>
</div>
```

Note that `*ngIf` is a structural directive that renders the node it is in only if the condition contained in its argument evaluates to `true`. Structural directives are described in depth in the *Structural directives and content projection* section in `Chapter 12`, *Angular Advanced Features*. Error messages are shown if and only if the input field has a red border, that is, if the input is invalid and it is either dirty, or touched, or if the form has been unsuccessfully submitted. All inner `*ngIf` select the appropriate error message. The `ngModel errors` property contains a property for each validator used by the input field. That property has a JavaScript `true` value if and only if the corresponding validation rule failed. The first inner `*ngIf` selects the message to display when the input is empty, while the second one selects the message to show when either the `minlength` or the `maxlength` rule fails.

If one also adds an input of the `number` type, it is easy to verify that the `min`, `max`, and `step` attributes do not add the corresponding validators automatically:

```
<div class="form-group">
    <label for="quantity">Quantity</label>
    <input type="number" class="form-control" [(ngModel)]="Model.Quantity"
            required min="1" max="10"
            step="1"
            id="quantity" name="quantity" #quantity="ngModel" >
</div>
```

Validators should be added manually through **responsive forms**, but this subject will not be covered in this book, since it is difficult and tedious. Instead, the *Attributes* section in Chapter 12, *Angular Advanced Features*, will show how to define directives that bind the min, max, and step attributes with the corresponding validators. The *Further reading* section contains links to the official Angular *responsive forms* documentation.

The Size property can be selected from a predefined list of available sizes with an HTML select. As a first step, let's define a property that contains all possible sizes in form-test.component.ts:

```
allSizes = [
    'small','medium','large',
    'x-large','xx-large'
];
```

After this definition, it is possible to add a select input field:

```
<div class="form-group">
  <label for="name">Size</label>
  <select class="form-control" [(ngModel)]="Model.Size"
          required
          id="size" name="size" #size="ngModel" >
    <option >none selected</option>
    <option *ngFor="let size of allSizes" [value]="size">
    {{size}}
    </option>
  </select>
</div>
```

The *ngFor structural directive repeats the node it is in for all elements of either an iterable or an array, which, in the preceding case, is the array contained in the allSizes property. At each iteration, a new instance of the variable that follows let is created and bound to the current element of the iterable.

Pipes

Pipes modify binding behavior by transforming values while they move from class properties to templates. They are placed after the binding expression, preceded by the | character. Several pipes may be stacked one after the other in the same binding, each separated from the others by a | symbol:

```
'<binding expression>|pipe1|pipe2...'
```

Pipes may have arguments that are placed after the pipe name and separated by colons:

```
'<binding expression>|pipe1:arg1:arg2|pipe2...'
```

Since arguments are identified by their positions, when an argument that is specified is preceded by other absent arguments, : separators must be added as placeholders for the missing arguments:

```
'<binding expression>|pipe1::arg2|pipe2...'
```

In the *Modules, components and data binding* section in Chapter 10, *Angular ASP.NET Core Project Template*, the app-smart-date component uses the Date pipe to render a date in a smart format: {roughDate|date}. The date pipe also accepts a format argument that customizes the way the date is rendered. For example, {roughDate|date: 'yyyy-MM-dd'} specifies a date with no time information in an international format.

Angular comes with the following predefined pipes: uppercase, lowercase, json, slice, currency, decimal, percent, date, and async.

- uppercase and lowercase transform strings, respectively, into uppercase and lowercase.
- json returns the JSON string of any JavaScript type.
- slice performs a slice array operation. It has two arguments; the first argument is the index where to start slicing the array, while the second argument is the index of the last element to take. If the second argument is omitted, the array is taken till the end; if the second argument is negative, the index of the last element to take is counted from the end of the array.
- The async pipe takes Promise as input and returns a value when the promise is resolved. It enables direct use of promises in templates. Async pipes may also be bound to RxJS observables that are not discussed in this book but the *Further reading* section gives links for interested readers.
- The way currency, decimal, percent, and date behave depends on the application localization settings, in particular on the current locale chosen for the application. As a default, the current locale is *en-US*, which means English for the United States. The *Application localization* subsection of this section discusses how to set the application locale.

- `currency` adds a currency symbol to a number. If it is specified without arguments, it adds the currency symbol of the current locale. Its first argument is used to specify a different symbol. For example, `{{myCost|currency|'CAD'}}` specifies the Canadian dollar. As a default, the complete format of the currency symbol is shown, which in the previous example is `CA$`. The second optional argument specifies the symbol format. If it is `'symbol-narrow'`, the short format for the symbol is added. In the previous example, `$`. `'symbol'` displays the complete symbol as in the default case, and finally `'code'` adds the international code of the currency, which in the previous example is `'CAD'`, that is, the same string added as the first argument. Moreover, `currency` also accepts a third `'digits format'` argument and a a fourth `'locale'` argument that are the same as the first and second arguments of `decimal`, described here.

- `decimal` and `percent` display a number in the current locale format, but `percent` renders it as a percentage. Thus, for instance, if `myNumber` is `0.1258`, `{{myNumber|percent}}` displays `12.8%`. The first argument of both pipes supplies constraints on the number of digits in this format: `<minimum number of integer digits>-<minimum number of decimal digits>.<maximum number of decimal digits>`. Thus, for instance, `{{myNumber|decima:'2-4.7'}}` displays `00.1280`. The second argument of both pipes overrides the current locale (it is a local string, like `'en-GB'` or `'it-IT'`). However, locales that differ from the application locale must be loaded before being used, as explained in the *Application localization* subsection.

- `date` displays a date in the application locale. Its first optional argument specifies the date format, while the second argument is the timezone in a `+/-hhmm` format, like, for instance, `'+0230'` or `'-0200'`. Finally, the third argument, when provided, overrides the application locale.

The format is one of two options as follows:

- `'shortDate'` (6/15/15), `'mediumDate'` (Jun 15, 2015), `'longDate'` (June 15, 2015), `'fullDate'` (Monday, June 15, 2015), which are date-only formats. `'shortTime'` (9:03 AM), `'mediumTime'` (9:03:01 AM), `'longTime'` (9:03:01 AM GMT+1), and `'fullTime'` (9:03:01 AM GMT+01:00) are time-only formats. `'short'` (6/15/15, 9:03 AM), `'medium'` (Jun 15, 2015, 9:03:01 AM), `'long'` (June 15, 2015 at 9:03:01 AM GMT+1), and `'full'` (Monday, June 15, 2015 at 9:03:01 AM GMT+01:00) are date-time formats. All examples are for the `'en-US'` locale. In other locales, the same information is displayed but in a different order, and with different symbols.

- A custom format string, like `'MM/dd/yyyy hh:mm:ss'`, specifies the exact format independently of which locale is selected. The full list of symbols allowed in a custom format string may be found in the Angular official documentation (links are listed in the *Further reading* section).

Defining custom pipes

A pipe is a TypeScript class decorated with the `@Pipe` decorator that implements the `PipeTransform` interface. The `PipeTransform` interface has a unique `transform` method that specifies the transformation applied by the pipe:

```
interface PipeTransform {
  transform(value: any, ...args: any[]): any
}
```

The first parameter is the value received either by the binding expression or by the previous pipe. All other parameters are the pipe arguments. As an example, let's define a `capitalize` pipe that transforms into uppercase the first character of any string. Let's scaffold it with the following Angular CLI command: `ng generate pipe Capitalize`. The scaffolder automatically declares the new pipe in the declaration section of `app.module.ts`, and adds all the needed imports to `capitalize.pipe.ts`. The developer must write just his implementation of the `transform` method, which, for the `capitalize` pipe, is straightforward:

```
transform(value: string): string {
    if (!value) return value;
    if (value.length == 1) return value.toUpperCase();
    return value.slice(0, 1).toUpperCase() + value.slice(1)
}
```

The pipe may be tested by applying it to the text of the `select` options in `form-test.component.html`:

```
<option *ngFor="let size of allSizes" [value]="size">
  {{size|capitalize}}
</option>
```

As a default, pipes are *pure*; that is, they react even if the root value passed to them changes—if the simple value (number, Boolean, or string) passed to them changes, or if the pointer of an object passed to them changes.

They do not react by causing a template update if a property of an object passed to them changes. Pipes that must also react to changes in properties and nested objects must be declared as *impure* in their `@Pipe` decorator:

```
@Pipe({
  name: 'capitalize',
  pure:false
})
```

Impure pipes are quite inefficient and should be avoided when possible.

Application localization

The locale to use for building the application is specified in each build configuration of the `Angular.json` files as follows:

```
"build": {
        ...
        "configurations": {
          "production": {
            ...
            "i18nLocale": "it-IT"
```

This way, the developer may define various configurations if the application must be localized in different languages. It is also possible to specify a file containing string translations for each configuration:

```
"i18nLocale": "it-IT",
"i18nFile": "src/locale/messages.it-IT.xlf",
"i18nFormat": "xlf",
```

The *Further reading* section contains links to the procedures for generating these files, and for specifying where to place all the translated strings.

When in development mode, the current locale must be injected into the main application module, as shown here:

```
import { LOCALE_ID, NgModule } from '@angular/core';
....
@NgModule({
    ...
    providers: [ { provide: LOCALE_ID, useValue: 'it-IT' } ]
    ...
})
```

If pipes explicitly specify locales that differ from the application locale, these locales must be loaded by placing the following code at the top of `app.module.ts`:

```
import { registerLocaleData } from '@angular/common';
import localeGB from '@angular/common/locales/en-GB';

registerLocaleData(localeGB , 'en-GB');
```

Summary

Angular life cycle hooks are the way to initialize components and directives and to extend Angular with non-Angular widgets. They also allow the limited customization of Angular change detection.

Angular enhances HTML forms and input fields with additional status information to handle input validation. Angular also automatically adds CSS classes to input fields and forms that reflect their validation state and that the developer can use to give adequate feedback to the user. These additional features are provided to forms by the `ngForm` directive, and to input fields by the `ngModel` directive.

Pipes are Angular's way to customize the data's appearance when moved to templates through bindings. Angular furnishes predefined pipes for the most common needs, but custom pipes are very easy to define. Some pipes apply transformations that depend on the locale associated to the application (date, number formats, and currency symbols). Locales can be easily associated to each Angular build configuration.

The next chapter explains how to define attribute directives for attaching validators to the `max`, `min`, and `step` input attributes, how to inject a HTML body into the modal implemented in this section, how to write structural directives such as `*nFor` and `*ngIf`, and how to improve an application' appearance with animations.

Questions

1. Are you able to list all Angular life cycle hooks? What is the right place to initialize a component? Why?
2. What is the container for all the validation status information of an input field? And the one for a form?
3. How can you check whether a validation rule failed on an input field?
4. What is `ng-valid`?

5. What is the argument separator in Angular pipes?
6. How do you format a property containing an amount of money so that at least two integer digits and two decimal digits are shown?
7. What is `PipeTransform`?

Further reading

This chapter used the template-based approach to Angular forms since it is more immediate and increases code productivity. Angular also allows a code-based approach called **Reactive forms** to enhance forms with the validation status. Interested readers may read the official documentation on Reactive forms here: `https://angular.io/guide/reactive-forms`. Examples of how to define custom validators are given in the *Attributes* section in `Chapter 12`, *Angular Advanced Features*, since they are essentially attribute directives.

The discussion of pipes given here is not quite complete since it doesn't contain the complete list of the custom date/time formats that is available here: `https://angular.io/api/common/DatePipe`. Async pipes are a very useful tool when used with RxJS observables, which are not discussed in this book. Interested readers may find a short introduction to their usage in Angular at `https://angular.io/guide/observables`, and are referred to the RxJS official documentation for a complete description: `https://rxjs-dev.firebaseapp.com/`.

The localization of strings in Angular is discussed in detail in the official documentation here: `https://angular.io/guide/i18n`.

12
Angular Advanced Features

This chapter introduces advanced customization techniques, such as how to build custom attributes and structural directives, how to associate style states to HTML elements, and how to animate their transitions. The reader is required to practice all the concepts learned by modifying and adding animations to previously designed components. Custom directives are an essential part of professional web applications, since, like components, they factor out common behaviors, used throughout the whole application, into unique chunks of code. Animations are useful mainly in the design of appealing public websites, but they also ensure a more natural and pleasant interaction in business intranet applications.

In this chapter, you will learn the following topics:

- Defining attribute directives
- Using and defining structural directives
- Defining and using Angular animations

Technical requirements

For this chapter, we require Angular CLI, a version higher than 6 should be installed globally. For the installation of the Angular CLI, please refer to the *Technical requirements* section of `Chapter 10`, *Angular ASP.NET Core Project Template*.

The whole chapter uses a copy of the `InputAndInteractions` project created in `Chapter 11`, *Input and Interactions*. Make a copy of it and rename its root folder `AdvancedFeatures`.

All the code used in this chapter can be downloaded from the following GitHub link: `https://github.com/PacktPublishing/Hands-On-TypeScript-for-CSharp-and-.NET-Core-Developers`.

Check out the following video to see the Code in Action: `http://bit.ly/2Rr8orB`.

Attribute directives

The previous two chapters on Angular (Chapter 10, *Angular ASP.NET Core Project Template*, and Chapter 11, *Input and Interactions*) already showed most of Angular's predefined attribute directives, such as ngModel, ngForm, ngSubmit, ngReset, ngClass, and ngStyle, and all routing-related attributes (Chapter 10, *Angular ASP.NET Core Project Template*): routerLink, which accepts and follows a router URL, and routerLinkActive, which adds a CSS class when the routerLink of the <a> tag contained in the element matches the current router URL. In general, an attribute directive somehow modifies the behavior of the HTML element or component it is attached to. This section shows how to define custom attribute directives.

Attribute directives are TypeScript classes decorated with the @Directive decorator. They receive a reference to the element they are attached to in their constructor, and modify it in the ngAfterViewInit or ngOInit life cycle hooks:

```
constructor(private el: ElementRef) { }
```

If needed, they also attach event handlers to the element with the help of the @HostListener decorator:

```
@HostListener('click', ['$event.target', '$event...'])
    onClick(el: HTMLElement, ...) ...
```

The @HostListener takes the event name as its first argument, and an array of properties to extract from $event as its second argument. All extracted arguments are passed in the same order they are defined to the method decorated with @HostListener. Events attached with @HostListener are automatically disposed of by Angular, thus saving the effort of disposing of them manually when the component/directive is destroyed.

As a first example, let's implement the lens attribute that, when applied to an HTML element, toggles its font size at each click to help the user to read its content. As the first step, let's add a directives folder under the app folder of the AdvancedFeatures project. Then, let's open a Window console in the new folder and let's scaffold a new directive with the Angular CLI command ng generate directive lens. The new directive is automatically imported in app.module.ts and added to its declarations. The code for this simple directive is straightforward:

```
import { Directive, HostListener, Input, ElementRef }
  from '@angular/core';
@Directive({
  selector: '[lens]'
})
```

```
export class LensDirective {
  @Input("lens") Magnification: number;
  @HostListener('click', ['$event.target'])
    onClick(el: HTMLElement) {
    if (el.style.fontSize) el.style.fontSize = null;
    else el.style.fontSize = this.Magnification+"%"
  }
  constructor(private el: ElementRef) { }
}
```

The directive may be tested by attaching it to the `h2` element of `app.component.html`:

```
<h2 [lens]="400">Here are some links to help you start:</h2>
```

The directive input property may be passed directly after the directive name because the attribute name specified in `@Input("lens")` is the same as the directive attribute name, `selector: '[lens]'`. Further input attributes, if needed, are placed as follows:

```
<h2 [lens]="400" [<aux. input attribute name 1>]="..." [<aux. input
attribute name 2>]="..." ....
```

Defining max, min, and step validation attributes

Once we understand how to define an attribute directive, defining validation attributes for the `max`, `min`, and `step` HTML attributes becomes quite an easy task. Each of these attributes does nothing other than adding the adequate validator to the list of validators applied to the input element. Validators are added to each input by adding them to a named list handled with a dependency injection (dependency injection is discussed in detail in `Chapter 13`, *Navigation and Services*). Type instances handled with a dependency injection are indexed either by class types (a class type is represented by the constructor function of the class), or by instances of the `InjectionToken` type (`InjectionToken` is described in detail in `Chapter 13`, *Navigation and Services* together with dependency injection). Validators must be associated to an `InjectionToken` instance contained in the `NG_VALIDATORS` constant defined in `'@angular/forms'`. The dependency injection is discussed in detail in the *Services and dependency injection* section in `Chapter 13`, *Navigation and Services*.

That said, all the skeleton classes of all validation attributes can be generated with Angular CLI in the `directives` folder, such as the `lens` directive, with commands such as `ng generate directive min` issued in a Window console rooted in the `directives` folder. The code for the `min` attribute is quite simple:

```
import { Directive, Input} from '@angular/core';
import { NG_VALIDATORS, Validator, AbstractControl, Validators }
   from '@angular/forms'

@Directive({
  selector: '[min]',
  providers: [{
    provide: NG_VALIDATORS,
    useExisting: MinDirective,
    multi: true
  }]
})
export class MinDirective implements Validator {
  @Input('min') minValue: number;
  validate(control: AbstractControl): { [key: string]: any } {
    return Validators.min(this.minValue)(control)
  }
}
```

The directive implements the `Validator` interface by implementing its `validate` method and then adding itself to the list of dependency injected providers associated to the input element. All providers added to the providers attribute of a directive are added to a unique list of providers associated to the HTML element they are applied to. Validators must be added under the `NG_VALIDATORS` key. `multi=true` in the record added to the `providers` directive, and says that the `NG_VALIDATORS` key may have several objects associated to it; otherwise, adding a new element under a given key would remove any previously added element.

Since the `min` and `max` validation logic is already implemented in Angular, the `validate` method just calls the existing validation function exposed as a static method of the `Validators` class defined in `'@angular/forms'`.

The code for the `max` attribute just differs for the `min` names replaced by `max`, and for the predefined function called by the `validate` method:

```
validate(control: AbstractControl): { [key: string]: any } {
    return Validators.max(this.maxValue)(control)
}
```

Since no validation logic is predefined for the `step` validator, the validation logic for this attribute must be implemented from scratch. The `validate` method is expected to return an object whose property names are validation error names, and whose values must be non-null if and only if the error associated to the property name is detected.

The `step` validator just has a single error associated with it that takes place when the value contained in the input field is not a multiple of the `step` value:

```
validate(control: AbstractControl): { [key: string]: any } {
  if (!control.value) return null
  let nVal = parseFloat(control.value);
  if (!nVal) return null
  if(nVal%this.stepValue)
    return { 'step': true }
  return null;
}
```

After the definition of the preceding directive, the numeric input contained in the `form-test` component should validate properly. The input field expects an integer (`step = 1`) in the `1-10` range. Launch the application and try it!

Content projection and structural directives

This section describes the techniques used to perform DOM manipulation in Angular. DOM manipulation is based on the following ideas:

- An Angular template that encodes a chunk of HTML to be inserted and possibly repeated several times somewhere
- The content placeholder that encodes a location to place the results of rendering Angular templates

The simplest form of DOM manipulation is content projection: content specified within the start and end tags of a component `C` is read as a template and projected in a location specified by a content placeholder inside of the `C` component template. Content projection adds the capability to include variable HTML furnished as input in the component template. The content placeholder used in content projection is the `<ng-content></ng-content>` tag. Content projection is completely automatic; it is enough to add a content placeholder into a component template and to place content between its start and end tags to have this content projected into the component.

As an example, let's modify the `modal-test` component to accept the modal body as projected content. We just need to place `<ng-content></ng-content>` in the modal body:

```
...
<div class="modal-body">
    <ng-content></ng-content>
</div>
...
```

To test content projection, it is enough to move `<app-form-test></app-form-test>` inside the `app-modal-test` tags. After that, the form will appear inside the modal:

```
<app-modal-test #modalToOpen
    Title="This is the modal title"
    (ModalClosed)="doAlert($event.Title+' was closed!')">
  <app-form-test></app-form-test>
</app-modal-test>
```

Try it!

It is also possible to project several content items in several different placeholders. In this case, placeholders must be named:

```
...
<ng-content select="[content1]"></ng-content>
...
<ng-content select="[content2]"></ng-content>
...
```

When the component is called, one must enclose all contents within a `multi-content` tag and then one must refer to the placeholder names in the root elements of the various contents, as shown here:

```
<my-component>
<multi-content>
    <div content1>....</div>
    <div content2>....</div>
</multi-content>
<my-component>
```

Structural directives are the most common way to manipulate HTML content in Angular. Several sections in the previous chapters on Angular show the use of the structural directives *ngFor and *ngIf. This section also analyzes the *ngSwitch directive, which is the last predefined Angular structural directive, and gives more insight on how a structural directive works and may be implemented by the user.

First of all, why are all structural directives preceded by an asterisk? Is this a convention or what?

It is not a convention, but syntactic sugar for a more complex syntax. In fact, structural directives should be applied to templates only, and not to standard HTML. Actually, the following markup is syntactic sugar:

```
<div *ngIf="name.errors.required">
    Name is required.
</div>
```

In fact, Angular translates it into this markup, before processing it further:

```
<ng-template [ngIf]="name.errors.required"="hero">
    <div >
        Name is required.
    </div>
</ng-template>
```

The `ngIf` structural directive reads the template contained inside the `<ng-template>` tag and renders it according to the condition that it receives as input. The template inside the `<ng-template>`, and a reference to a placeholder location to place the HTML that is passed to the constructor of the directive, should look like this:

```
constructor(
    private template: TemplateRef<any>,
    private viewContainer: ViewContainerRef) { }
```

Bindings in the template object are evaluated with respect to a context object computed by the directive, and then added to the content placeholder. This whole job is performed with a call to the `createEmbeddedView` method of `ViewContainerRef`:

```
this.viewContainer.createEmbeddedView(this.template, contextObject)
```

The preceding call may be performed several times if there are several context objects to render, as is the case for the `ngFor` directive. The result of each call is appended as the last child of the parent node that works as a content placeholder.

Properties of the context object are not used directly in the definition of the template bindings, since template bindings are based on the properties and variables available in the view context where the structural directive is used. Instead, their values are assigned to view variables defined by the user and specified in the structural directive binding. For instance, the context object of the `ngFor` directive contains the following properties: `index`, which is the sequence number of the current item being processed; `odd`, which is `true` when `index` is odd; `even`, which is `true` when `index` is even; `first`, which is `true` when the `first` item is being processed; and `last`, which is `true` when the last element is being processed. All these properties can't be used directly in the template but are bound to view variables that, in turn, are used in the template:

```
<div *ngFor="let x of collection; let myFirst=first; let myLast=last">
    ....myFirst....x....myLast
</div>
```

With the preceding technique, the `ngFor` template is still bound to a component class instance, and can continue using component class properties, while the context object properties are just added to this context through the `let` microsyntax. Renaming all context object properties with `let` is necessary to avoid name collisions when several structural directives are nested.

Since there is no explicit context object property name after `let x`, so x is bound to a special context property named `$implicit`. Thus, `let x of collection`, which resembles a JavaScript iteration statement, is actually composed of two independent parts—`let x` and `of collection`. The `of collection` part is a property name-value pair that assigns the value of `collection` to a directive input property named `<directivename>Of`. Thus, there is nothing special in `of`; it is not a keyword, but just the suffix of an input property name. You could define a custom directive that uses `from` instead of `of`, and that also has a further input property called `<directive name>With`. In this case, you could write something such as this:

```
*ngExtendedFor="let x from collection with mydictionary; let myFirst=first;
let myLast=last"
```

The whole syntax used within quotation marks immediately after the directive name is called a **microsyntax**. It consists of the following:

- `let` statements that bind template variables to directive properties. Just one `let` statement can omit the directive property, in which case it is bound to the `$implicit` property (in the preceding example `let x`).

- Identifier-template variable pairs `<identifier> <template variable>` like `from collection` and `with mydictionary` can be chained to to any `let` statement, in which case the directive property named `<directive name><identifier>` is bound to `<template variable>`. In the preceding example, `ExtendedForFrom` is bound to the template variable named `collection` and `ExtendedForWith` is bound to the `mydictionary` template variable.

The next subsection shows the preceding concepts in practice in the implementation of a directive that automatically adds a proper error message next to any input field.

The inputError directive

The basic idea is the definition of an `inputError` directive that would enable a syntax similar to this one:

```
<div *inputError="let error from quantity.errors">
    {{error}}
</div>
```

Here, `quantity` is a template reference bound to the `ngModel` input field with `#quantity="ngModel"`, so that `quantity.errors` is an object whose properties are the names of all error detected. The directive chooses just one of the error names and uses it to select an adequate error message. Then, it binds this error message to the `$implicit` context object property so that the error message is assigned to the `error` variable. `quantity.errors` will be bound to a directive input property named `inputErrorFrom`. The use of a `div` is just an example, since the `inputError` directive can be used with any HTML tag. Also, the content of the `div` tag is just a simple example of how to show the error message.

Let's scaffold the directive under the `directives` folder with the `ng generate directive inputError` command. Then, replace the existing code with the following class skeleton:

```
import { Directive, Input, TemplateRef, ViewContainerRef } from
'@angular/core';
@Directive({
  selector: '[inputError]'
})
export class InputErrorDirective {
  private static readonly allErrors =
    {
```

```
      . . .
    };
  @Input('inputErrorFrom') set errors(value: { [key: string]: any }) {
      . . .
  }
  private context = {
    $implicit: null
  };
  private previousError: string=null;
  constructor(
    private template: TemplateRef<any>,
    private viewContainer: ViewContainerRef) { }


}
```

`allErrors` is an object acting as a map that associates each error name to the corresponding error message. The `inputErrorFrom` input property is implemented as a setter so it may change the HTML produced by the directive each time the object containing all errors changes. All rendering logic will be placed in this setter. `previousError` stores the last error rendered, or is null if no error was detected. This way, the HTML created by the directive can be changed only when the new error name selected differs from the previous one. This is an essential performance tip since new error objects are created each time the user types a new character. A simple definition for the `allErrors` map is this:

```
{
    required: 'the field is required',
    minlength: 'minimum number of characters exceeded',
    maxlength: 'maximum number of characters exceeded',
    max: 'maximum value exceeded',
    min: 'minimum value exceeded',
    step: 'value is not a multiple of the step'
}
```

The code for the setter is this:

```
@Input('inputErrorFrom') set errors(value: { [key: string]: any }) {
    let newError = null;
    for (let x in value) {
      if (value[x]) {
        newError = x;
        break;
      }
    }
    if (this.previousError != newError) {
      this.previousError = newError;
      this.context.$implicit =
```

```
            InputErrorDirective.allErrors[newError];
        this.viewContainer.clear();
        if (newError) this.viewContainer.createEmbeddedView(
          this.template, this.context);
    }
  }
```

The `for` loop selects the first error name if a JavaScript `true` entry is found; otherwise, `newError` remains `null`. An HTML update is performed only if the new error differs from the one that was previously rendered.

As a first step, the error update code clears the previous HTML by calling the `clear()` method of `viewContainer`. Then, if `newError` contains an error, a new HTML is rendered by calling the `createEmbeddedView` method with the error message extracted from the `allErrors` map assigned to the `$implicit` property of the `context` object.

The new directive is easily tested by removing all previous error-displaying markup after the `name` input field in `form-test.component.html` and replacing it with this:

```
<div *ngIf="name.invalid && (name.dirty || name.touched || errorSubmitted)"
    class="alert alert-danger">
    <div *inputError="let error from name.errors">{{ error }}</div>
</div>
```

Similar markup can be added immediately after all other fields. It is enough to replace `name` with the template reference associated with the other input fields (`quantity` and `size`).

The `inputError` directive can be improved in several ways. First of all, fixed string messages can be replaced by customized messages that explain why the constraint was violated. In fact, in the error object, each error property contains an `error` object whose properties give information on the constraint violation. For instance, the `maxlength` error property contains an `error` object with a property that specifies the actual input value, and another property that specifies the limit that was exceeded. Therefore, fixed string messages may be replaced by functions that receive the `error` object as their unique argument, and use it to assemble a customized string.

A second improvement is injecting the map of all error messages with dependency injection. This way, it is quite easy to adapt error messages to the current locale selected for the applications. We will see how to handle error messages with dependency injection and build configurations in detail in the *Services and Dependency Injection* section in Chapter 13, *Navigation and Services*.

Predefined structural directories

`ngIf` doesn't use any context object. It receives the condition expression as its only input and renders its template only if the condition expression evaluates to `true`.

`ngFor` uses a context object containing the `index`, `odd`, `even`, `first`, `last`, and `$implicit`, properties, which have already been explained in the initial part of this *Content projection and structural directives* section. All options in the `type select` input of `form-test.component.html` are rendered with `ngFor`.

The collection following `from` is not the only input property of `ngFor`. `ngFor` also accepts another optional property, a function that receives the index and the current item as input and returns a value that uniquely identifies that item. Consider the following example:

```
*ngFor="let item of mtCollection;trackBy: myTrackByFn"
```

Here, `myTrackByFn` is a method available in the view context, and has the required two input arguments. `trackBy` is optional and has no impact on the final result but may have a great impact on performance (as explained in next paragraphs).

When the input array changes, `ngFor` must remove the templates of all deleted items and must add the templates of the newly added items. When item properties are modified, no action is required from `ngFor`, since property changes are automatically handled by Angular's change detection and update algorithm.

Angular doesn't know which items were added and which ones were deleted from the array, since it just has the old and the new copy of the array. Luckily, the **Levenshtein algorithm** is able to find the minimum number of deletes and inserts that transforms the old array into the new one. The Levenshtein algorithm needs a function that recognizes when two items represent the same entity. If `trackBy` is not provided, standard JavaScript equality is used. Thus, two objects are considered the same object if and only if they have the same pointer. Now, if the new array copy comes from the server, all pointers will be different, so all the old array templates are removed and the whole array is re-rendered from scratch. However, items coming from a server are likely to be extracted from some kind of database, or store, so they must have a key property that univocally identifies each item. Thus, when items are identified by a key property, `trackBy` must be passed as a function that returns each item's key value to maximize performance.

Angular also has an `ngSwitch` directive that mimics a TypeScript/JavaScript `switch` statement. It is used in conjunction with `*ngSwitchCase` and `*ngSwitchDefault` to render just one of `n` templates based on the value returned by the expression bound to `ngSwitch`. It is used like this:

```
<div [ngSwitch]="product.Color">
  <div *ngSwitchCase="'red'" >...</div>
  <div *ngSwitchCase="'green'" >...</div>
  ...
  <div *ngSwitchDefault >...</div>
</div>
```

Only the template whose `*ngSwitchCase` expression value is the same as the value bound to `ngSwitch` is rendered, if any; otherwise, the template with `*ngSwitchDefault` is rendered. `ngSwitchCase` and `ngSwitchDefault` are preceded by an asterisk, since they manipulate templates. `ngSwitch` doesn't need the asterisk, since it is a standard attribute directive that sets the context for the various `*ngSwitchCase` and `*ngSwitchDefault` directives.

Animations

Angular comes with a predefined animation framework that is contained in the `'@angular/animations'` package. The first step for using animations in Angular is to import `BrowserAnimationsModule` from `'@angular/platform-browser/animations'` in the main application module (`app.module.ts`), since it works as an interface with the browser for the animation's execution:

```
import { BrowserAnimationsModule } from '@angular/platform-
browser/animations';
...
@NgModule({
  ...
  imports: [
    ...
    BrowserAnimationsModule
```

Let's do this in the `AdvamcedFeatures` project. Then, all animations used by a component are placed in the `animations` property of its `@Component` decorator:

```
@Component({
    ...
    animations:[
        //animations go here
    ]
```

The code that defines each animation may be placed inline inside the `animations` array, or it may be assigned to an exported constant of an external file:

```
// file "animations/common.ts"
...
export const animation1 = trigger('animation1', [
    transition ('state2 => state1', [....],
    transition (.....
]);
...
export const animation2 = trigger(, [...
...
```

The first argument of the `trigger` function is the animation name, while its second argument lists all possible state transitions that compose the behavior encoded by the animation. The first argument of the `transition` function specifies a state transition, while the array passed as the second argument lists all animation steps to execute when the state transition takes place.

When animations are defined in external files, it is enough to import all constants and to place them in the `animations` array:

```
import { animation1, animation2 } from './animations/common.ts'
...
animations:[
    animation1,
    animation2,
    ...
]
```

For better reusability, it is also possible to define the animations steps contained in the second argument of a `transition` function in just external files. In this case, all steps are defined within the `animate` function and they can also contain parameters. Parameters must be placed within strings and enclosed inside the `{{...}}` symbols:

```
export const ItemsIn=
    animate ([
        query(':enter', style({ opacity: 0}), { optional: true }),
        query(':enter', [
          stagger('{{ delay }}', [
              animate('{{ time }}', style({ opacity: 1}))),
          ]),
        ], { optional: true })
    ]);
```

In this case, before being added to a `transition` function, all steps must be instantiated with the `useAnimation` function, which also accepts all values that must be bound to the animation parameters:

```
transition(* => *, [
    useAnimation(ItemsIn, {
        params: {
          delay : 100,
          time: '1s ease-out''
        }
      })
])
```

Parameters are specified through an object contained in the `params` property of the options object, passed as the second argument to `useAnimation`.

Triggers, states, and state transitions

Each Angular animation is encoded with a functional programming style, as a tree of function calls. The root function is always `trigger`, whose first argument is the name of the animation: `trigger('myAnimation', [...])`. The definition of the animation is contained in an array passed as the second argument. Once defined, the animation is applied to the HTML tag of the element to animate with this syntax: `[@myAnimation]='<binding expression>'`. All possible values returned by the expression define the animation states. For instance, an animation applied to a button might have two states identified by the strings `'opened'` and `'closed'`, or by the `true` and `false` Boolean values of a `closed` property.

Each element passed in the second argument of `trigger` defines either a style to apply to a state or how to handle a transition between two states. Styles are defined with the `style` function, which receives an object with all style properties and values as its unique argument. Styles are associated to states with the `state` function, which receives a string representation of the state as its first argument and the associated style as its second argument:

```
state('true', style({ backgroundColor: '#fbf4f3' }))
```

Style properties and values follow the same syntax as the JavaScript style properties of HTML elements. Style properties may also have an `'*'` value, in which case Angular takes the value assumed by that property before any state and any animation is applied as the property value. The `'*'` values are useful when the animation must be reused, and when the property value depends on browser settings such as the browser window size, or on the data bound to the template:

```
state('false', style({ backgroundColor: '*' }))
```

State transitions are defined with the `transition` function, whose first argument defines the state transition with strings such as `state1 => state2` (transition from `state1` to `state2`), `state1 <= state2` (transition from `state2` to `state1`), and `state1 <=> state2` (both transition from `state1` to `state2` and its inverse transition). The second argument contains the list of animation steps that defines the animation. Whenever a transition that matches the first argument of `transition` takes place, the animation steps listed in the second argument are executed.

In the simplest case, transition contains a call to the animate function as its unique animation step:

```
transition('false <=> true', [
    animate(500)
])
```

When the first argument of `animate` is a number, it is interpreted as the duration of the animation in milliseconds. It is also possible to use a string composed of a number followed by the unit of measure, which may either be `'s'` for seconds or `'ms'` for milliseconds. Thus, the duration in the previous transition may also be written as `animate('500ms')` or `animate('0.5s')`. If no other specification is supplied, Angular performs a linear interpolation of all style properties from their values in the initial and final states of the transition.

As an example, let's animate the background color of the form in the `form-test` component. Before writing the animation, all the required animation functions must be imported from `'@angular/animations'`:

```
import { trigger, state, style, animate, transition }
   from '@angular/animations';
```

The form will assume a pink appearance when it is submitted with errors, and its normal color in all other cases. There is a condition that may be `true` or false, so the animation states will be `'true'` and `'false'`:

```
@Component({
  ...
  animations: [
    trigger('formErrorInOut', [
      state('false', style({ backgroundColor: '*' })),
      state('true', style({ backgroundColor: '#fbf4f3' })),
      transition('false <=> true', [
        animate(500)
      ])
    ])
  ]
})
```

In the `false` state, `'*'` specifies the form's normal color defined in the overall CSS, while in the `'true'` state, a pink color is used. Both transitions have a duration of `500` milliseconds.

Now, it is enough to add the following binding to the form in `form-test.component.html`:

```
[@formErrorInOut] = "errorSubmitted&&mainForm.invalid"
```

Run the project and submit the form without writing anything; the form will transition to pink. As soon as all validation errors are corrected, the form will transition back to its original color.

After the duration, the string passed as the first argument to animate can also specify the kind of function to use for the interpolation. Predefined values are `ease-in` (starts slowly, and accelerates to reach a constant speed) `ease-out` (slows down at the end), `ease-in-out` (starts slowly, and accelerates to reach a constant speed, then slows down again at the end), and `ease` (similar to `ease-in-out`, but a little bit faster at the beginning). Let's try the following:

```
transition('false <=> true', [
  animate('800ms ease-in-out')
])
```

The reader is encouraged to try all options, with durations high enough to perceive the differences. However, differences are easily perceived with motion animations (which will be described soon) than with color animations. It is also possible to specify a generic cubic Bezier interpolation with custom parameters: `animate('800ms cubic-bezier(0.1, 0.7, 1.0, 0.1)')`. `animate` also admits a second argument, which can be either a style or a set of keyframes. Both possibilities will be described next.

`transition` also supports an asterisk in place of a specific state, in which case the transition will match any state in the asterisk position. For example, `'* => high'` matches transitions from any state to the `'high'` state.

Transitions can also have `void` as their final or start states, such as `'* => void'` and `'void => *'`. Now, `void` represents a state where the animated element is absent. Accordingly, `'* => void'` means *an HTML element in any state is removed*, while `'void => *'` means *an HTML element is created in any state*. They are used with structural directives such as `ngIf` and `ngFor` that create and destroy HTML elements, and are so frequently used that they are abbreviated with the shortcuts `':leave'` and `':enter'`. As an example of their use, let's animate the creation and destruction of the `<div @insertRemove *ngIf=...` error element that immediately follows each input element in `form-test.component.html`. Let's call `insertRemove` on this animation.

The `':leave'` and `':enter'` transitions usually don't use states since one doesn't animate the state changes of an HTML element, but its creation or destruction. As a first consequence, the animation is applied to the HTML element simply as `@insertRemove` with no square brackets, and with no binding expression after it. A second consequence is that the styles interpolated by the animation, not being defined in states, must be defined elsewhere. They are added as animation steps in the transition and/or as second arguments of the `animate` function:

```
trigger('insertRemove', [
    transition(':enter', [
      style({
        opacity: 0,
        transform: 'translateY(-100%)'
      }),
      animate('0.5s', style({
        opacity: 1,
        transform: 'translateY(0)'
      }))),
    ]),
    transition(':leave', [
      animate('0.5s', style({
```

```
      opacity: 0,
      transform: 'translateY(-100%)'
    }))
  ])
])
```

The animation consists of variations in the opacity, and of the vertical displacement of the `div` element. More specifically, as a first step of the *enter animation* triggered when the error `div` appears, a `style` step sets its opacity to completely invisible and displaces it upwards by an amount that is equal to its height. The subsequent `animate` step specifies a final state with `0` displacement and a completely opaque element. Thus, during the animation, the element always becomes less transparent, and moves downward until it reaches its final position.

The destruction animation starts from the current opacity and `0` displacement, and performs exactly the inverse transformation performed by `':enter'`. Test the animation by applying `@insertRemove` to all error `div`.

What if we would like to add a bouncing effect when the error `div` appears?

It is enough to replace the style in the `animate` functions with two `style` keyframes, the first one for the bounced position and the second one for the final position:

```
transition(':enter', [
  style({
    opacity: 0,
    transform: 'translateY(-100%)'
  }),
  animate('0.5s', keyframes([
    style({
      opacity: 1,
      transform: 'translateY(50%)',
      offset: 0.7
    }),
    style({
      opacity: 1,
      transform: 'translateY(0)',
      offset: 1
    })
  ])),
])
```

The `style` keyframe must be inserted inside a `keyframes` call, and the offset property added to all keyframe styles specifies the percentage of completion of the animation when the keyframe is reached. `0.7` means `70%` and `1` means the end of the animation.

Parallel and child animations

Animation steps listed in transition functions are executed sequentially. Animation steps that must be executed in parallel must be placed in a `group` function call:

```
group([step1, step2, step3,....])
```

If some of the animation processes to be executed in parallel are, in turn, composed of several sequential steps, the sequential steps nested in the `group` function must be grouped with the `sequence` function:

```
group([sequence(seq1, seq2, ...), par2, par2, ...])
```

The `group` function is not very useful in animations that animate a single HTML element, since in this case all properties to be animated in parallel can be placed in unique style objects, with no need to use the `group` function. The `group` function is typically used together with the `query` function, which allows the animation of elements that are descendants of the elements the animation is applied to. More specifically, the `query` function defines an animations step that involves some of the descendants of the element the application is applied to.

 When a descendant element that is being animated by `query` has pending animations directly applied to it, they are frozen, and executed when and if the ancestor animation executes an `animateChild()` animation step.

The first argument of the `query` function selects the descendants to animate. It is a string containing a CSS selector enriched with the following Angular-specific selection primitives:

- The `':leave'` and `':enter'` pseudo-classes select, respectively, descendants that are being destroyed and newly created descendants
- The `':animating'` pseudo-class selects all descendants that are already being animated
- `'@animationName'` selects all descendants that have an animation named `'animationName'` applied to them
- `'@*'` selects all descendants that have any animation applied to them
- The `':self'` pseudo-class adds the ancestor element to the set of descendants to be animated

The second argument of `query` is an array of animation steps, and the optional third argument contains an option object that can contain one or more of the following options:

- `limit`: If provided, it must contain an integer that specifies the maximum number of descendants to select.
- `optional`: As a default, if no descendant is found, `query` throws an error. Setting `optional` to `true` prevents this error.

One or more animation steps listed in the second argument of the `query` function may be grouped and enclosed in a `stagger` call:

```
query(':enter', [stagger(50, [step1, step2]), step3,....], {optional:
true})
```

In the preceding case, each descendant in the selected list starts `step1` 50 milliseconds after its predecessor in the list.

Often, to take advantage of the `stagger` effect, animations are applied to an ancestor element instead of applying them directly to each specific element to animate.

Let's see these concepts in practice by animating the elements in an `*ngFor` with an animation placed on an ancestor, so that we can use a `stagger` effect. The idea is that all created elements fade in, moving from the left to their final positions, one after the other, because of the `stagger` effect. Meanwhile, all destroyed elements fade out while moving to the right, one after the other, because of the `stagger` effect. We will call `enterLeaveAnimation` on this animation.

Let's open the `AngularVSTemplate` project created in `Chapter 10`, *Angular ASP.NET Core Project Template*, and let's add the `BrowserAnimationsModule` module to the application main module's `imports` array in `app.module.ts`, in order to enable animations.

Now, let's open `fetch-data.component.html`, and remove the `*ngIf` from the `table` HTML tag, so that it is immediately displayed:

```
<table class='table' >
```

Then, add the `enterLeaveAnimation` to the `tbody` HTML tag, so that the animation is triggered each time the number of elements in the `forecasts` array changes:

```
<tbody [@enterLeaveAnimation]="forecasts.length">
```

Finally, let's open `fetch-data.component.ts` to define the animation:

```
...
import {
  trigger, transition, query, style,
  stagger, animate, group
} from '@angular/animations'
...
@Component({
    ...
    animations: [
    trigger('enterLeaveAnimation', [
      transition('* => *', [
        query(':enter', style({
          opacity: 0,
          transform: 'translateX(-100%)'
        }), { optional: true }),
        group([
          query(':enter', [
            stagger(200, [
              animate('1s ease-out', style({
                opacity: 1,
                transform: 'translateX(0)'
              })),
            ]),
          ], { optional: true }),
          query(':leave', [
            stagger(200, [
              animate('1s ease-out', style({
                opacity: 0,
                transform: 'translateX(-100%)'
              })),
            ])
          ], { optional: true })
        ]),
      ])
    ])
  ]
})
...
```

There is an unique transition that is triggered each time the `forecasts` array's length changes. The first `query` call makes all created elements invisible and moves them to the left, in order to prepare them for the start of the animation. Then, two different animations for the created and destroyed elements are launched in parallel with `group`. `{ optional: true }` in all query calls prevents errors when either created or destroyed elements are absent. Run the project, go to the `fetch data` page, and enjoy the animation.

Summary

Angular attribute directives modify the standard behavior of HTML elements and components. Developers can use them to add features to HTML elements and to components, with no need to modify their source code, thus adding the possibility to modularize and to reuse not only components, but also single features.

Content projection increases the reusability of components by enabling the definition of parameterized components that can receive injected layout parts when they are used. Structural directives allow the dynamic manipulation of layout parts by adding/removing HTML nodes and by dynamically creating contents.

Angular animations are an easy-to-use interface to CSS3 animations. They allow the definition of states, behaviors, and animations with a simple functional language, thus leveraging the full power of CSS3 with an easy-to-use programming interface.

The next chapter shows how to build a complex application that communicates with the server and uses other services, and where user can navigate through several pages organized in loadable modules.

Questions

1. What is the advantage of using `@HostListener`?
2. How do you pass input values to a directive that accepts several input properties?
3. Is it possible to define something similar to `*ngFor` that uses `in`, instead of `of`? If yes, why is it possible?
4. What is the purpose of `trackBy`?
5. What is the asterisk that precedes structural directives?
6. What is the `ViewContainerRef` type passed in the constructor of a structural directive? Why is it needed?
7. Since all animation functions already accept a list of animation steps, why is the `sequence` function needed?
8. What is the purpose of the `query` animation function?
9. Is it possible to use `stagger` and group in non-child animations, and if so, why?

13
Navigation and Services

Up to now, we have learned how to build applications that perform simple tasks and whose content can be navigated by loading a few components on the HTML page. However, the main purpose of single page application frameworks, such as Angular, is the implementation of complex business applications that exchange non-trivial quantities of data with a remote server. In such complex applications, acceptable user interface and performance can only be ensured with complex navigation patterns, as well as with efficient data exchange techniques.

This chapter explains how to enable components to perform complex tasks, such as communicating with the server, with the help of service classes automatically injected in their constructors. It also explains how to mount and test a complete application with complex navigation patterns that optimize both performance and application loading time by means of lazy loading Angular modules. The reader is required to practice all concepts learned by adding new code to the one produced so far, and by modifying existing client-server communications.

More specifically, you will learn the following topics:

- Defining services and using them with Dependency Injection
- Using Angular HTTP Client to define services
- Defining SPA pages with routing and lazy loading
- Using Angular testing frameworks

Technical requirements

The technical requirements for this chapter are as follows:

- Visual Studio 2017, with the latest ASP.NET Core tools
- Visual Studio TypeScript SDK
- A version of Angular CLI installed globally (Version 6 or above)

For the installation of Angular CLI, please refer to the *Technical requirements* section of `Chapter 10`, *Angular ASP.NET Core Project Template*.

All the code used in this chapter can be downloaded from the following GitHub link: `https://github.com/PacktPublishing/Hands-On-TypeScript-for-CSharp-and-.NET-Core-Developers`.

Check out the following video to see the Code in Action: `http://bit.ly/2AzyHGs`.

Services and Dependency Injection

Application modularity requires that chunks of code performing the same task in several Angular components be factored out into separate classes. Actually, to improve software maintainability, it is best practice to factor out all code chunks that might be useful to other Angular component classes even when these other components have not yet been created. As a consequence, Angular components should only contain code that is specific to their internal peculiarities, that is, the code that defines their interaction with the user. Code that defines business logic, and localization rules, as well as code that handles application-level services, must be factored out in various specialized classes, which are usually referred to as services.

Thus, for instance, the code that takes care of retrieving and updating products from a database located on the server should be grouped in dedicated service classes. In general, the whole business logic that updates and retrieves data handled by a component must be factored out in service classes. Also, general-purpose error messages should be factored out in services, since they are application-level resources.

The simple approach of letting each component create all the services they need has several drawbacks:

- Service settings usually depend on the overall application state, which is unknown to each single component. Therefore, in general, components should be able to create services with the correct settings, so forcing them to do it would break application modularity, and would yield spaghetti code.
  Services that depend on the context are more common than they might appear, since possible contexts also include component testing. During unit testing, it is very difficult to arrange fake servers and other application parts that behave as required by each test. Therefore, when testing components, fake services are used that provide the data needed by the tests without actually interacting with a server and/or other application parts.

- Service creations may be expensive operations, so it is convenient that several components share the same service instance. Moreover, instance sharing becomes a necessity when service instances contain state information that must be shared among components.
  Implementing shared instances with static properties directly handled by the components breaks application modularity, creates problems during testing, and is likely to yield hard-to-find bugs during software maintenance because access to the static properties containing the shared services are spread throughout the code: they are hidden inputs/outputs that are difficult to track, and difficult to prepare, during testing.

Dependency Injection (DI) was conceived to overcome all of the aforementioned drawbacks. According to the DI paradigm, service instances are handled by a hierarchy of containers. Each container has a record for each service it can provide.

This record contains information on the following:

- How to create each service in a way that can be dependent on the overall application state?
- If the service is a singleton, or if a new instance is created each time the service is requested. When a service is not found in a container, it is searched up in the container hierarchy until it reaches the root. Thus, the structure of the hierarchy defines which requests share the same singletons, and which requests share the same service creation strategy.

Angular, like all frameworks relying on DI, allows the automatic injection of services in class constructors. Some DI engines also allow services to be injected into adequately tagged properties. All DI frameworks allow the recursive injection of services, that is, services mentioned in the constructor of other services are automatically created and injected into the service constructor, and this process is recursive. All requests caused by the recursion on the same initial request are resolved in the same container of the initial request (moving up in the containers hierarchy if the service is not found).

Angular containers are called **service injectors**, or simply injectors, and they contain only singletons; in other words, each service instance, once created in a container, is reused for all subsequent requests issued to that container. This is not an actual limitation, since Angular is a client-side framework, so *singleton* here means unique to the user session. Moreover, injector hierarchy also includes injectors associated with each component instance, so service instances placed there are unique, but only in the lifetime of that component instance.

Angular injects services in the constructors of all Angular building blocks: components, directives, pipes, and services themselves. Each parameter in the constructor of these class types is interpreted as a service retrieved in the current container, and injected into the constructor before creating an instance. The next subsection explains how the hierarchy of Angular injectors is organized and how to determine the current injector when components, directives, and pipes are created. Services mentioned in the constructor of other services use the same container as the initial request that caused their creation.

Angular injectors' hierarchy

Angular contains a unique platform injector that is populated when the application is bootstrapped. This injector contains services used by the framework itself, and other services that the developer can add in `main.ts` where the application is bootstrapped. The code scaffolded by the Visual Studio Angular template adds a service that returns the application base URL, as follows:

```
export function getBaseUrl() {
   return document.getElementsByTagName('base')[0].href;
}
const providers = [
   { provide: 'BASE_URL', useFactory: getBaseUrl, deps: [] }
];
platformBrowserDynamic(providers).bootstrapModule(AppModule)
   .catch(err => console.log(err));
```

In this case, the service is indexed by the string token BASE_URL. The singleton is itself a string that is computed by a factory function. The following subsection discusses in detail all the options Angular offers to index and select services, and to create their singleton instances.

Other injectors are also added to all instances of Angular modules and components. The records that describe all services provided by each injector are called **service providers**, or simply `providers`. They are added to the `providers` array property of the `@NgModule` and `@Component` decorators:

```
@NgModule({
   ...
   providers: [
      {...},
      {...}
      ...
   ],
   ...
})
```

```
...
@Component({
  ...
  providers: [
    ...
  ],
  ...
})
```

These injectors have the same lifetime of modules and component instances of which they are part. Module instances live until the end of the application. Accordingly, injectors associated with module instances span the entire lifetime of the application. Component instances and their injectors have a shorter lifetime, since they are removed from the DOM when the user navigates to other content, or when some DOM parts are destroyed for other reasons. For instance, components contained in an `*ngIf` directive are removed with all their descendants when the `*ngIf` condition becomes `false`. Components contained in an `*ngFor` instance are destroyed when the enumerable bound to the directive changes. Components contained in a `<router-outlet>` instance are removed with all their descendants when a router loads a different component instance in that `<router-outlet>`. Moreover, while modules are singletons, components may be instantiated several times in different places. Thus, injectors associated with components have a lifetime that is limited to the lifetime of each component instance, and that is usually shorter than the lifetime of the application.

All services added to each x module are merged into the application main module injector (`app.component.ts`) when the module is imported. Thus, when the application starts, there is just one application-level module injector containing all service providers of all imported modules. However, when a module is lazy loaded, its injector is not merged into the main application module and only remains available for requests originating in that module. In short, module injectors form a hierarchy that is parallel to the hierarchy of all lazy loaded modules, with the main application module injector also containing all providers contained in the modules that are not lazy loaded.

In each application state, there is also a hierarchy of component instances rooted in the component used to bootstrap the application (when the application is scaffolded with Angular CLI, the bootstrap component is called `app-root`). In this hierarchy, a component instance x is the parent of a component instance y if y is contained in x HTML, and there is no other component instance in between x and y.

But what happens when a request for a component originates in a component instance x? That is, when a pipe or a directive in x, or x itself, is created, and a service s has to be injected into its constructor?

s is searched for in the x injector. If it isn't found, it is searched in the injector of the x parent component instance, and then throughout the component instance hierarchy until the bootstrap component is reached, and then s is searched in the platform injector. If the service is not found, it is also searched in the hierarchy of lazy loaded modules, starting from the module that contains x. If there are no lazy loaded modules, the module's hierarchy just consists of the injector of the main application module where all the other module injectors have been merged.

As a default, if a service referred to by a constructor parameter is not found, Angular throws an exception. However, if a parameter is preceded by the @Optional() decorator, no exception is thrown, and the parameter is simply assigned to the null value. The following is an example of the utilization of the @Optional() decorator:

```
constructor(@Optional() private alternateCurrency: CurrencyDescriptor)...
```

In the preceding example, if the application is configured to also use an alternate currency for prices, then all product prices are shown in two different currencies. If no alternate currency is found, alternateCurrency is set to null, and so prices are shown just in the default application currency.

For each constructor parameter, the search for a service to bind to that parameter can be controlled with three parameter decorators:

- @Host(): When a parameter is preceded by the @Host decorator, the search for a service in the component's hierarchy stops at the injector of the component instance that hosts the pipe, directive, or component; in other words, in the case of a component, just the component injector and the injector of its parent component are searched. In the case of pipes and directives, Angular searches just the injector of the component where the pipe or directive instances are used.
- @Self():When a parameter is preceded by the @Self decorator, the search for a service is limited to the injector of the component that originated the request.
- @SkipSelf(): When a parameter is preceded by the @SkipSelf decorator, the injector of the component that originated the request is jumped in the search for a service in the component hierarchy.

The following is an example of the utilization of @Self and @SkipSelf:

```
//constructor of a service that performs price calculations
constructor(@Optional() @Self() private specificVAT: VATDescriptor,
            @SkipSelf() private defaultVAT: VATDescriptor)...
```

If the price calculation service whose constructor is shown here is used by a component that shows the price of a product with a non-standard VAT calculation, then that component will have a non-standard VATDescriptor instance defined in its injector. In this case, the component-specific VATDescriptor instance is bound to specificVAT; otherwise, specificVAT is set to null, because the search is limited to the component injector by @Self. In any case, defaultVAT is set to the default VAT calculator service defined in the main application module injector because defaultVAT jumps any component-specific service that might be contained in the component injector.

Service providers

The records added to injectors are called service providers, or simply providers. They specify two sets of information:

- Which requests are resolved by the service?
- How to create an instance of the service?

More specifically, providers have one of the following formats:

```
{provide: <token>, useClass: <class name>}
{provide: <token>, useFactory: <function>, deps: [<dependency>,..]}
{provide: <token>, useValue: <object or simple type instance>}
```

The token property specifies the kind of requests the provider is able to satisfy. Often, it is a class name, in which case the service is selected when this class name is identical to the type of the constructor parameter where the service must be injected:

```
{provide: ProductServerCommunicatior, useClass: ShirtsServerCommunicatior}
....
//component constructor
export class ProductListComponent{
    constructor(communicator: ProductServerCommunicatior)
```

Tokens may be instances of any other type. For instance, in main.ts, the application URL is injected into the platform injector using a string token, as follows:

```
{ provide: 'BASE_URL', useFactory: getBaseUrl, deps: [] }
```

Since strings might cause unwanted name collisions, usually instances of the `InjectionToken<T>` class are used, where `T` is the type of the service (in the preceding case, `T` is `string`). This way, collisions are avoided because pointers to class instances are unique. A better implementation of the base URL provider is as follows:

```
export const BASE_URL = new InjectionToken<string>('BASE_URL');
...
{ provide: BASE_URL, useFactory: getBaseUrl, deps: [] }
```

The description passed as an argument in the `InjectionToken` constructor is not used by the framework, but furnishes just a descriptive help during application debugging.

When the token is not a class name, the match with a constructor parameter cannot be executed through the parameter type, so the token value must be explicitly referenced with the `@inject(<token>)` decorator, as in the following example:

```
import {BASE_URL} from '../main.ts'
...
constructor(@inject(BASE_URL) public baseUrl: string)...
```

The second property contained in all providers specifies different ways to obtain the service instance. `useClass` is followed by a class type (that is, by the constructor function of the class in JavaScript that represents the class type). The class type is used by Angular to create a service instance with `new`. Once created, this instance is reused in all requests.

Frequently, `useClass` and `provide` specify the same class, in which case the whole provider can be replaced by the class type, as in the following example:

```
providers:[
    ...,
    //shortcut for:
    //{provide: WeatherForecastService, useClass: WeatherForecastService}
    WeatherForecastService
]
```

Sometimes, however, `provide` specifies a superclass of the class in `useClass`. This way, the service may be customized to satisfy the needs of different components by placing different subclasses in the component instance hierarchy.

For example, suppose there is a `ProductRetrieverService` abstract class with methods to retrieve products from the server (possibly paged and/or filtered). Also, suppose there is a `ProductListComponent` component that shows the list of products (possibly with a UI to page and filter them). The constructor of `ProductListComponent` should be something such as the following:

```
constructor(private retriever: ProductRetrieverService )...
```

`ProductListComponent` is placed in several components used in different application sections, where each section is dedicated to a different product type (shoes, shirts, and so on). Then, it is possible to define specialized subclasses of `ProductRetrieverService`, such as `ShoeRetriverService`, and `ShirtRetrieverService`, that retrieve just one type of product, and place providers such as the following in the various ancestor components of `ProductListComponent` that are specific to the various product types:

```
//add this to the ShoesComponent
{provide: ProductRetrieverService , useClass: ShoeRetriverService}
. . .
add this to ShirtsComponent
{provide: ProductRetrieverService , useClass: ShirtRetrieverService }
```

In this way, `ProductListComponent` instances are injected classes specific to the product types that are associated with the components from which they originate.

In languages such as C# and Java, server-side DI frameworks allow interfaces in the `provide` part of provider records. This way, the only constraint on the service is that it implements that interface. This ensures a high degree of modularity and flexibility.

Unlikely, an analogous solution based on interfaces is not possible in TypeScript, since, in this case, interfaces are not actual types but just a trick to perform compilation-time checks. However, Angular developers may use either abstract classes, or fake classes, which, like interfaces, expose methods and properties required by the component without providing an actual implementation (fake classes must provide fake methods/properties in any case).

Classes used in `useClass` must be explicitly declared to be injectable with the `@Injectable` decorator, as in the following example:

```
@Injectable({
  providedIn: 'root'
})
export class WeatherForecastService {
. . .
```

The `providedIn` attribute is optional and, when provided, it specifies the Angular module to whose injector it must be added. `root` means the main application module. Hence, writing `providedIn: 'root'` is equivalent to writing `providedIn: AppModule. providedIn: <Module name>` is equivalent to adding the following record to the Angular module injector:

```
{provide: WeatherForecastService, useClass: WeatherForecastService}
```

However, if `providedIn: <Module name>` is used, the fact that the service must be placed in that module injector may be detected at compilation time, or, even better, when WebPack prepares Angular JavaScript bundles. When the module is lazy loaded, it makes a significant difference because Angular-specific WebPack optimizer realizes that the service may only be used together with the lazy loaded module, and adds it to the bundle of the lazy loaded Angular module instead of adding it to the Angular main JavaScript application bundle, thereby reducing the time to load the initial bundle.

When the second property of a provider is `useFactory`, the value of that property must be a factory function that, once invoked, must return an instance of the service. Once created, the service instance is reused in all subsequent requests of the same service issued to the same container. If the factory function has parameters, for each parameter, the array in the `dep` property must specify the token for retrieving the service to be bound to that parameter. In this way, factory functions such as constructors may recursively pass other services. Tokens in the `dep` array work in the exact same way as the tokens mentioned in constructor parameters; in other words, they must match the token referred to in the `provide` property of another provider record.

Factory functions are useful in the following situations:

- When the service class is not accessible because it is part of an external library, so it cannot be decorated with the `@Injectable` decorator.
- When the initial state of all service instances depends on parameters that are available only after the application is run; for instance, application localization information, or privileges of a logged user. In the example in the following subsection, a service factory is used to handle error string localization.

Finally, the provider with the `useValue` property is useful when the service instance is already available when the provider is added to an injector. `useValue` can contain any JavaScript value, objects, strings, numbers, and so on. It is worth pointing out that `useValue` can't be used when the constructor of the service, in turn, depends on other services. This is because no recursive dependency resolution can be performed when the service instance is provided directly.

The next subsection shows an example of DI based on `useFactory`. An example based on `useClass` is provided in the *Client-server communication* section of this chapter.

Injecting localized error messages

The `*inputError` directive defined in *The inputError directive* subsection of `Chapter 12`, *Angular Advanced Features*, uses a predefined table of standard error messages, placed in a static property of the same directive class. As discussed at the beginning of this section, sharing a resource through a static property is not a best practice. DI should always be preferred to share resources. As a side effect of using DI for injecting the errors table, each application configuration may use a different version of the table that is localized for the language chosen for that configuration. Application localization is discussed in the *Application localization* section of `Chapter 11`, *Input and Interactions*, while application configurations are discussed in the *Configuring and building an Angular application* section of `Chapter 10`, *Angular ASP.NET Core Project Template*.

In any case, it is worth remembering that in `Angular.json`, the developer may define several application configurations, where each configuration is specific to a language and/or deployment environment (development, staging, production). During application development, a default configuration is used, while, when the application is built, a specific configuration may be selected by passing its name as an argument of the Angular CLI build command. In turn, each configuration can specify a file under the `environments` folder containing some configuration-specific code that will replace the default `environment.ts` file when the application is built with that configuration. The default `environment.ts` file itself is used by the default configuration, in other words, during application development.

This section shows how to modify the project in `Chapter 12`, *Angular Advanced Features*, so that error messages are defined as a service and injected into the `inputError` directive.

As a first step, let's prepare a copy of the project under `Chapter 12`, *Angular Advanced Features*, and let's rename the copied project root folder as `DependencyInjection`. Then, add a new TypeScript file called `AppTokens.ts` to the `app` folder. Here, we will collect DI tokens used by the application:

```
import { InjectionToken } from '@angular/core';

export const INPUT_ERROR_MESSAGES =
  new InjectionToken<{ [key: string]: string }>
    ("Input error messages");
```

`INPUT_ERROR_MESSAGES` is the token we will use to inject input error messages.

Then, let's create an en-US folder under the app folder. This folder will contain code that is specific to the en-US locale. If the application supports more locales, similar folders for all other locales should be added.

Now, let's add an input-error-messages.ts file under the en-US folder, and let's define there the table containing all the error messages:

```
export const inputErrorMessages: { [key: string]: string } =
  {
  required: 'the field is required',
  minlength: 'minimum number of characters exceeded',
  maxlength: 'maximum number of characters exceeded',
  max: 'maximum value exceeded',
  min: 'minimum value exceeded',
  step: 'value is not a multiple of the step'
} ;
```

Finally, each environment file under the environments folder will define service providers that are localized for the language of the Angular configuration associated with that environment. environment.ts and environment.prod.ts are the development and production environments associated with the en-US locale, but you are free to add more application configurations to angular.json, each with its own associated environment file. Let's replace the code of environment.ts with the following:

```
import { INPUT_ERROR_MESSAGES } from "../app/app-tokens"
import { inputErrorMessages } from "../app/en-US/input-error-messages";

export const environment = {
  production: false,
  rootProviders: [
    {
      provide: INPUT_ERROR_MESSAGES,
      useFactory: () => inputErrorMessages
    }
  ]
};
```

The rootProviders property contains providers that are specific to each different environment, that is, to each different Angular configuration. They will be merged in the main application module injector. The inputErrorMessages error table is imported from ../app/en-US/input-error-messages, but environments that support different locales should import the same constant from files localized in other languages, such as, for instance, ../app/fr-FR/input-error-messages.

The code for `environment.prod.ts` is identical, but contains `production: true` instead of `production: false`.

At this point, the `rootProviders` from the environment selected by the current Angular configuration must be merged with the providers of `app.module.ts`. So, let's add the necessary import statement to `app.module.ts`:

```
import {environment } from "../environments/environment"
```

Then, merge the environment providers into the `app.module.ts` injector:

```
...
providers: [].concat(environment.rootProviders),
...
```

Done! Now, the input error messages for the locale associated with the selected configuration are available for injection throughout the Angular application. The final step is the modification of the `inputError` directive in `input-error.directive.ts`.

Let's import the application DI tokens:

```
import { INPUT_ERROR_MESSAGES} from "../app-tokens"
```

Then, replace the existing constructor with one that accepts the input error messages table:

```
constructor(
   private template: TemplateRef<any>,
   private viewContainer: ViewContainerRef,
   @Inject(INPUT_ERROR_MESSAGES) private allErrors:
     { [key: string]: string })
 { }
```

Now, the static property named `allErrors` must be removed, since its content is now injected by Angular DI in an instance property with the same name (`allErrors`). Accordingly, the `InputErrorDirective.allErrors` reference in the `set errors` setter must be replaced with `this.allErrors`.

Providers with the same token

Adding several providers with the same token in the same injector is an error, since each newly added provider replaces the previous one with the same token. Moreover, the search for providers matching a given token stops as soon as the first match is found in the injector hierarchies. However, if all providers associated with the same token are declared as multiproviders; that is, if they have the `multi` property set to `true`, then several providers with the same token are allowed in the same container, and the search in the injector hierarchies collects all providers instead of stopping when the first one is encountered. Accordingly, in this case, the result of a search is a list of services instead of a single service. Therefore, dependencies must be arrays of the type specified by the multiproviders. In the *Defining max, min, and step validation attributes* section of `Chapter 12`, *Angular Advanced Features*, all validator providers are associated with the same `NG_VALIDATORS` `InjectionToken`, and have the `multi` property set to `true` because validation must use all available validators, not just one, since each validator performs a different type of validation.

Client-server communication

Client-server communication can be handled directly with the `XMLHttpRequest` standard JavaScript object, or with the modern `fetch` API described in the *fetch API* section of `Chapter 9`, *Decorators and Advanced ES6 Features*. Anyway, Angular has its own `HttpClient` object that is a wrapper around the `XMLHttpRequest` object. Angular `HttpClient` has a style that is similar to one of the `fetch` API, but that supports both RxJS Observables and Promises to handle asynchronous operations.

This book doesn't contain an exhaustive description of RxJS Observables. This section only uses them when they are the only option. In all other cases, an approach based on Promises handled with the async/await paradigm is preferred, since it produces more readable code. A description of the TypeScript async/await features and of their advantages can be found in the *Promises and async/await notation* section of `Chapter 9`, *Decorators and Advanced ES6 Features*.

Angular `HttpClient` is contained in the `HttpClientModule` module of the `@angular/common/http` Angular package. So, the first step for using it is to import it into the main application module (`app.module.ts`):

```
import { HttpClientModule } from '@angular/common/http';
...
imports: [
    ...
```

```
HttpClientModule,
...
],
...
```

The `HttpClient` service provider is registered in the `HttpClientModule` injector, which is merged into the main application module injector when the `HttpClientModule` injector is imported. Thus, after the preceding setting, `HttpClient` is ready to be injected throughout the application.

This section may use either the `Animate` project created in `Chapter 12`, *Angular Advanced Features*, or the original `AngularVSTemplate` project created in `Chapter 10`, *Angular ASP.NET Core Project Template*. Make a copy of any of the two previous projects and rename the root folder of the copied project as `ServicesAndRouting`.

The `fetch-data.component.ts` component uses the `HttpClient` that is injected into its constructor and used there immediately. Moreover, it uses observables instead of the more readable async/await notation:

```
constructor(http: HttpClient, @Inject('BASE_URL') baseUrl: string) {
  http.get<WeatherForecast[]>(baseUrl +
      'api/SampleData/WeatherForecasts').subscribe(result => {
    this.forecasts = result;
  }, error => console.error(error));
}
```

The application base URL has been injected into the platform injector in `main.ts`. As a default, the `get<T>` method retrieves information from the server in JSON format and automatically transforms it into JavaScript objects. The `get<T>` generic parameter is the type of the returned data that, in the preceding example, is an array of `WeatherForecast` classes. Filters and other preferences may be added directly to the URL string as URL parameters, but `get` also accepts a second options object that, *inter alia*, can be used to add URL parameters in a simpler way:

```
const options = {
  params: new HttpParams().set("name", "Francesco")
    .set("surname", "Abbruzzese")
};
  http.get<Teacher[]>(url, options)....
```

The `options` object can also be used to set request headers as an authentication token, as in the following example:

```
const options = {
  params: ...,
```

```
headers: new HttpHeaders({
  'Authorization': 'my-auth-token'
})
```

New headers may be added to an existing `HttpHeaders` object with its `set` method:

```
let myNewHeader =myHeaders.set('Authorization','my-auth-token');
```

`get`, like all other `HttpClient` methods, returns an observable, but the observable can be easily turned into a Promise by calling its `toPromise()` method. After that, and after having declared as `async` the method that invokes `get`, the call may be awaited:

```
let result = await resulthttp.get<T>(url, options)
      .toPromise():
```

Before transforming the observable into a Promise, the observable can be applied to some transformations through the `pipe` observable method. An example of transformation is the `retry` function, which retries the request several times in the event of failure:

```
let result = await resulthttp.get<T>(url, options)
      .pipe(retry(3))
      .toPromise();
```

If the response header is also required, the `get` method may be instructed to return the whole response object, instead of the data contained in the response body. It is sufficient to add `observe: 'response'` to the option object:

```
let wholeResponse =  await http.get<T>(url, {observe: 'response'})
      .toPromise();
```

In this case, the option object must be passed as a constant directly in the call; otherwise, TypeScript is unable to select the method overload that returns `HttpResponse<T>` instead of `T`.

The response object contains properties such as `status`, `statusText`, and `headers`, and obviously `body` as well. `body` contains the result that is an an instance of `T`, while headers contain an `HttpHeaders` object. `HttpHeaders` is the same type used to add request headers to the `headers` property of the `get` options object. `wholeResponse.headers.keys()` returns a list of all header names. The value corresponding to each header name (for example, `key`) is obtained with `wholeResponse.headers.get(key)`.

If the server is not sending JSON data, but, for instance a file `get` may be instructed to return the body as it is without trying a JSON parsing. It is enough to remove the generic parameter of the `get` method and to add `responseType: "text"` to the `get` option object, shown as follows:

```
let text = await http.get(url, { responseType: "text" })
        .toPromise();
```

`responseType: "text"` and `observe: 'response'` can be used together to get a whole response object with a string body.

Now we are ready to give a better design to the `fetch-data.component.ts` component. We will use the async/await pattern, and we will define a `WeatherForecastService` instead of using directly the `HttpClient` from within the `fetch-data` component.

As a first step, let's add a `services` folder under the `app` folder. Then, let's scaffold a new service from within a Windows console rooted in the newly created `services` folder with the Angular CLI command: `ng generate service WeatherForecast`.

Then, replace the code scaffolded by Angular CLI with the following code:

```
import { Injectable, Inject } from '@angular/core';
import { HttpClient } from '@angular/common/http';

@Injectable({
  providedIn: 'root'
})
export class WeatherForecastService {

  constructor(private http: HttpClient,
      @Inject('BASE_URL') private baseUrl: string)
      { }

  async getAll(): Promise<WeatherForecast[]> {
     return await this.http.get<WeatherForecast[]>
          (this.baseUrl + 'api/SampleData/WeatherForecasts')
     .toPromise();
  }

}
export interface WeatherForecast {
  dateFormatted: string;
  temperatureC: number;
  temperatureF: number;
  summary: string;
}
```

All services injected into the constructor are placed in private properties, so they can be used in the `getAll()` method that returns all data received by the server. `getAll()` is declared `async`, so it can await the `HttpClient get` method.

`providedIn: 'root'` adds the service to the injector of the main application module, so it is available throughout the application.

Now, the `fetch-data.component.ts` component just needs to define a `WeatherForecastService` parameter in its constructor, so an instance of the service is automatically injected when each component instance is created. However, the `getAll` method can't be called directly in the constructor of the `FetchDataComponent` component for two reasons:

- It is not best practice to execute time-consuming operations in the `class` constructors.
- `getAll` must be awaited, so it must be placed in an `async` method, and a `class` constructor can't be declared as `async`.

For these reasons, the `FetchDataComponent` constructor will just store the service in a private property, while the `getAll` method will be called in the `ngOnInit` lifetime hook. Accordingly, the `HttpClient` import is replaced by the following:

```
import { Component, OnInit } from '@angular/core';
import { WeatherForecastService, WeatherForecast }
  from '../services/weather-forecast.service'
```

Then, the `WeatherForecast` interface definition must be removed from the `fetch-data.component.ts` since it has been moved into the `WeatherForecastService` file.

The component constructor becomes the following:

```
constructor(private ws: WeatherForecastService) {}
```

The class must implement the `OnInit` interface:

```
export class FetchDataComponent implements OnInit
```

Finally, there is the `ngOnit` method, which must be declared as `async` so that it can await the `getAll()` method:

```
async ngOnInit(): Promise<void> {
  try {
    this.forecasts = await this.ws.getAll();
  }
  catch (ex) {
```

```
        console.error(ex);
    }
}
```

The following subsection explains how to send data to the server with Angular's `HttpClient`.

Sending data to the server

`HttpClient` also supports all other HTTP Verbs that exchange data with the server, namely: `head`, `post`, `put`, `patch`, and `delete`. Descriptions of these are as follows:

- `get` performs an HTTP `get`, already described previously in this section.
- `head` performs the same action as `get`, but it returns a response without a body; that is, it returns just the appropriate headers. It has the same usage and syntax of `get`, but the body is empty.
- `delete` destroys a resource on the server. The information needed to identify the resource to destroy is passed as URL parameters. The server may, or may not, return an entity describing the status after the action has been executed on the server. If the server returns a status entity, the status of the response is `200` (OK); if the action has been successfully queued for execution (but not executed, yet) the return status is `202` (Accepted). Finally, if the action is successfully executed but no status entity is returned, the response status is `204` (No content). If the entity to delete is not found, a `404` status (Not found) is returned. Clearly, it is the responsibility of the server to return the correct status. `delete` accepts the same parameters of `get`, with the same meaning. If a generic argument is passed, it must be the type of the entity returned by the server, not the type of the entity that has been destroyed.

- `post` creates a new resource. Servers may, or may not, return an entity describing the status following resource creation. Often, the status entity is the created object itself. If the created resource has its own URL, the response has a `201` status code (Created), and the server returns a status entity and a location header whose value is the URL of the created resource. If no specific URL can be associated with the resource created, the server returns a `200` code if a status entity is returned anyway, or a `204` status code if no status entity is returned. The Angular `post` method accepts three arguments: the URL, the object to create on the server, and the same option object used by all other verbs. The URL must identify the collection where to place the newly created entity. If no such collection exists, that is, if the URL path is unknown, the server returns a `404` error code. The object passed as a second argument is added to the body of the request that `post` issues to the server. If a generic argument is passed, it must be the type of entity returned by the server, not the type of entity created. In practice, post requests are also used as a generic way to pass data to the server when a REST interpretation of the request is not possible.

- `put` works in the same way as `post`, but it must be used to replace an existing resource. Therefore, the URL passed to the method must identify the already existing resource; hence, the unique key that identifies the object must be placed in the URL somehow, either as a parameter, or as part of the path. The syntax and the status code returned are the same as for the `post` method. A `404` status code is returned when the resource to replace is not found.

- `patch` updates an existing resource by issuing a sequence of modification commands to the server. Update commands can replace single object properties, or add/remove/replace whole objects from a collection. The following is an example of a command sequence:

```
[
{ "op": "remove", "path": "/Persons/5" },
{ "op": "add", "path": "/Persons/", "value": {id=7,...} },
{ "op": "replace", "path": "/Persons/6/Name", "value": "John" },
]
```

The syntax is a REST standard, and should not be replaced by custom commands. The response status is `200` (OK) when a status object is returned, or `204` (No content) when no content is returned. If the resource to modify is not found, a `404` code is returned. If a generic argument is passed, it must be the type of entity returned by the server, not the type associated with the sequence of update commands.

As an example, let's add a post-based method to the `WeatherForecastService` to inform the server of data measured by the local instrumentation:

```
async newData(x: WeatherForecast): Promise<string> {
    try {
      let response = await this.http.post<WeatherForecast>(
        this.baseUrl + 'api/SampleData/', x, { observe: 'response' })
        .toPromise();
      if (response.status == 201)
        return response.headers.get("Location");
      else return null;
    }
    catch (error) {
      ...
    }
  }
```

The `observe: 'response'` instance causes the whole response to be returned by `put`. If the status code is `201`, the response contains a location header with the URL of the newly created resource that is returned by `newData`; otherwise, `newData` returns `null`. The following is a simple error handling code for placing in the `catch` statement:

```
if (error instanceof ErrorEvent) {
  throw "error in client-server communication: " + error.message;
}
else if (error instanceof HttpErrorResponse) {
  throw "server returned the following error: " + error.message;
}
else throw "unknown error";
```

If the exception is an instance of `ErrorEvent`, the exception was created locally, either by a client error or by a network error; otherwise, the exception is caused by a `4xx` status code returned by the server. If the exception is not an `HttpErrorResponse` at all, the error is not due to the interaction with the server but can be attributed to a possible bug.

Let's also add a fake action method that answers to the `newData` request submitted to `SampleDataController.cs`:

```
[HttpPost("")]
public IActionResult Post(WeatherForecast x)
{
    //add here creation logics
    return Created("api/SampleData/3", x);
}
```

Let's also add a `sendLocalData()` method to the `fetch-data.component.ts` that invokes `newData` to send fake local measurements to the server:

```
async sendLocalData() {
  try {
    let result = await this.ws.newData({
      dateFormatted: new DatePipe("en-US")
        .transform(new Date(), 'shortDate'),
      temperatureC: 20,
      temperatureF:0, //not processed because redundant
      summary:'Warm'
    });
    if (result) alert("local data recorded: " + result);
    else alert("local data succesfully recorded");
  }
  catch (errorMessage) {
    alert("Unsuccesfull operation. " + errorMessage);
  }
}
```

Data passed to `newData` are fake. The only parameter that is actually computed is the date, which is formatted by creating a `DatePipe` (refer to the *Pipes* section in `Chapter 11`, *Input and Interactions*).

`sendLocalData` may be bound to a button click by adding the following code immediately after the table in `fetch-data.component.html`:

```
<div>
  <button (click) ="sendLocalData()" type="button"
          class="btn btn-primary">
    send local data
  </button>
</div>
```

Communication progress events

The `XMLHttpRequest` object of modern browsers offers progress events that can be used to give users a visual feedback of the percentage of completion of long server uploads/downloads (files, media, and so on). While, in all probability, low-level operations such as a file transfer are better handled directly with the `XMLHttpRequest` object, also Angular `HttpClient` offers options for tracking the progress of events.

Files can be sent to the server by appending them to a `FormData` object:

```
let files = event.srcElement.files;
const formData: FormData = new FormData();
for (let i = 0; i < files.length; i++) {
  formData.append(i.toString(), files[i], files[i].name);
}
```

Here, `event` is a parameter bound to the `$event` object of the `change` event of an input type file.

Then, the `formData` object can be passed to an instance of a lower-level `HttpRequest` object, with progress events enabled with the `reportProgress: true` option:

```
const request = new HttpRequest('POST', '/upload/file', file, {
  reportProgress: true
});
```

Then, the request object must be passed to the lower-level `HttpClient.request` method that also passes progress events to the observable it returns:

```
let result = await this.myHttpClient.request(req).pipe(
  tap(event => this.processEvent(event)),
  last()
).toPromise();
```

`tap` processes each event passed to the observable without replacing it in the pipe. All events are processed by `processEvent`, and `last()`, instead, removes from the pipe all events but the last one that contains the response sent by the server.

`processEvent` has the following structure:

```
private processEvent(event: HttpEvent<any>) {
  switch (event.type) {
    case HttpEventType.Sent:
      //handle here start trasmission event
    case HttpEventType.UploadProgress:
      const percentage = Math.round(100 * event.loaded / event.total);
      //handle here upload progress event
    case HttpEventType.Response:
      //handle here transmission completed event (if needed)
    default:
      //can't arrive here.
  }
```

Preventing XSRF attacks

In an XSRF attack, a hacker forces the user to submit a request to a website where they are already authenticated with an authentication cookie. Suppose, for instance, you click a link in an email while your browser is authenticated in the page of your bank, or that you click that link while the browser is closed but last time you provided authentication to your bank's website in the form of a persistent cookie. If, once the hacker page is opened with the email link, that page automatically submits a properly filled out form to your bank's website, then that request will be authenticated, since the active authentication cookie is automatically sent whenever a request to the website of your bank is issued.

Avoiding cookie-based authentication is the simplest way to avoid this kind of attack when the application is an SPA, since JSON API calls may efficaciously authenticate using authentication headers instead of authentication cookies that are better suited for standard server-based applications. A common authentication header is the bearer-token that contains inside of it the entire set of user permissions encoded as claims. Authentication tokens are returned to the client by the server when the application sends user login information to the server (typically, a username and password). Together with the authentication cookie, the server should also return a data structure with all user privileges that the application uses to show/hide elements of the user interface. All authentication and authorization data are stored in a class instance that is shared as a service. This service is injected into the login component, which fills it with all the data, and then is used throughout the application, which reads the data it contains.

Anyway, Angular offers automatic support for the typical anti-XSRF strategies used by all web servers. The usual strategy adopted by all servers with non-SPA applications is as follows:

- The server generates a random token and inserts it into a cookie, after having encrypted it with the server encryption key. To increase security, that cookie is defined as HTTP Cookie, that is, a cookie that can't be read from JavaScript.
- The server also then inserts the same token into a hidden input. However, this time, before encrypting it, it adds other data so that the two encrypted values are different and can't be computed one from the other without knowing the encryption key.

- When the form is submitted during normal software operations, the server receives both the cookie and the hidden input, and after having decrypted them, it can verify that they contain the same token.
- During hacker operations, the content of the hidden field can't be filled, also if the hacker is able to steal the cookie value, since creating a hidden field that is compatible with the cookie would require the server encryption key.

When the application is an SPA, the server can't provide the hidden field, since requests do not use forms, but JSON data. Therefore, Angular expects the information that should be inserted in the hidden input field into another cookie named XSRF-TOKEN to be assigned to the web application domain. Then, each time it sends a PUT/POST/DELETE/PATCH request, it reads the content of this cookie and adds it to the the request header under the X-XSRF-TOKEN header name. This transfer operation cannot be performed by the hacker website, since XSRF-TOKEN can be read only by JavaScript code running in the same domain assigned to XSRF-TOKEN, that is, by JavaScript running in the website page, not by JavaScript running in the hacker page.

Now the server must be instructed to read the second value from the X-XSRF-TOKEN header, instead of reading it from the standard hidden input. ASP.NET Core can be instructed to also look for the token in the X-XSRF-TOKEN header by changing the default anti-forgery options. Let's do this in the ServicesAndRouting project. Open Startup.cs and add the following code to the ConfigureServices method, immediately before services.AddMvc()....:

```
services.AddAntiforgery(options => options.HeaderName = "X-XSRF-TOKEN");
```

Now we must instruct ASP.NET Core to add the X-XSRF-TOKEN cookie to the response as soon as the Angular HTML page is loaded. This can be done by injecting an IAntiforgery service into the Startup.cs Configure method:

```
public void Configure(IApplicationBuilder app, IHostingEnvironment env,
        IAntiforgery antiforgeryService)
```

Then, add the following code immediately before app.UseMvc....:

```
app.Use(async (context, next) =>
{
    string path = context.Request.Path.Value;
    if (path != null && !path.ToLower().Contains("/api"))
    {
        var tokens = antiforgeryService
        .GetAndStoreTokens(context);
        context.Response.Cookies.Append("XSRF-TOKEN",
            tokens.RequestToken, new CookieOptions
```

```
                    {
                        HttpOnly = false,
                        Secure = true,
                        Path = "/"
                    }
                );
            }
        await next();
    });
```

The `if` condition ensures that `XSRF-TOKEN` is injected only at the Angular application startup, not each time an API request is received. The `tokens` object contains both the cookie token and the token that should be inserted in the hidden field, in other words, `tokens.RequestToken`. We need the last one, since the cookie token is automatically added to another cookie by the anti-forgery service. Thus, it is sufficient to create a secure, non-HTTP (otherwise, Angular can't read it) cookie named `XSRF-TOKEN` with `tokens.RequestToken` as the value, and adding it to the `Response`.

Now the cookie token and the header token will be tested in each action method decorated with `[ValidateAntiForgeryToken]`. Let's add the verification to the `Post` action method of `SampleDataController.cs`:

```
[HttpPost("")]
[ValidateAntiForgeryToken]
public IActionResult Post(WeatherForecast x)
{
    //add here creation logics
    return Created("api/SampleData/3", x);
}
```

Before everything works properly, the absolute URL in the `WeatherForecastService.newData` method must be replaced by a relative URL, since Angular only adds the `X-XSRF-TOKEN` header when URLs are relative to avoid also sending the token to cross-site calls (CORS calls to other websites). It is sufficient to perform the following substitution:

```
this.baseUrl + '/api/SampleData/' => '/api/SampleData/'
```

Run the project and click the **send local data** button in the **Fetch data** page. Everything should work properly. However, if you again use an absolute URL, Angular doesn't add the `X-XSRF-TOKEN` header, so the ASP.NET Core anti-forgery test fails and ASP.NET Core rejects the request with a `400` status code (bad request).

Interceptors

Angular offers transformations modules that can be piped after each `HttpClient` request. Each of them can modify the request received either from the `HttpClient` or from the module that precedes it in the pipe, and can also modify the response received either from the network or from the module that follows it in the pipe. They are called **interceptors**, and are completely analogous in functionality and structure to ASP.NET Core middleware.

Each interceptor is a service that implements the `HttpInterceptor` interface whose unique method is `intercept`. The following is a typical interceptor definition, with all the needed imports:

```
import { Injectable } from '@angular/core';
import { Observable } from 'rxjs';
import {
  HttpRequest, HttpEvent, HttpInterceptor, HttpHandler
} from '@angular/common/http';

@Injectable()
export class ExampleInterceptor implements HttpInterceptor {

  intercept(req: HttpRequest<any>, next: HttpHandler):
    Observable<HttpEvent<any>> {
    //modify request contained in req here
    let returnedEvent = next.handle(req);
    //modify returned event here
    return returnedEvent;
  }
}
```

Each interceptor passes the request to the next interceptor in the pipe after having applied its modifications by calling `next.handle(req)`. This call returns an observable of all events returned either by the network or from the previous interceptors. The final event usually is the `HttpResponse`. The `instanceof` operator can be used to recognize and process the `HttpResponse`. Since `returnedEvent` is an observable, HTTP response modifications must be performed by applying a transformation to the observable with the help of the RxJS `map` observable method:

```
return returnedEvent
    .pipe(map(event => {
        if (event instanceof HttpResponse ) {
            //modify response here
            event = event.clone({ ... })
        }
        return event;
```

```
    }));
```

To modify the response, you must clone it since it is an immutable object whose properties can't be modified. This is easily performed by calling the `clone` method, which creates another immutable object, with all new property values specified in the anonymous object passed as an argument. In short, we will show a complete example of `clone` usage.

In general, all request and response objects are immutables, so either they are modified with `clone`, or, by calling other more specific methods. For instance, a new header may be added to an `HttpHeader` object with the `set` method that creates a new `HttpHeader` with the new header added. The following is an example of an interceptor that automatically adds to all requests an authentication token taken from an authentication service whose data are filled when the user logs in. It shows the usage of `clone` and `set`:

```
@Injectable()
export class AuthenticationInterceptor implements HttpInterceptor {
  constructor(private authentication: AuthenticationService) {}

  intercept(req: HttpRequest<any>, next: HttpHandler) {
    const token = this.authentication.Token;
    const newReq = req.clone({
      headers: req.headers.set('Authorization', token )
    });
    return next.handle(newReq );
  }
}
```

The authentication service, being a service, is automatically injected into the interceptor constructor.

Once created, interceptors must be associated with the `HTTP_INTERCEPTORS` provider token as multi-valued providers. This way, Angular engine can take them all for building the entire interceptor's pipeline. Usually, all interceptor providers defined in an application are assembled into an array that is merged into the main application module injector:

```
//In "all-interceptors.ts"
import { HTTP_INTERCEPTORS } from '@angular/common/http';
import {Interceptor1} from...
...
import {Interceptorn} from...

export export const allInterceptorProviders = [
  { provide: HTTP_INTERCEPTORS, useClass: Interceptor1, multi: true },
  ...
  { provide: HTTP_INTERCEPTORS, useClass: Interceptorn, multi: true }
];
```

```
//In "app.module.ts"
import {allInterceptorProviders } from './all-interceptors.ts'
...
providers[...]
    .concat(allInterceptorProviders)
...
```

Interceptors are piped in the order they are defined in `allInterceptorProviders`.

Routing and navigation

The *Angular architecture* section of `Chapter 10`, *Angular ASP.NET Core Project Template*, gives the basics of Angular routing, and the *Angular modules* section of the same chapter also explains how to define routes in external modules. This section gives more details and introduces some advanced routing features, such as route guards and module lazy loading.

Each application must have just a single router that must be defined with `RouterModule.forRoot(...)` in the main application module that accepts an array of routes as its argument. If other modules define their own routes, they must do that with `RouterModule.forChild(...)`, which doesn't add another router, but which allows just the definitions of other routes to be merged into the ones of the unique router defined in the application main module. Routes defined in other modules are added in the same order the modules are imported in `imports[...]`. The `ExtraFeaturesModule` defined in the `extra-features` folder shows an example of how `RouterModule.forChild(...)` is used.

> It is best practice that Angular modules that provide new components for some `<router-outlet>` instance also define their associated routes, such as the `ExtraFeaturesModule` instance does. This way, the application is more modular, since module components don't need to be exported, and remains hidden to the remainder of the application.

The actions associated to the routes are executed, and recorded in the browser history in three ways:

- At application startup, when a link containing the website domain, plus a specific route, is written in the browser navigation bar. For instance, once `ServicesAndRouting` is run, if you write `https://localhost:44346/counter` in the browser navigation bar, the application will open directly in the counter page.

- When a link containing the `[routerLink]   ='`
  `["/...."]'` or `routerLink='<route url>'` is clicked.
- When the `navigate` method of the router instance is called with the same kind of argument passed to the `routerLink` directive.

URLs used with the browser are clearly absolute, while URLs used with `routerLink` and with the `navigate` method are relative to the base URL declared in the `<base href="...">` declaration in the header of the HTML page where the Angular application runs. When a new project is scaffolded, Angular CLI sets `<base href="/">`; that is, it assumes the URL of the HTML page where Angular runs as a base URL.

The URL can be passed as a string when it is constant and doesn't depend on variables defined in the template; otherwise, the URL is assembled by joining the various parts passed to an array. For example, a route link such as `"/customers/orders/<customer id>/<customer order id>"` (`/customers/orders/13/121`), may be written as `["/customers/orders", customeId, orderId ]`, where `customeId`, and `orderId` are variables defined in the HTML template context. Query parameters are passed in the `queryParams` directive of the link, as properties of an object, such as, for instance, `[queryParams]="{payment: transfer, days: 60}"`. When navigation is triggered by calling the router `navigate` method, query parameters are passed in a property of the second option argument of `navigate`:

```
this.router.navigate(["/customers/orders", customeId, orderId ], {
  queryParams: {payment: transfer, days: 60
})
```

An instance of the router can be obtained in the constructor with Dependency Injection, since the router is a service. As an example of utilizing the `Router.navigate` method, let's add a **go home** button to the `fetch-data.component.ts` component.

As a first step, let's add the requisite import:

```
import { Router } from '@angular/router';
```

Then, modify the constructor and add the `goHome` method as follows:

```
constructor(private ws: WeatherForecastService,
    private router: Router) {}
goHome() {
 this.router.navigate(["/"]);
}
```

Finally, add a `go home` button immediately after the `send local data` button in `fetch-data.component.html`:

```
...
<span> </span>
<button (click)="goHome()" type="button" class="btn btn-primary">
    go home
</button>
```

URLs passed to `routerLink` or `navigate` can also be relative to the current URL. Notation is similar to the usual file path notation. For instance, if the current URL is `/customers/orders/13/121`, the `./122` relative URL causes the router to navigate to `/customers/orders/13/122`, while the `../11/101` URL navigates to `/customers/orders/11/101`.

Required and optional parameters

Components placed in a `<router-outlet>` may need parameters. For instance, a component that shows order details needs the ID of the order to retrieve a specific order from the server. Routes used up to now have a format similar to the following:

```
{ path: 'counter', component: CounterComponent }
```

What if the counter needs an initial value? If this initial value is obligatory, it must be inserted as part of the `path` string in the route, so if it is not provided, then routing fails. In this case, `path` is modified as `counter/:init`, which defines the obligatory `init` parameter. Then, the `routerLink` or the `navigate` method may use either a string such as `/counter/2`, or an array such as `['/counter', 2]`, or else `['/counter', initValue]`. Here, `initValue` is a variable defined in the template context that contains the initial value to pass to the `CounterComponent`. Analogously, a path to a component that shows an order detail for a specific customer could be defined as `"/customers/orders/:customerid/:orderid"`, which can be navigated with an array such as `['/customers/orders/', 11, 101]`.

Optional parameters are not specified at all in the routing rules, since they don't constrain the navigation process. They may be passed either with query parameters, or with an Angular-specific notation for optional parameters. A URL with optional parameters appears as follows:

```
<oblicatory part>; param1 = value1; param2 = value2.......?<query
parameters>
```

All optional parameters are added to a URL by adding them to an object at the end of the array that defines the URL:

```
["/counter", {init: <value>}]
```

All parameters passed to a component are available in an `ActivatedRoute` object that contains detailed information on the active route. More specifically the following:

- `paramMap` is an observable containing a map of all mandatory and optional parameters.
- `queryParamMap` is an observable containing a map of all query parameters.
- `snapshot.paramMap` and `snapshot.queryParamMap` are the current values of the preceding observables.

In general, the use of observables cannot be avoided, since parameters may change dynamically. For instance, if a counter is invoked with `init = 2`, and then the user clicks another link that invokes the same counter component, but with `init = 3`, the component in the `<router-outlet>` doesn't change, so it is not re-initialized. Therefore, if you don't subscribe to the observable, the counter is not reset to the new `3` value, while if the counter is updated from within an observable subscription, the counter is updated each time the observable changes.

By way of an example of using parameters passed to a component, let's pass an initial value to the counter component. As a first step, `counter.component.ts` needs the appropriate imports:

```
import { Router, ActivatedRoute } from '@angular/router';
```

Then it is sufficient to add the following constructor:

```
constructor(private router: Router,
    private route: ActivatedRoute) {
    route.paramMap.subscribe(params => {
      this.currentCount = params.has('init') ?
          parseInt(params.get('init')) : 0;
    })
```

The constructor adds a subscription to the `route.paramMap` observable that updates `this.currentCount` each time the observable value changes, that is, each time the parameters passed to the component change. Since the `'init'` parameter is optional, a check on the presence of the parameter is performed with `has` before obtaining the parameter value using the `get` method. Parameter collections also have a `keys` property that contains an array with all parameter names.

The code can be modified by changing the counter link in `nav-menu.component.ts` from `["/counter"]` to `["/counter", {init: 2}]`.

Each route can also have a `data` property containing any data. This data is available in the `data` property of the `ActivatedRoute` object. Like `paramMap`, `data` is also an observable that must be subscribed. Developers can use this field to make a component activation dependent on the route it was called from.

Improving routes

In the `ServicesAndRouting` project, the home page is associated with the following route:

```
{ path: '', component: HomeComponent, pathMatch: 'full' }
```

`patMatch` is set to `full` to prevent the routing rule to trigger on all routes, since, as a default, routing rules trigger when `path` matches the start of the URL. `pathMatch: 'full'`, instead, requires a complete match.

The `[routerLinkActive]` directive in `nav-menu.component.html` has the `[routerLinkActiveOptions]='{ exact: true }'` input parameter that is analogous to `pathMatch: 'full'`, since it styles the element as active only when there is a complete match with the current URL.

`path=''` sets the home page as the default page. However, it is best practice to define the home page URL similar to all others, and then to add another route that defines which route is the default route:

```
{ path: '', redirectTo: "home", pathMatch: 'full' },
{ path: 'home', component: HomeComponent}
```

The `redirectTo` attribute causes an immediate redirect to the `/home` URL. `redirectTo` is a modular way of associating the same behavior with several URLs. Also, the link in `nav-menu.component.ts` must be changed from `["/"]` to `["/home"]`.

Usually, a route that matches all routes is added as a final route in the main application module, so that a `page not found` error page can be shown. Let's add a similar route to the `ServicesAndRouting` project, but to keep it simple, let's redirect to the `home` page instead of to an `error` page:

```
{ path: '**', redirectTo: "home"}
```

Here, `'**'` matches all URLs.

Children routes and named router-outlets

A component x placed inside a router outlet may have, in turn, another router outlet where other components inside its template may be loaded. In this case, the routing rules that decide which component to load in the child router outlet must be defined inside the `children` property of the rule that loads the x component:

```
{path: 'xPath', component: x,
    children: [
       { path: 'subpath1', component: Child1Component },
       ...
    ]
},
```

All `path` properties in the children routes contain sub-paths that come after the `/xPath` string to yield a final path , such as `/xPath/subpath1`.

As an example, let's add a child router outlet in `test-component.component.html`. Before starting the implementation, it is good practice to turn on route resolution tracing for discovering possible bugs in the way routes are defined. This can be done by setting the `enableTracing` property in the options object that is passed as a second argument to `RouterModule.forRoot`:

```
RouterModule.forRoot([
       ...
    ]
    , { enableTracing: true })
```

As a first step, let's place the following CSS in `test-component.component.css` to give a an acceptable styling to the new HTML component that we are going to define:

```
div {
   min-height:50px;
}
```

Then, we should remove the previous content of `test-component.component.html` and replace it with the following:

```
<div>
   <a [routerLink]='["./child1"]'>Child 1</a>
   <a [routerLink]='["./child2"]'>Child 2</a>
</div>
<div>
   <router-outlet></router-outlet>
</div>
```

The two preceding links contain relative paths to move in sub-paths of /test, namely, /test/child1, and /test/child2. All sub-paths of /test have TestComponentComponent loaded in the main application router outlet, so the child1 and child2 sub-paths merely determine which component is loaded in the child router outlet that is inside test-component.component.html.

Now let's create some components to load in the new router outlet. With a Windows console rooted in the extra-features folder, let's create three new components, named child1, child2, and child3, with Angular CLI.

The final step is the definition of the children routes of the /test path route. In extra-features.module.ts, replace the unique existing route with the following:

```
{
  path: 'test', component: TestComponentComponent,
  children: [
    { path: 'child1', component: Child1Component },
    { path: 'child2', component: Child2Component },
    { path: '', redirectTo: 'child1', pathMatch: 'full' }
  ]
}
```

The children routes define the child1 sub-path as the default sub-path that determines which component is initially loaded in the child router outlet. Then, the two links inside the TestComponentComponent template allow navigation inside the child router outlet.

A component may also contain several router outlets, but just one can be unnamed; all the others must be given a name that is then used to define routes that are specific to each outlet. When a route has no outlet name associated with it, it is associated with the default unnamed router outlet.

Let's append a div with another router outlet inside of it to test-component.component.html, as follows:

```
<div>
  <router-outlet name="extra"></router-outlet>
</div>
```

Outlet-specific routes must be defined to decide which component to place in the extra router outlet. Let's define them:

```
{
  path: 'test', component: TestComponentComponent,
  children: [
    { path: 'child1', component: Child1Component },
```

```
    { path: 'child2', component: Child2Component },
    { path: '', redirectTo: 'child1', pathMatch: 'full' },
    { path: 'add', component: Child3Component, outlet: 'extra' },
    { path: 'remove', component: null, outlet: 'extra', children: [] }
  ]
}
```

When the `add` sub-path is selected, `Child3Component` is loaded in the `extra` router outlet. When the `remove` sub-path is selected, a `null` component is added to the `extra` router outlet, that is, it is cleared. The `remove` route contains an empty `children` property since `null` component routes are only allowed in routes whose `children` property is defined.

Finally, let's add two more links to `test-component.component.html` that toggles the content of the `extras` router outlet:

```
<div>
  <a [routerLink]='["./child1"]'>Child 1</a>
  <a [routerLink]='["./child2"]'>Child 2</a>
  <a [routerLink]='{ outlets: { extra: ["add"] } }'>Add extra content</a>
  <a [routerLink]='{ outlets: { extra: ["remove"] } }'>Remove extra
content</a>
</div>
```

Outlets are dealt with as separate links, so each outlet has its own URL associated with it. All outlet URLs are specified as properties of the anonymous object contained in the `outlets` property. Angular combines all URLs. Named outlet URLs are combined with the main URL as follows:

```
/path1/path2.../(pathn//outlet1:outleturl1//outlet2:outleturl1....)
```

Thus, for instance, when the main URL is `/test/child1`, and the `extra` outlet URL is `/add`, then the overall URL is `/test/(child1//extra:add)`. In general, the place where parentheses are opened is the sub-path associated with the unnamed sibling of the named router outlet.

Guards

Each route may have various types of guards that are called at different times in the lifetime of an activated route. They may stop the current task, and/or perform certain activities before the current routing task continues. Each guard type is a service that implements a specific interface. Moreover, each guard is passed in a dedicated property of the route the guard must be applied to.

The following is a list of all available guards:

- `CanActivate` interface. Method to implement: `canActivate`. Route property where to place the implementation: `canActivate`. Used to prevent access to a route when certain conditions are not verified, for instance, when a user is not authenticated. An example of implementation is as follows:

```
@Injectable({
  providedIn: 'root',
})
export class AuthGuard implements CanActivate {
  constructor(private auth: AuthInfoService,
        private router: Router) {}
  canActivate(
    next: ActivatedRouteSnapshot,
    state: RouterStateSnapshot): boolean {
    if(auth.isAuthenticated) return true;
    auth.logingRedirect=state.url;
    this.router.navigate(['/login']);
    return false;
  }
}

//in the route
{...., canActivate=[AuthGuard]}
```

`AuthInfoService` must be implemented by the developer. If a user is authenticated, `canActivate` returns `true` and routing proceeds normally; otherwise, it redirects to a login page after having stored the current URL, so a user can be redirected there after logging in. After navigating to the login, the method returns `false` to stop the current routing action.

- `CanActivateChild` interface. Method to implement: `canActivateChild`. Route property where to place the implementation: `canActivateChild`. Works in the same way as `CanActivate`, but the guard is applied to all children routes instead of applying it to the route itself.

- `CanDeactivate<componentType>` interface. Method to implement: `canDeactivate`. Route property where to place the implementation: `canDeactivate`. Used to abort the exit from the current route. A typical use involves asking the user to save unsaved changes before leaving. The following is an example of such a use:

```
@Injectable({
  providedIn: 'root',
})
export class SaveChangesGuard implements
```

```
              CanDeactivate<MyComponent> {
         canDeactivate(component: MyComponent) {
           If(!component.dirty) return true;
           return window.confirm("Exit without saving changes?");
         }
       }
```

If there are no unsaved changes, `canDeactivate` immediately returns `true`; otherwise, it seeks confirmation from the user.

- `Resolve<T>` interface. Method to implement: `resolve`. Route property where to place the implementation: `resolve`. Used to pre-fetch data required by the component before it is loaded. If data is not available, component loading is aborted and application remains in the previous route. `T` is the type of data to pre-fetch. A detailed example follows after the list of all the guards.
- `CanLoad` interface. Method to implement: `canLoad`. Route property where to place the implementation: `canLoad`. Similar to `CanActivate`, but it prevents the loading of lazy loaded modules when certain conditions are not verified. `CanActivate` prevents component loading, but if routes are contained in a lazy loaded module, that lazy loaded module is loaded anyway. By adding a `CanLoad` guard, together with the `CanActivate` guard, the developer can also prevent module loading. `CanLoad` guards are not a replacement for `CanActivate` guards, since they stop routing only when the module has not yet been loaded. Once loaded, subsequent verifications must be carried out using a `CanActivate` guard. The following is an example of such usage:

```
@Injectable({
  providedIn: 'root',
})
class CanLoadAuthGuard implements CanLoad {
  constructor(private auth: AuthInfoService) {}
  canLoad(route: Route):
Observable<boolean>|Promise<boolean>|boolean {
    return auth.isAuthenticated;
  }
}
```

A `CanLoad` guard is only allowed on routes that trigger the lazy loading of other Angular modules, that is, on routes with a non-empty `loadChildren` property. Lazy loading is discussed in the next subsection.

By way of an example of `Resolve` usage, let's preload all data used by the `fetch-data.component.ts`. With a Windows console rooted in the `services` folder, use Angular CLI to scaffold a `WeatherForecastPrefetch` service. Then replace the existing code with the following:

```
import { Injectable } from '@angular/core';
import { WeatherForecastService, WeatherForecast }
  from './weather-forecast.service';
import { Resolve, ActivatedRouteSnapshot, RouterStateSnapshot } from
'@angular/router';
@Injectable({
  providedIn: 'root'
})
export class WeatherForecastPrefetchService
  implements Resolve<WeatherForecast[]> {
  constructor(private ws: WeatherForecastService) { }
  async resolve(route: ActivatedRouteSnapshot, state: RouterStateSnapshot):
    Promise<WeatherForecast[]> {
    return await this.ws.getAll();
  }
}
```

The `resolve` method uses the injected `WeatherForecastService` constructor to obtain all data, and to return it.

The `fetch-data` route in `app.module.ts` must be modified as follows:

```
{
  path: 'fetch-data', component: FetchDataComponent,
  resolve: {
    weatherForecast: WeatherForecastPrefetchService
  }
}
```

Angular uses an instance of `WeatherForecastPrefetchService` to create a `{weatherForecast: <data returned by resove method>}` object that it assigns to the observable contained in the `data` property of the route (the `data` property contains general-purpose data associated with the route).

The `fetch-data.component.ts` component must accept the active route in its constructor:

```
constructor(private ws: WeatherForecastService,
    private router: Router, private route: ActivatedRoute) {}
```

Then, in the `ngOnInit()` method, instead of retrieving the data itself, it must extract it from the `route.data` observable:

```
async ngOnInit(): Promise<void> {
    try {
      this.route.data
        .subscribe((data: { weatherForecast: WeatherForecast[] }) => {
          this.forecasts = data.weatherForecast;
      });
    }
    catch (ex) {
      console.error(ex);
    }
}
```

Lazy loaded modules

Modules containing other routes, and the code required to run those routes, can be lazy loaded only when required, instead of increasing the size of the initial JavaScript to load when the application starts. The routes that trigger the module lazy loading must be children routes of a given route. However, in this case, instead of listing all children routes, a `loadChildren` property specifies the name of the file containing the module post fixed with a # symbol, followed by the module class name, as in the following example:

```
{
    path: 'test',
    loadChildren:
      './extra-features/extra-features.module#ExtraFeaturesModule'
}
```

This route may be added to `app.module.ts` to lazy load the `extra-features.module.ts` module. Once the module is lazy loaded, in `app.module.ts`, all imports mentioning the lazy loaded module must be commented out:

```
...
//import { ExtraFeaturesModule }
//   from './extra-features/extra-features.module'
..
imports: [
    ...
    //ExtraFeaturesModule,
    ...
]
```

Moreover, the single route in `ExtraFeaturesModule` must become a child of the `test` path route defined in `app.module.ts`. It is sufficient to replace `path: "test"` with `path: ""`. Hence, the single `ExtraFeaturesModule` route becomes as follows:

```
{
  path: '', component: TestComponentComponent,
  children: [
    { path: 'child1', component: Child1Component },
    { path: 'child2', component: Child2Component },
    { path: '', redirectTo: 'child1', pathMatch: 'full' },
    { path: 'add', component: Child3Component, outlet: 'extra' },
    { path: 'remove', component: null, outlet: 'extra', children: [] }
  ]
}
```

At this point, the main application doesn't know anything about the `ExtraFeaturesModule` code, and all module code is bundled in a chunk that is loaded dynamically.

Run the application and open the browser development tools to trace all browser requests. When the external page menu item is selected, the browser downloads a file called `extra-features-extra-features-module.js`. It is the bundle containing all the lazy loaded module code.

Once in the external page menu item, the `Child 1` and `Child 2` links work properly, but the *Add extra content* and *Remove extra content links* do not work at all! This is due to an Angular bug that wasn't completely fixed, at least until version 6.1.7. (see `https://github.com/angular/angular/issues/10981`). The problem can be patched by avoiding the empty string as follows:

```
path: '', component: TestComponentComponent,
```

For instance, we can add a `loaded` string:

```
path: 'loaded', component: TestComponentComponent
```

Since `loaded` will be added after `test` to get `test/loaded`, we must also change the link of the external page navigation menu item:

```
<li [routerLinkActive]='["link-active"]'>
  <a [routerLink]='"/test/loaded"]' (click)='collapse()'>
    <span class='glyphicon glyphicon-th-list'></span> external page
  </a>
</li>
```

With this patch, the application works properly.

If some modules are lazy loaded just when they are required, the application start time is decreased, but, then, when a module is loaded, the user must wait until loading is completed. If some modules are likely to be used, a better strategy would be to load them after the application starts, but before they are required. This way, they are loaded in the background while the user is doing something else, and no delay is experienced when the user moves to a lazy loaded route.

The choice as to which lazy loaded modules to preload in the background is performed by a preloading strategy that is a service that implements the `PreloadingStrategy` interface. If no preloading strategy is provided, no module is preloaded, otherwise a preloading strategy must be specified in the option object passed as a second argument to `RouterModule.forRoot`.

Angular comes with the `PreloadAllModules` predefined strategy. It is sufficient to specify it, as having all lazy loaded modules preloaded is demonstrated as follows:

```
{
  //enableTracing: true,
  preloadingStrategy: PreloadAllModules
}
```

You may experiment with these settings, while keeping browser development tools open to see what happens.

The developer can also provide a custom implementation of `PreloadingStrategy` in the preceding `preloadingStrategy` property. For instance, the following implementation just preloads all lazy loaded modules with a non-empty route, `data` property:

```
@Injectable({
  providedIn: 'root',
})
export class MyPreloadingStrategyService implements PreloadingStrategy {
  preload(route: Route, load: () => Observable<any>): Observable<any> {
    if (route.data ) return load();
    else return of(null);
  }
}
```

When the strategy decides to load a module, it calls the `load` function that is automatically passed as an argument in the `preload` method by the framework. If the route passed as an argument must not be preloaded, the `preload` method must return a `null` observable.

Testing

Angular unit tests are performed with Jasmine that was described in the *Testing your library with Jasmine* section of `Chapter 8`, *Building TypeScript Libraries*. Angular uses Karma to run all tests in a browser, and adds some facilities to handle component compilation, Dependency Injection, and HTML manipulation.

When an Angular entity is generated, Angular automatically generates a test file skeleton to unit test that entity. All existing tests may be run by launching the `ng test` command in a Windows console rooted in the `ClientApp` folder. Once the command is activated, the browser opens and Karma displays the results of all tests. Since some tests are incomplete, or not aligned to the modifications done to some components, Karma, for sure, will signal a number of errors. The `counter.component.spec.ts` file contains tests that should pass, so let's open it. It contains a Jasmine `beforeEach` function call with the following code inside of it:

```
TestBed.configureTestingModule({
  declarations: [ CounterComponent ]
})
.compileComponents();
```

`TestBed.configureTestingModule(...)` accepts the same object passed to each `@NgModule` directive. `TestBed` acts as a mock Angular module where the developer may configure components and mock services to use in all tests. All services are usually mock objects whose methods return fixed values. When `compileComponents` is called, all declared components are compiled and their HTML templates are bound to the component classes.

A second `beforeEach` call creates a component instance:

```
fixture = TestBed.createComponent(CounterComponent);
component = fixture.componentInstance;
```

Then it calls `fixture.detectChanges()` to reflect the component state in its HTML template.

A user can test just the component properties and methods without performing verifications on the modifications happening in the HTML, in which case calls to `fixture.detectChanges()` are not needed since their purpose is just to update the component template. Otherwise, calls to `fixture.detectChanges()` must be done each time a property bound to the template is modified by the code to reflect that change on the component template.

The majority of tests should not involve the HTML component, since it changes more frequently, and also a small change might invalidate all HTML-based tests. Let's define a test for the counter increment that doesn't involve the component template, and place it immediately after the second `beforeEach`:

```
it('should start with count 0, then increments by 1 when clicked',
  async(() => {
  expect(component.currentCount).toBe(0);
  component.incrementCounter(null);
  expect(component.currentCount).toBe(1);
  component.incrementCounter(null);
  expect(component.currentCount).toBe(2);
}));
```

Later on, the same file contains another version of the same test that makes the same verification, but, this time, on the HTML component. As a first step, let's replace 0 with `$0.00`, and 1 with `$1.00`, since the component was modified to give a currency format to the number manipulated by the counter. `fixture.nativeElement` returns the root of the HTML template. Other HTML elements can be retrieved from there with `querySelector`:

```
const countElement = fixture.nativeElement
    .querySelector('strong');
```

The element containing the count is retrieved through its tag name. In general, this is not a good idea, since, during component maintenance, some other elements with the same tag might be added, so a better strategy is to add unique CSS classes to all elements that must be tested.

The initial value is tested as follows:

```
expect(countElement.textContent).toEqual('$0.00');
```

Then, the increment button is retrieved:

```
const incrementButton =
    fixture.nativeElement.querySelector('button');
```

The button is clicked, and, immediately after, a call to `fixture.detectChanges()` updates the HTML component:

```
incrementButton.click();
fixture.detectChanges();
```

Finally, the modified value is tested:

```
expect(countElement.textContent).toEqual('$1.00');
```

Angular documentation contains detailed procedures for testing all Angular entity types. Links are listed in the *Further reading* section.

When a new project is created, Angular CLI also sets up Protractor, which is an integration test framework that simulates user interaction with the whole application. Protractor tests can be run by launching the `ng e2e` command in a Windows console rooted in the `ClientApp` folder. All Protractor tests are grouped in the `e2e` folder. The scaffolded project contains just a single `app.e2e-spec.ts` file. While unit tests are part of the code, and accompany a software product throughout its lifetime, Protractor tests that are very sensitive to the application user interface are likely to change almost completely in new product releases, so that they are more suited to acceptance tests. A description of Protractor is beyond the scope of this book, but the *Further reading* section contains links to the official documentation.

Summary

Angular offers an advanced Dependency Injection framework capable of injecting services recursively into the constructor of Angular pipes, components, and directives. A significant degree of flexibility is reached by searching services within two hierarchies of containers: the hierarchy of component instances, and the hierarchy of lazy loaded modules. The `HttpClient` class is capable of handling easily all HTTP Verbs, while returning JavaScript data structures directly. It also offers the possibility of accessing lower-level entities, such as headers and progress events.

Angular routing features handle nested routes, and multiple router outlets, in a simple way. The developer has full control of routing dynamics through Angular guards that control route activation/deactivation and module loading. Modules may be lazy loaded and loaded in the background.

Angular CLI automatically scaffolds Angular unit test skeleton files. Tests are based on Jasmine and can also involve component templates because of Angular-specific extensions. Angular also offers mock modules that a user can use to inject mock services. Angular CLI also scaffolds a Protractor application that the developer may use to simulate the behavior of users across the application as a whole.

Questions

1. How many injector hierarchies are visited by Angular on each service search? Can you describe them?
2. What is the advantage of using `providedIn: 'root'` instead of listing a service in the `providers` array of a module?
3. How many ways are there to supply an instance of a service? How many providers may have the same token?
4. Can you list all HTTP Verbs supported by Angular's `HttpClient` class?
5. How are progress events handled by Angular's `HttpClient` class?
6. Can you explain what an XSRF attack is? What is the safest way to handle authentication in Angular?
7. Is it possible to automatically add an authentication token to each request issued with Angular `HttpClient`?
8. Which is the route property involved in module lazy loading?
9. How can all lazy loaded modules be preloaded in the background ?
10. What is the purpose of the `CanActivate` guard? Can you list all the other guards?

Further reading

The description of services presented in this chapter is quite complete, like the description of the Angular `HttpClient` object. A list of all method overloads may be found in the official documentation here: `https://angular.io/api/common/http/HttpClient`. More details on RxJS observables are available on the RxJS official website at `https://rxjs-dev.firebaseapp.com`.

All properties and methods of the `Router` object are available in the following Angular official documentation: `https://angular.io/api/router/Router`. The *Testing* section just describes the basics of Angular testing. Angular official documentation on testing contains detailed procedures to test any Angular class type (services, components, pipes, and so on): `https://angular.io/guide/testing`. Detailed documentation on end-to end testing with Protractor can be found on Protractor's official website: `https://www.protractortest.org/#/`.

Finally, Angular API documentation is indexed here: `https://angular.io/api`.

To speed up commercial application development, the use of Angular component libraries is advised. Those available include NG Bootstrap, which contains Bootstrap 4 widgets as Angular 5+ directives (`https://ng-bootstrap.github.io/#/home`), and Angular Material (`https://material.angular.io/`).

Assessments

This chapter contains the solutions to the assessments of all the chapters.

Chapter 1

1. Performing compilation-time checks, and getting suggestions from VS IntelliSense.
2. No, TypeScript types only exist at compilation time. They disappear in the generated JavaScript code.
3. No, there is no chance, since TypeScript is Types+JavaScript of the future, and there is no official proposal to include operator overloading in any future JavaScript version.
4. `var myVar: number|string`.
5. `void`.
6. In JavaScript, variables used without having been declared are defined in the global scope and may collide with other variable names defined in the global scope. Often, similar errors cause hard-to-find bugs. TypeScript's obligatory variable declarations prevent developers from accidentally declaring a variable in the global scope.
7. `var` generates a single variable instance, since the scope of variables declared with `var` is the function they are in. Thus, when the `var` statement is repeated several times, no new variable is created. On the other hand, `let` would declare 100 different variables, since the scope of `let` is a code block; that is, the code block of the loop that is repeated 100 times.
8. The statement is `false`. Strings are allowed to have `null` values only if the `strictNullChecks` compiler option is `false`.
9. To define them as `const enum`.
10. All TypeScript enums can be handled as bit flags and combined with the bitwise operators `&`, `|`, and `~`.

Chapter 2

1. The JavaScript equivalent of TypeScript tuples are arrays.
2. Function types can be defined with two notations: the interface notation, and the arrow notation (see the *Anonymous functions and function types* section).
3. No. Declarations of interface implementations are not obligatory in TypeScript. TypeScript automatically infers the interface implementation from the structure of the object.
4. You must specify just the header of all possible overloads, and then a complete function that is compatible with all overloads (see the *Function overloads* section).
5. No, they differ in the meaning they give to `this`. See the *Arrow functions* section.
6. They are used in both array destructuring and array spread. See the *Array destructuring* and *array spread* subsections. They are also used in object destructuring to capture all remaining properties that have not been mentioned in the destructuring syntax.
7. Yes, they can.
8. No, they can't.

Chapter 3

1. It is not correct, since `parentNode` may also return `null`. A `null` test must be done before calling `appendChild`.
2. A variable declaration may appear in a declaration file but must be preceded by declare, as in `declare myVar:....` This way, TypeScript understands that it is a declaration only and no memory location must be allocated. In fact, the actual variable is already allocated elsewhere.
3. Any property that is specific for an HTML page, such as `domain`.
4. Yes, you must install the `npm` package containing all jQuery TypeScript declarations.
5. By using the `HTMLElement.matches(selector:string)` method.
6. No `insertAfter` method exists. You must use `insertBefore` on the element successor, if any; otherwise, use `append`.
7. Using string interpolation (see *Declarations and scoping* in `Chapter 1`, *Introduction to TypeScript*).

Chapter 4

1. Protected members can be used by successor classes, while private members can't. No, abstract members can't be declarated private, otherwise no successor could provide a definition for them.
2. When the method doesn't use `this`.
3. Yes, classes may have several constructor overloads. They are defined like function overloads.
4. No, it is not possible because abstract classes are incomplete.
5. Yes, abstract classes can also have constructors. Abstract class constructors can be called by successor classes to initialize properties of the abstract class.
6. By preceding the method with `super`.
7. By calling `super(<parent constructor arguments>)` in its constructor.
8. Write-only properties can be defined with setters.
9. When several classes have some common methods but implement them in different ways. This way, they may be processed uniformly by the same chunks of code that depend just on those common methods.
10. There is no limit to the number of interfaces a class can implement. However, each class can inherit only from a single other class. This limitation has been conceived for performance reasons, and to avoid collisions among members with the same name inherited along different paths.

Chapter 5

1. No, not possible. Generics, like all TypeScript-type stuff, disappear in the compiled JavaScript code.
2. a) With a variable function, passed once the type is known; b) Manipulating the type with an interface whose implementation depends on a type that will be bound to the variable type; c) Manipulating the variable type with abstract methods whose implementations depend on a type that will be bound to the variable type.
3. By using TypeScript constructor types. See the *Creating instances of generic variables* section.
4. `type Nullable<T> = { [P in keyof T]: T[P] | null }`.
5. `keyof K | keyof T`.
6. `T&K`.
7. `Nullable<T&K>`.

8. Loop on all properties of `T` , then on all properties of `K`, and then add them to an empty object.

Chapter 6

1. Name collisions. JavaScript implements namespaces with objects.
2. See the *Pitfalls of namespaces and ES6 modules* section.
3. You must mention all of them in the import statement: `import {Person, ....} from ...`
4. Both at compilation time by the TypeScript compiler to get all necessary declarations, and at runtime to load the corresponding compiled JavaScript modules in the browser.
5. They are needed for library packages, because library packages don't know the exact position of all other packages in the filesystem.
6. When the choice of which modules to load depends on runtime user choices, or on browser capabilities.
7. No, but it should be included in ECMAScript 2018/2019.
8. Either with the help of bundlers, or by generating JavaScript code for JavaScript loaders, instead of ES6. This is achieved by setting the `module` compiler option to `UMD`, `AMD`, `System`, or `CommonJs`.
9. They must be preceded by `declare` to avoid the TypeScript compiler creating the JavaScript code, they need to work properly.
10. Non-relative paths are not supported in ES6. Therefore, projects containing non-relative paths must be processed with JavaScript bundlers such as WebPack.

Chapter 7

1. Just three. Entries depend only on the main bundles that must be created, not on their dependencies.
2. Yes, it is possible, but the names of the modules that might be loaded dynamically must be computable at bundling time. This way, WebPack knows which modules it must process. Usually, they are passed as constant strings in the import instruction, and the decision of whether or not to load each module is taken with `if`.
3. By letting the WebPack configuration object be returned by an arrow function that receives the environment as its argument. See the *Production and development configurations* section.

4. Yes, it is. Each entry may also be passed an array of independent files.

5. Once `Microsoft.AspNetCore.SpaServices` is installed and configured, it is enough to set the `HotModuleReplacement` property of the `WebPackDevMiddlewareOptions` option object to `true`. Then it is necessary to inform WebPack on the name of the endpoint where to download new code chunks. This is done by setting `WebPack output.publicPath` to `dist/`. See the *Integrating WebPack in ASP.NET Core middleware* section.

6. `DllPlugin` and `SplitChunksPlugin`.

7. Because it is compatible with Hot Module Replacement, so the developer can see immediately the result of any change. Moreover, using it is faster than bundling all the CSS in separated bundles, so it is more adequate for development.

8. You must add the following XML to the `.csproj` file:

```
<Target Name="PublishRunWebPack"
AfterTargets="ComputeFilesToPublish">
    <Exec Command="node node_modules/webpack/bin/webpack.js --
env.prod" />
</Target>
```

   See the *Production and development configurations* section.

9. You must use the `SourceMapDevToolPlugin` plugin with adequate settings. See the *WebPack plugins – recovering Visual Studio debugger* section.

10. It is enough to set `cachedGroups.minSize=3`. The required chunk name is `default~bundle1~bundle2~bundle3`.

Chapter 8

1. Go to **File** | **Preferences** | **Settings** and add the following setting:

```
{
    ...
    "typescript.tsdk": "./node_modules/typescript/lib"
    ...
}
```

2. Once in the **DEBUG** window, click the checkbox at the top of VS Code and select **Add Configuration....** See the *Debugging tests* subsection.

3. **Tasks** | **Configure Tasks** opens the task configuration window.

4. It contains the path to the declaration file associated with the package main module (for instance, `dist/index.d.ts`).

5. Because tests are performed in the Node.js environment, which contains no DOM.

6. Developer must define an appropriate debugger configuration. See the *Debugging tests* subsection.

7. Preparing the environment before executing tests. `beforeEach` is executed before each test, and `beforeAll` before all tests enclosed in `describe("....",` . . . .

8. It is `expect`.

Chapter 9

1. Because they are unique.
2. A predefined symbol that is available as a static property of the `Symbol` class.
3. For the definition of iterables.
4. `for...of....`
5. An iterator function mimics an actual loop, so it is easy to write.
6. No, it can't.
7. A maps accepts any type as its index.
8. Promises transform a tree of nested callbacks into a sequence of `then` calls. In turn, async/await restores the standard instruction sequence of synchronous code.
9. Decorators add declarative information to JavaScript entities. They can be applied to classes, methods, fields, setters/getters, and method arguments. They are the preferred way of defining metadata.
10. Decorator factories.

Chapter 10

1. In the `exports` array.
2. No, the interpolation operator works just with strings. Non-string properties must be handled with property bindings: `[propertyName]="<expression>"`.
3. `ng generate component <component name>`. AN application is started in development mode with `ng serve`.
4. Since `colspan` exists just as an attribute and not as a DOM property, its name must be preceded by the `attr.` prefix: `[attr.colspan]='<expression>'`.

5. With `ngModel`.

6. By setting the `sourceMap` property of the production configuration to `true` in `Angular.json`.

7. In the configurations section of `Angular.json`. Code is made aware of configuration through adequate `environment.<conf>.ts` files that, when the configuration is selected, will replace the default `environment.ts` file.

8. By adding its package reference into the `scripts` array in `Angular.json`.

9. In the `polyfills.ts` file.

10. Variables/properties that are defined either in the component class or in the template itself.

Chapter 11

1. `ngOnInit`, `ngAfterContentInit`, `ngAfterViewInit`, `ngOnDestroy`, `ngOnCha nges`, `ngDoCheck`, `ngAfterContentChecked`, and `ngAfterViewChecked`. The right place for initialization is `ngOnInit`, since it is not best practice to insert complex code in a class constructor.

2. `ngModel` and `ngForm`.

3. The `valid` and `invalid` properties of `ngModel`.

4. A CSS class added automatically by Angular when an input field is valid.

5. The colon.

6. `myCost|currency:::2.2`.

7. The interface that must be implemented by all pipes.

Chapter 12

1. Angular automatically handles all events, such as removing the event when the component is destroyed.

2. All input parameters of a directive must be added to the element the directive is attached to.

3. Yes, because `of` is just an identifier that is assigned the collection that follows it. Therefore, it can be given any name when the directive is defined.

4. Improving the efficiency of collection rendering.

5. The * means that the directive is a shortcut for a more complex syntax that contains also a template. See the *Content projection and structural directives* section.

6. There the directive adds the created HTML.
7. Because you might have parallel animations that, in turn, are composed of sequences of animations.
8. Selecting the descendant node of the animated element.
9. `stagger` makes sense only for a collection of nodes, so it can't be used on the single animated node. `group` can be used also for non-child animations, but it is not very useful, since parallel animations on a single element may be specified together in the same state definitions.

Chapter 13

1. Two hierarchies: the hierarchy of component instances and the hierarchy of lazy-loaded components.
2. Angular bundler is able to perform better optimization, adding services only to the bundles where they are needed.
3. Three ways: direct creation, direct specification of an instance, and a farm function. Normally, a token can be associated to just one service in a container, but if the provider `multi` property is set to `true`, several services can be added to the same token.
4. `get`, `head`, `post`, `put`, `delete`, and `patch`.
5. See the *Communication progress events* subsection.
6. In an XSRF attack, a hacker forces the user to submit a request to a website where they are already authenticated with an authentication cookie. The safest way to handle authentication in SPAs is with authentication tokens placed in each request header.
7. Yes, with the help of interceptors.
8. `loadChildren`.
9. `preloadingStrategy: PreloadAllModules`.
10. `CanActivate` verifies whether a route can be followed. All the guards are `CanActivate`, `CanActivateChild`, `CanDeactivate`, `Resolve`, and `CanLoad`.

Other Books You May Enjoy

If you enjoyed this book, you may be interested in these other books by Packt:

C# 7 and .NET Core 2.0 High Performance
Ovais Mehboob Ahmed Khan

ISBN: 978-1-78847-004-9

- Measure application performance using BenchmarkDotNet
- Explore the techniques to write multithreaded applications
- Leverage TPL and PLinq libraries to perform asynchronous operations
- Get familiar with data structures to write optimized code
- Understand design techniques to increase your application's performance
- Learn about memory management techniques in .NET Core
- Develop a containerized application based on microservices architecture
- Learn tools and techniques to monitor application performance

C# Data Structures and Algorithms
Marcin Jamro

ISBN: 978-1-78883-373-8

- How to use arrays and lists to get better results in complex scenarios
- Implement algorithms like the Tower of Hanoi on stacks of C# objects
- Build enhanced applications by using hashtables, dictionaries and sets
- Make a positive impact on efficiency of applications with tree traversal
- Effectively find the shortest path in the graph

Leave a review - let other readers know what you think

Please share your thoughts on this book with others by leaving a review on the site that you bought it from. If you purchased the book from Amazon, please leave us an honest review on this book's Amazon page. This is vital so that other potential readers can see and use your unbiased opinion to make purchasing decisions, we can understand what our customers think about our products, and our authors can see your feedback on the title that they have worked with Packt to create. It will only take a few minutes of your time, but is valuable to other potential customers, our authors, and Packt. Thank you!

Index

www.ingramcontent.com/pod-product-compliance
Lightning Source LLC
Chambersburg PA
CBHW060645060326
40690CB00020B/4520